PETERSON'S
College Guide for
Visual *Arts*
Majors
2009

PETERSON'S
A **nelnet** COMPANY

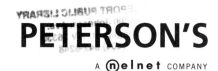

PETERSON'S

A ⓝelnet COMPANY

About Peterson's, a Nelnet company

Peterson's (www.petersons.com) is a leading provider of education information and advice, with books and online resources focusing on education search, test preparation, and financial aid. Its Web site offers searchable databases and interactive tools for contacting educational institutions, online practice tests and instruction, and planning tools for securing financial aid. Peterson's serves 110 million education consumers annually.

For more information, contact Peterson's, 2000 Lenox Drive, Lawrenceville, NJ 08648; 800-338-3282; or find us on the World Wide Web at www.petersons.com/about.

ISSN 1552-7751
ISBN-13: 978-0-7689-2564-7
ISBN-10: 0-7689-2564-9

Printed in the United States of America

10 9 8 7 6 5 4 3 2 1   10 09 08

Fourteenth Edition

Ultimately, artists communicate through their work. They express their ideas, their dreams, their perspectives and their personal stories in forms that may endure for generations and speak to millions. An arts-centered educational community enables students to explore their talents and learn how best to articulate their unique perceptions to the world.

Sandra Reed
Former Dean of Graduate Studies
Savannah College of Art and Design

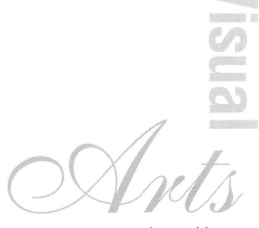

Liberal Arts Education vs. Specialized Education

Jon Fraser

If you are planning to major in art, it's important to choose the college art program that's right for you and an environment that nurtures you as an artist. That's what a good school can do for you: develop and nurture the talent you may already have and prepare you, in some cases, for a professional career.

The difference between a liberal arts education and a specialized education is significant. A specialized school usually awards a Bachelor of Fine Arts degree and offers intense training in your art form, with little emphasis on other subjects. A liberal arts education offers you a broad training that attempts to make you a well-rounded, well-educated member of society. Some programs offer a specialized approach in a liberal arts environment, where you'll study other subjects while receiving intense training in your art form. And some programs are highly specialized and preprofessional. Which one is best for you?

B.A./B.F.A./B.S.

Colleges offer three types of degrees in the visual arts: a general degree, called a Bachelor of Arts (B.A.), a preprofessional degree called a Bachelor of Fine Arts (B.F.A.), and a Bachelor of Science (B.S.) for areas such as art therapy. The main difference between the types of degree programs is the number of classes you will be required to take in your major. The goals of these various types of degrees are also different.

B.F.A. programs allow students to focus most of their studies in art—up to 70 percent of all course work—and don't usually permit as many electives in areas outside the major as B.A. programs. These programs are meant for those who intend to pursue a professional career in their field of study. The B.F.A. program in the visual arts at a university will be rigorous and professional, typically offering a broad range of courses and electives. Universities vary, though, as to whether or not areas for specialization are available.

The B.A. program is meant for those who want a broad-based education with plenty of room for electives and who may not be sure what they want to do after they graduate.

The B.S. is generally a more technically oriented degree in a subject like art therapy, where the career is related to art but requires other skills.

Some schools offer two or three degrees in the same subject and let you choose which program to pursue. Other schools have stricter entrance requirements for the B.F.A. or B.S. degree programs than for the B.A. program.

As a general rule of thumb, if you're not sure or you have to ask, it's probably best to pursue a B.A. degree. If you feel you have no choice, that your art form is what you must do for the rest of your life, the B.F.A. or B.S. is probably the right choice. Another thing to keep in mind is that in many schools with several degree programs, you may switch from one to the other once you get there.

LIBERAL ARTS COLLEGE OR SPECIALIZED COLLEGE

Once you've decided on a degree program, you need to decide which type of school is right for you. The choice between attending a liberal arts college and a specialized college is highly individual. It is not about which one will make you successful. Both types of school may or may not help you to become a success at what you do. You don't get a "better" education at one or the other. What you get is a different sort of education that may or may not serve your needs.

Competition within a specialized school tends to be more intense than in a liberal arts environment. Moreover, liberal arts schools may have a minimum grade point average requirement for staying in their programs. So, a word of warning: If you're planning on majoring in the arts, plan on working hard!

As someone who has worked for a liberal arts institution (Long Island University's C.W. Post Campus) for many years, I have my prejudice about which one you should choose. For most people, I feel that a liberal arts education makes a better artist, in the holistic sense that any art form is more than simply good technique. It requires intelligent inquiry and critical thinking about the world around you. A good liberal arts undergraduate education in the arts should develop not only your artistic skills and talent, but your intellectual and critical skills as well. Usually offered outside the department or school of art, liberal arts programs

Making the Most of Your Campus Visit

Dawn B. Sova, Ph.D.

The campus visit should not be a passive activity for you and your parents. You will see many important indicators during your visit that will tell you a lot about the true character of the college and its students. Most organized campus visits include tours of such campus facilities as dorms, dining halls, libraries, student activity and recreation centers, and the health and student services centers. Some may only be pointed out, while you will walk through others. As an art student, you will of course be interested in seeing the facilities that pertain to your particular major, and those might be a major factor when considering a school. However, the general environment of the campus is important as well and merits close attention. Colleges do not train their tour guides to deceive prospective students, but they do caution guides to avoid unflattering topics and campus sites. Does this mean that you are destined to see only a sugarcoated version of life on a particular college campus? Not at all—especially if you are observant.

VISITOR CENTER/ADMISSIONS OFFICE

Your first stop on a campus visit is the visitor center or admissions office. Begin your investigation with the visitor center staff members. As a student's first official contact with the college, these staff members should make every effort to welcome prospective students and to project a friendly image.

- How do they treat you and other prospective students who are waiting? Are they friendly and willing to speak with you, or do they try their hardest to avoid eye contact and conversation?

- Are they friendly with each other and with students who enter the office, or are they curt and unwilling to help?

If the visitor center staff members seem indifferent to *prospective* students, there is little reason to believe that they will be warm and welcoming to current students.

SCHOOL NEWSPAPER

If time permits, look through several copies of the school newspaper, which should reflect the major concerns and interests of the students. The paper is also a good way to learn about the campus social life.

- Does the paper contain a mix of national and local news?

- What products or services are advertised?

- How assertive are the editorials?

- With what topics are the columnists concerned?

- Are movies and concerts that meet your tastes advertised or reviewed?

- What types of ads appear in the classified section?

The newspaper should be a public forum for students, and, as such, should reflect the character of the campus and of the student body. A paper that deals only with seemingly safe and well-edited topics on the editorial page and in regular feature columns might indicate administrative censorship. A lack of ads for restaurants might indicate either a lack of good places to eat or that area restaurants do not welcome student business. A limited mention of movies, concerts, or other entertainment might reveal a severely limited campus social life. Even if ads and reviews are included, you can also learn a lot about how such activities reflect your tastes.

BULLETIN BOARDS

Bulletin boards in the dorms and student centers contain a wealth of information about campus activities, student concerns, and campus groups. Read the posters, notices, and messages to learn what *really* interests students. Unlike ads in the school newspaper, posters put up by students advertise both on- and off-campus events, so they will give you an idea of what is also available in the surrounding community. Art exhibits, poetry readings, jam sessions, writers' groups, and other activities may be announced and show diversity of student interests on that campus. Even the brief bulletin board messages offering objects for sale and noting objects that people want to purchase reveal a lot about a campus. Are most of the items computer-related? Or do the messages specify compact discs, audio equipment, or musical instruments? Don't

- Is the emphasis on grades or social life or a mix of both?

- How hard do students have to work to receive high grades?

Current students can also give you the inside line—the true highs and lows of campus life. Ask them about drug use, partying, dating, drinking, and anything else that may affect your life as a student.

- Which are the most popular club activities?

- What do students do on weekends? Do most go home?

- How frequently do concerts occur on campus? Ask them to name groups that have recently performed.

- How can you become involved in specific activities (name them)?

- How strictly are campus rules enforced, and how severe are penalties?

- What counseling services are available?

- Are academic tutoring services available?

- Do they feel that the faculty really cares about students, especially freshmen?

You will receive the most valuable information from current students, but you will only be able to speak with them after the tour is over. And you might have to risk rejection as you try to initiate conversations with students who might not want to reveal how they feel about the school.

SURROUNDING COMMUNITY

Make a point of at least driving through the community surrounding the college, because you will be spending time there shopping, dining, working in a part-time job, or attending events. Even the largest and best-stocked campus will not meet all of your social and personal needs. If you can spare the time, stop in several stores to see if they welcome college students.

- Is the surrounding community suburban, urban, or rural?

- Does the community offer stores of interest, such as bookstores, craft shops, and boutiques?

- Do the businesses employ college students?

- Does the community have a movie or stage theater?

- Are there several types of interesting restaurants?

- Do there seem to be any clubs that court a college clientele?

- Is the center of activity easy to walk to, or do you need a car or other transportation?

REVIEW YOUR NOTES

You might feel that a day is not enough to answer all of your questions, but even answering some questions will provide you with a stronger basis for choosing a college. Many students visit a college campus several times before making their decision. Keep in mind that not only will you spend the next four years of your life at a college, but for the rest of your life you will be associated with that college. The effort of spending several days to collect information to make your decision is worthwhile.

FOLLOWING UP

Your connection with a college does not end when you return home, no matter what your impression might be. Whether or not you wish to attend the school, you should take the time to follow up. Write a letter to thank people specifically for taking the time to meet with you. Beyond common courtesy, this also leaves the college officials with a positive view of you, and the letter will most likely be placed in your file. Will it make the difference between being accepted or rejected? No one can say. Write to the visitor center to thank counselors for their time, even if your experience was less than pleasant. You may have contact with them in the future and there is no reason not to leave them with a good impression.

Dawn B. Sova is a former newspaper reporter and columnist who teaches creative and research writing as well as scientific and technical writing, newswriting, and journalism.

Searching for Art Programs and Scholarships Online

Choosing a college art program involves a serious commitment of time and resources. Therefore, it is important to have the most up-to-date information about institutions and their programs at your fingertips. The Internet can be a great tool for gathering that information, and one of the best sites to visit during the college selection process is Peterson's Visual & Performing Arts (VPA) channel at www.petersons.com/arts.

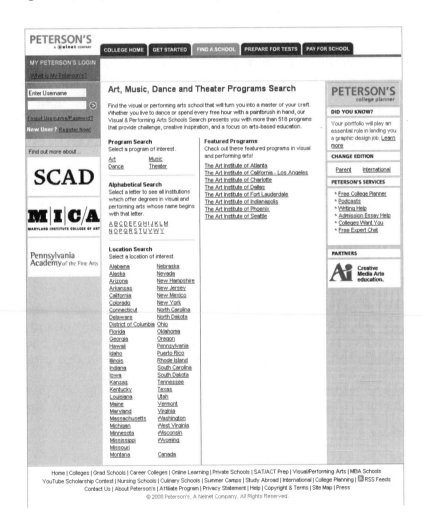

PETERSON'S VISUAL & PERFORMING ARTS CHANNEL

The VPA channel at www.petersons.com is a one-stop source of information on college art programs in the U.S. and Canada. Under "Colleges and Universities," click on "Art, Music, Dance and Theater Programs" in the Quick Links box to access Peterson's comprehensive database of arts programs. If you know what area of art you're interested in, you can locate a school or program by clicking on "Art" on the Program Search menu, which gives you a list of art majors or concentrations. Simply click one of these, and you will get a list of schools that offer a degree program in that field. Or, if you'd like to search by location, you can access lists of schools offering art programs in any U.S. state or in Canada. Finally, if you have a particular school in mind and want to see what art programs it offers, you can do an alphabetical search on the school's name and get information about their programs.

You can also request information from some schools by clicking on "Get Free Info." Within minutes, the school will receive your message and mail a catalog, an application, or information on financial aid to you. If you find the perfect school for a friend, you can even send the page to him or her with a message. There also are links to the school's Web site.

PETERSON'S FREE SCHOLARSHIP SEARCH

Petersons.com is a great site for any college-bound student. There is a wealth of information on undergraduate, graduate, online learning, and study-abroad programs and also some of the best financial aid advice available.

With Peterson's free Scholarship Search on the financial aid channel of Petersons.com (www.petersons.com/finaid), you can explore more than 1.7 million scholarships, grants, and prizes totaling nearly $8 billion and do an individualized search for awards that match your financial and educational needs. In just three easy steps, you can register and complete a customized profile indicating your scholastic and personal background, including intended major, work experience, and a host of other criteria that will allow you to access a list of scholarships that match your needs. Each scholarship is described in detail with eligibility and application requirements, contact information, and links to its e-mail address and Web site. Finding money for college couldn't be easier.

So, what are you waiting for? Log on to Petersons.com and let us help you with your college planning!

FFEL Stafford Student Loan, and the Parent Loan (PLUS) program are not based on need, and these loans accrue interest while the student is in school.

There are also a number of federal tax–based programs that help families with incomes up to $110,000. Additional information about the Hope Scholarship, Lifetime Learning tax credits, and other education assistance tax–based programs is available from the IRS. You should consult a tax adviser for other educational tax deductions, since income cutoffs can vary from program to program.

IF YOU DON'T QUALIFY FOR NEED-BASED AID

If you are not eligible for need-based aid, or the aid you have been awarded is not sufficient, you should look into three other funding sources.

First is the search for merit scholarships, which you can start during your junior year of high school at the initial stages of the aid application process. Merit-based awards are becoming an increasingly important part of college financing plans, and many colleges award these grants to students they especially want to attract. As a result, applying to a school at which your qualifications put you at the top of the entering class may be a good idea since you may receive a merit award. It is also a good idea to look for private scholarships and grants, especially from local service and community groups.

The second source of aid is employment, during both the summer and the academic year. The student employment office at your college should be able to help you locate a job in the area, either on or off campus.

The third source is borrowing through the Unsubsidized FFEL Stafford Student Loan or the Unsubsidized Direct Stafford Student Loan, both of which are open to all students. The terms and conditions are similar to the subsidized loans. The biggest difference is that the borrower is responsible for the interest while still in college, although most lenders permit students to delay paying the interest right away and add the accrued interest to the total amount owed.

After you've secured what you can through scholarships, work, and loans, your parents will have to figure out how they will meet the balance of the college bill. Most colleges offer monthly payment plans that spread the cost out over the academic year. For many parents, the monthly payments still turn out to be more than they can afford, so they can borrow through the Federal Parent Loan for Undergraduate Students

constraints, very few colleges make the interview mandatory. If you do decide to have an interview, never drop in; be sure to make the arrangements well in advance. Often, specialized colleges do not hold interviews but just require that you send in your portfolio. At liberal arts colleges the interview is usually with an admissions representative, who might ask you briefly about your work but does not see your portfolio, which is submitted directly to the appropriate art department or school of art for evaluation. For advice on having a successful college interview, see "Acing Your College Interview" in this guide.

When evaluating portfolios, liberal arts universities usually use faculty members from the department or school of art. Art colleges use trained admissions staff members who are usually artists themselves, as well as faculty members. Portfolio evaluators at the more selective art colleges and universities are looking for more than raw talent. They are looking for a particular level of competency and technical skill as well as conceptual ability. The emphasis placed on conceptual ability versus skill varies from college to college because each has a different philosophy of education and programmatic thrust and looks for students who are a good match for that institution. What all colleges look for, however, are students who demonstrate through their artwork that they are creative, intellectually curious, and seriously invested and committed—even compelled—to make art. For more in-depth advice on preparing a portfolio, see "Developing an Undergraduate Visual Portfolio" and "Portfolio Advice from Admissions Directors" in this guide.

Deadlines

Do yourself and the admissions office a favor by submitting your application before it is actually due. Remember to proofread your application before you mail or transmit it and to keep a copy of it for your files. If sent by standard "snail mail," it is a good idea to include a self-addressed, stamped postcard saying, "College X has received the application from Mary Jones. Signed by admissions: Date: __," for the admissions office to return to you. Also, watch for a canceled check, or check the statement of the credit card you used. Things do get lost in postal and electronic mail, and you want to be sure that your application does not go astray. And, if you are using e-mail or otherwise filing electronically, remember to print out a hard copy of whatever you transmit to save for your files, too.

Refer to the College Admissions Timetable on pages 41–45 and use it as a guideline for the admission process.

ADMISSIONS OUTCOMES

After the application and portfolio review, admissions committees meet to determine whether to admit you, reject you, or place your name on a waiting list. Beware that the weight of the letter or size of the envelope does not necessarily indicate the admissions decision.

If you are admitted to more than one school, weigh the pros and cons of each institution, perhaps visit again, ask lots of questions, and try to respond to the Office of Admissions in plenty of time, before their acceptance deadline. Most institutions comply with the guidelines established by the National Association for College Admission Counseling (NACAC) and the College Board, which set the Candidate's Reply Deadline (CRD) as May 1. If a school requires you to make a decision before that deadline or before you have heard from all of your schools, you have every right to question that institution. If, in order to make an informed decision about your college choice, you need more information, or if your financial aid package has not arrived in time to meet the deadline, call the college and request an extension of the deadline. If you do not contact the college at all by the college's deadline, the admissions staff may assume that you have decided to attend another institution and offer your place to someone on the wait list. Be certain to contact your college by the deadline stipulated.

The wait list is a positive place to be. It means that a college realized your strengths, but because of a limited number of openings, it was not able to offer you admission at this time. Your initial response will probably be disappointment and irritation, but wait a few days before you do anything. Then you should be able to make a rational decision about whether to remain active on a wait list or to accept the offer of another college that admitted you.

If you want to be considered from the wait list, now is the time to be even more proactive in demonstrating your desire to attend. Call, send an e-mail, and/or write to the college to say that you want to be considered from the wait list. Include any new information about yourself since the school reviewed your application. If it is true, let a college know that if taken off the wait list, you will enroll. Talk to your guidance counselor about any further steps you should take—and then be patient. You should probably submit a deposit to your second-choice school to protect yourself, in the event that the first choice does not accept anyone from the wait list. If you are admitted from the wait list, however, and you intend to accept the offer of admission and enroll, be sure to immediately contact the school where you gave your deposit so that they may possibly offer your place to someone else. You should never make a deposit at more than one school; multiple deposits are considered unethical in college admissions.

If You Want To Defer Admission

Often, a student who has been admitted will want to take a year to travel or work before enrolling. Many colleges and universities are pleased to grant a deferral of a year. They may give you guidelines about what they will allow you to do with the year. For instance, attending another college usually is not allowed, and they may give a new deadline for committing to enrollment. Some schools may ask for an account of what you have done with your time off.

INTERNATIONAL STUDENTS' CHECKLIST

Any student who is not a citizen or permanent resident of the United States is usually considered an "international" or "foreign" student (the term varies at schools). Many schools recruit abroad and most schools welcome students from abroad. The admissions procedures at most schools are the same for international students as for U.S. applicants. However, there are a few additional aspects international students should take into account.

- Begin your search extra early. International mail takes additional time and catalogs cannot be faxed at this point.

- Take advantage of the Internet and e-mail in expediting your questions, but always print a hard copy for yourself.

- Determine from each college or university whether you must take the TOEFL (Test of English as a Foreign Language), if English is not your native language. Arrange to take the test, if necessary, so that your scores can be submitted at the required time. Contact www.TOEFL.org or ETS at 609-771-7100.

- Be sure to study English intensively. There are many good English as a Second Language (ESL) programs both in the United States and abroad and many summer programs in the United States. An Internet search should help you to discover ESL programs available to you.

- Investigate the visa process early. Many conservatories or colleges will issue you a letter to present to a consulate in order to obtain a B-2 Prospective Student Visa. An I-20 will be issued to admitted students only. Everything regarding visas does take time, so plan ahead.

- Determine a school's policy on financial aid for international students. Government or state loans are not available to students from abroad, and many schools reserve their limited scholarship funds for domestic students. Some schools will not admit a qualified international student who has applied for financial aid. Be sure to ask for the current policy, and do not hesitate to ask for clarification of the policy if you are in doubt.

- Find out whether the school requires a guarantee of financial support in advance.

- Ask about tape or application pre-screening or regional auditions in your country.

- Complete the application on your own, especially the essays. If your English is not good enough to write an acceptable essay, you probably won't be able to understand the lectures or complete the assignments at a U.S. school.

- Be sure that schools know about your academic history in terms of the grading and overall educational system in your country. For instance, if no one from your high school has ever applied to schools in the United States before, you should send a prospectus or profile of your school.

- Some colleges and universities may require that your official transcript be reviewed or translated by the World Education Service (WES). Ask about the requirements of the specific schools. The Web address for WES is www.wes.org.

- Find out whether it is possible for international students to work while attending the program.

- Ask whether there are quotas on the number of students from a certain country or on foreign students in general.

- Find out about advisers and other support services for students from abroad.

- Find out if the program is authorized to grant Practical Training status to international students.

FINANCIAL AID

Many art students considering postsecondary education need some form of financial aid. Do not eliminate a school from your list just because of the school's cost. Often, the most expensive schools have the largest endowments and are able to be particularly generous in financial aid. In order to qualify for financial aid, you must apply for it. Many middle-income families, in particular, assume that financial assistance is not available to them; this may not be true. Read the catalog and any financial aid information very carefully, and be sure to speak to a financial aid officer at the college to which you are applying. Ask questions about the financial aid process and find out exactly what forms you will need. It is essential that you submit all the required forms and documents and meet deadlines in applying for financial aid. For safety's sake, keep photocopies of every form you send, whether you file these via regular mail or electronically.

Aside from scholarships, there are a variety of grants, loans, and work-study opportunities to help you finance your education. The Foundation Center, http://foundationcenter.org; 79 Fifth Avenue, New York, NY 10003 (212-620-4230 or 800-424-9836), is an excellent resource and has regional branches in the United States. There are also many helpful financial aid guides at libraries and in guidance offices. Do not overlook religious organizations, community and civic organizations, or state programs in your quest for funding. There are also many fine Web sites, such as Petersons.com, CollegeScholarships.com, or Collegetoolkit.com, that have fine information about funding higher education—but beware of Internet sites that advertise and request a fee for finding you funds. Ask your parents to check if they work for a company or belong to an association or union that sponsors scholarships.

Here are some questions that you will want to ask about financial aid:

- Are scholarships based on merit? On need? On a combination of both?

- Are financial aid decisions made separately from admissions decisions?

- What percentage of students receives scholarships? Other financial aid?

- What are the most common mistakes people make in filling out financial aid forms?

- Should I assume that if my parents make (some dollar amount) as their income I would not be eligible for any aid?

- Do you have payment plans?

- What happens if I do not meet deadlines in filing forms for financial aid?

- Do you give financial aid to applicants admitted from the waiting list?

Deadlines are very important when applying for financial aid. It is critical that the FAFSA (Free Application for Federal Student Aid) and the CSS/PROFILE® be completed and submitted as early as possible. Many colleges have January and February deadlines for submission of the PROFILE. If parents have not completed their income tax returns by February, estimate income as accurately as possible, and submit corrections later in the process.

If the financial aid package you are offered is not adequate, or if your first-choice school offers less than a second or third choice, call the admissions or financial aid office of your first-choice school and discuss this with them. Schools may reconsider their original financial aid offer. They may ask you to send a copy of the other school's offer and then make you a counter-offer. In general, there is a great deal more comparative shopping and negotiating in financial aid these days.

- Last chance to take the SAT and ACT.

February–March

- Check to make sure that all your financial aid documents are in order.

April

- Make your decision. Consider with your parents and adviser the pros and cons of each institution.

- Revisit any college if your decision to attend is not crystal clear.

- Notify colleges of your decision by May 1. If a school asks for a decision response before May 1, you have a right to request an extension until the May 1 Candidate's Reply Deadline (CRD).

May

- Be sure to notify all colleges by May 1, even if you are on the waiting list.

- Take any AP exams, if applicable.

COLLEGE ADMISSIONS CHECKLIST

Use this convenient checklist to remind yourself of individual college admissions requirements and to record the progress of your application procedures.

	Registration Deadline	Testing Date	Registration Deadline	Testing Date	Registration Deadline	Testing Date	Registration Deadline	Testing Date
College Name								
College Address								
Application Deadline								
Application Fee								
Required Tests:								
PSAT/NMSQT								
SAT								
ACT								
Others								
Course Requirements Fulfilled								
Personal Interview Required								
Interview Date								
Portfolio Required								
Portfolio Date								
Applications Requested								
References Required								
Names/Addresses of References								
References Completed								
Application Filed								
Transcript Forwarded								
College Reply Date								
Financial Interview Required								
Required Financial Forms:								
CSS/PROFILE								
FAFSA								
Other								
Housing Deadline								
Housing Fee								
Housing Application Mailed								

a senior to show someone your portfolio, you could be creating an unnecessary problem for yourself. So start early, and do your research at least in the beginning of your junior year.

WHAT MEDIA SHOULD I INCLUDE IN MY PORTFOLIO?

Most schools do not require you to present particular media. However, most do expect you to have a number of works in pencil and a few works done in other media. The most common media are pencil, charcoal (soft or hard), pastels (oil or dry), paint (oil, acrylic, watercolor, or colored inks or dyes), photography, computer-generated work, printmaking (block, etching, silk screen, or lithography), and collage. You are not required to have all, and the most important aspect of the media you choose is that you use them well and the works are strong. If possible, your portfolio should have works in black & white, color, and a few three-dimensional works. Variety and quality are the key points when deciding on media. If you cannot seem to master a particular medium, don't include it. Quality should not be compromised for variety.

WHAT IS A HOME EXAM/HOME TEST?

A home exam or home test is required at some college(s) in addition to the general portfolio. These home exams/tests give you a particular problem to solve and typically ask for this problem to be solved in particular dimensions. Some schools require that the original home exam/test work be mailed to them directly, and in some cases you cannot have this work back. Therefore, it is important that you document all of your work so that you have a record of your early works. You should check with all your potential school(s) to find out what requirements they may have for the home exam/test. These home exams/tests can get very detailed in terms of the particular requirements such as size, medium, etc. Pay close attention to the fine print.

HOW CAN I EDIT MY VISUAL PORTFOLIO?

The first and most obvious way of editing your work is to have your high school art teacher help you out. The second way is to have a classmate or family member help you critique your work and edit using this information. The third way is to have a pre-review by one of your potential colleges. (See How Can I Get Advice on My Work?) The fourth way is to make sure you are not keeping works in your portfolio that are weak just because they have sentimental value. If you did a work in seventh grade and everyone thought it was the greatest work you'd ever done, don't assume it's still great. You have grown, and hopefully your work has grown too. Finally, the most important aspect of editing your work is you. After you have collected all necessary opinions, remember you have the final word on what stays in and what is left out.

HOW DO I PRESENT OR SUBMIT MY VISUAL PORTFOLIO?

Each school has its own requirements in regards to how you should and how you can submit work. Most schools do not require your work to be matted or framed and some even encourage you not to do so. Some schools will review your work in person and grade your portfolio and require no other reproductions. Other schools may review your work in person but also require reproductions to be sent with your applications. Still other schools may not offer personal interviews and may require all applicants to submit reproductions. Therefore, you need to get the details of what your potential school(s) requires. Don't wait to find out this information in your senior year. Do your research early and learn what will be expected of you.

However, no matter what the requirements of your potential school(s), it is recommended that you take slides of your visual work to keep as a visual record of your artwork history. To this day, I still have my slides from high school and I am grateful to my high school art teacher for stressing the importance of visual documentation. Most schools will accept slides and some even require them. However, some schools will accept images of your work either on a VHS, CD-ROM, DVD, via the Internet, or printed out, typically in an 8 × 10 format. It is extremely important that you find out the format required and/or accepted by your potential school(s). There may be size requirements and program requirements that are critical to the application process. At Pratt, we often receive CDs and DVDs with files that cannot be opened, and I am sure we are not alone.

Reproducing Your Work

35-mm Slides

You can take your own slides easily, provided you have or can borrow a 35-mm camera, a tripod, and daylight 200-slide film. Most high schools that offer photography have a 35-mm camera and tripod that you may be able to borrow or use at the school to take your slides. Even if your school doesn't have a photography department, you may want to talk to your art teacher or guidance counselor to see if there is any assistance or equipment available at your school.

Once you have your 35-mm camera, tripod, and daylight 200-slide film, the rest is pretty easy. First, set your 35-mm camera according to the to colleges, universities, and professional institutions that are actively recruiting students in the creative and performing arts.

NFAA is also the exclusive agent for nominating selected ARTS winners to the Commission on Presidential Scholars, which names the Presidential Scholars in the Arts. For an application form and more information, contact the NFAA at 800-970-ARTS (toll-free) or apply online at www.NFAA.org.

PERFORMING AND VISUAL ARTS COLLEGE FAIRS

The NACAC (National Association for College Admission Counseling) Performing and Visual Arts College Fairs are events for college and college-bound students interested in pursuing undergraduate and graduate programs of study in the areas of music, dance, theater, visual arts, graphic design, and other related disciplines. Attendees learn about educational opportunities, admission and financial aid, portfolio days, audition and entrance requirements, and much more by meeting with representatives from colleges, universities, conservatories, festivals, and other educational institutions with specialized programs in the visual and performing arts.

For information about NACAC's Performing and Visual Arts College Fairs, call the national office at 800-822-6285 (toll-free). For a schedule, visit www.nacacnet.org.

You're In! What's Next?

You have followed your dream and it has paid off. What will your life be like as a full-time art major? And what lies ahead for you if you decide to become a professional artist? Turn the page and find out from those in the know.

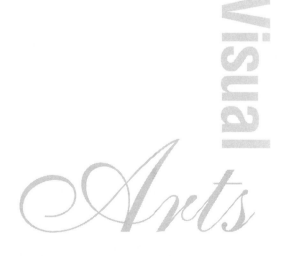

The Importance of Foundation Studies

Maureen Garvin

Foundation studies programs are an integral part of a visual arts education. These programs are a series of studio classes taken during the first year of study in an art college or program. The primary function of foundation programs is to prepare all students to be successful in their major programs.

The names of the foundation programs are variations on the terms "Visual Fundamentals" and "Preliminary Courses," which were used to describe the first year in the Bauhaus, a design school founded in Germany that migrated to Chicago in 1937. The structure and content of many of today's foundation programs developed from traditions established in the Bauhaus: material exploration and an understanding of form, color, and composition. More contemporary terms such as "Core Studio Practice" and the more common "Foundation Studies" are used to describe a sequence of classes that teach both the technical and conceptual skills needed to pursue any area of art and design.

LEARNING THE VISUAL LANGUAGE

While the sequence and titles of the foundation courses vary from college to college, the common goal is to teach visual literacy. Visual literacy is about understanding the language used in art and design. In the same manner that one learns French or Italian, one can learn about the elements of visual language: line, shape, value, color, and how to manipulate and compose these elements to visually communicate ideas. Georgia O' Keeffe said, "I found I could say things with color and shapes that I couldn't say any other way."

The elements and the principles of design are the language students use in their majors. In these first-year studio classes, students learn to handle a variety of media that can range from the traditional—charcoal, graphite, and gouache—to digital versions of these traditional tools. Foundation programs teach how to develop ideas, how to understand the terminology of visual language, and how to evaluate or critique the work. Most programs include drawing classes to train a student's eye and hand to see and translate information out in the real world into a visual representation or response. Learning to draw has been used as a method to train artists since the Renaissance.

Students often perceive foundation courses as something to get through to move on to "real" courses in the major. It can be a struggle to see the purpose of taking courses that appear unrelated to a major. The reality is that the visual language and skills learned in foundation courses are the common denominator in all the fields. Designing an ad, creating visual effects for a film, constructing a garment, and designing a building all begin with knowing how to manipulate visual language to relay content, an idea.

NEW WAYS OF SEEING

As a result of your foundation classes, you literally will begin to see in different ways. You will start to understand how artists and designers think—how one thought, sketch, or doodle leads to another and another and to a series of ideas that generate new designs or images. Another frequent outcome of taking foundation classes is that students accomplish what they never believed they could do. An example would be the drawing-phobic student who slowly realizes that he or she can actually draw and even reach a point where he or she wants to draw and enjoys the process of drawing. You will begin to make connections between the design principles you learn: balance, repetition, rhythm, emphasis, and why an image can look calm, boring, or comforting. You will look at an artist's work and understand what he or she was aiming to accomplish and how he or she went about it. (This can impress and amaze relatives.) New ideas will occur when looking at familiar objects. You might think, "The chair could be more comfortable and better looking if the back was a different shape."

ADVANTAGES OF TAKING FOUNDATION COURSES

One advantage of beginning your career with the foundation courses is that you can picture yourself pursuing a variety of careers. You will be in classes with students who are interested in architecture, fashion, animation, furniture design, painting, and maybe a few majors you have never even heard of, such as sound design, broadcast design, or information architecture. Most first-year programs include the opportunity to take several electives to try out different areas of interest. Some students arrive with the desire to be a graphic designer and after taking an elective in ceramics or glass begin to see an entirely new future for themselves.

A second advantage of that first-year program is that you learn how to be disciplined, that good art and design come from practice and perseverance, and that creativity occurs with the willingness to go beyond what is obvious, to see, to visualize in new ways. Mary Stewart is a noted artist and author of a text frequently used in foundation studies courses, titled *Launching the Imagination: A Comprehensive Guide to Basic Design.* She writes about the seven characteristics of thinking: receptivity, curiosity, a wide range of interests, attentiveness, connection-seeking, conviction, and complexity. Throughout the sequence of foundation courses, you will learn not only the mechanics—the tools, techniques, and concepts— but how to think and see in new ways. You will be developing the ability to be a creative thinker.

A third advantage to foundation studies is that you will start to see the common language used in all the fields you could choose as a major. The edges of an architectural detail will remind you of lines in a drawing and a pattern on a fabric. This brings into play some of the characteristics to which Mary Stewart refers: connection-seeking, curiosity, and attentiveness.

SUMMING IT UP

- The primary function of foundation programs is to prepare all students to be successful in their major programs.

- The common goal is to teach visual literacy.

- Foundation programs teach how to develop ideas, understand the terminology of visual language, and how to evaluate or critique the work.

- You are not only learning to draw but to see.

- One result of foundation classes is that you will begin to literally see in different ways.

- You will accomplish what you never believed you could do.

- A student can arrive with the desire to be a graphic designer and after taking an elective in ceramics or glass begin to see an entirely new future for himself.

- You will be acclimated to hard work and confident in your ability to learn. You will be ready.

Maureen Garvin is Dean of the School of Fine Arts, Savannah College of Art and Design

Typical First-Year Schedules

While all schools differ in their degree requirements, the following samples of first-year schedules for B.F.A. programs at a typical specialized college give you an idea of what a week in the life of an art major is like.

Computer Graphics

Mon	Survey of World Art	12:00–2:50
Tues	Imaging Techniques	9:00–11:50
Wed	Drawing	9:00–2:50
Thurs	Language and Literature	9:00–11:50
Fri	Introduction to Animation	2:00–6:50

Fine Arts

Mon	Painting	9:00–2:50
Tues	Sculpture	12:00–5:50
Wed	Drawing	9:00–2:50
Thurs	Free	
Fri	Survey of World Art	12:00–2:50
	Language and Literature	3:00–5:50

Photography

Mon	Free	
Tues	Digital Imaging	9:00–11:50
	History of Photography	3:00–5:30
Wed	Language and Literature	9:00–11:50
Thurs	Photo Workshop	9:00–2:50
	Studio Workshop	6:30–9:20
Fri	Free	

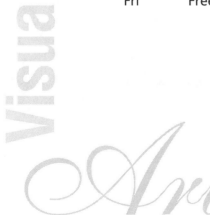

Visual Arts

Current Art Majors Tell All

LAURA
Graphic Design
American University

For students thinking about majoring in any of the visual arts, I advise you to first consider whether an art school (e.g., Pratt Institute, Maryland Institute College of Art, Rhode Island School of Design) or a liberal arts school is a better fit for you. In my experience attending a liberal arts school, I feel as though I've been exposed to much more of the so-called college experience than I might encounter at a school devoted to visual arts only. American University has Greek life, athletics, and a multicultural student body. If this is what you're looking for, you may not feel comfortable in an art school, where you may experience more competition, both among classmates and schoolwide.

If you're not quite certain what you want from an art degree, a liberal arts school might also allow you time to explore other disciplines, or even to minor in a completely different subject. Evaluate how focused and developed you are as an artist; this is crucial in deciding whether you should major in art and/or attend an art school. If you already know that visual art—and only visual art—is your calling, then I would suggest focusing your search only on arts schools.

What should a prospective visual arts student look for in a school? I believe you should first consider the school's visual arts facilities. Are they modern and extensive? Are they well developed? If not, you can assume that visual arts is probably not a major focus for the school. On the other hand, if you visit a college with a large arts building or center that offers a range of visual art major programs, you can bet that it would be a better choice than one without such amenities.

Be sure to find out about offerings for art majors who plan to enter the business world. For example, some institutions will host job or internship fairs, in which students can speak with representatives of potential employers and have their portfolios critiqued. Review the level of popularity the visual arts program enjoys among the total population of students. A strong program is likely to have a greater percentage of students than one with an underdeveloped program.

You can begin preparing to be a visual arts major while you're still in high school. I suggest taking as many art courses as you can (without overloading yourself, of course). Choose courses that focus on different media; for example, I

75

took Clay, Advanced Painting, Advanced Drawing, Computer Arts, and Printmaking. Getting a taste of a variety of visual art forms helped me narrow my focus and decide what I really had a passion for.

What's a day in the life of a visual arts major like? My typical daily schedule includes two or three classes, usually separated by an hour or two. In the time between classes, I catch up on reading assignments. I usually lunch with friends, and I have dinner at the school cafeteria. On pleasant days, I'll try to spend some time outside. I usually do my homework on weeknights.

Some of the projects I've worked on include designing a CD cover and a series of postal stamps, creating an original bitmap font, designing a set of greeting cards, and—my favorite—planning and creating a ten-page booklet about Frederic Goudy, a famous typographer.

One aspect of college life that surprised me was the fact that a school of about 6,000 undergraduates can seem like a small community. I was also surprised by the amount of reading I was assigned—and by how much time it took to complete seemingly simple assignments. As I adjusted to college life, however, I believe that I became more self-confident, more independent, and more aware of fellow students who may have vastly different backgrounds than my hometown friends.

With a degree in the visual arts, I hope to find a job in advertising or magazine layout. My greatest interest lies in experimenting with the way information appears on the printed page and how to come up with the most creative solutions for reaching the targeted customer.

ED MOORMAN
Comic Art
Minneapolis College of Art and Design

If you want to major in art, it's obvious to make sure that your portfolio is your focus; you want to have a variety of work, and you want to make sure that it's about something. Art is how you communicate, and you want to have something to communicate. The more specific your work is to you and the way that you feel, the more you'll stand out to admissions officers. Also, do as much work as you can outside of school and just push yourself. Sequester yourself in your room with your materials and follow all the ridiculous ideas you might have. Study history and artists that interest you and/or work within your chosen field. Trust your obsessions. Read, watch films, listen to music, and go to museums as much as you can. Everything you take in will feed and inform what you're doing.

When you go to Portfolio Days, pay attention to what the admissions officers are looking for. If, for example, they're looking to see if your proportions are dead-on or that you have included a landscape, a figure, etc., that says something about what the school cares about, because they're instructing their employees to find people who have these things. I went to a Portfolio Day and a popular school that shall remain nameless focused on those things alone while quickly sifting through my stuff. I went to the table for the Minneapolis College of Art and Design, and the admissions officer talked with me for a long time about my intentions and what I was doing, laughed at my comics, commented on my line quality, and generally seemed to be in tune with caring about me and how I was growing and would grow as an artist—instead of staunch criteria that has nothing to do with how a piece will affect the viewer. Lo and behold, MCAD is a great school.

As for once you're in school: I could advise you to learn how to manage your time, but you will learn through experience and stupidity (as we all do) that sleeping and eating are not negotiable enterprises.

Pay very close attention to selecting your teachers. Art school can cost your mortal soul in debts, and there's no reason you shouldn't have all fantastic instructors.

If you're going to a good school, you will be amazed how easy it is to make friends, no matter how alienated or awkward you may have felt beforehand. As it always is, your friends will be your saving grace in art school, and what's more, they'll be your artistic peers. I always know that if I have trouble with a project and I need an objective viewpoint, there are certain friends of mine whose opinion I respect to the highest degree who will help out.

I'm majoring in comic art and will try my hand with independent publishers after college for awhile. Then, at some point, I'll go to graduate school and get a master's in art education, since I really want to be an art teacher.

As an artist, you may never make a great deal of money. You must make peace with this idea. My sculpture teacher talks about the janitors who are great novelists, the art museum guards who are great painters, etc., and there is always the possibility that that will be you. But if you think that your passion for art can drive you through school and life, you're blessed, because you will always have that and you will always be okay because of it.

DANIELLE SMITH
Film and Television, with a Minor in Sound Design
Savannah College of Art and Design

Visiting my sister who was attending a large university while I was still in high school allowed me to experience college life at an early age. I went to parties, football games, and sat in on a few of her classes—in an auditorium with hundreds of other students she barely knew. I can remember thinking, "Is something wrong with me or is this just not that appealing?" I mean, the only thing she did for fun was go to parties and sporting events. Right then and there, I promised myself I would make a different college decision—not for my parents, not for my friends, but for my future.

I requested catalogs from several different colleges with good film programs. I had decided I wanted to study film and that was that. By chance, I went with my video production club on a tour of the Savannah College of Art and Design and the rest is history. I brought my dad back for a visit, and I remember thinking about it being the best college visit we had had out of the many colleges we visited up and down the East Coast. I applied, got in, and have never regretted my decision.

When I arrived at SCAD, I didn't know anyone. But that was a good thing. I knew that if I had gone to any of the other in-state colleges, I'd basically be living a rerun from high school. I knew that to grow I would need to expand my horizons by leaving my comfort zone. I can remember calling my friend during my first year of college to see how she was enjoying the new college life. The conversation went a little something like this:

"Hey, Jerry, what's going on? What are you up to?"

"Nothing much," she replied. "I'm just studying for this stupid science test I have tomorrow. What are you up to?"

"Oh, nothing really. I'm on a film shoot right now, so that's really cool. I got to work on a graduate student's film just yesterday too."

I wasn't trying to brag, but I couldn't help but to express my excitement. She was amazed that I was already working in my major too.

At SCAD, everyone is passionate about something. We love going to class and getting the chance to work with our favorite media. The best part about it is that our classmates love their work too, and they're excited to share it with you. It's never just busy work either. Every little thing you do can contribute to your portfolio if you want it to, and that makes students work even harder.

The networking possibilities are endless from the day you get here. From meeting graphic designers, architects, textile designers, and Hollywood directors, we experience it all. And we make connections with students in other majors. For instance, when I need an actor, I ask media and performing arts students. When

My college education has been instrumental in my career as an artist, both in theater and in fine arts. It has given me the knowledge, skill, and fortitude necessary to forge through my occupation as an artist. Today, as a wife and a mother of five young boys, my vocational focus is more on fine arts. I paint prolifically while my children slumber or attend school. When they are home, they delight in watching me paint, often offering invaluable criticism and support. They boast about my art shows to their teachers and peers. My children tangibly benefit from my college education; I impart to them many of the invaluable lessons in art that I gained as a college student. Clearly, my college education has enriched my life, not only as an artist, but also as a mother.

My studio is in the premier art gallery district of Chung King Road in Chinatown, Los Angeles. The studio is large, over 2,000 square feet, with three levels—a "store front" level that is all windows, a large functional basement, and a loft. Upon my easels, taped in random order, are inspirational photographs and words, most smudged with paint and charcoal. The hardwood floors beneath my easels are splattered in paint. There is always music playing in the background that relates to the subject I am painting. I often dance when I paint and sometimes speak to the canvas, as if it has a life of its own. Painting is always a joy-filled experience. One of my goals is to share with viewers a small portion of the joy I am blessed to feel, all within the process of creating art.

The subjects of my paintings range from the spiritual, through the natural, to the ancestral. I paint in oils, sans thinning agents. One of the most time-consuming and yet therapeutic aspects in my painting is the mixing of colors on the pallet. I tend to derive hues that are brightly colored, which reflect rather than absorb light.

It is always rewarding to see how positively my paintings impact people. This is most evident at the opening of an art show. I measure the success of a painting by the length of time people stand in front of it and stare or by the questions they ask, regarding the work. My acting career has helped me with the Questions & Answers portion of art show openings when I have had to stand before more than 100 people and speak about my inspiration and creative process.

I look at every venue to display and sell my work as an utter blessing. This is particularly true in the context of relatively few women and people of color being represented in the art world. One of my most gratifying experiences as an artist is being able to commune with other artists, of all types. I enjoy the soul connection that invariably exists between artists and benefit from listening to the reflections and insights of artists who are more experienced in the professional world of art than I am.

In the eve of a career as a professional fine artist, my plans for the future involve applying to graduate school so that I may pursue a Master of Fine Arts (M.F.A.) for my own personal edification and fortification. I look forward to benefiting from the relationships I will form with other graduate students as well as with professors who themselves are experienced artists. Being equipped with an M.F.A. will also give me the option to pursue a career as an instructor of art at the college level, should I so desire. My other plans for the future involve my continuing to develop a nonprofit organization I recently incorporated called ¡HABLA! (Harvesting Asian, Black, Latino Artists). The purpose of ¡HABLA! is to provide a platform for the voices of Asian, Black, and Latino fine artists in the mainstream art world, where artists of color are grossly underrepresented. ¡HABLA! achieves this goal through its all-inclusive youth-mentoring programs and its scholarships for artists of color to graduate and undergraduate art schools.

How to Use This Guide

Peterson's College Guide for Visual Arts Majors offers detailed information on professional degree programs in art offered at institutions in the U.S., its territories, and Canada. The guide should be used as a first step toward identifying potential programs; students are encouraged to consult with their school counselors and arts teachers for additional guidance.

QUICK-REFERENCE CHART

If you want to find out quickly which professional degrees are offered by a specific school, turn to the **Art Programs At-a-Glance** chart. Organized geographically, the chart provides the most basic information about each school in this guide, including:

- *Institution name and location*

- *Professional degrees offered in art*

- *Total enrollment*

- *Tuition and fees for the 2008–09 or 2007–08 academic year*

- *Profile page reference*

PROFILES OF VISUAL ARTS PROGRAMS

This guide profiles professional degree programs only. The **Profiles of Visual Arts Programs** section is organized alphabetically by institution name.

Each profile consists of the following elements:

Institutional control: Private institutions are designated as *independent* (nonprofit), *independent/religious* (sponsored by or affiliated with a religious group or having a non-denominational or interdenominational religious orientation), or *proprietary* (profit-making). Public institutions are designated by their primary source of support, such as *federal, state, commonwealth* (Puerto Rico), *territory* (U.S. territories), *county, district* (an administrative unit of public education, often having boundaries different from units of local government), *city, state, and local* ("local" refers to county, district, or city), or *state-related* (funded primarily by the state but administered autonomously).

Student body type: Categories are *men* (100 percent of student body), *primarily men, women* (100 percent of student body), *primarily women,* and *coed.* A few schools are designated as *undergraduate: women only; graduate: coed* or *undergraduate: men only; graduate: coed.*

Campus setting: Setting is designated as *urban, suburban, small town,* or *rural.*

Degrees: Many of the degrees listed (both undergraduate and graduate) are purely professional in scope and definition. Institutions may also offer B.A., B.S., M.A., and M.S. degrees that are considered professional, based on the prescribed curriculum and course load within the discipline. In a professional degree program, the majority of the curriculum is made up of course work within the particular arts field, while the rest of the program involves traditional liberal arts course work. A professional degree program allows students to focus most of their studies in art and emphasizes professional training and acquiring professional skills. This section also lists program accreditation by national arts organizations.

Enrollment: This data element cites the number of matriculated undergraduate and (if applicable) graduate students in the arts program, both full-time and part-time, as of fall 2007 (or 2006 if 2007 information was not available).

Student profile: Whole-figure percentages are given for the total program enrollment broken down into the following categories: *minorities, female, male, international.*

Faculty: Numbers are given for undergraduate and (if applicable) graduate faculty members teaching full-time and part-time in the respective area of study. The percentage of full-time faculty members who have appropriate terminal degrees in their field is listed, as is the ratio of undergraduate students to faculty members teaching undergraduate courses. Finally, mention is made if graduate students teach undergraduate courses in the program.

Student life: This section lists program-related organizations and campus activities in which visual arts students may participate. The availability of housing opportunities designated solely for visual arts students is mentioned here as well.

Expenses: Figures are given for the 2008–09 academic year (actual or estimated) or for the 2007–08 academic year if more recent figures were not yet available at the time of data collection. Annual expenses may be

Quick-Reference Chart

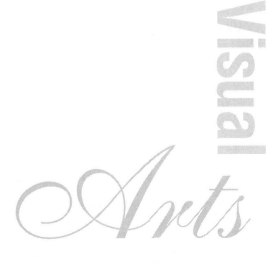

	Art	Enrollment	Tuition and Fees	Summer Programs	Page
Indiana—*continued*					
Indiana University Bloomington	BFA, MA, MAT, MFA, PhD	38,990	7837*		174
Saint Mary's College	BA, BFA	1,604	26,875*		247
University of Evansville	BFA	2,898	24,340*		283
University of Indianapolis	BFA	4,598	19,730*		288
University of Notre Dame	BFA, MA, MFA	11,733	35,187*		301
Iowa					
Clarke College	BFA	1,230	21,312*		145
Drake University	BA, BFA	5,617	23,692*		162
Iowa State University of Science and Technology	BFA, MFA	26,160	6360**		176
Maharishi University of Management	BFA	948	24,430**		191
The University of Iowa	BFA, MA, MFA, PhD	29,117	6544**		289
Kansas					
Emporia State University	BFA, BSEd	6,354	3926*		165
Kansas State University	BA, BFA, MFA	22,530	6235*		182
University of Kansas	BFA, MFA	28,569	7146*		289
Washburn University	BFA	6,901	5636*		316
Kentucky					
Murray State University	BFA	10,149	5748**	Art	210
Northern Kentucky University	BFA	14,785	6528**		218
University of Louisville	BFA, MA, MAT, PhD	20,592	7564**		290
Louisiana					
Louisiana Tech University	BFA, MFA	10,564	4548**		188
Loyola University New Orleans	BA, BFA	4,360	28,044**		189
Northwestern State University of Louisiana	BFA	9,037	3528*	Art	219

* Expenses for 2007–2008.   ** Estimated expenses for 2008–2009.   NR = Not reported.
For public institutions where tuition differs according to residence, the in-state tuition and fees are shown.

	Art	Enrollment	Tuition and Fees	Summer Programs	Page
Maine					
Maine College of Art	BFA, MFA	377	27,740**	Art	192
University of Southern Maine	BA, BFA	10,453	6866*	Art	303
Maryland					
Maryland Institute College of Art	BFA, BFA/ MA, BFA/ MAT, MA, MFA	1,899	30,680*	Art	194
Salisbury University	BFA	7,581	6412*		248
Massachusetts					
Anna Maria College	BA	1,244	24,617*		117
The Art Institute of Boston at Lesley University	BFA, BFA/ MA, BFA/ MEd, MFA	6,474	25,635**	Art	124
Boston University	BFA, MFA	32,053	37,050**	Art	133
Emmanuel College	BFA	2,467	26,250*		164
Massachusetts College of Art and Design	BFA, MFA, MS	2,315	7450*		197
Montserrat College of Art	BFA	285	22,300*	Art	206
School of the Museum of Fine Arts, Boston	BFA, MAT, MFA	797	27,970*	Art	257
Suffolk University	BFA, MA	9,083	24,250*	Art	268
University of Massachusetts Dartmouth	BA, BFA, MAE, MFA	9,080	8592*		291
Michigan					
Adrian College	BFA	1,308	23,390**		113
Albion College	BFA	1,938	27,530*		115
The Art Institute of Michigan	BFA		NR		128
College for Creative Studies	BFA, MFA	1,307	28,275**	Art	147
Grand Valley State University	BFA	23,464	7240*		169
Hope College	BA	3,226	23,800*		172
Kendall College of Art and Design of Ferris State University	BFA, BS, MFA		NR		183

* Expenses for 2007–2008.   ** Estimated expenses for 2008–2009.   NR = Not reported.
For public institutions where tuition differs according to residence, the in-state tuition and fees are shown.

	Art	Enrollment	Tuition and Fees	Summer Programs	Page
Oklahoma					
Oklahoma Baptist University	BFA		15,468**		221
Oregon					
The Art Institute of Portland	BFA		NR		128
Oregon College of Art & Craft	BFA		19,085*	Art	223
Southern Oregon University	BFA	4,801	5409*		265
University of Oregon	BFA, MFA	20,332	6036*		302
Pennsylvania					
Arcadia University	BA, BFA	3,592	29,700**	Art	119
Carnegie Mellon University	BFA, MFA	10,493	39,564**	Art	143
Drexel University	BARC, BS, MARC, MS	20,682	30,440**	Art	162
Edinboro University of Pennsylvania	BFA, BS, MA, MFA	7,686	6686**		164
Moore College of Art & Design	BFA	557	27,848**	Art	208
Pennsylvania Academy of the Fine Arts	BFA, MFA		NR	Art	228
Pennsylvania College of Art & Design	BFA	253	15,205*	Art	230
Point Park University	BA	3,592	18,990*	Art	233
Rosemont College	BFA	940	22,835*		245
Seton Hill University	BFA, MA	1,967	25,006*		260
Temple University	BARC, BFA, MA, MEd, MFA, PhD	34,696	10,802*	Art	274
The University of the Arts	BFA, BS, MA, MAT, MFA, MID	2,396	30,600**	Art	308
West Chester University of Pennsylvania	BA, BFA	13,219	6676*		320

* Expenses for 2007–2008.   ** Estimated expenses for 2008–2009.   NR = Not reported.
For public institutions where tuition differs according to residence, the in-state tuition and fees are shown.

Visual *Arts*

	Art	Enrollment	Tuition and Fees	Summer Programs	Page
Rhode Island					
Rhode Island School of Design	BDG, BFA, BID, MA, MARC, MAT, MFA, MIARC, MID, MLARC	2,259	33,118*	Art	239
Roger Williams University	BA	5,166	25,942*		245
South Carolina					
The Art Institute of Charleston	BFA	224	NR		127
Tennessee					
The Art Institute of Tennessee–Nashville	BFA	266	21,936**		129
Austin Peay State University	BA, BFA	9,094	5238*		129
Belmont University	BFA	4,756	21,110**		131
Memphis College of Art	BFA, MA, MAT, MFA	341	21,560**	Art	198
Tennessee Technological University	BFA	10,321	4980*		118
The University of Tennessee	BFA, MFA	29,937	6188**		305
The University of Tennessee at Martin	BFA	7,173	5005*		305
Watkins College of Art and Design	BFA	393	14,160**	Art	318
Texas					
Abilene Christian University	BFA, BS	4,675	17,410*		111
The Art Institute of Austin	BFA		NR		123
The Art Institute of Dallas	BFA		NR		127
The Art Institute of Houston	BFA		NR		127
Southern Methodist University	BFA, MFA	10,829	33,198**		265
Texas A&M University–Commerce	BA, BFA, BS, MFA	8,882	5126**		270
Texas A&M University–Corpus Christi	BFA, MFA	8,585	5640*		270
Texas Christian University	BFA, MA, MFA	8,668	24,868*		271
Texas Tech University	BFA, MFA, DA	28,257	6783*	Art	271

* Expenses for 2007–2008.   ** Estimated expenses for 2008–2009.   NR = Not reported.
For public institutions where tuition differs according to residence, the in-state tuition and fees are shown.

Undergraduate Contact Admissions, The Art Institute of California–San Diego, 7650 Mission Valley Road, San Diego, California 92108; 866-275-2422, fax: 619-291-3206.

The Art Institute of California–San Francisco

San Francisco, California

Proprietary, coed. Urban campus.

Degrees Bachelor of Fine Arts. Majors and concentrations: fashion design. Graduate degrees offered: Master of Fine Arts in the area of computer animation.

Expenses for 2007–2008 Contact school for current expenses.

Web Site http://www.artinstitutes.edu/sanfrancisco

Contact Admissions, The Art Institute of California–San Francisco, 1170 Market Street, San Francisco, California 94102-4928; 888-493-3261, fax: 415-863-6344.

The Art Institute of Charleston

Charleston, South Carolina

Proprietary, coed. Urban campus. Total enrollment: 224.

Degrees Bachelor of Fine Arts. Majors and concentrations: graphic design, interior design, photographic imaging, Web design and interactive media.

Expenses for 2007–2008 Tuition cost varies by program. Prospective students should contact the school for current tuition costs. Other charges include a starting kit for all first-quarter students. Kits vary in price depending on the program of study.

Web Site http://www.artinstitutes.edu/charleston

Undergraduate Contact Admissions, The Art Institute of Charleston, 24 North Market Street, Charleston, South Carolina 29401-2623; 866-211-0107, fax: 843-727-3440.

The Art Institute of Dallas

Dallas, Texas

Proprietary, coed. Urban campus. Art program established 1964.

Degrees Bachelor of Fine Arts. Majors and concentrations: advertising design, digital filmmaking and video production, fashion and retail management, fashion design, graphic design, interior design, media arts/animation, Web design and interactive media.

Expenses for 2007–2008 Contact school for current expenses.

Web Site http://www.artinstitutes.edu/dallas

Undergraduate Contact Admissions, The Art Institute of Dallas, 8080 Park Lane, Suite 100, Dallas, Texas 75231-5993; 800-275-4243, fax: 214-750-9460.

The Art Institute of Houston

Houston, Texas

Proprietary, coed. Urban campus.

Degrees Bachelor of Fine Arts. Majors and concentrations: digital filmmaking and video production, graphic design, interior design, media arts/animation, photography, Web design and interactive media. Program accredited by CIDA.

Expenses for 2007–2008 Contact school for current expenses.

Web Site http://www.artinstitutes.edu/houston

Undergraduate Contact Admissions, The Art Institute of Houston, 1900 Yorktown Street, Houston, Texas 77056-4197; 800-275-4244, fax: 713-966-2797.

The Art Institute of Jacksonville

Jacksonville, Florida

Proprietary, coed. Suburban campus.

Degrees Bachelor of Fine Arts. Majors and concentrations: digital filmmaking and video production, graphic design, interior design, Web design and interactive media.

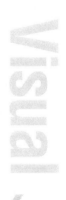

The Art Institute of Jacksonville (continued)

Expenses for 2007–2008 Contact school for current expenses..

Web Site
http://www.artinstitutes.edu/jacksonville/

Undergraduate Contact Admissions, The Art Institute of Jacksonville, 8775 Baypine Road, Jacksonville, Florida 32256-8528; 800-924-1589, fax: 904-732-9423.

The Art Institute of Michigan

Novi, Michigan

Proprietary, coed.

Degrees Bachelor of Fine Arts. Majors and concentrations: interior design, visual communication, Web design and interactive media.

Expenses for 2007–2008 Tuition cost varies by program. Prospective students should contact the school for current tuition costs. Other charges include a starting kit for all first-quarter students. Kits vary in price depending on the program of study.

Web Site http://www.artinstitutes.edu/detroit

Undergraduate Contact Admissions, The Art Institute of Michigan, 28125 Cabot Drive, Suite 120, Novi, Michigan 48377; 800-479-0087, fax: 248-675-3830.

The Art Institute of Portland

Portland, Oregon

Proprietary, coed. Urban campus.

Degrees Bachelor of Fine Arts. Majors and concentrations: advertising, apparel accessory design, apparel design, design, digital film and video, fashion marketing, game art and design, graphic design, interior design, media arts/animation, visual effects and motion graphics.

Expenses for 2007–2008 Contact school for current expenses.

Web Site http://www.artinstitutes.edu/portland

Undergraduate Contact Admissions, The Art Institute of Portland, 1122 NW Davis Street, Portland, Oregon 97209-2911; 888-228-6528, fax: 503-227-1945.

The Art Institute of Seattle

Seattle, Washington

Proprietary, coed. Urban campus. Total enrollment: 2,352.

Degrees Bachelor of Fine Arts. Majors and concentrations: digital filmmaking and video production, fashion design, game art and design, graphic design, interior design, media arts/animation, photography.

Expenses for 2007–2008 Application fee: $50. Comprehensive fee: $30,652 includes full-time tuition ($19,968) and college room and board ($10,684). Tuition cost varies by program. Prospective students should contact the school for current tuition costs. Other charges include a starting kit for all first-quarter students. Kits vary in price depending on the program of study.

Web Site http://www.artinstitutes.edu/seattle

Undergraduate Contact Admissions, The Art Institute of Seattle, 2323 Elliott Avenue, Seattle, Washington 98121-1642; 800-275-2471, fax: 206-269-0275.

The Art Institute of Tampa

Tampa, Florida

Proprietary, coed. Suburban campus. Total enrollment: 881.

Degrees Bachelor of Fine Arts. Majors and concentrations: digital filmmaking and video production, digital photography, game art and design, graphic design, interior design, media arts/animation, visual effects and motion graphics, Web design and interactive media.

Expenses for 2007–2008 Application fee: $50. Tuition cost varies by program. Prospective students should contact the school for current tuition costs. Other charges include a starting kit for all first-quarter students. Kits vary in price depending on the program of study.

Web Site http://www.artinstitutes.edu/tampa

Undergraduate Contact Admissions, The Art Institute of Tampa, 4401 North Himes Avenue, Suite 150, Tampa, Florida 33614-7086; 866-703-3277, fax: 813-873-2171.

The Art Institute of Tennessee–Nashville

Nashville, Tennessee

Proprietary, coed. Urban campus. Total enrollment: 266.

Degrees Bachelor of Fine Arts. Majors and concentrations: digital filmmaking and video production, graphic design, interior design, photographic imaging, Web design and interactive media.

Expenses for 2008–2009 Application fee: $50. One-time mandatory fee: $150. Tuition: $21,936 full-time. College room only: $5433.

Web Site http://www.artinstitutes.edu/nashville

Undergraduate Contact Admissions, The Art Institute of Tennessee–Nashville, 100 Centerview Drive, Suite 250, Nashville, Tennessee 37214-3439; 866-747-5770, fax: 615-874-3530.

The Art Institute of Washington

Arlington, Virginia

Proprietary, coed. Urban campus. Total enrollment: 1,700.

Degrees Bachelor of Fine Arts. Majors and concentrations: digital filmmaking and video production, game art and design, graphic design, interior design, media arts/animation, photographic imaging, visual effects and motion graphics, Web design and interactive media.

Expenses for 2008–2009 Application fee: $50. Tuition: $20,880 full-time. College room only: $8385.

Web Site http://www.artinstitutes.edu/arlington

Undergraduate Contact Admissions, The Art Institute of Washington, 1820 North Fort Myer Drive, Arlington, Virginia 22209-1802; 877-303-3771, fax: 703-358-9759.

The Art Institutes International Minnesota

Minneapolis, Minnesota

Proprietary, coed. Urban campus. Art program established 1997.

Degrees Bachelor of Fine Arts in the area of photography. Majors and concentrations: graphic design, interactive media, interior design, media arts/animation, photography, visual effects and motion graphics.

Expenses for 2007–2008 Students should contact school for current tuition costs.

Web Site http://www.artinstitutes.edu/minneapolis

Undergraduate Contact Admissions, The Art Institutes International Minnesota, 15 South 9th Street, Minneapolis, Minnesota 55402; 800-777-3643.

Augusta State University

Augusta, Georgia

State-supported, coed. Urban campus. Total enrollment: 6,588. Art program established 1958.

Web Site http://www.aug.edu/

Austin Peay State University

Clarksville, Tennessee

State-supported, coed. Suburban campus. Total enrollment: 9,094.

Degrees Bachelor of Arts in the area of art education/licensure K-12; Bachelor of Fine Arts in the areas of studio arts, visual communication. Majors and concentrations: art education, ceramics, drawing, graphic design, illustration, painting, photography, printmaking, sculpture. Program accredited by NASAD.

Enrollment 280 total; all undergraduate.

Art Student Profile 60% females, 40% males, 15% minorities, 10% international.

Art Faculty 13 undergraduate (full-time), 8 undergraduate (part-time). 95% of full-time faculty have terminal degrees. Graduate stu-

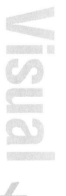

Austin Peay State University (continued)

dents do not teach undergraduate courses. Undergraduate student–faculty ratio: 20:1.

Student Life Student groups/activities include Student Art League/ Student Art Show, Capsule Magazine, Student Chapter NAEA (art education).

Expenses for 2007–2008 Application fee: $15. State resident tuition: $4058 full-time. Nonresident tuition: $14,334 full-time. Mandatory fees: $1180 full-time. Full-time tuition and fees vary according to location and program. College room and board: $5510. College room only: $3400. Room and board charges vary according to board plan and housing facility.

Financial Aid Program-specific awards: 1 Tom Malone Scholarship for studio arts students ($1000), 1 Claudell Wootten Scholarship for art education students ($500), 2 Friends of Photography Scholarships for photography students ($250), 1 Jewel Birdsong Scholarship for art history/conservation students ($1000), 1 Art Alumni Scholarship for design/photography students ($500), 1 US Bank Scholarship for those with outstanding portfolios and demonstrating need ($1000), Friends of the Art Scholarship ($500), Helena Haskill Scholarship for typography students ($500).

Application Procedures Students apply for admission into the professional program by junior year. Required: high school transcript, college transcript(s) for transfer students, SAT or ACT test scores (minimum composite ACT score of 19). Recommended: letter of recommendation, interview. Portfolio reviews held once on campus; the submission of slides may be substituted for portfolios.

Web Site http://www.apsu.edu/art/

Undergraduate Contact Chair, Department of Art, Austin Peay State University, PO Box 4677, Clarksville, Tennessee 37044; 931-221-7333, fax: 931-221-7432.

Ball State University

Muncie, Indiana

State-supported, coed. Suburban campus. Total enrollment: 19,849.

Degrees Bachelor of Fine Arts in the area of art; Bachelor of Science in the area of art education. Majors and concentrations: animation, ceramics, drawing, electronic arts, jewelry and metalsmithing, painting, photography, printmaking, sculpture, visual communication. Graduate degrees offered: Master of Arts in the area of art. Program accredited by NASAD.

Enrollment 573 total; 447 undergraduate, 19 graduate, 107 nonprofessional degree.

Art Student Profile 55% females, 45% males, 3% minorities, 2% international.

Art Faculty 30 total (full-time), 4 total (part-time). 100% of full-time faculty have terminal degrees. Graduate students do not teach undergraduate courses. Undergraduate student–faculty ratio: 15:1.

Student Life Student groups/activities include National Art Education Association Student Chapter, Fine Arts League, Crafts Guild.

Expenses for 2007–2008 Application fee: $25. State resident tuition: $6672 full-time. Nonresident tuition: $17,740 full-time. Mandatory fees: $476 full-time. College room and board: $7240. Room and board charges vary according to board plan and housing facility.

Financial Aid Program-specific awards: 4–6 freshmen scholarship awards for outstanding freshmen program applicants ($1000), 8 Fine Art Scholarships for outstanding freshmen program applicants ($4000), 5 Ruth Swain Scholarships for outstanding sophomores, juniors, or seniors ($1000), 2 Roberta Law Scholarships for outstanding sophomores, juniors, seniors ($1000), 1 Dorotha Stock Scholarship for outstanding sophomores, juniors, or seniors ($500), 1 Alice Nichols Scholarship for outstanding art education students ($360), 1 Indiana Arts and Craftsman Scholarship for outstanding art majors ($250), 5 Presidential Scholar in the Arts Awards for outstanding freshmen.

Application Procedures Students admitted directly into the professional program freshman year. Deadline for freshmen: April 1; transfers: continuous. Notification date for freshmen: May 1. Required: high school transcript, college transcript(s) for transfer students, portfolio, SAT or ACT test scores. Recommended: minimum 2.0 high school GPA. Portfolio reviews held once on campus; the submission of slides may be substituted for portfolios if a campus visit is impossible.

Web Site http://www.bsu.edu/art/

Undergraduate Contact Ms. Barbara Giorgio-Booher, Primary Department Advisor, Department of Art, Ball State University, Muncie, Indiana 47306-0405; 765-285-5841, fax: 765-285-5838, e-mail address: bgiorgio@bsu.edu

Graduate Contact Prof. Kenton Hall, Graduate Director, Department of Art, Ball State University, Muncie, Indiana 47306-0405; 765-285-5838, fax: 765-285-5838, e-mail address: khall@bsu.edu

Barton College

Wilson, North Carolina

Independent, coed. Small town campus. Total enrollment: 1,130. Art program established 1902.

Degrees Bachelor of Fine Arts in the areas of art and design (emphasis in design, ceramics, painting, photography); Bachelor of Science in the area of art education K-12. Majors and concentrations: art education, ceramics, design, painting, photography.

Enrollment 70 total; 60 undergraduate, 10 nonprofessional degree.

Art Student Profile 50% females, 50% males, 15% minorities, 1% international.

Art Faculty 4 undergraduate (full-time), 3 undergraduate (part-time). 100% of full-time faculty have terminal degrees. Graduate students do not teach undergraduate courses. Undergraduate student–faculty ratio: 16:1.

Expenses for 2008–2009 Application fee: $25. Comprehensive fee: $26,720 includes full-time tuition ($18,460), mandatory fees ($1478), and college room and board ($6782). College room only: $3178. Special program-related fees: $43 per studio for supplies, $110 for photography supplies.

Financial Aid Program-specific awards: 1 Bessie Massengill Award for sophomores and juniors, 1 TEAM Award for sophomores and juniors ($1000), 1 National Scholastic Award for freshmen ($1000), 1 Art Faculty Scholarship for sophomores, juniors, seniors ($750), 1 Triangle East Advertising and Marketing Association Scholarship for sophomores, juniors, seniors ($1000), 1 Stuart Walston Scholarship for those with minimum 2.5 GPA ($500).

Application Procedures Students admitted directly into the professional program freshman year. Deadline for freshmen and transfers: continuous. Required: high school transcript, college transcript(s) for transfer students, letter of recommendation, SAT or ACT test scores. Recommended: minimum 2.0 high school GPA, interview, portfolio. Portfolio reviews held by appointment on campus; the submission of slides may be substituted for portfolios.

Web Site http://www.barton.edu/

Undergraduate Contact Ms. Susan B. Fecho, Chair, Art Department, Barton College, PO Box 5000, Wilson, North Carolina 27893-7000; 252-399-6480, fax: 252-399-6571.

Baylor University

Waco, Texas

Independent Baptist, coed. Urban campus. Total enrollment: 14,174.

Web Site http://www.baylor.edu/

Belmont University

Nashville, Tennessee

Independent Baptist, coed. Urban campus. Total enrollment: 4,756. Art program established 1984.

Degrees Bachelor of Fine Arts in the areas of studio, art education, design communications. Majors and concentrations: art education, design communication, studio art. Cross-registration with O'More College. Program accredited by NASAD.

Enrollment 106 total; all undergraduate.

Art Student Profile 70% females, 30% males, 10% minorities, 1% international.

Art Faculty 5 undergraduate (full-time), 13 undergraduate (part-time). 100% of full-time faculty have terminal degrees. Graduate students do not teach undergraduate courses. Undergraduate student–faculty ratio: 21:1.

Student Life Student groups/activities include Art Association, Blvd Gallery and Design (student-run, on-campus business).

Expenses for 2008–2009 Application fee: $35. Comprehensive fee: $31,110 includes full-time tuition ($20,070), mandatory fees ($1040), and college room and board ($10,000). College room only: $6300. Special program-related fees: $100 per semester for design communi-

Belmont University (continued)

cation courses, $100 per semester for photography lab fee, $100 per semester for model fees, materials fee for studio courses.

Financial Aid Program-specific awards: 4 Leu Art Scholarships for freshmen art majors ($2000), 1 rising senior award ($1000).

Application Procedures Students admitted directly into the professional program freshman year. Deadline for freshmen and transfers: continuous. Required: essay, high school transcript, college transcript(s) for transfer students, minimum 2.0 high school GPA, letter of recommendation, portfolio, SAT or ACT test scores. Recommended: interview. Portfolio reviews held by arrangement on campus; the submission of slides may be substituted for portfolios whenever needed (DVD preferred).

Web Site http://www.belmont.edu/art/

Undergraduate Contact Dr. Judy Bullington, Chair, Department of Art, Belmont University, 1900 Belmont Boulevard, Nashville, Tennessee 37212-3537; 615-460-6770, fax: 615-460-6757, e-mail address: bullingtonj@mail.belmont.edu

More About the University

The Department of Art is part of Belmont's College of Visual and Performing Arts and is located in the 40,000-square-foot Leu Center for the Visual Arts. This facility combines the latest technology with traditional studio space, including two Macintosh graphics labs and a student gallery. There are large studios specifically for drawing, painting, printmaking, photography, sculpture, and ceramics as well as a 118-seat audiovisual room for slide lectures and other multimedia presentations. In addition, the Leu Art Gallery in the Lila D. Bunch Library provides more than 1,000 square feet of exhibit space for traveling exhibits, regional art exhibitions, and regional and national artists.

Faculty Faculty members are practicing artists and designers who exhibit both regionally and nationally.

Exhibition Opportunities Each year, the Department of Art exhibits student work in a large art show. In addition, seniors exhibit their work during their last semester of study.

Special Programs International residencies in art are offered in France, Great Britain, Germany, Greece, Russia, and in Italy at the Lorenzo de Medici Art Institute of Florence. Course work in Florence may include photography, painting and drawing, textiles, fashion design, oil and fresco painting restoration, graphics, sculpture, jewelry, and art history. Internship programs allow students to gain valuable, practical work experience. In addition, the Belmont University Career Office offers assistance with career planning.

Birmingham-Southern College

Birmingham, Alabama

Independent Methodist, coed. Urban campus. Total enrollment: 1,389. Art program established 1946.

Degrees Bachelor of Fine Arts in the area of studio art. Majors and concentrations: art history, painting, photography, printmaking, sculpture. Cross-registration with University of Alabama at Birmingham, University of Montevallo, Samford University.

Enrollment 350 total; 190 undergraduate, 160 nonprofessional degree.

Art Student Profile 60% females, 40% males, 10% minorities, 5% international.

Art Faculty 7 undergraduate (full-time), 2 undergraduate (part-time). 100% of full-time faculty have terminal degrees. Graduate students do not teach undergraduate courses. Undergraduate student–faculty ratio: 15:1.

Student Life Student groups/activities include Art Students League.

Expenses for 2008–2009 Application fee: $25. Comprehensive fee: $34,691 includes full-time tuition ($24,780), mandatory fees ($806), and college room and board ($9105). College room only: $5245. Special program-related fees: $30–$80 per unit for materials.

Financial Aid Program-specific awards: 10–15 art scholarships for art majors ($1300–$8000).

Application Procedures Students admitted directly into the professional program freshman year. Notification date for freshmen and transfers: continuous. Required: essay, high school transcript, college transcript(s) for transfer students, minimum 2.0 high school GPA, SAT or ACT test scores (minimum composite ACT score of 21), interview for scholarship consideration. Recommended: 2 letters of recommendation, interview, portfolio. Portfolio reviews held once on campus; the submission of slides may be substituted for portfolios when distance is prohibitive, or work is too large to carry.

Web Site http://www.bsc.edu

Undergraduate Contact Ms. Sheri Salmon, Associate Vice President of Admissions, Birmingham-Southern College, 900 Arkadelphia Road, Box 549008, Birmingham, Alabama 35254; 205-226-4696, fax: 205-226-3074.

Boston University

Boston, Massachusetts

Independent, coed. Urban campus. Total enrollment: 32,053. Art program established 1954.

Degrees Bachelor of Fine Arts in the areas of painting, sculpture, graphic design, art education. Majors and concentrations: art education, ceramics, glassblowing, graphic design, painting, photography, printmaking, sculpture. Graduate degrees offered: Master of Fine Arts in the areas of painting, sculpture, graphic design, art education, studio teaching. Cross-registration with Boston College, Brandeis University, Tufts University.

Enrollment 306 total; 230 undergraduate, 65 graduate, 11 nonprofessional degree.

Art Student Profile 60% females, 40% males, 10% minorities, 14% international.

Art Faculty 21 total (full-time), 10 total (part-time). 100% of full-time faculty have terminal degrees. Graduate students do not teach undergraduate courses. Undergraduate student–faculty ratio: 16:1.

Student Life Student groups/activities include American Institute of Graphic Arts, Copley Society, Boston University Art League. Special housing available for art students.

Expenses for 2008–2009 Application fee: $75. Comprehensive fee: $48,468 includes full-time tuition ($36,540), mandatory fees ($510), and college room and board ($11,418). College room only: $7420. Special program-related fees: $35–$50 for lab fee, $100 for studio fee for painting majors.

Financial Aid Program-specific awards: 160 grants-need/performance awards for enrolled program students ($17,000).

Application Procedures Students admitted directly into the professional program freshman year. Deadline for freshmen: January 1; transfers: April 1. Notification date for freshmen: April 15; transfers: May 30. Required: essay, high school transcript, college transcript(s) for transfer students, portfolio, SAT or ACT test scores. Recommended: minimum 3.0 high school GPA, 3 letters of recommendation. Portfolio reviews held continuously on campus; the submission of slides may be substituted for portfolios.

Web Site http://www.bu.edu/cfa/visual

Undergraduate Contact Jeannette Guillemin, Assistant Director/Director of Admissions and Student Affairs, School of Visual Arts, College of Fine Arts, Boston University, 855 Commonwealth Avenue, Boston, Massachusetts 02215; 617-353-3371, fax: 617-353-7217, e-mail address: visuarts@bu.edu

More About the University

Boston University College of Fine Arts (CFA) is a small, conservatory-style school within a major university, offering outstanding professional training in music, the theater, and visual arts. The college was founded as the College of Music in 1873 and has a long and distinguished history of training artists. The Division of Applied Arts, now known as the School of Visual Arts, was added in 1919, and it currently enrolls approximately 250 students.

The student painters, sculptors, graphic designers, and art educators at the School of Visual Arts prepare for leading positions in the art world by engaging in its present and understanding its past. With a faculty composed of practicing professional artists, the school offers an intensive program of studio training combined with liberal arts studies leading to the Bachelor of Fine Arts (B.F.A.) and Master of Fine Arts (M.F.A.).

Campus Surroundings Boston University—independent, coeducational, nonsectarian—is an internationally recognized center of higher education and research. The University is located in the heart of Boston, along the banks of the Charles River and adjacent to the historic Back Bay district of Boston. Boston University is perfectly situated to enjoy both the charm and beauty of the city and its cultural and recreational attractions. School of Visual Arts students benefit from the many major museums and galleries as well as the theaters and musical organizations that make Boston a rich and varied environment for the art student.

Program Facilities The School of Visual Arts offers painting, drawing, and sculpture studios; a welding

Boston University (continued)

and wood shop; computer labs; photography and printmaking studios; a book and slide library; and exhibition spaces, including the Boston University Art Gallery, the 808 Showroom Gallery, the Sherman Gallery, and the Commonwealth Gallery.

Faculty, Resident Artists, and Alumni The faculty of dedicated teachers includes some of the finest painters, sculptors, graphic designers, and art educators in the country. Distinguished faculty members include John Walker, painter; Richard Raiselis, painter; Harold Reddicliffe, painter; Lynne Allen, printmaker; Judith Simpson, art educator; and Alston Purvis, graphic designer. Visiting artists include Charles Close, painter; Peter Schjeldahl, art critic; Vincent Desiderio, painter; Greg Amenoff, painter; William Tucker, sculptor; William Bailey, painter; Rackstraw Downes, printmaker; Mags Harries, sculptor, Jonathan Shahn, painter; Pat Steir, painter; Tim Rollins, educator; Al Leslie, painter; and Suzanne Coffey, painter. Alumni include the distinguished American artists Pat Steir and Brice Martin; designer Ira Yoffe, Vice President and Creative Director for *Parade Magazine;* Penelope Zencks, sculptor; and Richard Heinrichs, sculpture and production/set designer, whose credits include *Planet of the Apes, Fargo,* and *Pirates of the Caribbean.*

Exhibition Opportunities Each year, the School of Visual Arts exhibits student work in its spring show. Additional exhibition opportunities exist throughout the year for students, faculty members, and alumni in the Boston University Art Gallery, the Sherman Gallery, the 808 Gallery, and the Commonwealth Gallery.

Special Programs Through the Boston University Collaborative Degree Program (BUCOP), students may obtain a dual degree in the College of Fine Arts and another of the University's schools or colleges. Students may minor in liberal arts, business, or communications. Painting and graphic design students are encouraged to study abroad at the Scuola Internazionale di Graphica in Venice, Italy, in their junior year. A five-year B.F.A./M.F.A. is available to students interested in majoring in a studio area along with art education.

Bowling Green State University

Bowling Green, Ohio

State-supported, coed. Small town campus. Total enrollment: 18,619.

Web Site http://www.bgsu.edu/

Bradley University

Peoria, Illinois

Independent, coed. Suburban campus. Total enrollment: 6,053.

Degrees Bachelor of Arts in the areas of studio art, art education, art history; Bachelor of Fine Arts in the area of studio art; Bachelor of Science in the areas of studio art, art education. Majors and concentrations: art education, art history, studio art. Graduate degrees offered: Master of Arts in the area of studio art; Master of Fine Arts in the area of studio art. Program accredited by NASAD.

Enrollment 153 total; all undergraduate.

Art Student Profile 54% females, 46% males, 11% minorities, 4% international.

Art Faculty 9 total (full-time), 8 total (part-time). 100% of full-time faculty have terminal degrees. Graduate students teach a few undergraduate courses. Undergraduate student–faculty ratio: 11:1.

Student Life Student groups/activities include Spectrum, American Institute of Graphic Arts (AIGA), Potters Guild, Art History Club, National Art Education Association Students (NAEAS).

Expenses for 2007–2008 Application fee: $35. Comprehensive fee: $28,410 includes full-time tuition ($21,200), mandatory fees ($160), and college room and board ($7050). College room only: $4100. Full-time tuition and fees vary according to student level. Room and board charges vary according to board plan. Special program-related fees: $25 per credit hour for supplies.

Financial Aid Program-specific awards: 33 art scholarships for art majors ($992).

Application Procedures Students apply for admission into the professional program by sophomore year. Deadline for freshmen and transfers: continuous. Required: high school

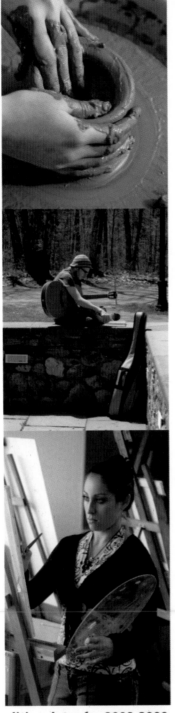
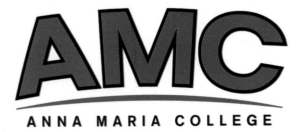

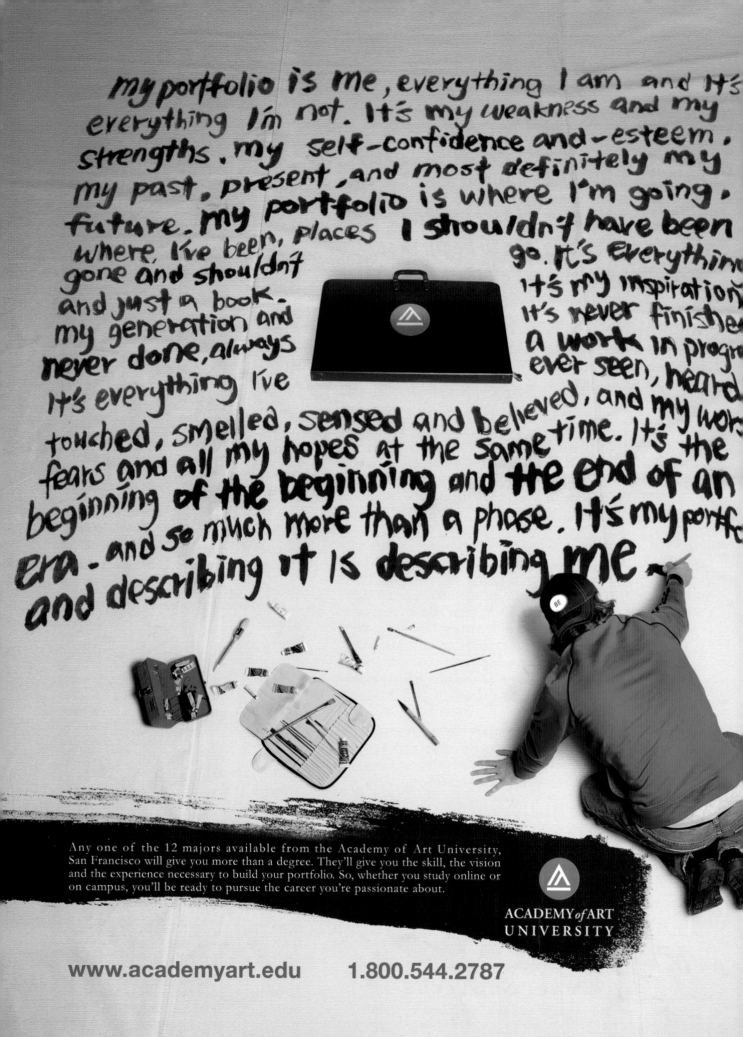

My portfolio is me, everything I am and it's everything I'm not. It's my weakness and my strengths. My self-confidence and -esteem, my past, present, and most definitely my future. My portfolio is where I'm going, where I've been, places I shouldn't have been and shouldn't go. It's everything gone and just a book. It's my inspiration. My generation and it's never finished never done, always a work in progress It's everything I've ever seen, heard touched, smelled, sensed and believed, and my work fears and all my hopes at the same time. It's the beginning of the beginning and the end of an era. and so much more than a phase. It's my portfolio and describing it is describing me.

transcript, college transcript(s) for transfer students, minimum 2.0 high school GPA, portfolio, SAT or ACT test scores. Recommended: 2 letters of recommendation. Portfolio reviews held 3 times on campus; the submission of slides may be substituted for portfolios (slides preferred for scholarship decisions).

Web Site http://art.bradley.edu

Undergraduate Contact Ms. Nickie Roberson, Director of Admissions, Office of Undergraduate Admissions, Bradley University, Swords Hall, Peoria, Illinois 61625; 800-447-6460, fax: 309-677-2797, e-mail address: admissions@bradley.edu

Graduate Contact Leslie Betz, Director of Graduate Enrollment Management, Graduate School, Bradley University, 1501 West Bradley Avenue, Peoria, Illinois 61625; 309-677-2375.

Brenau University

Gainesville, Georgia

Independent, women only. Small town campus. Total enrollment: 916. Art program established 1973.

Web Site http://www.brenau.edu/

Brigham Young University

Provo, Utah

Independent, coed. Suburban campus. Total enrollment: 34,174. Art program established 1925.

Degrees Bachelor of Arts in the areas of art history, art education; Bachelor of Fine Arts in the areas of studio art, graphic design, photography, illustration, animation. Majors and concentrations: animation, art education, art history, graphic design, illustration, photography, studio art. Graduate degrees offered: Master of Fine Arts in the area of studio art. Program accredited by NASAD.

Enrollment 659 total; 625 undergraduate, 34 graduate.

Art Student Profile 70% females, 30% males.

Art Faculty 33 total (full-time), 30 total (part-time). 78% of full-time faculty have terminal degrees. Graduate students teach more than half of undergraduate courses.

Student Life Student groups/activities include Art History Student Association, National Art Education Association Student Chapter.

Expenses for 2007–2008 Application fee: $30. Comprehensive fee: $14,140 includes full-time tuition ($7680) and college room and board ($6460). Room and board charges vary according to board plan and housing facility. Latter Day Saints full-time student $3840 per year. Special program-related fees: $200 per semester for supplies.

Financial Aid Program-specific awards: 150 talent awards for program majors ($200–$1000), 1–5 J. Roman Andrus Printmaking Awards for printmaking majors ($200–$300), 5 Demery Scholarships for program majors ($200–$300), 5 Anna F. Sommers Scholarships for program majors ($200–$400), 25 Olena K. and George K. Lewis Scholarships for painting majors ($200–$400), 15 Betty M. and Paul J. Boshard Scholarships for program majors ($200–$300), 15 Cory Nathan Belleau Scholarships for program majors ($200–$700), 1–5 Max Dickson and Ruth Kimball Weaver Scholarships for ceramics majors ($200–$300).

Application Procedures Students apply for admission into the professional program by freshman, sophomore year. Deadline for freshmen: February 15; transfers: March 15. Notification date for freshmen: April 15; transfers: May 1. Required: essay, high school transcript, college transcript(s) for transfer students, minimum 3.0 high school GPA, letter of recommendation, portfolio, ACT test score only (minimum composite ACT score of 25), 10 pieces of best work, creative exercise. Portfolio reviews held 3 times on campus.

Web Site http://cfac.byu.edu/

Undergraduate Contact Sonya Schiffman, Department Secretary, Department of Visual Arts, Brigham Young University, Provo, Utah 84602; 801-422-8773, fax: 801-422-0695, e-mail address: sonya_schiffman@byu.edu

Graduate Contact Ms. Sharon Heelis, Secretary to Chair, Department of Visual Arts, Brigham Young University, E-509 HFAC, Provo, Utah 84602; 801-422-4429, fax: 801-422-0695, e-mail address: sharon_heelis@byu.edu

Brooklyn College of the City University of New York

Brooklyn, New York

State and locally supported, coed. Urban campus. Total enrollment: 15,947 (2007). Art program established 1967.

Degrees Bachelor of Fine Arts in the area of art. Majors and concentrations: computer art, painting/drawing, photography, printmaking, sculpture. Graduate degrees offered: Master of Arts in the area of art education (K-12); Master of Fine Arts in the area of art. Cross-registration with City University of New York System.

Enrollment 84 total; 20 undergraduate, 34 graduate, 30 nonprofessional degree.

Art Student Profile 55% females, 45% males, 25% minorities, 15% international.

Art Faculty 17 total (full-time), 9 total (part-time). 100% of full-time faculty have terminal degrees. Graduate students teach a few undergraduate courses. Undergraduate student–faculty ratio: 16:1.

Student Life Student groups/activities include Art Group, Graduate Art Student Union.

Expenses for 2007–2008 Application fee: $65. State resident tuition: $4000 full-time. Nonresident tuition: $8762 full-time. Mandatory fees: $150 full-time. Special program-related fees: $15–$20 per course for supplies and model fees.

Financial Aid Program-specific awards: 10–20 Charles G. Shaw Memorial Awards for studio art majors ($400–$1000), 2–3 Bernard Horlick Awards for program majors ($500–$750), 1–2 Jerome J. Viola Memorial Scholarships for program majors ($350–$500), 1–2 Bernard Cole Memorial Scholarships for photography majors ($150–$250), 1 Thomas S. Buechner Award for program majors ($500), 2 Diana and Lewis Sills Memorial Scholarships for program majors ($500), 10–20 Walter Cerf Awards for program majors ($400–$1000).

Application Procedures Students apply for admission into the professional program by sophomore year. Deadline for freshmen and transfers: continuous. Notification date for freshmen and transfers: continuous. Required: high school transcript, college transcript(s) for transfer students, portfolio, minimum 2.8 high school GPA. Recommended: interview, SAT or ACT test scores. Portfolio reviews held once on campus; the submission of slides may be substituted for portfolios for large works of art.

Web Site http://depthome.brooklyn.cuny.edu/art/

Undergraduate Contact Prof. Michael Mallory, Chair, Department of Art, Brooklyn College of the City University of New York, 2900 Bedford Avenue, Brooklyn, New York 11210-2889; 718-951-5181, fax: 718-951-4728, e-mail address: mmallory@brooklyn.cuny.edu

Graduate Contact Prof. Janet Carlile, Deputy Chair, Department of Art, Brooklyn College of the City University of New York, 2900 Bedford Avenue, Brooklyn, New York 11210-2889; 718-951-5572, fax: 718-951-4728, e-mail address: artmfa@brooklyn.cuny.edu

California College of the Arts

San Francisco, California

Independent, coed. Urban campus. Total enrollment: 1,614. Art program established 1907.

Degrees Bachelor of Arts in the areas of writing and literature, visual studies; Bachelor of Architecture; Bachelor of Fine Arts in the areas of furniture, glass, ceramics, sculpture, painting, drawing, printmaking, photography, textiles, jewelry/metal arts, graphic design, illustration, industrial design, fashion design, media arts, community arts, interior design, animation. Majors and concentrations: animation, architecture, ceramic art and design, creative writing, fashion design, furniture design, glass, graphic design, illustration, industrial design, interior design, jewelry and metalsmithing, media arts, painting/drawing, photography, printmaking, public art studies, sculpture, textile arts, visual studies. Graduate degrees offered: Master of Arts in the areas of curatorial practice, visual and critical studies; Master of Architecture; Master of Fine Arts in the areas of design, writing, fine arts; Master of Business Administration in the area of design strategy. Cross-registration with Mills College, Holy Names College. Program accredited by NAAB, NASAD, CIDA.

Enrollment 1,579 total; 1,284 undergraduate, 295 graduate.

Art Student Profile 60% females, 40% males, 26% minorities, 7% international.

Art Faculty 61 undergraduate (full-time), 372 undergraduate (part-time), 5 graduate (full-time), 47 graduate (part-time). 62% of full-time faculty have terminal degrees. Graduate students do not teach undergraduate courses. Undergraduate student–faculty ratio: 14:1.

Student Life Student groups/activities include American Institute of Graphic Arts, American Institute of Architects, American Society of Interior Designers. Special housing available for art students.

Expenses for 2008–2009 Application fee: $50. Tuition: $31,032 full-time. Mandatory fees: $350 full-time. College room only: $6600. Special program-related fees: $50–$275 per year for lab fees, $120 for student activity fee, $230 per year for registration fee.

Financial Aid Program-specific awards: 405 Creative Achievement Awards for freshmen ($5418), 108 Faculty Honors Awards for transfer students ($5144), 826 CCA Scholarships for students demonstrating need ($6349), 247 named scholarships for those demonstrating need ($2876), 48 diversity scholarships for under-represented populations ($6223).

Application Procedures Students admitted directly into the professional program freshman year. Deadline for freshmen and transfers: continuous. Required: essay, high school transcript, college transcript(s) for transfer students, minimum 2.0 high school GPA, 2 letters of recommendation, portfolio, minimum TOEFL score of 550 (paper-based) or 213 (computer-based), or 79 (internet-based) for international applicants. Recommended: interview, SAT or ACT test scores. Portfolio reviews held continuously on campus and off campus at National Portfolio Days; the submission of slides may be substituted for portfolios (digital portfolio preferred).

Web Site http://www.cca.edu

Undergraduate Contact Ms. Robynne Royster, Director of Undergraduate Admission, Enrollment Services, California College of the Arts, 1111 Eighth Street, San Francisco, California 94107; 415-703-9532, fax: 415-703-9539, e-mail address: enroll@cca.edu

Graduate Contact Mr. Noel Dahl, Director of Graduate Admission, Enrollment Services, Cali-

fornia College of the Arts, 1111 Eighth Street, San Francisco, California 94107; 415-703-9537, fax: 415-703-9539, e-mail address: graduateprograms@cca.edu

More About the College

California College of the Arts (CCA) was founded in 1907 and offers twenty undergraduate majors in the areas of art, architecture, design, and writing. It is located in the San Francisco Bay Area, home to world-class museums, galleries, theaters, film festivals, and performance spaces. CCA has two campuses, one in San Francisco and one in Oakland.

At CCA, students make art that makes a difference. They develop their individual voices and styles as part of a dynamic conversation that engages global currents of thought and practice. Their work is informed by a multidisciplinary context in which crossing boundaries is encouraged and celebrated. The First Year Program is based on the Oakland campus and emphasizes skill building, experimentation, and critical thinking in a year of cross-disciplinary study. Through a combination of core studios and academic courses, the program orients students to the rigor of building a creative practice while introducing them to foundational skills that apply to all programs. Students officially choose a major in their second year. The average class size is 14.

The faculty members—a diverse group of artists, architects, designers, and writers—support students in their explorations while challenging them to take risks, clarify and deepen their processes of inquiry,

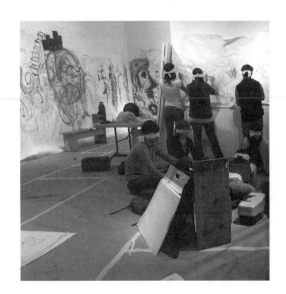

California College of the Arts (continued)

and refine their techniques. Visiting artists and scholars bring fresh perspectives through stimulating lectures and studio visits.

CCA undergraduates regularly win major recognition: Architecture student Jessica Kmetovic was a finalist in the World Trade Center competition while she was completing her degree. In 2008, four students won student filmmaking awards at the Cannes Film Festival and several architecture students were selected to compete in the Solar Decathlon in Washington, D.C. CCA's graphic design students win awards almost every year from Graphic Design USA, How, Type Directors Club, Adobe, and Graphis. *BusinessWeek* named CCA one of the world's best design schools in a 2007 issue. CCA students have participated in Yahoo!'s Annual University Design Expo, shown their films at the Venice Biennale, won the VH1 and IFILM Show Us Your Junk competition, and presented their product designs at the Milan Furniture Fair, the International Contemporary Furniture Fair, and the International Home and Housewares Show.

Program Facilities CCA's beautiful, historic, 4-acre Oakland campus is home to the spacious Treadwell Ceramic Arts Center, the Barclay Simpson Sculpture Studio (which has one of the largest working college foundries), the Blattner Print Studio (with facilities for silkscreening, papermaking, and photographic printing), and dedicated studios for animation, glass, jewelry, metal arts, textiles, and interactive media. There are also several galleries with regularly rotating exhibitions of student, faculty, and alumni work.

CCA's San Francisco campus is home to the programs in architecture, the design disciplines, illustration, media arts (film/video), and painting/drawing as well as all of the graduate programs. It includes the Boyce Fashion Design Studio (with facilities for cutting, draping, knitting, and sewing), the Wornick Wood and Furniture Studios (with a bench room, a machine room, and a spray booth), and a new facility for digital film and media (with a 2,000-square foot production/shooting stage, three film/video editing suites, an audio recording/editing suite, and a media lab). The campus also houses spacious studios for painting, drawing, and architecture. There is a newly expanded graduate center and a new graduate writing building. The CCA Wattis Institute, located on campus, presents international exhibitions of contemporary art, and another gallery regularly features work by CCA graduate students.

Both campuses have a wireless network and several computer labs with the latest hardware and software, open to students 16 to 24 hours daily.

Faculty, Resident Artists, and Alumni Works by CCA faculty members and alumni are in the collections of the Museum of Modern Art, the Whitney Museum of American Art, the Smithsonian, and many other major art institutions. Noted alumni include the painters Raymond Saunders and Squeak Carnwath, the ceramicists Robert Arneson and Peter Voulkos, the conceptual artists David Ireland and Dennis Oppenheim, the filmmaker Wayne Wang, and the designers Lucille Tenazas and Michael Vanderbyl. The Wattis Institute's Capp Street Project residency program brings acclaimed artists to campus each year. The Graduate Studies Lecture Series features some of the world's most influential and innovative artists, architects, writers, scholars, designers, and curators.

Student Exhibitions Undergraduate and graduate exhibitions rotate regularly in dedicated galleries on both campuses. The Baccalaureate Exhibition and the Graduate Exhibition are major events each spring, featuring work by students in all disciplines. There is also a juried fashion design show each spring, and several programs host junior review exhibitions that are open to the public.

Special Programs CCA students may earn credit for study off campus, either through cross-registration at Mills College or Holy Names College in Oakland, or at another art school through the Association of Independent Colleges of Art and Design mobility program. Through the international exchange program, students may study at schools of art and design in Canada, Denmark, France, Germany, Ireland, Israel, Japan, the Netherlands, Sweden, and the United Kingdom. Financial aid is available for study abroad. CCA also hosts its own summer study-abroad courses in Europe and Central and South America.

A precredential teaching concentration, open to students in all majors, satisfies prerequisites for application to postgraduate art teacher credentialing programs. Through CCA's Center for Art and Public Life, students serve as teaching assistants in public schools, mentor young artists, and create their own community art projects. Students may also undertake internships (required for some programs, and encouraged for all), gaining practical experience and professional connections while earning academic credit. The college facilitates internships at design and architecture firms, galleries, museums, nonprofit organizations, publishing houses, and fine-art studios.

School of Film/Video
California Institute of the Arts

Valencia, California

Independent, coed. Suburban campus. Total enrollment: 1,324. Art program established 1961.

Degrees Bachelor of Fine Arts in the areas of character animation, experimental animation, film/video. Majors and concentrations: animation, film and video production. Graduate degrees offered: Master of Fine Arts in the areas of experimental animation, film/video, film directing.

Enrollment 372 total; 241 undergraduate, 131 graduate.

Art Student Profile 44% females, 56% males, 33% minorities, 24% international.

Art Faculty 31 total (full-time), 40 total (part-time). 80% of full-time faculty have terminal degrees. Graduate students do not teach undergraduate courses. Undergraduate student–faculty ratio: 6:1.

Student Life Student groups/activities include Community Arts Partnership, Integrated Media. Special housing available for art students.

Expenses for 2008–2009 Application fee: $70. Comprehensive fee: $42,084 includes full-time tuition ($32,860), mandatory fees ($576), and college room and board ($8648). College room only: $4985. Special program-related fees: $475 per year for technology fee.

Financial Aid Program-specific awards: CalArts Scholarships for students demonstrating talent and need ($1000–$10,000).

Application Procedures Students admitted directly into the professional program freshman year. Deadline for freshmen and transfers: January 6. Required: essay, high school transcript, college transcript(s) for transfer students, 2 letters of recommendation, portfolio. Portfolio reviews held at National Portfolio Days.

Web Site http://www.calarts.edu

Contact Libby Hux, Admissions Counselor, California Institute of the Arts, 24700 McBean Parkway, Valencia, California 91355; 661-255-1050 ext. 7884, fax: 661-253-7710, e-mail address: lhux@calarts.edu

California Institute of the Arts

Valencia, California

Independent, coed. Suburban campus. Total enrollment: 1,324. Art program established 1961.

Degrees Bachelor of Fine Arts in the areas of art, graphic design, photography and media. Majors and concentrations: art/fine arts, graphic design, photography. Graduate degrees offered: Master of Fine Arts in the areas of art, graphic design, photography and media. Program accredited by NASAD.

Enrollment 299 total; 207 undergraduate, 92 graduate.

Art Student Profile 56% females, 44% males, 28% minorities, 8% international.

Art Faculty 36 total (full-time), 20 total (part-time). 90% of full-time faculty have terminal degrees. Graduate students do not teach undergraduate courses. Undergraduate student–faculty ratio: 7:1.

Student Life Student groups/activities include Community Arts Partnership (CAP), Integrated Media Program, interdisciplinary project. Special housing available for art students.

Expenses for 2008–2009 Application fee: $70. Comprehensive fee: $42,084 includes full-time tuition ($32,860), mandatory fees ($576), and college room and board ($8648). College room only: $4985. Special program-related fees: $50 per year for studio fee, $475 per year for technology fee.

Financial Aid Program-specific awards: CalArts Merit Scholarships for those demonstrating merit ($1000–$5000), CalArts Strategic Scholarships for minority students ($1000–$31,290), CalArts Scholarship for those demonstrating financial need and merit ($1000–$31,290).

Application Procedures Students admitted directly into the professional program freshman year. Deadline for freshmen and transfers: January 5. Notification date for freshmen and transfers: April 1. Required: essay, high school transcript, college transcript(s) for transfer students, portfolio, personal statement. Recommended: 2 letters of recommendation, video (if applicable). Portfolio reviews held continuously on campus and off campus at

Visual *Arts*

California Institute of the Arts (continued)

National Portfolio Days; the submission of slides may be substituted for portfolios (slides preferred).

Web Site http://www.calarts.edu

Contact Ms. Taryn Wolf, Associate Director of Admissions, California Institute of the Arts, 24700 McBean Parkway, Valencia, California 91355; 661-255-1050, fax: 661-253-7710, e-mail address: twolf@calarts.edu

More About the Institute

The School of Art at California Institute of the Arts (CalArts) offers undergraduate and graduate programs in the areas of art, graphic design, and photography and media. The undergraduate programs lead to a Bachelor of Fine Arts (B.F.A.) degree and the graduate programs to a Master of Fine Arts (M.F.A.) degree.

Faculty, Resident Artists, and Alumni The School's faculty is made up of innovators and leaders in contemporary art practice. Since all faculty members are working artists with an abundance of real-world experience, they prepare students for the creative and professional demands of contemporary art and design.

A faculty mentor serves as each student's artistic adviser, guiding them through the program and assisting the student in customizing a curriculum to fit their personal interests and artistic goals. To supplement the expertise of the faculty members, the School of Art regularly invites a wide range of visiting artists, designers, photographers, performers, writers, and theorists to share their experience and vision with students. The School of Art alumni are prominent in the art and design communities at the local, national, and international levels and can often be found on faculty rosters of some of the most esteemed colleges.

Programs of Study Admission into the programs of study within the School of Art is focus-specific. Students must apply directly to the area of interest with a portfolio that demonstrates technical and conceptual interest and ability. The School of Art at CalArts does not have a general foundation year; students begin their studies within their chosen program.

Encompassing both studio practice and theory, The Program in Art offers instruction in a wide range of media, including but not limited to painting, drawing, printmaking, photography, digital imaging, sculpture, installation, video, film, writing, and performance. The program does not require students to concentrate on a particular medium; instead, it relies on a flexible structure of individualized instruction and mentoring to emphasize the articulation of ideas.

The four-year B.F.A. curriculum begins with a selection of foundation course options, along with critical studies, where students investigate various media, art-historical traditions, and theoretical positions. Additional course work includes a combination of seminars, group critique classes, technical workshops, and independent studies. By the third year in residence, undergraduates are expected to pursue independent projects.

The Program in Graphic Design prepares students for a wide range of professional options—from Web design and motion graphics to editorial design and environmental graphics, from film title and broadcast design to exhibitions and careers in education. The program emphasizes both practical and conceptual skills and enables each designer to integrate a command of visual language with imagination, theory, and new technology. The highly structured B.F.A. curriculum begins with courses covering basic design principles, imagemaking, typography, history, and theory.

The Program in Photography and Media is committed to educating independent artists in a world where photographic imagery and new media representations and strategies are omnipresent. The program encourages debate and experimentation, and students are encouraged to challenge conventions in a genre that includes many new practices. The B.F.A. curriculum begins with a year of intensive photographic foundation work, followed by a mixture of courses that includes classes on specific issues in photography, video and Internet practice, the histories of photography and film, and media theories and semiotics as well as critique classes, technical workshops, and independent studies. Students are welcome work in darkroom photography, digital imaging, time-based formats, and beyond.

Program Facilities The MacLab is used for creating digital and print-based work, including drawing, painting, photo manipulation, editorial design, type design, 3-D rendering, motion graphics, sound design and Web, and CD and DVD authoring.

The Photography and Media Lab includes high-capacity black-and-white and color processors, a 52-inch capacity Cibachrome color processor, black-and-white printing bays, and individual color darkrooms, including an 8-by-10-inch color mural enlarger. The digital photography and video lab is equipped with eight Final Cut Pro Stations, digital imaging software, a negative scanner, and two large Epson digital photographic printers.

The Print and Media Lab is used for producing multiples through silk-screening, etching, lithography, and letterpress. It contains light tables, work tables, paper cutters, an exposure unit, various presses, and a digital imaging lab with a large output capacity printer and a vinyl cutter.

The Super Shop is the Institute's main sculpture studio and features work areas and equipment for woodworking, metalworking, machining, sandblasting, spraying, and mold making.

The Video Lab offers an assortment of high-quality equipment for time-based media production and post-production, as well as facilities for classroom instruction and student use. Digital video and Hi-8 cameras, tripods, microphones, lighting kits, mini-disc sound recorders, and other production equipment are available for checkout.

Beginning undergraduates in the Programs in Art and Photography and Media have shared studios, while most upper-level undergraduates work in individual studios. Graphic design students have individual workspace cubicles in larger studios that have adjoining critique rooms.

Student Performance/Exhibit Opportunities

School of Art students exhibit their work in seven on-campus galleries, and in various unconventional or informal settings around campus. First- and second-year undergraduates participate in several group shows, while upper-level undergraduates are required to mount solo exhibitions. Shows are often accompanied by opening receptions, which are organized by students and open to the public as well as the CalArts community.

California State University, Chico

Chico, California

State-supported, coed. Small town campus. Total enrollment: 17,034.

Degrees Bachelor of Fine Arts in the areas of studio art, interior design, electronic arts. Majors and concentrations: ceramic art and design, electronic arts, glass, interior design, painting/drawing, photography, printmaking, sculpture. Graduate degrees offered: Master of Fine Arts in the area of studio art. Cross-registration with California State University System. Program accredited by NASAD.

Enrollment 398 total; 25 undergraduate, 8 graduate, 365 nonprofessional degree.

Art Faculty 17 undergraduate (full-time), 15 undergraduate (part-time). 100% of full-time faculty have terminal degrees. Graduate students teach a few undergraduate courses. Undergraduate student–faculty ratio: 19:1.

Student Life Student groups/activities include General Student Art Club, Ceramics Student Art Club, Glass Art Club.

Expenses for 2008–2009 Application fee: $55. Nonresident tuition: $13,220 full-time. Mandatory fees: $4144 full-time. Special program-related fees: $10–$100 per course for materials fee.

Financial Aid Program-specific awards: academic and performance awards for incoming freshmen.

Application Procedures Students apply for admission into the professional program by junior year. Deadline for freshmen: November 30. Notification date for freshmen: continuous. Required: high school transcript, college transcript(s) for transfer students, minimum 3.0 high school GPA, 2 letters of recommendation, portfolio, SAT or ACT test scores, minimum 3.0 college GPA in art for entry into BFA program. Portfolio reviews held twice on campus; the submission of slides may be substituted for portfolios whenever necessary.

Web Site http://www.csuchico.edu

Undergraduate Contact Mr. Michael Bishop, Chairman, Department of Art and Art History, California State University, Chico, Chico, California 95929-0820; 530-898-5331, e-mail address: mbishop@csuchico.edu

Graduate Contact Cameron Crawford, Professor, Department of Art and Art History, California State University, Chico, Chico, California 95929-0820; 530-898-5331, e-mail address: ccrawford@csuchico.edu

California State University, Fullerton

Fullerton, California

State-supported, coed. Suburban campus. Total enrollment: 37,130. Art program established 1962.

Degrees Bachelor of Fine Arts in the areas of entertainment art/animation, drawing/paint-

California State University, Fullerton (continued)

ing, printmaking, sculpture, crafts, ceramics and glass, graphic design, illustration, creative photography. Majors and concentrations: ceramics, crafts, entertainment art/animation, glass, graphic design, illustration, jewelry and metalsmithing, painting/drawing, photography, printmaking, sculpture. Graduate degrees offered: Master of Arts in the areas of drawing/painting, printmaking, sculpture, ceramics and glass, graphic design, creative photography, illustration, jewelry and metalsmithing, exhibition design, art history, crafts; Master of Fine Arts in the areas of drawing/painting, printmaking, sculpture, ceramics and glass, crafts, graphic design, creative photography, illustration, jewelry and metalsmithing, exhibition design. Cross-registration with California State University System. Program accredited by NASAD.

Enrollment 1,559 total; 1,448 undergraduate, 111 graduate.

Art Student Profile 57% females, 43% males, 34% minorities, 5% international.

Art Faculty 32 total (full-time), 66 total (part-time). 76% of full-time faculty have terminal degrees. Graduate students teach a few undergraduate courses. Undergraduate student–faculty ratio: 19:1.

Student Life Student groups/activities include Pencil Mileage Club, The Art Network, Graphic Design Club. Special housing available for art students.

Expenses for 2007–2008 Application fee: $55. Nonresident tuition: $13,512 full-time. Mandatory fees: $3342 full-time. Full-time tuition and fees vary according to course load. College room and board: $9035. Special program-related fees: $10 per course for ceramic glaze fee, $10–$16 per course for lab fees.

Financial Aid Program-specific awards: 2 Mert Purkiss Awards for incoming freshmen ($1000), 2–4 Florence Arnold Awards for continuing students ($500), 1–3 John Olson Awards for design/crafts majors ($700), 2–3 Tribute Fund Awards for transfer students ($750), 1 California China Painters Association Award for traditional/descriptive art majors ($1000), 2 Costa Mesa Art League Awards for juniors or seniors ($500), 1 Jeff and Rosalie Bacon Award for incoming students ($2000), 2 Orange County Fine Arts Awards for new and continu-

ing students ($500), 2 Art Alliance Scholarships for transfer students from community colleges ($1000).

Application Procedures Students apply for admission into the professional program by sophomore year. Deadline for freshmen and transfers: continuous. Required: high school transcript, college transcript(s) for transfer students, minimum 2.0 high school GPA, SAT test score only.

Web Site http://www.art.fullerton.edu/

Undergraduate Contact Ms. Rachel Yunn, Undergraduate Secretary, Department of Visual Arts, California State University, Fullerton, PO Box 6850, Fullerton, California 92834-6850; 714-278-3471, fax: 714-278-2390.

Graduate Contact Ms. Jackie Reynolds, Graduate Secretary, Department of Visual Arts, California State University, Fullerton, PO Box 6850, Fullerton, California 92834-6850; 714-278-3471, fax: 714-278-2390, e-mail address: jreynolds@fullerton.edu

California State University, Long Beach

Long Beach, California

State-supported, coed. Suburban campus. Total enrollment: 36,868. Art program established 1949.

Web Site http://www.csulb.edu/

Capital University

Columbus, Ohio

Independent, coed. Suburban campus. Total enrollment: 3,713.

Degrees Bachelor of Fine Arts. Majors and concentrations: art education, art therapy. Cross-registration with Higher Education Council of Columbus.

Enrollment 30 total; all undergraduate.

Art Student Profile 92% females, 8% males, 11% minorities.

Art Faculty 3 undergraduate (full-time), 2 undergraduate (part-time). 67% of full-time faculty have terminal degrees. Graduate students do not teach undergraduate courses. Undergraduate student–faculty ratio: 9:1.

Student Life Student groups/activities include Capital University Student Art Therapy Association, Phi Beta.

Expenses for 2007–2008 Application fee: $25. Comprehensive fee: $33,180 includes full-time tuition ($26,360) and college room and board ($6820). Full-time tuition varies according to course load, degree level, program, and student level. Room and board charges vary according to board plan and housing facility.

Financial Aid Program-specific awards available.

Application Procedures Students admitted directly into the professional program freshman year. Deadline for freshmen and transfers: continuous. Required: high school transcript, college transcript(s) for transfer students, SAT or ACT test scores (minimum composite ACT score of 18), minimum 2.6 high school GPA, minimum 2.5 cumulative college GPA for transfer students, high school counselor form, 880 reading/math only, application end of freshman year (art education only). Recommended: interview, portfolio. Portfolio reviews held as needed on campus; the submission of slides may be substituted for portfolios for large works of art.

Web Site http://www.capital.edu

Undergraduate Contact Ms. Lisa McKitrick, Associate Director of Admission, Capital University, 1 College and Main, Columbus, Ohio 43209; 614-236-6101, fax: 614-236-6926, e-mail address: admissions@capital.edu

Carnegie Mellon University

Pittsburgh, Pennsylvania

Independent, coed. Urban campus. Total enrollment: 10,493. Art program established 1910.

Degrees Bachelor of Fine Arts. Majors and concentrations: art. Graduate degrees offered: Master of Fine Arts in the area of art. Cross-registration with Chatham College, University of Pittsburgh, Duquesne University, Point Park College, Community College of Allegheny County, Pittsburgh Theological Seminary, LaRoche College, Robert Morris University, Carlow University. Program accredited by NASAD.

Enrollment 169 total; 151 undergraduate, 18 graduate.

Art Student Profile 60% females, 40% males, 34% minorities, 9% international.

Art Faculty 5 undergraduate (part-time), 1 graduate (part-time), 24 total (full-time). 100% of full-time faculty have terminal degrees. Graduate students do not teach undergraduate courses. Undergraduate student–faculty ratio: 6:1.

Student Life Student groups/activities include weekly exhibitions, student-managed gallery exhibitions, Surg (undergraduate research grant projects).

Expenses for 2008–2009 Application fee: $70. Comprehensive fee: $49,614 includes full-time tuition ($39,150), mandatory fees ($414), and college room and board ($10,050). College room only: $5890. Special program-related fees: $20–$215 per 10 units for materials fees for various courses.

Financial Aid Program-specific awards: Jacques and Natasha Gelman Scholarships, Scholastic Art Awards, Ethel Murdock Kirk Awards, Eleanor Zygler Awards for junior and senior painting majors.

Application Procedures Students admitted directly into the professional program freshman year. Deadline for freshmen: October 1; transfers: December 1. Notification date for freshmen: continuous; transfers: April 15. Required: essay, high school transcript, college transcript(s) for transfer students, 3 letters of recommendation, portfolio, SAT or ACT test scores. Recommended: minimum 3.0 high school GPA, interview. Portfolio reviews held 11 times on campus and off campus at National Portfolio Day Associations locations; the submission of slides may be substituted for portfolios.

Web Site http://artserver.cfa.cmu.edu

Undergraduate Contact Michael Steidel, Director of Admission, Carnegie Mellon University, 5000 Forbes Avenue, Warner Hall 212, Pittsburgh, Pennsylvania 15213-3890; 412-268-2082.

Graduate Contact Ms. Cynthia Lammert, Facilities and Project Manager, School of Art, Carnegie Mellon University, College of Fine Arts Building, Room 300, 5000 Forbes Avenue, Pittsburgh, Pennsylvania 15213-3890; 412-268-6707, fax: 412-268-7817, e-mail address: cl2w@andrew.cmu.edu

Visual

Arts

Cazenovia College

Cazenovia, New York

Independent, coed. Small town campus. Total enrollment: 1,006. Art program established 1982.

Degrees Bachelor of Fine Arts in the areas of interior design, studio art, visual communications, fashion design. Majors and concentrations: advertising graphic design, fashion design, interior design, photography, studio art, visual communication, Web design.

Art Faculty 13 undergraduate (full-time), 20 undergraduate (part-time). 79% of full-time faculty have terminal degrees. Graduate students do not teach undergraduate courses. Undergraduate student–faculty ratio: 13:1.

Student Life Student groups/activities include Art Club, Fashion Design Club, New York State Eleven Albany Conference (Interior Design).

Expenses for 2007–2008 Application fee: $30. Comprehensive fee: $30,440 includes full-time tuition ($21,280), mandatory fees ($220), and college room and board ($8940). Full-time tuition and fees vary according to class time and course load. Room and board charges vary according to board plan and housing facility. Special program-related fees: $78 per semester for required fee.

Financial Aid Program-specific awards available.

Application Procedures Students admitted directly into the professional program freshman year. Deadline for freshmen and transfers: continuous. Required: essay, high school transcript, college transcript(s) for transfer students, letter of recommendation. Recommended: minimum 2.0 high school GPA, minimum 3.0 high school GPA, interview, portfolio, SAT or ACT test scores. Portfolio reviews held as needed on campus; the submission of slides may be substituted for portfolios when distance is prohibitive or if scheduling is difficult.

Web Site http://www.cazenovia.edu

Undergraduate Contact Robert Croot, Dean for Enrollment Management, Admissions and Financial Aid, Cazenovia College, 3 Sullivan Street, Cazenovia, New York 13035; 315-655-7208, fax: 315-655-4486, e-mail address: admission@cazenovia.edu

Centenary College

Hackettstown, New Jersey

Independent, coed. Suburban campus. Total enrollment: 3,028.

Web Site http://www.centenarycollege.edu/

Central Michigan University

Mount Pleasant, Michigan

State-supported, coed. Small town campus. Total enrollment: 26,611. Art program established 1971.

Web Site http://www.cmich.edu/

Central State University

Wilberforce, Ohio

State-supported, coed. Rural campus. Total enrollment: 2,022.

Degrees Bachelor of Arts in the area of art; Bachelor of Science in the area of art education. Majors and concentrations: advertising graphic design, art education, drawing, painting. Cross-registration with Consortium of Ohio State Universities.

Enrollment 40 total; all undergraduate.

Art Student Profile 60% females, 40% males, 90% minorities.

Art Faculty 4 total (full-time), 5 total (part-time). 100% of full-time faculty have terminal degrees. Graduate students do not teach undergraduate courses. Undergraduate student–faculty ratio: 6:1.

Student Life Student groups/activities include Art Club.

Expenses for 2007–2008 Application fee: $20. State resident tuition: $5294 full-time. Nonresident tuition: $11,462 full-time. Full-time tuition varies according to course load. College room and board: $7402. College room only: $3978. Room and board charges vary according to board plan.

Financial Aid Program-specific awards: 15 Fine and Performing Arts Scholarships ($400–$1200).

Application Procedures Students admitted directly into the professional program freshman year. Deadline for freshmen and transfers: continuous. Required: high school transcript, SAT or ACT test scores, minimum 2.0 high school GPA for in-state students, minimum 2.5 high school GPA for out-of-state students, minimum ACT score of 15 for in-state students, minimum ACT score of 18 for out-of-state students. Recommended: portfolio. Portfolio reviews held by appointment on campus; the submission of slides may be substituted for portfolios.

Web Site http://www.centralstate.edu

Undergraduate Contact Admissions Department, Central State University, Wilberforce, Ohio 45384; 937-376-6348.

Chowan University

Murfreesboro, North Carolina

Independent Baptist, coed. Rural campus. Art program established 1978.

Degrees Bachelor of Arts in the area of studio art; Bachelor of Science in the areas of studio art, graphic design.

Enrollment 55 total; 8 undergraduate.

Art Student Profile 50% females, 50% males, 50% minorities.

Art Faculty 3 undergraduate (full-time), 3 undergraduate (part-time). 67% of full-time faculty have terminal degrees. Graduate students do not teach undergraduate courses. Undergraduate student–faculty ratio: 12:1.

Student Life Student groups/activities include "Artisus" Art Club, trips to Smithsonian (Washington, DC), Europe, Chrysler Museum, Gallery Exhibitions in Green Hall Galleries.

Expenses for 2007–2008 Application fee: $20. Comprehensive fee: $24,030 includes full-time tuition ($16,750), mandatory fees ($280), and college room and board ($7000). College room only: $3300. Room and board charges vary according to board plan.

Financial Aid Program-specific awards available.

Application Procedures Students admitted directly into the professional program freshman year. Required: essay, high school transcript, college transcript(s) for transfer students, letter of recommendation, interview, audition,

portfolio, SAT or ACT test scores. Portfolio reviews held on campus.

Web Site http://www.chowan.edu/academics/school-arts-sciences-visual-art.htm

Undergraduate Contact Christina Rupsch, MS, Chair, Department of Visual Art, Department of Visual Art, Chowan University, 1 University Place, Murfreesboro, North Carolina 27855; 252-398-6306, e-mail address: rupscc@chowan.edu

Clarke College

Dubuque, Iowa

Independent Roman Catholic, coed. Urban campus. Total enrollment: 1,230. Art program established 1843.

Degrees Bachelor of Fine Arts in the areas of studio art, graphic design. Majors and concentrations: art history, ceramics, drawing, graphic design, painting, printmaking, sculpture. Cross-registration with Loras College, University of Dubuque.

Enrollment 60 total; 35 undergraduate, 25 nonprofessional degree.

Art Student Profile 65% females, 35% males, 3% minorities, 3% international.

Art Faculty 5 undergraduate (full-time), 2 undergraduate (part-time). 80% of full-time faculty have terminal degrees. Graduate students do not teach undergraduate courses. Undergraduate student–faculty ratio: 12:1.

Student Life Student groups/activities include gallery exhibits, visiting artists workshops.

Expenses for 2007–2008 Application fee: $25. Comprehensive fee: $27,886 includes full-time tuition ($20,666), mandatory fees ($646), and college room and board ($6574). College room only: $3198. Room and board charges vary according to board plan and housing facility. Special program-related fees: $20–$50 per course for lab fees.

Financial Aid Program-specific awards: 12–15 art scholarships for art students (renewable) ($1000–$3000).

Application Procedures Students apply for admission into the professional program by sophomore year. Deadline for freshmen and transfers: continuous. Required: high school transcript, college transcript(s) for transfer students, minimum 2.0 high school GPA, letter

Clarke College (continued)

of recommendation, portfolio, SAT or ACT test scores (minimum composite ACT score of 21), portfolio review for scholarship consideration. Recommended: essay, interview. Portfolio reviews held by appointment from January to April on campus and off campus in Chicago, IL; St. Louis, MO; Minneapolis, MN; the submission of slides may be substituted for portfolios when distance is prohibitive.

Web Site http://www.clarke.edu

Undergraduate Contact Andy Schroeder, Director, Office of Admissions, Clarke College, 1550 Clarke Avenue, Dubuque, Iowa 52001; 563-588-6366, fax: 563-588-6789, e-mail address: andy.schroeder@clarke.edu

The Cleveland Institute of Art

Cleveland, Ohio

Independent, coed. Urban campus. Total enrollment: 485. Art program established 1882.

Degrees Bachelor of Fine Arts. Majors and concentrations: ceramics, digital art, drawing, enameling, fibers, glass, graphic design, illustration, industrial design, interior design, medical illustration, metals, painting, photography, printmaking, sculpture. Graduate degrees offered: Master of Fine Arts in the area of medical illustration and digital arts. Cross-registration with members of the Northeast Ohio Council on Higher Education. Program accredited by NASAD.

Enrollment 485 total; 482 undergraduate, 3 graduate.

Art Student Profile 53% females, 47% males, 10% minorities, 3% international.

Art Faculty 43 undergraduate (full-time), 46 undergraduate (part-time). 80% of full-time faculty have terminal degrees. Graduate students do not teach undergraduate courses. Undergraduate student–faculty ratio: 8:1.

Student Life Student groups/activities include Industrial Design Society of America. Special housing available for art students.

Expenses for 2007–2008 Application fee: $30. Comprehensive fee: $38,859 includes full-time tuition ($28,100), mandatory fees ($1990), and college room and board ($8769). Full-time

tuition and fees vary according to program. Room and board charges vary according to board plan. Special program-related fees: $55 per credit hour for technology fee (under 12 credit hours), $65 per credit hour for lab fees (under 12 credit hours), $280 per semester for lab fees (12-15 credit hours), $315–$575 per semester for technology fee (depending on major).

Financial Aid Program-specific awards: 437 renewable portfolio merit awards for freshman transfers ($5000–$28,100).

Application Procedures Students admitted directly into the professional program freshman year. Deadline for freshmen and transfers: continuous. Required: essay, high school transcript, college transcript(s) for transfer students, minimum 2.0 high school GPA, 2 letters of recommendation, SAT or ACT test scores, slides or CD of portfolio. Recommended: interview. Portfolio reviews held bi-monthly on campus.

Web Site http://www.cia.edu

Undergraduate Contact Mrs. Sheila Wendeln, Interim Director of Admissions, The Cleveland Institute of Art, 11141 East Boulevard, Cleveland, Ohio 44106; 216-421-7422, fax: 216-754-3634, e-mail address: swendeln@cia.edu

Graduate Contact Dr. Gary Sampson, Director of Graduate Studies, The Cleveland Institute of Art, 11141 East Boulevard, Cleveland, Ohio 44106; 216-421-7369, fax: 216-421-7438, e-mail address: gsampson@cia.edu

More About the Institute

The Cleveland Institute of Art (CIA) offers one of America's most comprehensive educational programs in the field of visual arts.

Drawing, color, design, art history, literature, and digital art classes make up the core curriculum of the Foundation. Both traditional and conceptual approaches to drawing and painting are emphasized. Composition, design theory, and the organization of 2-D and 3-D space are the focus of design classes. Art history includes the Paleolithic era through contemporary works of the late twentieth to early twenty-first centuries, which are discussed in the last semester of study. The contemporary writings of each era are studied in the literature classes, which encompass composition and critical analysis of those works. Digital art courses are required and serve as an introduction to both the Macintosh platform and the use of graphics software as a tool for art and design.

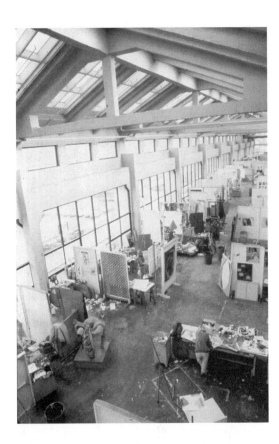

Foundation students take an open environmental elective, which helps students make informed decisions, based on experience, regarding which major they wish to study during the later years of their education.

Each major at CIA is categorized into one of four environments—visual arts and technologies, design, material culture-craft, or integrated media. Cross-discipline study is an integral part of the curriculum. Regardless of their major, all students take courses outside their discipline, and everyone graduates with a Bachelor of Fine Arts (B.F.A.) degree.

Liberal arts electives continue to play an important role in a student's development as a professional artist or designer during the later years of study. An array of subjects in the humanities and social sciences are offered each term. The structure of the program ensures a broad distribution by requiring students to pursue advanced studies across six areas.

The culmination point of the program is the B.F.A. thesis exhibition and review. During this requirement for graduation, the candidates present their work throughout the school and receive formal critique by

peers and faculty members. Much of the final year is spent independently preparing for this review, much the same way that one would prepare work for an agency or develop a body of work for a gallery show.

Program Facilities Individual studio spaces are provided for all majors. The facilities at the Cleveland Institute of Art include big, bright, professional art and design studios. Available to students are high-output printers; woodshops; darkrooms; a foundry; Macintosh, Silicon Graphics, and IBM computer labs; printmaking equipment; glass furnaces; metal lathes; milling machines; kilns; critique spaces; and the Jessica Gund Memorial Library.

Faculty, Resident Artists, and Alumni Studio faculty members are practicing artists and designers. Their work can be found in national and international, public and private collections, including the Hirshhorn Museum; the Corcoran Gallery; the Library of Congress; the Smithsonian Institution of Washington, D.C.; the Metropolitan Museum of Art; the Museum of Modern Photography in New York City; the Cleveland Museum of Art; and the Victoria and Albert Museum in London. Liberal arts faculty members are historians, poets, and researchers. The Visiting Artist program offers learning through the firsthand experiences of prominent artists. Alumni work in a variety of art fields at distinguished institutions and industry leaders, including Fisher Price, General Electric, Disney, Yale University, Rubbermaid, Mattel, the Metropolitan Museum of Art, General Motors, and American Greetings.

Student Performance and Exhibit Opportunities The Cleveland Institute of Art offers generous student gallery space, library gallery space, the annual Student Independent Exhibition, and various local restaurants, coffeehouses, and galleries.

Special Programs Students attending the Cleveland Institute of Art have the opportunity to participate in the New York Studio program, extensive internship opportunities, cross-registration with other colleges and universities, intensive summer workshops, and liberal arts tutoring. Biomedical art students work with the medical and dental schools of Case Western Reserve University, University Hospitals, and the Cleveland Clinic Foundation. A wide range of study-abroad opportunities are available.

College for Creative Studies

Detroit, Michigan

Independent, coed. Urban campus. Total enrollment: 1,307. Art program established 1906.

College for Creative Studies (continued)

Degrees Bachelor of Fine Arts in the areas of fine arts, crafts, photography, graphic design/illustration, transportation design, interior design, animation/digital media, advertising design, product design. Majors and concentrations: advertising design, art/fine arts, crafts, entertainment arts, graphic design, illustration, interior design, painting/drawing, photography, printmaking, product design, sculpture, transportation design. Graduate degrees offered: Master of Fine Arts in the areas of transportation design, design. Cross-registration with Association of Independent Colleges of Art and Design. Program accredited by NASAD.

Enrollment 1,307 total; all undergraduate.

Art Student Profile 42% females, 58% males, 13% minorities, 4% international.

Art Faculty 52 undergraduate (full-time), 220 undergraduate (part-time). Graduate students do not teach undergraduate courses. Undergraduate student–faculty ratio: 11:1.

Student Life Student groups/activities include Student Government, Black Artists Researching Trends, Industrial Design Society of America. Special housing available for art students.

Expenses for 2008–2009 Application fee: $35. Tuition: $27,090 full-time. Mandatory fees: $1185 full-time. College room only: $4300. Special program-related fees: $400–$900 per year for lab/material fees.

Financial Aid Program-specific awards: 15 Walter B. Ford, II Award of Excellence Scholarships for entering students ($20,000), CCS Scholarships for entering students ($3500–$10,000).

Application Procedures Students admitted directly into the professional program freshman year. Deadline for freshmen and transfers: continuous. Notification date for freshmen and transfers: August 15. Required: high school transcript, college transcript(s) for transfer students, SAT or ACT test scores, minimum 2.5 high school GPA, minimum 2.0 college GPA for transfer students, portfolio (must be digital images or actual work; slides are not acceptable). Recommended: essay, 2 letters of recommendation. Portfolio reviews held throughout the year on campus and off campus in during National Portfolio Days and during high school visits.

Web Site http://www.collegeforcreativestudies.edu

Contact Lori Watson, Director of Admissions, College for Creative Studies, 201 East Kirby Street, Detroit, Michigan 48202; 800-952-ARTS, fax: 313-872-2739, e-mail address: admissions@collegeforcreativestudies.edu

More About the College

The College for Creative Studies (CCS) is among the nation's leading colleges of art and design. Students can pursue a Bachelor of Fine Arts degree in the following majors: advertising design, animation and digital media, art education, crafts, fine arts, graphic design, illustration, interior design, photography, product design, and transportation design.

At the College for Creative Studies, first-year students can enter their chosen department and concentrate their studies in one area or spend their first semester "undeclared" and take an orientation class to learn about the eleven studio majors. While students are immersed in their chosen area of study immediately upon entering CCS, they are also encouraged to take classes outside of their major to broaden their skills.

Each department emphasizes four distinct components of a visual arts education: technical skill, aesthetic sensibility, conceptual ability, and practical experience, combining studio and academic classes with more individualized instruction. Upper-level students have the opportunity to begin working independently in private and semiprivate studio settings. While these students have the freedom to cultivate their own personal vision and style, they are regularly visited by faculty members for critiques and guidance. Internships give students an opportunity to work side-by-side with art and design professionals.

CCS' faculty consists of professional artists and designers who are also working and exhibiting in their fields of expertise. They provide students with an immediate connection to the real world by bringing new trends, practical insights, and networking opportunities to the College, shedding a realistic light on theoretical classroom exercises. Students are assigned a faculty academic adviser in their department upon entering the school.

Studies at CCS are also fully supported by state-of-the-art facilities. The College has woodworking, metalsmithing, and hot glass studios; a foundry; a clay modeling studio; a Thermwood 5-axis CNC milling machine; a rapid prototyping studio for creating 3-D color models from computer-generated

Application Procedures Students apply for admission into the professional program by sophomore year. Deadline for freshmen and transfers: continuous. Required: high school transcript, college transcript(s) for transfer students, minimum 2.0 high school GPA, SAT or ACT test scores, portfolio for scholarship consideration. Portfolio reviews held as needed on campus; the submission of slides may be substituted for portfolios when distance is prohibitive.

Web Site http://www.ccis.edu/departments/arts/

Undergraduate Contact Ms. Regina Morin, Director of Admissions, Columbia College, 1001 Rogers Street, Columbia, Missouri 65216; 573-875-7352, fax: 573-875-8765, e-mail address: admissions@ccis.edu

Art and Design Department
Columbia College Chicago

Chicago, Illinois

Independent, coed. Urban campus. Total enrollment: 11,499. Art program established 1970.

Degrees Bachelor of Arts in the area of art and design; Bachelor of Fine Arts in the areas of advertising art direction, product design, fashion design, interior design, graphic design, illustration. Majors and concentrations: advertising art direction, art and design, art/fine arts, fashion design, graphic design, illustration, interior architecture and design, product design. Graduate degrees offered: Master of Fine Arts in the areas of architectural studies, interior design.

Enrollment 1,644 total; 1,619 undergraduate, 25 graduate.

Art Student Profile 68% females, 32% males, 28% minorities, 2% international.

Art Faculty 35 undergraduate (full-time), 128 undergraduate (part-time), 1 graduate (part-time). Graduate students do not teach undergraduate courses. Undergraduate student–faculty ratio: 10:1.

Student Life Student groups/activities include Arts Community, Columbia College Fashion Association, International Interior Design Association.

Expenses for 2007–2008 Application fee: $35. Comprehensive fee: $29,652 includes full-time tuition ($17,104), mandatory fees ($530), and college room and board ($12,018). College room only: $9048. Special program-related fees: $5–$415 per course for class fees.

Financial Aid Program-specific awards: 1 Pougialis Fine Arts Award for continuing fine arts majors ($2500).

Application Procedures Students admitted directly into the professional program freshman year. Deadline for freshmen and transfers: continuous. Notification date for freshmen and transfers: continuous. Required: essay, high school transcript, college transcript(s) for transfer students, letter of recommendation, meeting with admissions counselor for a personal interview and possible remediation program attendance for students with less than a 2.0 GPA, portfolio for transfer students. Recommended: minimum 2.0 high school GPA, interview, SAT or ACT test scores. Portfolio reviews held continuously on campus.

Web Site http://www.colum.edu

Undergraduate Contact Mr. Murphy Monroe, Director, Office of Admissions, Columbia College Chicago, 600 South Michigan Avenue, Chicago, Illinois 60605; 312-344-7133, fax: 312-344-8024, e-mail address: admissions@colum.edu

Graduate Contact Mr. Robert Garcia, Director of Graduate Admission, Graduate School Admissions, Columbia College Chicago, 600 South Michigan Avenue, Chicago, Illinois 60605; 312-344-7262, fax: 312-344-8047, e-mail address: rgarcia@colum.edu

Film/Video Department
Columbia College Chicago

Chicago, Illinois

Independent, coed. Urban campus. Total enrollment: 11,499. Art program established 1967.

Degrees Bachelor of Arts in the area of film/video. Majors and concentrations: alternative forms, audio for visual media, cinematography, computer animation, critical studies, directing, documentary, editing, post-produc-

Columbia College Chicago (continued)

tion, producing, screenwriting, traditional animation. Graduate degrees offered: Master of Fine Arts in the area of film/video.

Enrollment 2,284 total; 2,223 undergraduate, 61 graduate.

Art Student Profile 26% females, 74% males, 23% minorities, 2% international.

Art Faculty 34 total (full-time), 154 total (part-time). Graduate students do not teach undergraduate courses. Undergraduate student–faculty ratio: 12:1.

Student Life Student groups/activities include Documentary Film Group, Japanese Animation Club, Sunrayz Film Society.

Expenses for 2007–2008 Application fee: $35. Comprehensive fee: $29,652 includes full-time tuition ($17,104), mandatory fees ($530), and college room and board ($12,018). College room only: $9048. Special program-related fees: $5–$415 per course for class fee (varies by class and class-related activities).

Application Procedures Students admitted directly into the professional program freshman year. Deadline for freshmen and transfers: continuous. Notification date for freshmen and transfers: continuous. Required: essay, high school transcript, college transcript(s) for transfer students, letter of recommendation, meeting with admissions counselor for a personal interview and possible remediation program attendance for students with less than a 2.0 GPA, portfolio for transfer students. Recommended: minimum 2.0 high school GPA, interview, SAT or ACT test scores. Portfolio reviews held continuously on campus.

Web Site http://www.colum.edu

Undergraduate Contact Mr. Murphy Monroe, Director, Office of Admissions, Columbia College Chicago, 600 South Michigan Avenue, Chicago, Illinois 60605; 312-344-7133, fax: 312-344-8024, e-mail address: admissions@colum.edu

Graduate Contact Robert Garcia, Director of Graduate Admission, Graduate School Admissions, Columbia College Chicago, 600 South Michigan Avenue, Chicago, Illinois 60605; 312-344-7262, fax: 312-344-8047, e-mail address: rgarcia@colum.edu

Photography Department
Columbia College Chicago

Chicago, Illinois

Independent, coed. Urban campus. Total enrollment: 11,499. Art program established 1968.

Degrees Bachelor of Arts in the area of photography; Bachelor of Fine Arts in the area of photography. Majors and concentrations: fine art photography, photojournalism, professional photography. Graduate degrees offered: Master of Fine Arts in the area of photography.

Enrollment 733 total; 709 undergraduate, 24 graduate.

Art Student Profile 65% females, 35% males, 16% minorities, 1% international.

Art Faculty 16 total (full-time), 63 total (part-time). Undergraduate student–faculty ratio: 9:1.

Expenses for 2007–2008 Application fee: $35. Comprehensive fee: $29,652 includes full-time tuition ($17,104), mandatory fees ($530), and college room and board ($12,018). College room only: $9048. Special program-related fees: $5–$415 per course for class fees.

Financial Aid Program-specific awards: Kodak Scholarship for photography majors ($2000).

Application Procedures Students admitted directly into the professional program freshman year. Deadline for freshmen and transfers: continuous. Notification date for freshmen and transfers: continuous. Required: essay, high school transcript, college transcript(s) for transfer students, letter of recommendation, meeting with admissions counselor for a personal interview and possible remediation program attendance for students with less than a 2.0 GPA, portfolio for transfer students. Recommended: minimum 2.0 high school GPA, interview, SAT or ACT test scores. Portfolio reviews held continuously on campus.

Web Site http://www.colum.edu

Undergraduate Contact Mr. Murphy Monroe, Director, Office of Admissions, Columbia College Chicago, 600 South Michigan Avenue, Chicago, Illinois 606050; 312-344-7133, fax: 312-344-8024, e-mail address: admissions@colum.edu

Graduate Contact Robert Garcia, Director of Graduate Studies, Graduate School Admissions, Columbia College Chicago, 600 South Michigan Avenue, Chicago, Illinois 60605; 312-344-7262, fax: 312-344-8047, e-mail address: rgarcia@colum.edu

Columbus College of Art & Design

Columbus, Ohio

Independent, coed. Urban campus. Total enrollment: 1,623. Art program established 1879.

Degrees Bachelor of Fine Arts in the areas of fine art, visual communication, interior design, industrial design, media studies, illustration, fashion design. Majors and concentrations: art/fine arts, fashion design, graphic design, illustration, industrial design, interior design, media studies, visual communication. Cross-registration with Higher Education Council of Columbus. Program accredited by NASAD.

Enrollment 1,374 total; all undergraduate.

Art Student Profile 57% females, 43% males, 18% minorities.

Art Faculty 80 undergraduate (full-time), 100 undergraduate (part-time). 41% of full-time faculty have terminal degrees. Graduate students do not teach undergraduate courses. Undergraduate student–faculty ratio: 12:1.

Student Life Special housing available for art students.

Expenses for 2007–2008 Application fee: $25. Comprehensive fee: $29,062 includes full-time tuition ($21,768), mandatory fees ($644), and college room and board ($6650). Room and board charges vary according to housing facility and student level. Special program-related fees: $25–$160 for lab/studio fees.

Financial Aid Program-specific awards: 300 International Scholarship Competition Awards for incoming freshmen ($4500–$11,000), 150 Art Competition Awards for members of National Art Honor Society ($2000).

Application Procedures Students admitted directly into the professional program freshman year. Deadline for freshmen and transfers: continuous. Required: essay, high school transcript, college transcript(s) for transfer students, minimum 2.0 high school GPA, letter of recommendation, portfolio, SAT or ACT test scores. Recommended: interview. Portfolio reviews held continuously by appointment on campus and off campus; the submission of slides may be substituted for portfolios if a campus visit is impossible.

Web Site http://www.ccad.edu

Undergraduate Contact Thomas E. Green, Director of Admissions, Columbus College of Art & Design, 107 North Ninth Street, Columbus, Ohio 43215; 614-224-9101, fax: 877-869-5897, e-mail address: admissions@ccad.edu

Concordia University

Montreal, Quebec, Canada

Province-supported, coed. Urban campus. Total enrollment: 32,416. Art program established 1975.

Web Site http://www.concordia.ca/

Concordia University, Nebraska

Seward, Nebraska

Independent, coed. Small town campus. Total enrollment: 1,279. Art program established 1963.

Web Site http://www.cune.edu/

The Cooper Union School of Art
Cooper Union for the Advancement of Science and Art

New York, New York

Independent, coed. Urban campus. Total enrollment: 957. Art program established 1859.

Degrees Bachelor of Fine Arts in the area of fine arts. Majors and concentrations: art/fine arts. Cross-registration with Parsons School of Design-New School University. Program accredited by NASAD.

Enrollment 291 total; all undergraduate.

Art Student Profile 54% females, 46% males, 30% minorities, 9% international.

Cooper Union for the Advancement of Science and Art (continued)

Art Faculty 9 undergraduate (full-time), 49 undergraduate (part-time). 90% of full-time faculty have terminal degrees. Graduate students do not teach undergraduate courses. Undergraduate student–faculty ratio: 7:1.

Student Life Student groups/activities include End of the Year Show, Cultural Show, open mike nights.

Expenses for 2008–2009 Application fee: $65. Comprehensive fee: $15,150 includes full-time tuition ($0), mandatory fees ($1450), and college room and board ($13,700). College room only: $9700. All students are awarded full-tuition scholarships. Living expenses are subsidized by college-administered financial aid.

Financial Aid Program-specific awards: full-tuition scholarships for all admitted students ($31,500).

Application Procedures Students admitted directly into the professional program freshman year. Deadline for freshmen and transfers: January 10. Notification date for freshmen and transfers: April 1. Required: essay, high school transcript, college transcript(s) for transfer students, minimum 2.0 high school GPA, portfolio, SAT or ACT test scores, home test. Recommended: 2 letters of recommendation, portfolio review. Portfolio reviews held 4 times during fall semester on campus and off campus at National Portfolio Days (about 20/year); the submission of slides may be substituted for portfolios for large works of art.

Web Site http://www.cooper.edu

Undergraduate Contact Mr. Mitchell L. Lipton, Dean of Admissions and Records and Registrar, Cooper Union for the Advancement of Science and Art, 30 Cooper Square, Suite 300, New York, New York 10003; 212-353-4120, fax: 212-353-4342, e-mail address: admissions@cooper.edu

The Cooper Union School of Art

See Cooper Union for the Advancement of Science and Art

Corcoran College of Art and Design
Washington, District of Columbia

Independent, coed. Urban campus. Total enrollment: 698. Art program established 1890.

Degrees Bachelor of Fine Arts in the areas of fine art, graphic design, photography, photojournalism, digital media design, art education, interior design; Bachelor of Fine Arts/Master of Arts in Teaching in the area of fine art/teaching. Majors and concentrations: art education, art/fine arts, ceramics, digital art, digital media, drawing, graphic design, interior design, painting, photography, photojournalism, printmaking, sculpture. Graduate degrees offered: Bachelor of Fine Arts/Master of Arts in Teaching in the area of fine art/teaching; Master of Arts in the areas of interior design, history of decorative arts, art education, exhibition design. Cross-registration with Washington Consortium of Colleges. Program accredited by NASAD.

Enrollment 664 total; 480 undergraduate, 184 graduate.

Art Student Profile 69% females, 31% males, 25% minorities, 9% international.

Art Faculty 22 undergraduate (full-time), 3 graduate (full-time), 174 total (part-time). 64% of full-time faculty have terminal degrees. Graduate students do not teach undergraduate courses. Undergraduate student–faculty ratio: 4:1.

Student Life Student groups/activities include Student Government, Off The Walls Art Sale, student exhibitions, WPA/C. Special housing available for art students.

Expenses for 2008–2009 Application fee: $45. Comprehensive fee: $39,534 includes full-time tuition ($27,180), mandatory fees ($200), and college room and board ($12,154). College room only: $9694.

Financial Aid Program-specific awards: 91 Dean's Scholarships for freshmen and transfers ($1500–$6500), 20 departmental scholarships for continuing students ($1000–$2500), 125 President's Awards for freshmen and transfers, 4 Delaware College of Art and Design Grants for transfer students from DCAD ($4000–$9000), 3 Faculty Chairs' Grants for entering freshmen ($6500–$26,000), 3 Scholastic Art and Writing Awards for freshmen ($1500–$7000).

Application Procedures Students admitted directly into the professional program freshman year. Deadline for freshmen and transfers: continuous. Required: high school transcript, college transcript(s) for transfer students, minimum 2.0 high school GPA, interview, portfolio, SAT or ACT test scores. Recommended: essay, minimum 3.0 high school GPA, 3 letters of recommendation. Auditions held numerous times on campus and off campus. Portfolio reviews held continuously by appointment on campus and off campus in various cities in the U.S.; the submission of slides may be substituted for portfolios for applicants living beyond 200-mile radius.

Web Site http://www.corcoran.edu

Contact Elizabeth Smith Paladino, Director of Admission, Corcoran College of Art and Design, 500 17th Street, NW, Washington, District of Columbia 20006-4804; 202-639-1814, fax: 202-639-1830, e-mail address: admissions@corcoran.org

More About the College

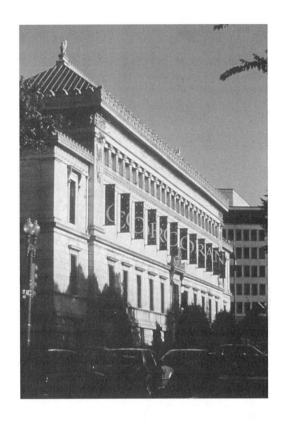

The Corcoran College of Art and Design is one of the oldest art schools in the United States and upholds a long tradition of partnership between art schools and museums. Studying at one of the few museum-schools in the country, Corcoran students are surrounded by great art and frequently by the contemporary masters whose work is regularly exhibited. The Corcoran Museum of Art has one of the finest collections of American art in the world, which is supplemented by holdings in European painting and sculpture, classical antiquities, and the decorative arts. As Washington's first museum of art, the Corcoran has played a central role in the development of American culture for more than 125 years. The aspiring young professionals who study today at the Corcoran College of Art and Design join a great and long tradition of quality and impact on the development of American and international art and design.

Corcoran undergraduate students take the integrated first-year Foundation program, which includes an introduction to the many art collections of Washington. After their first year, students select a major field of study in art education, fine art, digital media design, graphic design, photography, or photojournalism. Fine Art majors may choose to concentrate in ceramics, digital art, drawing, painting, printmaking, or sculpture. At the graduate studies level, a master's degree is offered in art education, interior design, and the history of decorative arts.

Location Washington is a city of monuments and museums set off by the neoclassical architecture of government buildings, parks, trees, and greenery. With dozens of major colleges and universities in the metropolitan area, there exists a feeling of a giant "campus" in which restaurants, coffee shops, movie theaters, and night spots are intermingled with bookstores, clothing boutiques, and academic facilities. Within a mile of the Corcoran, the city offers numerous museums and galleries, including the National Gallery of Art, the Phillips Collection, the Hirshhorn Museum and Sculpture Garden, and the Smithsonian National Museum of Natural History. Also a short walk from Corcoran are the world-famous Mall and performing arts institutions such as the Kennedy Center, Ford's Theater, and the National Theater. Rock Creek Park, a 1,700-acre public park that has a golf course, bicycle path, picnic area, nature center, playgrounds, tennis center, and Horse Center, is nearby as well.

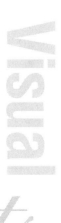

*Corcoran College of Art and Design
(continued)*

Program Facilities The Downtown Campus of the Corcoran College of Art and Design is located in the same building as the Corcoran Gallery of Art, one block from the White House, with additional facilities in proximity. The building is one of America's finest examples of Beaux-Arts architecture, with wings designed by Ernest Flagg and Charles Platt.

Freshmen students spend their class time in the downtown and Georgetown buildings. Juniors and seniors in Fine Art have designated studio space as well as generous studio hours.

The Corcoran's nearby Georgetown Campus is home to the design and printmaking departments, papermaking and silkscreen facilities, jewelry studio, and state-of-the-art computer laboratories.

As an appealing alternative to crowded traditional dormitory housing, the College provides new students with attractive, spacious supervised apartments. These furnished apartments are subway accessible, close to downtown and Georgetown, and have 24-hour security.

Student and Alumni Exhibit Opportunities
Students of all levels have several opportunities to exhibit their work. In the College/Museum space, there are several exhibition areas, including the White Walls Gallery and the Corcoran Gallery for the annual student sale of art work.

The Corcoran is the only college of art and design that incorporates an exhibition in a prominent museum into its curriculum. For three months of every year, graduating seniors showcase their thesis projects in the Corcoran Museum in a series of weeklong rotating exhibitions. The students are responsible for all aspects of these shows, from exhibition design to installation. These exhibitions culminate in a final exhibition featuring at least one work by every graduating senior. Through the formal presentation of their work in the museum, students make the transition to professional artists and designers and are introduced to the public as emerging talents.

The Corcoran Museum is also the site of the annual juried Corcoran Alumni Association exhibition, presenting works by some of the College's most accomplished alumni, all with extensive lists of exhibitions to their credit and many with gallery affiliations. The Visiting Artists Program also holds its exhibitions in the museum, allowing renowned contemporary artists, scholars, and critics to visit the Corcoran's campus each semester.

The Alumni Gallery, located off the main atrium of the Corcoran Gallery of Art, is dedicated to works by artists and designers who have received their degree from the Corcoran College of Art and Design.

Cornell University

Ithaca, New York

Independent, coed. Small town campus. Total enrollment: 19,800. Art program established 1921.

Degrees Bachelor of Fine Arts. Majors and concentrations: combined media, electronic imaging, painting/drawing, photography, printmaking, sculpture. Graduate degrees offered: Master of Fine Arts.

Enrollment 130 total; 120 undergraduate, 10 graduate.

Art Student Profile 70% females, 30% males, 30% minorities, 8% international.

Art Faculty 10 total (full-time), 6 total (part-time). 100% of full-time faculty have terminal degrees. Graduate students do not teach undergraduate courses. Undergraduate student–faculty ratio: 8:1.

Student Life Student groups/activities include Minority Organization of Architecture, Art, and Planning, Art Majors Organization (AMO). Special housing available for art students.

Expenses for 2007–2008 Application fee: $65. Comprehensive fee: $45,971 includes full-time tuition ($34,600), mandatory fees ($181), and college room and board ($11,190). College room only: $6680. Room and board charges vary according to board plan and housing facility. Special program-related fees: $50–$150 for departmental fees.

Application Procedures Students admitted directly into the professional program freshman year. Deadline for freshmen: January 1; transfers: March 15. Notification date for freshmen: April 1; transfers: May 1. Required: essay, high school transcript, college transcript(s) for transfer students, minimum 3.0 high school GPA, 2 letters of recommendation, SAT or ACT test scores, portfolio containing 15-20 slides. Recommended: interview. Portfolio reviews held by appointment on campus.

Web Site http://www.aap.cornell.edu

Undergraduate Contact Ms. Deborah Durnam, Director of Admissions, College of Architecture, Art and Planning, Cornell University, B-1 West Sibley Hall, Ithaca, New York 14853;

607-255-4376, fax: 607-254-2848, e-mail address: aap_admissions@cornell.edu

Graduate Contact Mr. Buzz Spector, Chair, Department of Art, Cornell University, 224 Olive Tjaden Hall, Ithaca, New York 14853; 607-255-3558, fax: 607-255-3462.

Art Department
Cornish College of the Arts

Seattle, Washington

Independent, coed. Urban campus. Total enrollment: 768 (2006). Art program established 1914.

Degrees Bachelor of Fine Arts in the area of art. Majors and concentrations: art/fine arts, painting/drawing, photography, printmaking, sculpture, video art. Program accredited by NASAD.

Enrollment 153 total; all undergraduate.

Art Student Profile 65% females, 35% males, 14% minorities, 3% international.

Art Faculty 11 undergraduate (full-time), 5 undergraduate (part-time). 58% of full-time faculty have terminal degrees. Graduate students do not teach undergraduate courses. Undergraduate student–faculty ratio: 9:1.

Expenses for 2007–2008 Application fee: $35. Tuition: $23,700 full-time. Mandatory fees: $300 full-time. Special program-related fees: $500 per semester for lab fees.

Financial Aid Program-specific awards: Nellie Scholarships for new students ($2000–$5000), departmental scholarships for new and continuing students ($500–$7500), Presidential Scholarships for continuing students ($2000–$5000).

Application Procedures Students admitted directly into the professional program freshman year. Deadline for freshmen and transfers: August 15. Notification date for freshmen and transfers: August 30. Required: essay, high school transcript, college transcript(s) for transfer students, minimum 2.0 high school GPA, portfolio. Recommended: minimum 3.0 high school GPA, 2 letters of recommendation, interview, SAT or ACT test scores. Auditions held multiple times throughout fall and spring on campus and off campus. Portfolio reviews

held continuously on campus and off campus in various cities; the submission of slides may be substituted for portfolios when distance is prohibitive.

Web Site http://www.cornish.edu

Undergraduate Contact Sharron Starling, Director of Admission, Cornish College of the Arts, 1000 Lenora, Seattle, Washington 98121; 800-726-ARTS, fax: 206-720-1011, e-mail address: sstarling@cornish.edu

More About the College

For more than ninety years, Cornish College of the Arts has educated students and nurtured artists who, as professionals, have consistently contributed to the culture of society. The Cornish School was founded in 1914 when Nellie Cornish, a woman of profound vision and unlimited energy, realized her vision of a school that offered arts training based on inspirational encouragement and guidance of student self-expression. While Cornish's mission is to "provide students aspiring to become practicing artists with an educational program of the highest quality," its role is far broader. Cornish students, alumni, and faculty members are working artists—theater directors, visual artists, set and lighting designers, dancers, and musicians—making art in and for the community. They are also innovative designers, business leaders, teachers, passionate and supportive audience members, and torchbearers for the arts.

Cornish College of the Arts, one of only three private, nonprofit performing and visual arts colleges in the nation, offers a Bachelor of Music degree and

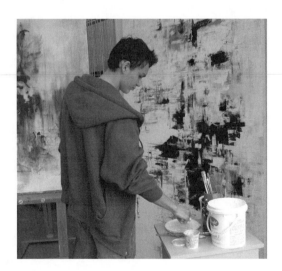

Cornish College of the Arts (continued)

Bachelor of Fine Arts degrees in art, dance, design, music, theater, and performance production. The academic programs are a distinctive blend of visual and performing arts grounded in a core curriculum of humanities and sciences. With more than 145 faculty members and an enrollment of over 775, Cornish has the lowest student-faculty ratio (8:1) in the country for an institution of its kind. Individualized attention and mentoring for every student are emphasized, and students thrive in their chosen artistic disciplines. They are encouraged to exchange ideas, to experiment and find their unique artistic voices, and to share them in both innovative and traditional projects. Cornish challenges artists to broaden their artistic perspectives and engage in creative collaboration by encouraging students to select from a wide range of elective studio courses outside their majors. The educational programs are of the highest possible quality, and the environment at Cornish nurtures creativity and intellectual curiosity and also prepares students to contribute to society as artists, citizens, and innovators.

The Art Department is devoted to realizing the individuality and full potential of each student. The faculty members support artistic play and risk, rigor, and a strong work ethic. Students are challenged to be involved in cross-disciplinary creation and collaboration and to engage with their peers in rich, critical discourse; studio projects; and exhibitions. They become adept at both traditional and contemporary technical approaches to art-making, develop fluency in various visual languages, and learn to understand their work in the context of history and culture and within the larger world of contemporary artistic endeavor.

Campus and Surroundings Seattle has more cultural construction projects in the works than any other urban area in the U.S., with more than $1.2 billion in cultural infrastructure for concert halls, museums, and theaters. The city has 190 galleries, five cultural heritage museums, five art museums, a dance company, a symphony, and twenty-nine professional theater companies and fifty-six fringe theater companies as well as more than eighty clubs with live music. Cornish serves as a focal point for public presentation, artistic criticism, participation, and discussion of the arts in this artistically rich community.

Faculty, Resident Artists, and Alumni The faculty at Cornish represents the largest concentration of practicing artists in the Northwest. They are nationally renowned in their fields and are dedicated to instruction of the arts. Their art can be found in major galleries, theaters, dance troupes, and other prestigious art organizations around the nation. Dedication to Cornish College and the stability of its programs is demonstrated by a faculty retention rate of more than 90 percent.

Since its earliest days, the College has fostered influential artists, arts movements, and arts organizations in the local community and beyond. Prominent members of the Northwest School of Artists, including Mark Tobey, Morris Graves, Guy Anderson, and William Cumming, taught at Cornish College, as did Martha Graham, an inventor of modern dance. Merce Cunningham, the legendary contemporary dancer/choreographer, and broadcast pioneer Chet Huntley were Cornish students. Revolutionary composer John Cage worked and invented the prepared piano at Cornish. In more recent years, the College has nurtured the talents of Heart's Nancy Wilson, Brendan Fraser, and award-winning composer Wendell Yuponce.

Cornish has hosted elite members of the artistic community as artists-in-residence, including Meredith Monk (performance), Mark Morris (dance), Bill Frisell (music), Rinde Eckert (theater), Syvilla Fort (dance), Imogen Cunningham (photography), and Lou Harrison (music). These acclaimed artists provide Cornish students with unique and invaluable educational experiences.

Design Department
Cornish College of the Arts

Seattle, Washington

Independent, coed. Urban campus. Total enrollment: 768 (2006). Art program established 1914.

Degrees Bachelor of Fine Arts in the area of design. Majors and concentrations: advertising design, animation, computer animation and interactive media, interior design, visual communication. Program accredited by NASAD.

Enrollment 164 total; all undergraduate.

Art Student Profile 65% females, 35% males, 14% minorities, 3% international.

Art Faculty 10 undergraduate (full-time), 21 undergraduate (part-time). 58% of full-time faculty have terminal degrees. Graduate students do not teach undergraduate courses. Undergraduate student–faculty ratio: 9:1.

Student Life Student groups/activities include American Society of Interior Designers, American Institute of Graphic Arts.

Expenses for 2007–2008 Application fee: $35. Tuition: $23,700 full-time. Mandatory fees: $300 full-time.

Financial Aid Program-specific awards: Nellie Scholarships for new students, departmental scholarships for new and continuing students, Presidential Scholarships for continuing students.

Application Procedures Students admitted directly into the professional program freshman year. Deadline for freshmen and transfers: August 15. Notification date for freshmen and transfers: August 30. Required: essay, high school transcript, college transcript(s) for transfer students, minimum 2.0 high school GPA, portfolio. Recommended: minimum 3.0 high school GPA, 2 letters of recommendation, interview, SAT or ACT test scores. Portfolio reviews held 12 times on campus and off campus at National Portfolio Days (California, Colorado, Oregon, Washington, Illinois, Minnesota, Hawaii); the submission of slides may be substituted for portfolios when distance is prohibitive.

Web Site http://www.cornish.edu

Undergraduate Contact Sharron Starling, Director of Admission, Cornish College of the Arts, 1000 Lenora, Seattle, Washington 98121; 800-726-ARTS, fax: 206-720-1011, e-mail address: sstarling@cornish.edu

Culver-Stockton College

Canton, Missouri

Independent, coed. Rural campus. Total enrollment: 849. Art program established 1900.

Degrees Bachelor of Fine Arts in the area of art. Majors and concentrations: graphic design, studio art.

Enrollment 42 total; 30 undergraduate, 12 nonprofessional degree.

Art Student Profile 60% females, 40% males, 8% minorities, 4% international.

Art Faculty 2 undergraduate (full-time), 3 undergraduate (part-time). 100% of full-time faculty have terminal degrees. Graduate students do not teach undergraduate courses. Undergraduate student–faculty ratio: 12:1.

Student Life Student groups/activities include Images Unlimited (art club).

Expenses for 2007–2008 Application fee: $0. Comprehensive fee: $23,450 includes full-time tuition ($16,600) and college room and board ($6850). College room only: $3100. Room and board charges vary according to board plan.

Financial Aid Program-specific awards: scholarship awards for program majors ($500–$1750).

Application Procedures Students admitted directly into the professional program freshman year. Deadline for freshmen and transfers: August 31. Required: high school transcript, portfolio, SAT or ACT test scores. Portfolio reviews held once in November (formally), and as needed on campus; the submission of slides may be substituted for portfolios.

Web Site http://www.culver.edu

Undergraduate Contact Mr. Joseph E. Jorgensen, Head, Art Department, Culver-Stockton College, Herrick Center, 1 College Hill, Canton, Missouri 63435-1299; 217-231-6368, fax: 217-231-6611, e-mail address: jjorgensen@culver.edu

Daemen College

Amherst, New York

Independent, coed. Suburban campus. Total enrollment: 2,511. Art program established 1948.

Degrees Bachelor of Fine Arts in the areas of applied design, graphic design, fine art. Majors and concentrations: applied design, drawing, graphic design, illustration, painting, printmaking, sculpture. Cross-registration with 17 institutions in the Western New York Consortium of Higher Education.

Enrollment 109 total; 68 undergraduate, 41 nonprofessional degree.

Art Student Profile 68% females, 32% males, 55% minorities.

Art Faculty 5 undergraduate (full-time), 6 undergraduate (part-time). 60% of full-time faculty have terminal degrees. Graduate students do not teach undergraduate courses. Undergraduate student–faculty ratio: 6:1.

Student Life Student groups/activities include Art Club, Academic Festival, art exhibits.

Expenses for 2007–2008 Application fee: $25. Comprehensive fee: $27,360 includes full-time tuition ($18,300), mandatory fees ($450), and

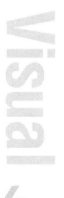

Daemen College (continued)

college room and board ($8610). Room and board charges vary according to board plan and housing facility.

Financial Aid Program-specific awards: 6 Visual Art Scholars Awards for freshmen enrolling in fine arts curriculum ($5000), 7 high school art show scholarships for entering first year students (award becomes available upon enrollment) ($1357).

Application Procedures Students admitted directly into the professional program freshman year. Deadline for freshmen and transfers: continuous. Notification date for freshmen and transfers: continuous. Required: high school transcript, college transcript(s) for transfer students, portfolio, SAT or ACT test scores (minimum composite ACT score of 16), "C" average in prior college work for transfer students. Recommended: 3 letters of recommendation, interview. Portfolio reviews held continuously on campus; the submission of slides may be substituted for portfolios when distance is prohibitive.

Web Site http://www.daemen.edu/academics/visual_performing_arts/

Undergraduate Contact Admissions Counselor, Admissions Office, Daemen College, 4380 Main Street, Amherst, New York 14226; 716-839-8225, fax: 716-839-8229, e-mail address: admissions@daemen.edu

Dorothy F. Schmidt College of Arts and Letters

See Florida Atlantic University

Drake University

Des Moines, Iowa

Independent, coed. Suburban campus. Total enrollment: 5,617. Art program established 1881.

Degrees Bachelor of Arts in the areas of art history, graphic design, studio art; Bachelor of Fine Arts in the areas of studio art, graphic design. Majors and concentrations: art history, drawing, graphic arts, painting, printmaking,

sculpture. Cross-registration with The Institute of Italian Studies (Italy). Program accredited by NASAD.

Enrollment 140 total; all undergraduate.

Art Student Profile 75% females, 25% males, 5% minorities, 5% international.

Art Faculty 9 undergraduate (full-time), 5 undergraduate (part-time). 100% of full-time faculty have terminal degrees. Graduate students do not teach undergraduate courses. Undergraduate student–faculty ratio: 12:1.

Student Life Student groups/activities include Art Student Club, American Institute of Graphic Arts (AIGA), Art Directors Association of Iowa.

Expenses for 2007–2008 Application fee: $25. Comprehensive fee: $30,612 includes full-time tuition ($23,280), mandatory fees ($412), and college room and board ($6920). College room only: $3500. Full-time tuition and fees vary according to class time, course load, and student level. Room and board charges vary according to board plan.

Financial Aid Program-specific awards: 25–30 art scholarships for entering freshmen and transfers ($500–$6000).

Application Procedures Students admitted directly into the professional program freshman year. Deadline for freshmen and transfers: continuous. Required: essay, high school transcript, college transcript(s) for transfer students, SAT or ACT test scores, portfolio for scholarship consideration. Portfolio reviews held as needed on campus; the submission of slides may be substituted for portfolios.

Web Site http://www.drake.edu

Undergraduate Contact Robert Craig, Chair, Department of Art and Design, Drake University, 25th and University Avenue, Des Moines, Iowa 50311; 515-271-2863, fax: 515-271-2558, e-mail address: robert.craig@drake.edu

Drexel University

Philadelphia, Pennsylvania

Independent, coed. Urban campus. Total enrollment: 20,682. Art program established 1963.

Degrees Bachelor of Architecture; Bachelor of Science. Majors and concentrations: architecture, digital media, fashion design, fashion design and merchandising, film and video production, graphic design, interior design, music industry, photography, playwriting, screenwriting. Graduate degrees offered: Master of Architecture in the area of architecture; Master of Science in the areas of fashion and interior design, arts administration, digital media, television management. Program accredited by NAAB, CIDA, NASAD.

Enrollment 1,765 total; 1,598 undergraduate, 167 graduate.

Art Student Profile 58% females, 42% males, 3% international.

Art Faculty 70 total (full-time), 170 total (part-time). 90% of full-time faculty have terminal degrees. Graduate students do not teach undergraduate courses. Undergraduate student–faculty ratio: 15:1.

Student Life Student groups/activities include Graphics Group (graphic design students only).

Expenses for 2008–2009 Application fee: $75. Comprehensive fee: $42,575 includes full-time tuition ($28,500), mandatory fees ($1940), and college room and board ($12,135). College room only: $7275. Special program-related fees: $500 per term for music lessons (private).

Financial Aid Program-specific awards: 2 Suzanne Roberts Awards for graphic and fashion design students with financial need ($15,000).

Application Procedures Students admitted directly into the professional program freshman year. Deadline for freshmen: March 1; transfers: May 1. Notification date for freshmen and transfers: continuous. Required: high school transcript, college transcript(s) for transfer students, minimum 2.0 high school GPA, 2 letters of recommendation, portfolio, SAT or ACT test scores, essay for architecture applicants, portfolio for fashion design applicants, graphic design, photo, essay for screenwriting, film and video, interior design, design and merchandising. Recommended: minimum 3.0 high school GPA. Portfolio reviews held by appointment on campus; the submission of slides may be substituted for portfolios.

Web Site http://www.drexel.edu/comad

Contact David Miller, Director of Recruitment, Office of the Dean, College of Media Arts and Design, Drexel University, 33rd and Market Streets, Philadelphia, Pennsylvania 19104; 215-895-1675, fax: 215-895-4917, e-mail address: ddm22@drexel.edu

East Carolina University

Greenville, North Carolina

State-supported, coed. Urban campus. Total enrollment: 25,990. Art program established 1909.

Degrees Bachelor of Fine Arts in the areas of art, art education. Majors and concentrations: art education, ceramic art and design, graphic design, illustration, jewelry and metalsmithing, painting/drawing, photography, printmaking, sculpture, surface design, textile arts, weaving, woodworking design. Graduate degrees offered: Master of Fine Arts in the area of art. Program accredited by NASAD.

Enrollment 550 undergraduate, 45 graduate, 25 nonprofessional degree.

Art Student Profile 60% females, 40% males, 20% minorities, 1% international.

Art Faculty 48 total (full-time), 10 total (part-time). 98% of full-time faculty have terminal degrees. Graduate students teach a few undergraduate courses. Undergraduate student–faculty ratio: 16:1.

Student Life Student groups/activities include Visual Art Forum, North Carolina Art Education Association Student Chapter.

Expenses for 2007–2008 Application fee: $60. State resident tuition: $2431 full-time. Nonresident tuition: $12,945 full-time. Mandatory fees: $1937 full-time. College room and board: $7150. College room only: $4150. Room and board charges vary according to board plan and housing facility. Special program-related fees: $25–$75 per course for supplies in selected classes.

Financial Aid Program-specific awards: 2 University Book Exchange Scholarships for program majors ($500), 1 Art Enthusiasts Scholarship for freshmen ($500), 1 K Eastern Carolina Advertising Federation Scholarship for communication art majors, 40 out-of-state special talent awards for out-of-state freshmen ($950).

Application Procedures Students admitted directly into the professional program freshman year. Deadline for freshmen: May 15; transfers: April 15. Required: high school transcript, SAT or ACT test scores, minimum 2.5 high school GPA.

Web Site http://www.ecu.edu/art/

Undergraduate Contact Ms. Ann Melanie, Academic Advisor, School of Art and Design, East

East Carolina University (continued)

Carolina University, Jenkins Fine Arts Center, East Fifth Street, Greenville, North Carolina 27858-4353; 252-328-6665, fax: 252-328-6441, e-mail address: melaniea@ecu.edu

Graduate Contact Mr. Scott Eagle, Director of Graduate Studies, School of Art and Design, East Carolina University, Jenkins Fine Arts Center, East Fifth Street, Greenville, North Carolina 27858-4353; 252-328-6665, fax: 252-328-6441, e-mail address: eagles@ecu.edu

Edinboro University of Pennsylvania

Edinboro, Pennsylvania

State-supported, coed. Small town campus. Total enrollment: 7,686. Art program established 1920.

Degrees Bachelor of Fine Arts in the areas of applied media arts, studio arts; Bachelor of Science in the area of art education. Majors and concentrations: art education, art history, ceramics, drawing, film/animation/video, furniture design, graphic design, jewelry and metalsmithing, painting, photography, printmaking, sculpture, weaving and fibers. Graduate degrees offered: Master of Arts in the area of art; Master of Fine Arts in the area of art. Program accredited by NASAD.

Enrollment 960 total; 950 undergraduate, 10 graduate.

Art Faculty 42 total (full-time), 7 total (part-time). Graduate students do not teach undergraduate courses. Undergraduate student–faculty ratio: 18:1.

Student Life Student groups/activities include Student Art League, clubs in every studio area.

Expenses for 2008–2009 Application fee: $30. State resident tuition: $5177 full-time. Nonresident tuition: $7766 full-time. Mandatory fees: $1509 full-time. College room and board: $5718. College room only: $3600. Special program-related fees for lab fees for art studio courses.

Financial Aid Program-specific awards: 1 alumni departmental award for general art majors ($500–$1000), 1 Ralph and Mildred Bruce Award for art education majors ($500–$1000), 1 Hank Katzwinkle Award for jewelry or art

majors ($500–$1000), 1 George Nicholas Award for animation majors ($500–$1000).

Application Procedures Students admitted directly into the professional program freshman year. Deadline for freshmen and transfers: continuous. Required: high school transcript, college transcript(s) for transfer students, SAT or ACT test scores. Recommended: interview, personal statement.

Web Site http://www.edinboro.edu

Undergraduate Contact William Mathie, Chair, Department of Art, Edinboro University of Pennsylvania, DH 113, Edinboro, Pennsylvania 16444; 814-732-2406.

Graduate Contact Dr. Scott Baldwin, Graduate Dean, School of Graduate Studies, Edinboro University of Pennsylvania, Edinboro, Pennsylvania 16444; 814-732-2856.

Emerson College

Boston, Massachusetts

Independent, coed. Urban campus. Total enrollment: 4,380.

Web Site http://www.emerson.edu/

Emmanuel College

Boston, Massachusetts

Independent Roman Catholic, coed. Urban campus. Total enrollment: 2,467. Art program established 1957.

Degrees Bachelor of Fine Arts in the areas of painting and printmaking, graphic design. Majors and concentrations: graphic arts, studio art. Cross-registration with Simmons College, Wheelock College, Wentworth Institute of Technology, Massachusetts College of Pharmacy and Allied Health Sciences, Massachusetts College of Art.

Enrollment 121 total.

Art Student Profile 70% females, 30% males, 5% international.

Art Faculty 4 undergraduate (full-time), 5 undergraduate (part-time). 100% of full-time faculty have terminal degrees. Graduate students do not teach undergraduate courses. Undergraduate student–faculty ratio: 15:1.

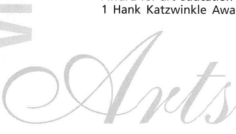

Student Life Student groups/activities include professional gallery on campus, membership in Boston Museum of Fine Arts.

Expenses for 2007–2008 Application fee: $40. Comprehensive fee: $37,450 includes full-time tuition ($26,100), mandatory fees ($150), and college room and board ($11,200). Full-time tuition and fees vary according to course load, degree level, and program. Room and board charges vary according to housing facility. Special program-related fees: $35–$75 per course for materials fee for studio classes.

Financial Aid Program-specific awards available.

Application Procedures Students admitted directly into the professional program freshman year. Deadline for freshmen and transfers: September 1. Notification date for freshmen and transfers: September 16. Required: essay, high school transcript, college transcript(s) for transfer students, minimum 2.0 high school GPA, 2 letters of recommendation, interview, SAT test score only. Recommended: portfolio. Portfolio reviews held twice on campus; the submission of slides may be substituted for portfolios when time constraints exist (digital media also acceptable).

Web Site http://www.emmanuel.edu

Undergraduate Contact Director of Admissions, Emmanuel College, 400 The Fenway, Boston, Massachusetts 02115; 617-735-9715, fax: 617-735-9877.

Emporia State University

Emporia, Kansas

State-supported, coed. Small town campus. Total enrollment: 6,354. Art program established 1863.

Degrees Bachelor of Fine Arts in the areas of ceramics, painting, photography, printmaking, sculpture and glassforming, graphic design, engraving arts, metals; Bachelor of Science in Education in the area of art. Majors and concentrations: art education, art therapy, ceramics, engraving arts, glassworking, graphic design, painting/drawing, photography, printmaking, sculpture. Program accredited by NASAD.

Enrollment 175 total; 95 undergraduate, 80 nonprofessional degree.

Art Student Profile 60% females, 40% males, 5% minorities, 3% international.

Art Faculty 13 undergraduate (full-time), 6 undergraduate (part-time). 100% of full-time faculty have terminal degrees. Graduate students do not teach undergraduate courses. Undergraduate student–faculty ratio: 15:1.

Student Life Student groups/activities include Alpha Rho Theta, Glass Guild, Kansas Art Education Association Student Chapter.

Expenses for 2007–2008 Application fee: $30. State resident tuition: $3140 full-time. Nonresident tuition: $11,190 full-time. Mandatory fees: $786 full-time. Full-time tuition and fees vary according to degree level. College room and board: $5581. College room only: $2832. Room and board charges vary according to board plan and housing facility. Special program-related fees: $10–$120 per class for expendable supplies.

Financial Aid Program-specific awards: 1 Timothy Sharp Memorial Scholarship for art majors ($250), 2 Jerry Ely Awards for art majors ($1000), 1 Hazelrigg Memorial Award for art majors ($250), 3 Art Faculty Awards for art majors ($250), 4 Beulah Holton Memorial Awards for art education majors ($1700), 1 Linda Ball Memorial Award for art majors ($250), 1 Cremer Family Memorial Award for art majors ($500), 1 Jean Hesenbart Memorial Award for art majors ($500), 1 Art 96 Award for art majors ($2000), 4 Ames Family Memorial Awards for art majors ($225).

Application Procedures Students admitted directly into the professional program freshman year. Deadline for freshmen and transfers: continuous. Required: high school transcript, college transcript(s) for transfer students, minimum 3.0 high school GPA, ACT test score only (minimum composite ACT score of 21), portfolio for scholarship consideration. Portfolio reviews held once on campus; the submission of slides may be substituted for portfolios (slides preferred; digital media also accepted).

Web Site http://www.emporia.edu/art/

Undergraduate Contact Elaine O. Henry, Chair, Department of Art, Emporia State University, Campus Box 4015, 1200 Commercial, Emporia, Kansas 66801-5087; 620-341-5246, fax: 620-341-6246, e-mail address: ehenry@emporia.edu

Visual *Arts*

Fashion Institute of Technology

New York, New York

State and locally supported, coed, primarily women. Urban campus. Total enrollment: 9,938. Art program established 1976.

Degrees Bachelor of Fine Arts. Majors and concentrations: accessories design and fabrication, advertising design, art/fine arts, computer animation and interactive media, fabric styling, fashion design, graphic design, illustration, interior design, packaging design, photography, textile/surface design, toy design. Graduate degrees offered: Master of Arts in the areas of exhibition design, art market: principles and practice, fashion and textile studies, illustration. Cross-registration with State University of New York System. Program accredited by NASAD, CIDA.

Enrollment 3,119 total; 1,283 undergraduate, 128 graduate, 1,708 nonprofessional degree.

Art Student Profile 85% females, 15% males, 36% minorities, 11% international.

Art Faculty 47 undergraduate (full-time), 128 undergraduate (part-time), 7 graduate (full-time), 22 graduate (part-time). Graduate students do not teach undergraduate courses. Undergraduate student–faculty ratio: 13:1.

Student Life Student groups/activities include literary publications, professional clubs and societies.

Expenses for 2007–2008 Application fee: $40. State resident tuition: $4567 full-time. Nonresident tuition: $11,140 full-time. Mandatory fees: $440 full-time. College room and board: $10,095. College room only: $9705.

Application Procedures Students apply for admission into the professional program by junior year. Deadline for freshmen and transfers: continuous. Required: essay, high school transcript, college transcript(s) for transfer students, minimum 2.0 high school GPA, portfolio. Portfolio reviews held several times on campus; the submission of slides may be substituted for portfolios with permission of the chair.

Web Site http://www.fitnyc.edu

Undergraduate Contact Ms. Dolores Lombardi, Director of Admissions, Fashion Institute of Technology, 7th Avenue at 27th Street, New York, New York 10001-5992; 212-217-3760, fax: 212-217-7481, e-mail address: fitinfo@fitnyc.edu

Graduate Contact Ms. Carole DeSantis, Secretary, School of Graduate Studies, Fashion Institute of Technology, 7th Avenue at 27th Street, New York, New York 10001-5992; 212-217-4300, fax: 212-217-4301, e-mail address: gradinfo@fitnyc.edu

More About the Institute

The Fashion Institute of Technology (FIT) is New York City's celebrated urban college for creative and business talent. A selective State University of New York (SUNY) college of art and design, business, and technology, FIT is a creative axis for a rich mix of innovative achievers, original thinkers, and industry pioneers, with more than forty programs of study leading to the Associate in Applied Science (A.A.S.), Bachelor of Fine Arts (B.F.A.), Bachelor of Science (B.S.), Master of Arts (M.A.), and Master of Professional Studies (M.P.S.) degrees.

FIT serves approximately 10,000 students from the greater New York metropolitan area, across the country, and around the world, offering full- and part-time study options, evening/weekend programs, and online studies. The college provides a singular approach to higher education—balancing a real-world-based curriculum and hands-on instruction with a rigorous liberal arts foundation, marrying design and business, supporting individual creativity in a collaborative environment, and encouraging faculty members

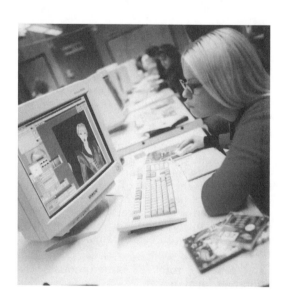

to match pedagogy with professional experience. It offers a complete college experience with a vibrant student life.

FIT's mission is to produce well-rounded graduates: doers and thinkers who raise the professional bar to become the next generation of business pacesetters and creative icons. Each degree program builds upon a traditional core of courses in the sciences and humanities, providing students with a global perspective, critical thinking skills, and the ability to communicate effectively.

The college offers fifteen A.A.S. and twenty-two baccalaureate programs. Most students complete a two-year A.A.S. program in their major area of study and the liberal arts, and then typically continue in a related, two-year B.F.A. or B.S. program. If students choose, they may begin their careers with the A.A.S. degree, which qualifies them for entry-level positions in a wide range of creative and/or business professions. Students with a degree or credits equivalent to an FIT A.A.S. (from an accredited and approved college) may apply directly to a baccalaureate program.

The School of Art and Design offers eleven A.A.S. and thirteen B.F.A. degree programs, the Jay and Patty Baker School of Business and Technology offers four A.A.S. and eight B.S. degree programs, and the School of Liberal Arts offers one B.S. degree program. The School of Graduate Studies offers six programs leading to either an M.A. or M.P.S. degree. Graduate students complete a capstone/thesis project that serves as the culmination of their studies and a professional-level addition to their portfolio or resume. FIT is accredited by the Middle States Association of Colleges and Schools, National Association of Schools of Art and Design, and Council for Interior Design Accreditation.

Campus and Surroundings The college's campus comprises an entire city block in Manhattan's Chelsea neighborhood, and the college makes extensive use of the city's vast resources, providing students with unrivaled internship opportunities and valuable professional connections. A wide range of cultural and entertainment options—from art galleries to theater to world-class dining—are available within short walking distance of campus, as is easy and convenient access to several subway and bus routes and the city's major rail and bus transportation hubs.

Program Facilities FIT's classrooms, laboratories, and studios reflect the most advanced educational and professional practices. Art and design facilities include drawing, painting, photography, printmaking, and sculpture studios; a graphics printing service bureau with high-resolution, large-format printers and laminating, scanning, slide-duplication, and wire-binding machines; a design/research lighting laboratory; display and exhibit design rooms; knitting and weaving labs; model-making and toy design workshops; and a multimedia foreign languages laboratory. Twenty-three computer labs house nearly 700 Mac and PC workstations, with several additional labs offering computers and specialized software reserved for students in specific programs. A computer-aided design and communications center provides the latest technological advancements in the fields of animation, design, and photography, offering specialized peripheral equipment and software such as Adobe Creative Suite, Shockwave Studio, Accumark, Modaris, Primavision, U4ia, Colour Matters, Karat Designer, 3D Studio Max, Final Cut Pro, Form Z, Softimage, Vellum 3D, and more.

Construction is currently underway on 50,000 square feet of new laboratories and studios. Set to open in the 2009–10 academic year, they will provide the latest in professional-quality equipment and workspace for art and design students majoring in accessories design, fashion design, jewelry design, textile/surface design, and toy design.

The Museum at FIT is the repository for one of the most important collections of fashion and textiles in the world, and is used year-round by students, historians, and designers for research and inspiration. The Gladys Marcus Library contains more than 300,000 volumes, 90 searchable databases, and specialized resources like clipping and sketch files and trend forecasting services.

All full-time, degree-seeking students are eligible for FIT housing. Four residence halls house 2,300 in fully furnished single, double, triple, and quad rooms, and students have the option of either traditional (meal plan included) or apartment-style accommodations.

Faculty and Alumni FIT's faculty is drawn equally from top professionals in academia, art, and business who bring their experience to the classroom and introduce students to the real-life opportunities and challenges of their disciplines through field trips, guest lectures, and sponsored competitions. Academic departments consult with industry advisory boards of noted experts in their fields, who ensure that the course work and classroom technology adapt to mirror evolving industry practices. Student-instructor interaction is encouraged, with a maximum class size of 25, and courses are structured to foster participation, independent thinking, and self-expression.

Well-known alumni include Calvin Klein, Nanette Lepore, and Chris Madden, and there are thousands more—from interior designers to toy designers, from

Fashion Institute of Technology (continued)

animators and illustrators to graphic and fine artists. Alumni often serve on FIT advisory boards, as guest lecturers in classes, and as project critics.

Student Exhibit Opportunities Exhibitions of student work are held throughout the year. Every spring, the college hosts its Art and Design Graduating Student Exhibition and the Fashion Design BFA show, a runway show whose judges include leading names in the industry and media. Each year, graduate students in Art Market: Principles and Practices curate a group show at a New York City gallery, and graduate students in Fashion and Textile Studies: History, Theory, Museum Practice curate an exhibition at The Museum at FIT. Sponsored competitions promote student work to prospective employers and in prominent trade publications, and clubs like Urban Studio provide public art opportunities in venues citywide—recent projects include a 600-square-foot, mixed-media mural in the Empire State Building.

Special Programs FIT's International Programs provide students the option of studying abroad for a year, a semester, or a summer or winter session in countries from Australia to China, Italy to Mexico.

The Presidential Scholars Program, available to academically exceptional students in all disciplines, offers special liberal arts courses, projects, colloquia, extracurricular activities, and off-campus visits designed to broaden horizons and stimulate discourse. Past areas of study have included urban archeology, theories of public space, Greek mythology, and cultural studies. Presidential Scholars are also awarded priority course registration and an annual merit stipend.

Precollege Programs are available to high school students during the fall, spring, and summer. More than forty-five courses help students develop their portfolios, explore a range of creative careers, and discover talents and abilities. Courses for middle school students are available in the summer.

The School of Continuing and Professional Studies provides evening/weekend classes to students and working professionals. Four art and design degrees are available through evening/weekend programs: Communication Design A.A.S., Fashion Design A.A.S., Graphic Design B.F.A., and Illustration B.F.A.

Cooperative Agreements FIT's extraordinary location at the center of New York City—world capital of the arts, business, and media—allows it to maintain close ties with the professions it serves. Field trips, guest lectures, internships, and sponsored competitions introduce students to the opportunities and challenges of their discipline. Internships are a required element of most programs, and available to all students. Sponsor organizations have included Calvin Klein, Fairchild Publications, MTV, and Saatchi & Saatchi.

Career Placement Services and Opportunities FIT's Career Services offers lifetime placement and career-building workshops to all of its students and alumni, with a graduation employment rate of nearly 90 percent. Approximately one third of student internships result in job offers by the sponsoring organizations.

Dorothy F. Schmidt College of Arts and Letters
Florida Atlantic University

Boca Raton, Florida

State-supported, coed. Suburban campus. Total enrollment: 26,275. Art program established 1961.

Web Site http://www.fau.edu/

Florida International University

Miami, Florida

State-supported, coed. Urban campus. Total enrollment: 38,290. Art program established 1972.

Web Site http://www.fiu.edu/

Florida State University

Tallahassee, Florida

State-supported, coed. Suburban campus. Total enrollment: 40,555. Art program established 1973.

Degrees Bachelor of Fine Arts in the areas of studio art, graphic design. Majors and concentrations: graphic design, studio art. Graduate degrees offered: Master of Fine Arts in the area of studio art. Program accredited by NASAD.

Enrollment 632 total; 48 undergraduate, 24 graduate, 560 nonprofessional degree.

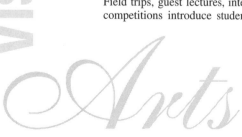

Art Student Profile 63% females, 37% males, 25% minorities, 5% international.

Art Faculty 25 total (full-time), 15 total (part-time). 100% of full-time faculty have terminal degrees. Graduate students teach a few undergraduate courses.

Student Life Student groups/activities include Art Student League.

Expenses for 2007–2008 Application fee: $30. State resident tuition: $3355 full-time. Nonresident tuition: $16,487 full-time. Full-time tuition varies according to location. College room and board: $8000. College room only: $4700. Room and board charges vary according to board plan and housing facility. Special program-related fees: $25–$50 per course for lab fee.

Financial Aid Program-specific awards: 2 Andy McLachlin Memorial Endowment Awards for sculpture students ($1000), 5 Ann Kirn Scholarships for graphic design students ($800).

Application Procedures Students apply for admission into the professional program by sophomore year. Deadline for freshmen and transfers: continuous. Required: essay, high school transcript, college transcript(s) for transfer students, minimum 2.0 high school GPA, portfolio, SAT or ACT test scores, portfolio review at end of second year for admission into BFA program. Recommended: minimum 3.0 high school GPA, letter of recommendation. Portfolio reviews held 3 times on campus; the submission of slides may be substituted for portfolios whenever necessary.

Web Site http://www.fsu.edu/~art

Undergraduate Contact Ms. Phyllis Straus, Undergraduate Admissions Coordinator, College of Visual Arts, Theatre and Dance, Florida State University, 220 FAB, Tallahassee, Florida 32306-1150; 850-644-6474, fax: 850-644-8977.

Graduate Contact Bunnie Hunter, Program Assistant, Department of Art, Florida State University, 220 FAB, Tallahassee, Florida 32306-1150; 850-644-6474, fax: 850-644-8977.

Fontbonne University

St. Louis, Missouri

Independent Roman Catholic, coed. Suburban campus. Total enrollment: 2,969.

Web Site http://www.fontbonne.edu/

Frostic School of Art

See Western Michigan University

Grand Valley State University

Allendale, Michigan

State-supported, coed. Small town campus. Total enrollment: 23,464. Art program established 1961.

Degrees Bachelor of Fine Arts. Majors and concentrations: ceramic art and design, graphic design, illustration, jewelry and metalsmithing, painting/drawing, printmaking, sculpture. Program accredited by NASAD.

Enrollment 271 total; 204 undergraduate, 67 nonprofessional degree.

Art Student Profile 73% females, 27% males, 5% minorities, 1% international.

Art Faculty 25 undergraduate (full-time), 5 undergraduate (part-time). 100% of full-time faculty have terminal degrees. Graduate students do not teach undergraduate courses. Undergraduate student–faculty ratio: 12:1.

Student Life Special housing available for art students.

Expenses for 2007–2008 Application fee: $30. State resident tuition: $7240 full-time. Nonresident tuition: $12,510 full-time. Full-time tuition varies according to program and student level. College room and board: $6880. College room only: $4930. Room and board charges vary according to board plan, housing facility, and location. Special program-related fees: $5–$15 per credit for studio maintenance.

Financial Aid Program-specific awards: 6 recruitment awards for freshmen ($1000), 1 Branstrom Award for program majors ($2000), 1 Calder Award for program majors ($1000–$1500), 1 Ox Bow Summer Program Award for program majors ($2000), 1 Margaret Warol Award for art education students ($500), 1 Nedra Otis Smith Award for program majors ($1200), 1 Koeze Award for program majors ($1000).

Application Procedures Students admitted directly into the professional program freshman year. Deadline for freshmen and transfers: August 1. Notification date for freshmen and transfers: continuous. Required: essay, high school transcript, minimum 3.0 high school

Grand Valley State University (continued)

GPA, portfolio, ACT test score only (minimum composite ACT score of 21). Portfolio reviews held 8 times on campus and off campus in various cities in Michigan and contiguous states; the submission of slides may be substituted for portfolios.

Web Site http://www.gvsu.edu/art/

Undergraduate Contact Dr. Patricia Clark, Interim Chair, Art and Design Department, Grand Valley State University, 1105 CAC, Allendale, Michigan 49401; 616-331-2575, fax: 616-331-3240, e-mail address: clarkp@gvsu.edu

Green Mountain College

Poultney, Vermont

Independent, coed. Small town campus. Total enrollment: 823. Art program established 1990.

Degrees Bachelor of Fine Arts. Majors and concentrations: studio art. Cross-registration with Castleton State College.

Art Faculty 4 undergraduate (full-time), 2 undergraduate (part-time). 100% of full-time faculty have terminal degrees. Graduate students do not teach undergraduate courses.

Student Life Student groups/activities include exhibitions.

Expenses for 2007–2008 Application fee: $30. One-time mandatory fee: $150. Comprehensive fee: $33,629 includes full-time tuition ($23,772), mandatory fees ($793), and college room and board ($9064). College room only: $5380. Full-time tuition and fees vary according to course load. Room and board charges vary according to housing facility. Special program-related fees: $10–$60 per semester for studio fees.

Financial Aid Program-specific awards: program scholarships for freshmen/sophomore/junior art majors, Peyser Painting Prize.

Application Procedures Students admitted directly into the professional program freshman year. Deadline for freshmen and transfers: continuous. Required: essay, high school transcript, college transcript(s) for transfer students, minimum 2.0 high school GPA. Recommended: letter of recommendation, interview, video, portfolio, SAT or ACT test scores. Portfolio reviews held once on campus; the submission of slides may be substituted for portfolios (slides preferred).

Web Site http://www.greenmtn.edu

Undergraduate Contact Dean of Admissions, Green Mountain College, 1 College Circle, Poultney, Vermont 05764-1199; 802-287-8208, fax: 802-287-8099, e-mail address: admiss@ greenmtn.edu

Guilford College

Greensboro, North Carolina

Independent, coed. Suburban campus. Total enrollment: 2,688. Art program established 1960.

Degrees Bachelor of Fine Arts in the area of studio art. Majors and concentrations: ceramics, painting/drawing, photography, printmaking, sculpture. Cross-registration with University of North Carolina at Greensboro.

Enrollment 60 total.

Art Student Profile 60% females, 40% males, 3% minorities, 2% international.

Art Faculty 3 undergraduate (full-time), 4 undergraduate (part-time). 100% of full-time faculty have terminal degrees. Graduate students do not teach undergraduate courses. Undergraduate student–faculty ratio: 13:1.

Student Life Student groups/activities include Annual Student Art Exhibition, senior thesis exhibition.

Expenses for 2008–2009 Application fee: $25. Comprehensive fee: $33,240 includes full-time tuition ($26,100) and college room and board ($7140).

Financial Aid Program-specific awards: 1–2 J. S. Laing Art Awards for sophomore and junior program majors ($800), 2 Merry Moore Winette Scholarships for photography majors ($800).

Application Procedures Students apply for admission into the professional program by junior year. Deadline for freshmen: February 1; transfers: May 1. Notification date for freshmen: March 15; transfers: June 1. Required: essay, high school transcript, minimum 2.0 high school GPA, SAT or ACT test scores. Recommended: letter of recommendation, interview, portfolio. Portfolio reviews held once at end of junior year or by appointment on campus; the submission of slides may be substituted for portfolios whenever necessary.

Web Site http://www.guilford.edu

Undergraduate Contact Roy Nydorf, Chair, Art Department, Guilford College, 5800 West Friendly Avenue, Greensboro, North Carolina 27410; 336-316-2249, fax: 336-316-2467.

Harding University

Searcy, Arkansas

Independent, coed. Small town campus. Total enrollment: 6,139. Art program established 1936.

Degrees Bachelor of Fine Arts in the areas of graphic design, painting, three-dimensional design; Bachelor of Science in the areas of art therapy, interior design, art (teacher certification). Majors and concentrations: art education, art therapy, graphic design, interior design, painting, three-dimensional studies. Program accredited by NCATE.

Enrollment 186 total; 150 undergraduate, 36 nonprofessional degree.

Art Faculty 9 undergraduate (full-time), 4 undergraduate (part-time). 75% of full-time faculty have terminal degrees. Graduate students do not teach undergraduate courses. Undergraduate student–faculty ratio: 18:1.

Student Life Student groups/activities include Kappa Pi (international honorary art fraternity), Red Brick Studio (graphic design club), American Society of Interior Designers.

Expenses for 2007–2008 Application fee: $35. Comprehensive fee: $17,938 includes full-time tuition ($11,940), mandatory fees ($420), and college room and board ($5578). College room only: $2810. Full-time tuition and fees vary according to course load. Room and board charges vary according to board plan and housing facility. Special program-related fees: $10–$200 per course for supplies.

Financial Aid Program-specific awards: 15 art scholarships for program majors ($350–$700).

Application Procedures Students apply for admission into the professional program by sophomore year. Deadline for freshmen and transfers: continuous. Required: high school transcript, college transcript(s) for transfer students, 2 letters of recommendation, SAT or ACT test scores (minimum composite ACT score of 19), portfolio for scholarship consider-ation. Recommended: interview, portfolio. Portfolio reviews held once on campus; the submission of slides may be substituted for portfolios.

Web Site http://www.harding.edu/

Undergraduate Contact Dr. John E. Keller, Chairman, Department of Art and Design, Harding University, Box 12253, Searcy, Arkansas 72149-0001; 501-279-4426, fax: 501-279-4717, e-mail address: art@harding.edu

Harrington College of Design

Chicago, Illinois

Proprietary, coed, primarily women. Urban campus. Total enrollment: 1,563 (2007). Art program established 1931.

Degrees Bachelor of Fine Arts in the areas of interior design, communication design. Majors and concentrations: communication design, interior design. Program accredited by NASAD, CIDA.

Enrollment 1,490 total; all undergraduate.

Art Student Profile 85% females, 15% males, 43% minorities, 2% international.

Art Faculty 19 undergraduate (full-time), 131 undergraduate (part-time). 43% of full-time faculty have terminal degrees. Graduate students do not teach undergraduate courses. Undergraduate student–faculty ratio: 16:1.

Student Life Student groups/activities include American Society of Interior Designers (ASID) Student Chapter, International Interior Design Association, American Institute of Graphic Arts (AIGA) Student Chapter.

Expenses for 2007–2008 Application fee: $60. Tuition: $18,000 full-time. Mandatory fees: $2520 full-time. College room only: $2600. Special program-related fees: $380 per semester for technology, library and resource, and CTA U-Pass fees for interior design program, $630 per semester for technology, graphic/photography, library and resource, and CTA U-Pass fees for communication design program.

Application Procedures Students admitted directly into the professional program freshman year. Deadline for freshmen and transfers: continuous. Required: high school transcript, college transcript(s) for transfer students,

Visual Arts

Harrington College of Design (continued)

interview. Recommended: essay, minimum 2.0 high school GPA, SAT or ACT test scores.

Web Site http://www.harringtoncollege.com

Undergraduate Contact Wendi Franczyk, Vice President of Admissions, Admissions, Harrington College of Design, 200 West Madison, Chicago, Illinois 60606; 877-939-4975 ext. 1188, fax: 312-697-8032, e-mail address: wfranczyk@harringtoncollege.com

Hartford Art School

See University of Hartford

Henry Radford Hope School of Fine Arts

See Indiana University Bloomington

Herron School of Art and Design

See Indiana University–Purdue University Indianapolis

Hope College

Holland, Michigan

Independent, coed. Suburban campus. Total enrollment: 3,226. Art program established 1949.

Degrees Bachelor of Arts in the area of fine arts. Majors and concentrations: art education, art history, studio art. Program accredited by NASAD.

Enrollment 51 total; all undergraduate.

Art Student Profile 78% females, 22% males, 10% minorities, 2% international.

Art Faculty 7 undergraduate (full-time), 4 undergraduate (part-time). 85% of full-time faculty have terminal degrees. Graduate students do not teach undergraduate courses. Undergraduate student–faculty ratio: 6:1.

Student Life Student groups/activities include GLCA New York Arts Program, DePree Gallery exhibition program, NYCAMS.

Expenses for 2007–2008 Application fee: $35. Comprehensive fee: $31,100 includes full-time tuition ($23,660), mandatory fees ($140), and college room and board ($7300). College room only: $3330. Full-time tuition and fees vary according to course load. Room and board charges vary according to board plan.

Financial Aid Program-specific awards: 9 Distinguished Artist Awards for freshman/transfer art students ($2500).

Application Procedures Students admitted directly into the professional program freshman year. Deadline for freshmen and transfers: continuous. Required: high school transcript, college transcript(s) for transfer students, SAT or ACT test scores. Recommended: portfolio. Portfolio reviews held once on campus; the submission of slides may be substituted for portfolios.

Web Site http://www.hope.edu/academic/art

Undergraduate Contact Steve Nelson, Chair, Department of Art and Art History, Hope College, PO Box 9000, Depree Art Center, Holland, Michigan 49424; 616-395-7503, fax: 616-395-7499, e-mail address: nelson@hope.edu

Idaho State University

Pocatello, Idaho

State-supported, coed. Small town campus. Total enrollment: 13,208. Art program established 1960.

Web Site http://www.isu.edu/

The Illinois Institute of Art–Chicago

Chicago, Illinois

Proprietary, coed. Urban campus.

Degrees Bachelor of Fine Arts. Majors and concentrations: digital filmmaking and video production, fashion design, game art and design, interior design, media arts/animation, visual communication, visual effects and motion graphics, Web design and interactive media. Program accredited by CIDA.

Expenses for 2007–2008 Contact school for current expenses.

Web Site http://www.artinstitutes.edu/chicago

Undergraduate Contact Admissions, The Illinois Institute of Art–Chicago, 350 North Orleans Street, Chicago, Illinois 60654-1593; 800-351-3450, fax: 312-280-8562.

The Illinois Institute of Art–Schaumburg

Schaumburg, Illinois

Proprietary, coed. Suburban campus.

Degrees Bachelor of Fine Arts. Majors and concentrations: digital filmmaking and video production, digital photography, game art and design, graphic design, interior design, visual effects and motion graphics, Web design and interactive media. Program accredited by CIDA.

Expenses for 2007–2008 Contact school for current expenses.

Web Site http://www.artinstitutes.edu/schaumburg

Undergraduate Contact Admissions, The Illinois Institute of Art–Schaumburg, 1000 North Plaza Drive, Suite 100, Schaumburg, Illinois 60173-4990; 800-314-3450, fax: 847-619-3064.

Illinois State University

Normal, Illinois

State-supported, coed. Urban campus. Total enrollment: 20,274. Art program established 1965.

Web Site http://www.ilstu.edu/

Illinois Wesleyan University

Bloomington, Illinois

Independent, coed. Suburban campus. Total enrollment: 2,094. Art program established 1850.

Degrees Bachelor of Fine Arts in the area of art and design. Majors and concentrations: art/fine arts, ceramic art and design, computer graphics, drawing, graphic arts, painting, photography, printmaking, sculpture, studio art. Cross-registration with Institute for European and Asian Studies.

Enrollment 80 total; 65 undergraduate, 15 nonprofessional degree.

Art Student Profile 52% females, 48% males, 8% minorities, 5% international.

Art Faculty 5 undergraduate (full-time), 2 undergraduate (part-time). 100% of full-time faculty have terminal degrees. Graduate students do not teach undergraduate courses. Undergraduate student–faculty ratio: 10:1.

Student Life Student groups/activities include Students in Design, Kappa Pi (international honorary art fraternity). Special housing available for art students.

Expenses for 2007–2008 Application fee: $0. Comprehensive fee: $37,780 includes full-time tuition ($30,580), mandatory fees ($170), and college room and board ($7030). College room only: $4330. Room and board charges vary according to board plan and housing facility. Special program-related fees: $100 for departmental fee.

Financial Aid Program-specific awards: 60 art talent awards for freshmen ($3000–$8500).

Application Procedures Students admitted directly into the professional program freshman year. Deadline for freshmen and transfers: continuous. Required: essay, high school transcript, college transcript(s) for transfer students, minimum 3.0 high school GPA, portfolio, SAT or ACT test scores. Recommended: interview. Portfolio reviews held by appointment on campus; the submission of slides may be substituted for portfolios for large works of art, three-dimensional pieces, or when distance is prohibitive.

Web Site http://titan.iwu.edu/~art/

Undergraduate Contact Tony Bankston, Director of Admissions, Illinois Wesleyan University, PO Box 2900, Bloomington, Illinois 61702-2900; 309-556-3031, fax: 309-556-3411, e-mail address: bankston@iwu.edu

Indiana State University

Terre Haute, Indiana

State-supported, coed. Small town campus. Total enrollment: 10,543. Art program established 1870.

Degrees Bachelor of Fine Arts in the area of studio art and design; Bachelor of Science in the area of art education. Majors and concentrations: art education, ceramic art and design,

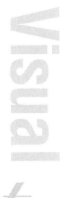

Indiana State University (continued)

graphic design, painting/drawing, photography, printmaking, sculpture, studio art. Graduate degrees offered: Master of Fine Arts in the area of studio art and design. Program accredited by NASAD.

Enrollment 195 total; 173 undergraduate, 22 graduate.

Art Student Profile 65% females, 35% males, 26% minorities, 8% international.

Art Faculty 10 total (full-time), 1 total (part-time). 90% of full-time faculty have terminal degrees. Graduate students teach a few undergraduate courses. Undergraduate student–faculty ratio: 15:1.

Student Life Student groups/activities include Student Gallery Program, Design Club, Art Club. Special housing available for art students.

Expenses for 2008–2009 Application fee: $25. State resident tuition: $6792 full-time. Nonresident tuition: $15,046 full-time. Mandatory fees: $356 full-time. Special program-related fees: $24 per course for studio lab fee.

Financial Aid Program-specific awards: 1 Hildegard Ping Art and Anthropology Scholarship for program majors ($400), 1 ISU Friends of Art Scholarship for program majors ($500), 10–12 Creative and Performing Arts Scholarships for freshmen ($2000), 1 Indiana Artist-Craftsmen/Talbot Street Art Fair Scholarship for program majors ($350), 1 Violet Helen Rich Scholarship for painting majors ($1500), 1 Elmer J. Porter Scholarship for program majors ($675), 1 Mark Hannig Scholarship for program majors ($1000), 3 Marian J. Frutiger Awards for art majors ($1000).

Application Procedures Students admitted directly into the professional program freshman year. Deadline for freshmen and transfers: August 15. Notification date for freshmen and transfers: continuous. Required: high school transcript, college transcript(s) for transfer students, minimum 2.0 high school GPA, SAT or ACT test scores, portfolio for scholarship consideration. Portfolio reviews held 6 times on campus and off campus in Vincennes, IN; Fort Wayne, IN; Louisville, KY; Indianapolis, IN; St. Louis, MO; Chicago, IL; the submission of slides may be substituted for portfolios when distance is prohibitive, if original work is unavailable, or for large works of art.

Web Site http://www.indstate.edu/art-dept/

Undergraduate Contact Fran Lattanzio, Undergraduate Advisor, Department of Art, Indiana State University, Fine Arts 108, Terre Haute, Indiana 47809; 812-237-8528, fax: 812-237-4369, e-mail address: artdept@isugw.indstate.edu

Graduate Contact Charles Mayer, Interim Chair, Department of Art, Indiana State University, Fine Arts 108, Terre Haute, Indiana 47809; 812-237-3697, fax: 812-237-4369, e-mail address: artdept@isugw.indstate.edu

Henry Radford Hope School of Fine Arts

Indiana University Bloomington

Bloomington, Indiana

State-supported, coed. Small town campus. Total enrollment: 38,990. Art program established 1896.

Degrees Bachelor of Fine Arts in the areas of ceramics, graphic design, jewelry and metalsmithing, painting, photography, printmaking, sculpture, textiles, digital art. Majors and concentrations: ceramic art and design, digital art, graphic design, jewelry and metalsmithing, painting/drawing, photography, printmaking, sculpture, textile arts. Graduate degrees offered: Master of Arts in the area of art history; Master of Arts in Teaching in the area of art education; Master of Fine Arts in the areas of ceramics, graphic design, jewelry and metalsmithing, painting, photography, printmaking, sculpture, textiles, digital art. Doctor of Philosophy in the area of art history. Program accredited by NASAD.

Enrollment 645 total; 74 undergraduate, 135 graduate, 436 nonprofessional degree.

Art Student Profile 70% females, 30% males, 8% minorities, 3% international.

Art Faculty 40 undergraduate (full-time), 8 undergraduate (part-time). 100% of full-time faculty have terminal degrees. Graduate students teach about a quarter of undergraduate courses. Undergraduate student–faculty ratio: 15:1.

Student Life Student groups/activities include Art History Association, Fine Arts Student Association, Graphic Design Student Association.

Expenses for 2007–2008 Application fee: $50. State resident tuition: $7000 full-time. Nonresident tuition: $21,479 full-time. Mandatory fees: $837 full-time. Full-time tuition and fees vary according to location and program. College room and board: $6676. College room only: $4172. Room and board charges vary according to board plan and housing facility. Special program-related fees: $23–$100 per course for material fees.

Financial Aid Program-specific awards: 10–15 Hope School of Fine Arts Student Awards for program majors ($150–$2500).

Application Procedures Students apply for admission into the professional program by sophomore, junior year. Deadline for freshmen and transfers: continuous. Notification date for freshmen and transfers: August 29. Required: high school transcript, college transcript(s) for transfer students, SAT or ACT test scores.

Web Site http://www.fa.indiana.edu/

Undergraduate Contact Nell Weatherwax, Undergraduate Advisor, Henry Radford Hope School of Fine Arts, Indiana University Bloomington, 1201 East 7th Street, Room 123, Bloomington, Indiana 47405; 812-855-1693, fax: 812-855-7498, e-mail address: nweather@indiana.edu

Graduate Contact Brad Wicklund, Graduate Services Coordinator, Henry Radford Hope School of Fine Arts, Indiana University Bloomington, 1201 East 7th Street, Room 123, Bloomington, Indiana 47405; 812-855-0188, fax: 812-855-7498, e-mail address: faoffice@indiana.edu

Herron School of Art and Design
Indiana University–Purdue University Indianapolis

Indianapolis, Indiana

State-supported, coed. Urban campus. Total enrollment: 29,854. Art program established 1902.

Web Site http://www.iupui.edu/

International Academy of Design & Technology

Tampa, Florida

Proprietary, coed. Urban campus. Art program established 1984.

Degrees Bachelor of Fine Arts. Majors and concentrations: computer animation, digital media production, digital photography, digital production, fashion design and marketing, graphic design, interior design, Web design. Graduate degrees offered: Master of Fine Arts in the areas of media design, management, animation, game and virtual space studies. Program accredited by CIDA.

Enrollment 2,000 total.

Art Faculty 27 undergraduate (full-time), 127 undergraduate (part-time). Graduate students do not teach undergraduate courses. Undergraduate student–faculty ratio: 17:1.

Student Life Student groups/activities include American Society of Interior Designers Student Chapter, Fashion Design Club, SIGGRAPH (graphics and animation).

Expenses for 2008–2009 Application fee: $50.

Financial Aid Program-specific awards: Florida High School Partnership Scholarships for entering freshmen ($1000), merit award scholarships for incoming freshmen ($1000–$10,000), Portfolio Review Scholarships for incoming freshmen ($150–$500), International Academy Scholarship for international students ($500–$2500), President's Institutional Scholarship for continuing students ($250–$1000), National Academy Scholarship for incoming freshmen ($500–$2500), Academy Local Applicant Award for incoming freshmen ($2000), Future Artist Scholarship for incoming freshmen ($250), Designers Scholarship for new or continuing students ($500–$7200), Florida Resident Scholarship for Interior or Graphic Design for incoming freshmen ($2000).

Application Procedures Students admitted directly into the professional program freshman year. Deadline for freshmen and transfers: continuous. Required: college transcript(s) for transfer students, interview, high school transcript or GED attestation. Recommended: essay, minimum 2.0 high school GPA, portfolio. Portfolio reviews held on campus.

Web Site http://www.academy.edu

Visual

Arts

International Academy of Design & Technology (continued)

Undergraduate Contact Heidi Demello, Associate Vice President, Admissions and Marketing, International Academy of Design & Technology, 5104 Eisenhower Boulevard, Tampa, Florida 33634; 800-ACADEMY ext. 8092, fax: 813-881-0008.

International Academy of Design & Technology

Chicago, Illinois

Proprietary, coed, primarily women. Urban campus. Art program established 1977.
Web Site http://www.iadtchicago.edu/

Iowa State University of Science and Technology

Ames, Iowa

State-supported, coed. Suburban campus. Total enrollment: 26,160. Art program established 1920.

Degrees Bachelor of Fine Arts in the areas of graphic design, interior design, integrated studio arts. Majors and concentrations: graphic design, integrated studio arts, interior design. Graduate degrees offered: Master of Fine Arts in the areas of graphic design, interior design, integrated visual arts. Program accredited by CIDA.

Enrollment 999 total; 550 undergraduate, 50 graduate, 399 nonprofessional degree.

Art Student Profile 60% females, 40% males, 6% minorities, 4% international.

Art Faculty 38 total (full-time), 12 total (part-time). 95% of full-time faculty have terminal degrees. Graduate students teach a few undergraduate courses. Undergraduate student–faculty ratio: 18:1.

Student Life Student groups/activities include Interior Design Student Association, American Institute of Graphic Arts Student Chapter, College of Design Art Club. Special housing available for art students.

Expenses for 2008–2009 Application fee: $30. State resident tuition: $5524 full-time. Nonresi-dent tuition: $16,514 full-time. Mandatory fees: $836 full-time. Special program-related fees: $5–$100 per course for in-studio expenses.

Financial Aid Program-specific awards: 10–12 art and design excellence awards for program majors ($500–$1500), 2 Garfield/Boody Awards for fine arts majors ($1600), 3 Kiser/Beard Awards for interior design majors ($1500), 2–4 art and design minority awards for program majors ($500–$1000), 1–2 graphic design sophomore scholarships for program majors ($500).

Application Procedures Students apply for admission into the professional program by freshman year. Deadline for freshmen and transfers: continuous. Required: high school transcript, college transcript(s) for transfer students, SAT or ACT test scores, minimum TOEFL score of 550 for international applicants, portfolio for graphic, interior design, and integrated studio arts. Recommended: minimum 2.0 high school GPA, standing in top half of graduating class. Portfolio reviews held once in spring on campus.

Web Site http://www.design.iastate.edu/

Undergraduate Contact Director of Admissions, Iowa State University of Science and Technology, 100 Alumni Hall, Ames, Iowa 50011-2010; 515-294-5836, fax: 515-294-2592, e-mail address: admissions@iastate.edu

Graduate Contact Mona Pett, Secretary, Department of Art and Design, Iowa State University of Science and Technology, 158 College of Design, Ames, Iowa 50011-2010; 515-294-6725, fax: 515-294-2725, e-mail address: grad_admissions@iastate.edu

Roy H. Park School of Communications
Ithaca College

Ithaca, New York

Independent, coed. Small town campus. Total enrollment: 6,660. Art program established 1986.

Degrees Bachelor of Fine Arts in the areas of film, photography, visual arts. Majors and concentrations: film/photography/visual arts. Cross-registration with Cornell University, Wells College.

Enrollment 79 total; all undergraduate.

Art Student Profile 41% females, 59% males, 9% minorities, 5% international.

Art Faculty 12 undergraduate (full-time), 6 undergraduate (part-time). 100% of full-time faculty have terminal degrees. Graduate students do not teach undergraduate courses. Undergraduate student–faculty ratio: 5:1.

Student Life Student groups/activities include television station, radio station, Production Unit.

Expenses for 2007–2008 Application fee: $60. Comprehensive fee: $39,398 includes full-time tuition ($28,670) and college room and board ($10,728). College room only: $5604.

Financial Aid Program-specific awards: 1 Kristen Landen Film Scholarship for cinema majors ($2305), 2 Mark Mazura Video Production Scholarships for video production students ($1530), 1 James B. Pendleton Filmmaking Award for film majors ($1000), 18 James B. Pendleton Scholarships for cinema and photography majors ($5000–$15,000), 1 Rod Serling Scholarship for video production students ($4845), 1 Mark Wilder Memorial Scholarship for video production students ($1420).

Application Procedures Students admitted directly into the professional program freshman year. Deadline for freshmen: February 1; transfers: March 1. Notification date for freshmen: April 15. Required: essay, high school transcript, college transcript(s) for transfer students, letter of recommendation, SAT or ACT test scores. Recommended: minimum 3.0 high school GPA, interview.

Web Site http://www.ithaca.edu/rhp.php

Undergraduate Contact Mr. Gerard Turbide, Director, Admission, Ithaca College, 100 Job Hall, Ithaca, New York 14850-7020; 607-274-3124, fax: 607-274-1900, e-mail address: admission@ithaca.edu

art. Majors and concentrations: art, art education. Cross-registration with Cornell University, Wells College.

Enrollment 40 total; 13 undergraduate, 27 nonprofessional degree.

Art Student Profile 73% females, 27% males, 15% minorities, 8% international.

Art Faculty 7 undergraduate (full-time), 3 undergraduate (part-time). 100% of full-time faculty have terminal degrees. Graduate students do not teach undergraduate courses. Undergraduate student–faculty ratio: 5:1.

Student Life Student groups/activities include Ithaca College Art Club.

Expenses for 2007–2008 Application fee: $60. Comprehensive fee: $39,398 includes full-time tuition ($28,670) and college room and board ($10,728). College room only: $5604. Special program-related fees: $25–$60 per semester for supplies.

Financial Aid Program-specific awards: 1 Donald and Martha Negus Scholarship for program majors ($875).

Application Procedures Students admitted directly into the professional program freshman year. Deadline for freshmen: February 1; transfers: March 1. Notification date for freshmen: April 15. Required: essay, high school transcript, college transcript(s) for transfer students, letter of recommendation, SAT or ACT test scores. Recommended: minimum 3.0 high school GPA, interview, portfolio. Portfolio reviews held continuously by appointment on campus; the submission of slides may be substituted for portfolios.

Web Site http://www.ithaca.edu/hs.php

Undergraduate Contact Mr. Gerard Turbide, Director, Admission, Ithaca College, 100 Job Hall, Ithaca, New York 14850-7020; 607-274-3124, fax: 607-274-1900, e-mail address: admission@ithaca.edu

School of Humanities and Sciences
Ithaca College

Ithaca, New York

Independent, coed. Small town campus. Total enrollment: 6,660. Art program established 1960.

Degrees Bachelor of Arts in the area of art education; Bachelor of Fine Arts in the area of

Jacksonville State University

Jacksonville, Alabama

State-supported, coed. Small town campus. Total enrollment: 9,077.

Degrees Bachelor of Fine Arts in the area of studio art. Majors and concentrations: ceram-

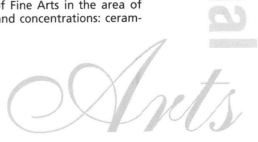

Jacksonville State University (continued)

ics, graphic design, painting/drawing, photography, printmaking. Program accredited by NASAD.

Enrollment 169 total; 102 undergraduate, 67 nonprofessional degree.

Art Student Profile 63% females, 37% males, 12% minorities, 2% international.

Art Faculty 8 undergraduate (full-time), 3 undergraduate (part-time). 100% of full-time faculty have terminal degrees. Graduate students do not teach undergraduate courses. Undergraduate student–faculty ratio: 14:1.

Student Life Student groups/activities include Student Art Alliance, The Potter's Guild.

Expenses for 2007–2008 Application fee: $20. State resident tuition: $5070 full-time. Nonresident tuition: $10,140 full-time. College room and board: $3763. Room and board charges vary according to board plan and housing facility.

Financial Aid Program-specific awards: 1 Art Department Award for incoming freshmen ($1000), 2 Art Department Awards for upperclassmen ($1000), 1 Lee Manners Scholarship for junior art majors with 3.0 minimum GPA ($150), 2 Visual Art Society/JSU Scholarships for upperclassmen ($2000).

Application Procedures Students apply for admission into the professional program by sophomore year. Deadline for freshmen and transfers: continuous. Required: high school transcript, portfolio, SAT or ACT test scores. Recommended: minimum 2.0 high school GPA. Portfolio reviews held twice on campus.

Web Site http://art.jsu.edu

Undergraduate Contact Mr. Charles Groover, Head, Department of Art, Jacksonville State University, 700 Pelham Road North, Jacksonville, Alabama 36265; 256-782-5625, fax: 256-782-5419.

Jacksonville University

Jacksonville, Florida

Independent, coed. Suburban campus. Total enrollment: 3,436. Art program established 1961.

Degrees Bachelor of Fine Arts in the areas of studio art, computer art and design, art history. Majors and concentrations: art history, computer art, studio art.

Enrollment 72 total; all undergraduate.

Art Student Profile 58% females, 42% males, 27% minorities, 3% international.

Art Faculty 10 undergraduate (full-time). 90% of full-time faculty have terminal degrees. Graduate students do not teach undergraduate courses. Undergraduate student–faculty ratio: 7:1.

Student Life Student groups/activities include Fine Art Society, volunteer city-wide art projects, student group shows.

Expenses for 2008–2009 Application fee: $30. Comprehensive fee: $32,660 includes full-time tuition ($23,900) and college room and board ($8760). College room only: $5000.

Financial Aid Program-specific awards: 2 Phillips Scholarships for those demonstrating exceptional talent ($1500–$6000), 2 Sheldon Bryan Scholarships for those demonstrating exceptional talent ($1000–$6000).

Application Procedures Students admitted directly into the professional program freshman year. Deadline for freshmen and transfers: continuous. Notification date for freshmen and transfers: continuous. Required: high school transcript, college transcript(s) for transfer students, minimum 2.0 high school GPA, portfolio, SAT or ACT test scores. Recommended: essay, letter of recommendation. Portfolio reviews held 5 times and by appointment on campus and off campus in various high schools in Duval County; the submission of slides may be substituted for portfolios if a campus visit is impossible.

Web Site http://www.ju.edu

Undergraduate Contact Ms. Miriam King, Vice President of Enrollment Management, Jacksonville University, 2800 University Boulevard North, Jacksonville, Florida 32211; 904-256-7000, fax: 904-256-7012, e-mail address: admissions@ju.edu

Johnson State College

Johnson, Vermont

State-supported, coed. Rural campus. Total enrollment: 1,867. Art program established 1982.

Degrees Bachelor of Fine Arts in the area of studio art. Majors and concentrations: ceramics, drawing, painting, sculpture. Graduate degrees offered: Master of Fine Arts in the areas of painting, sculpture, drawing, mixed media. Cross-registration with members of National Student Exchange Program, schools within the Vermont State College System.

Enrollment 116 total; 18 undergraduate, 24 graduate, 74 nonprofessional degree.

Art Student Profile 58% females, 42% males, 5% minorities, 4% international.

Art Faculty 5 total (full-time), 30 total (part-time). 100% of full-time faculty have terminal degrees. Graduate students do not teach undergraduate courses. Undergraduate student–faculty ratio: 4:1.

Student Life Student groups/activities include Student Art Coalition, gallery displays.

Expenses for 2008–2009 Application fee: $35. State resident tuition: $7500 full-time. Nonresident tuition: $16,000 full-time. Mandatory fees: $500 full-time. College room and board: $7581. College room only: $4500. Special program-related fees: $15–$35 per course for studio material fees.

Financial Aid Program-specific awards: 13 Dibden Talent Scholarships for talented artists ($250–$500).

Application Procedures Students apply for admission into the professional program by sophomore year. Deadline for freshmen and transfers: continuous. Notification date for freshmen and transfers: continuous. Required: essay, high school transcript, college transcript(s) for transfer students, minimum 2.0 high school GPA, 2 letters of recommendation, SAT or ACT test scores (minimum combined SAT score of 1350, minimum composite ACT score of 18), portfolio for entry into BFA program. Recommended: interview, portfolio. Portfolio reviews held twice on campus.

Web Site http://www.johnsonstatecollege.com

Undergraduate Contact Penny P. Howrigan, Associate Dean for Enrollment Services, Johnson State College, 337 College Hill, Johnson, Vermont 05656; 800-635-2356, fax: 802-635-1230, e-mail address: jscapply@badger.jsc.vsc.edu

Graduate Contact Ms. Cathy Higley, Administrative Assistant, Graduate Studies, Johnson State College, 337 College Hill, Johnson, Vermont 05656; 802-635-1244, e-mail address: higleyc@badger.jsc.vsc.edu

J. William Fulbright College of Arts and Sciences

See University of Arkansas

Kansas City Art Institute

Kansas City, Missouri

Independent, coed. Urban campus. Total enrollment: 676. Art program established 1885.

Degrees Bachelor of Fine Arts in the areas of ceramics, fiber, painting, printmaking, photography/digital filmmaking, sculpture, art history, creative writing, animation, graphic design, interdisciplinary arts. Majors and concentrations: animation, art history, ceramics, creative writing, fibers, graphic design, interdisciplinary studies, painting/drawing, photography/digital filmmaking, printmaking, sculpture. Cross-registration with University of Missouri at Kansas City. Program accredited by NASAD.

Enrollment 676 total; all undergraduate.

Art Student Profile 55% females, 45% males, 12% minorities, 1% international.

Art Faculty 51 undergraduate (full-time), 53 undergraduate (part-time). 84% of full-time faculty have terminal degrees. Graduate students do not teach undergraduate courses. Undergraduate student–faculty ratio: 12:1.

Student Life Student groups/activities include Student Gallery Committee, Ethnic Student Association, Student Film Series Committee. Special housing available for art students.

Expenses for 2007–2008 Application fee: $35. Comprehensive fee: $35,480 includes full-time tuition ($27,220) and college room and board ($8260). Full-time tuition varies according to program. Room and board charges vary according to board plan and housing facility. Special program-related fees: $45 per course for sculpture fee, $50 per course for painting fee, $50 per course for interdisciplinary arts fee, $60 per course for design fee, $60 per course for animation fee, $100 per course for

Kansas City Art Institute (continued)

printmaking fee, $150 per course for fiber fee, $175 per course for photo and digital filmmaking fee, $390 per course for ceramics materials.

Financial Aid Program-specific awards: 300–350 need-based scholarships for program majors ($2000–$8000), 100–125 merit-based scholarships for program majors ($2000–$8000).

Application Procedures Students apply for admission into the professional program by sophomore year. Deadline for freshmen and transfers: continuous. Required: essay, high school transcript, college transcript(s) for transfer students, 2 letters of recommendation, portfolio, SAT or ACT test scores (minimum combined SAT score of 1425, minimum composite ACT score of 20). Recommended: interview, minimum 2.5 high school GPA. Portfolio reviews held continuously on campus and off campus in various locations on National Portfolio Days; high school visits; the submission of slides may be substituted for portfolios (CD-DVD preferred).

Web Site http://www.kcai.edu

Undergraduate Contact Mr. Larry E. Stone, Vice President for Enrollment Management, Kansas City Art Institute, 4415 Warwick Boulevard, Kansas City, Missouri 64111; 800-522-5224, fax: 816-802-3309, e-mail address: admiss@kcai.edu

More About the Institute

Kansas City Art Institute (KCAI), founded in 1885, is a private and fully accredited distinguished four-year college of art and design. Kansas City Art Institute is accredited by the Higher Learning Commission, a commission of the North Central Association of Colleges and Schools, and by the National Association of Schools of Art and Design. KCAI's 670 students are from thirty-seven states and six foreign nations. Kansas City Art Institute combines intensive time in the classroom, extensive experience in the studio, a broad liberal arts background, focused learning opportunities, and a dynamic campus community. It is this rich combination that develops the "whole" student as an artist and a person.

Kansas City Art Institute is located in the heart of the cultural community of Kansas City. Across the street to the east is the Nelson-Atkins Museum of Art, consistently ranked in the top fifteen general art museums. The Kemper Museum of Contemporary Art

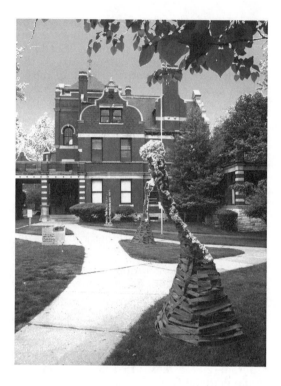

is across the street to the west. Galleries and studios, restaurants and cafés, the Country Club Plaza, and other entertainment spots are only a short distance from the campus.

Kansas City Art Institute provides an ideal environment to bring the students' art to life. A scenic 15-acre campus is complete with individual studio space as early as freshman year, cutting-edge technology, wide open spaces, and first-rate facilities that foster creative spirit. The commitment to high-quality resources provides materials that enhance a finished product. The Living Center is a hub of student life and very much the students' space, from the Foundation artwork displayed in the cafeteria to the places, indoors and outdoors, where students gather and talk about their work.

KCAI, consistently recognized for the rigor and diversity of its curriculum, provides quality academic programs that are strengthened by first-rate support services such as the Academic Resource Center, the Computer Graphics Center, the Media Center, the Central Shop, the Career Services Office, and the Library.

KCAI makes it possible for students to study at other schools in the United States and Canada as well as schools in Australia, Ecuador, England, Germany, Hungary, Ireland, Israel, Japan, New Zealand, the

Netherlands, Spain, and others. It is also possible for students to take part in internships at places such as Hallmark Cards, Industrial Light and Magic, Warner Bros., and Bernstein-Rein.

All serious students with a passion for art are encouraged to apply. While it is not mandatory that applicants follow a college preparatory program in high school and take courses in studio and art history, it is highly recommended to assure competitiveness with other applicants. Students are advised to follow a college preparatory curriculum based on the following: four years of English, three years of social sciences, and art courses if possible. Considerable emphasis is placed on abilities in the areas of drawing, color, and design. The criteria for admission requires evaluation of the student's portfolio, academic transcripts, standardized test scores, statement of purpose, letters of recommendation, and other indicators of potential success as a professional artist. Applicants must have successfully completed a recognized secondary school program (high school) or its equivalent, with a good academic record to be eligible for admission to KCAI. KCAI students' backgrounds are diverse, but they share a desire to pursue an education in the arts. The Admissions Committee looks for serious and motivated students who are willing to work hard and take risks. The committee evaluates each application with a great deal of sensitivity and open-mindedness before reaching an admission decision because the Committee knows each student's level of imagination, innovation, and academic achievement is highly individual.

KCAI makes every effort to help students who need financial aid. More than 90 percent of the students attending KCAI receive assistance from one or more financial aid sources. When awarding need-based assistance, KCAI first looks to the financial contribution of the parents and/or student. Students are expected to take an active part in the financing of their education through working, saving, and pursuing scholarships from outside sources. Grants, loans, employment, and monthly payment plans are available. KCAI offers a competitive scholarship competition and KCAI merit awards. Missouri Financial Assistance Grants provide grant funding from the State of Missouri for Missouri residents who are attending a Missouri institution and meet financial need requirements established by the State of Missouri. An Academic Competitiveness Grant of up to $750 for the first academic year of study and up to $1300 for the second academic year of study is available to students who meet the requirements. Applications from students seeking the full range of financial aid opportunities must include the Free Application for Federal Student Aid (FAFSA).

For more information about The Kansas City Art Institute in general, students should call 800-522-5224 (toll-free) or visit KCAI's Web site at http://www.kcai.edu.

Faculty The approximately 105 faculty members at KCAI are a distinguished group. They are recognized scholars, sought-after consultants, talented artists, and professional mentors. They bring impressive degrees from Cranbrook Academy of Art, Pratt Institute, Alfred University, Yale University, and other prestigious programs. Their work has been exhibited all around the world, and it resides in the permanent collections of places such as the Metropolitan Museum of Art, MoMA, The National Museum of Wales, The Nelson-Atkins Museum of Art, and the Smithsonian. They have professional experience through employment and consulting with companies such as Atlantic Records; Hallmark Cards, Inc.; Perry Ellis; and Time/Life Books.

Program Facilities KCAI's ceramics department contains a clay-mixing room, a plaster room, potter's wheels, kilns, and a pitfiring space. There are also various low, mid-range, and high-temperature gas and electric kilns. Glass has recently been introduced. Students in the painting program have individual studio space as well as studio facilities and resources for a range of painting media and techniques, including oil, acrylic, watercolor, collage, and mixed-media construction as well as art-making innovations in computer technology. Students in the printmaking program work in a well-equipped facility with access at all times to etching, lithography, monoprinting, screen and relief printing, photography, letterpress, digital imaging, and multimedia software. Students in the sculpture program work in both indoor and outdoor areas containing hoists, a forklift, loft studios, and video and slide projection equipment. It is also possible to access ceramic kilns, clay mixing facilities, a complete foundry, and metal fabrication facilities. In all programs, computer hardware and software are available in networked, multiplatform surroundings.

Special Programs In pursuit of the Bachelor of Fine Arts degree, students may complete a comprehensive liberal arts program that complements an emphasis in one of the following majors: animation, art history, ceramics, creative writing, digital filmmaking, fiber, graphic design, painting, photography, printmaking, sculpture, and interdisciplinary arts.

The School of the Foundation Year provides KCAI's first year studio program. Foundation pro-

Kansas City Art Institute (continued)

vides an ideal groundwork for upper-level studies and combines discovery, discipline, and dedication. Studio space is reserved solely for freshmen, giving them an ideal place in which to create.

The School of Liberal Arts offers a curriculum that adds a dimension to a B.F.A. degree that makes a vital difference in the student's education. The liberal arts enhance education by fostering critical-thinking skills and by opening the doors to new subjects in the arts and sciences. At KCAI, it is possible to pursue a major in art history or studio art with an emphasis in creative writing.

The School of Design prepares students to grow with the rapidly developing professional design and animation fields. Creative exploration is at the core of the animation curriculum and is prioritized in a suite of sequential classes that build relationships between traditional, experimental, and computer animation practice. The graphic design curriculum is formulated to differentiate graphic design as a distinct discipline and to better reflect and anticipate the actual evolving conditions of high-level professional practice in this field worldwide.

The School of Fine Arts offers majors in the following areas: ceramics, digital filmmaking, fiber, painting, photography, printmaking, sculpture, and interdisciplinary arts.

The ceramics program at KCAI provides a technical, visual, and conceptual basis for the education of artists. Traditions in ceramic history, pottery, the figure, architecture, and new forms in contemporary sculpture and installation are all explored in the curriculum.

The fiber program at KCAI encompasses not only textile processes, but also experimental techniques and the investigation of materials, issues, ideas, and forms of presentation. Students discover the vast potential of fiber, its history, and its place in contemporary art and design. Internationally prominent faculty members direct an integrated program involving surface design, weaving, papermaking, felting, basketry, clothing and costume construction, and sculptural form-making.

The photography and digital filmmaking department allows students to select one of two tracks or courses of study. Students produce innovative forms of contemporary image-making in a 20,000-square-foot facility with well-designed networked production and post-production equipment. Students are actively engaged in critical, historical, and theoretical discussions examining the interaction of media, art, and society. The program stresses experimentation, collaboration, self-motivation, research, mentoring, and professionalism through curating, exhibitions, and internships.

The painting program at KCAI covers painting's past and present and introduces students to an unusually broad foundation in drawing, painting, and printmaking. The program balances formal and technical experience with intellectual activity, perceptual acumen with conceptual skills, and an awareness of space with attention to effect.

The printmaking program provides a blend of basic studio practice—drawing, painting, collage—with a core of technologies specific to print, such as intaglio, wood block, lithography, letterpress, silkscreen, and book-making. Simultaneously, students learn to utilize digital and Web possibilities, including iMovie, Photoshop, Illustrator, InDesign, Dreamweaver, Flash, and FinalCut Pro.

The sculpture program at KCAI is known among undergraduate programs for providing a strong background in materials, techniques, aesthetics, and ideas. Students learn to carve stone, cast metal, choreograph performance, shoot video, program electronic media, and manipulate sound and light.

The interdisciplinary arts major establishes a dialogue between students and faculty members who are grounded in an established discipline yet are simultaneously investigating ideas and processes that are not easily categorized or defined. Audience, public art, community, ecology, and technology are all explored in order to discover new avenues for art to influence culture and to affect social and political change.

Kansas State University

Manhattan, Kansas

State-supported, coed. Suburban campus. Total enrollment: 22,530. Art program established 1964.

Degrees Bachelor of Arts in the area of art history; Bachelor of Fine Arts. Majors and concentrations: art education, art history, ceramic art and design, digital art, drawing, graphic design, illustration, jewelry and metalsmithing, painting, pre-art therapy, printmaking, sculpture. Graduate degrees offered: Master of Fine Arts. Cross-registration with Norwich School of Art and Design (England), Glasgow School of Art (Scotland), Trier School of Applied Arts and Sciences (Germany). Program accredited by NASAD.

Enrollment 456 total; 423 undergraduate, 28 graduate, 5 nonprofessional degree.

Art Student Profile 50% females, 50% males, 12% minorities, 8% international.

Art Faculty 16 total (full-time), 6 total (part-time). 100% of full-time faculty have terminal degrees. Graduate students teach about a quarter of undergraduate courses. Undergraduate student–faculty ratio: 15:1.

Student Life Student groups/activities include exhibitions, visiting artists, workshops.

Expenses for 2007–2008 Application fee: $30. State resident tuition: $5625 full-time. Nonresident tuition: $15,360 full-time. Mandatory fees: $610 full-time. College room and board: $6084. Room and board charges vary according to board plan. Special program-related fees: $2–$147 per semester for lab fees (materials).

Financial Aid Program-specific awards: 18 art scholarships for art majors ($150–$1000).

Application Procedures Students apply for admission into the professional program by sophomore year. Deadline for freshmen and transfers: continuous. Required: high school transcript, college transcript(s) for transfer students, ACT test score only, portfolio for scholarship consideration. Recommended: interview. Portfolio reviews held twice on campus; the submission of slides may be substituted for portfolios when distance is prohibitive.

Web Site http://www.ksu.edu/art

Undergraduate Contact Art Advisor, Department of Art, Kansas State University, Willard Hall 322, Manhattan, Kansas 66506; 785-532-1757, fax: 785-532-0334.

Graduate Contact Prof. Elliott Pujol, Director of Graduate Studies, Department of Art, Kansas State University, Willard Hall 322, Manhattan, Kansas 66506; 785-532-6605, fax: 785-532-0334, e-mail address: hepujol@ksu.edu

Kendall College of Art and Design of Ferris State University

Grand Rapids, Michigan

State-supported, coed. Urban campus. Art program established 1928.

Degrees Bachelor of Fine Arts in the areas of furniture design, industrial design, interior design, illustration, fine arts, metals/jewelry design, art with K-12 art education certificate; Bachelor of Science in the areas of art history-studio, art history-academics. Majors and concentrations: art education, art history, art/fine arts, digital media, furniture design, graphic design, illustration, industrial design, interior design, metals and jewelry, painting, photography, sculpture. Graduate degrees offered: Master of Fine Arts. Program accredited by NASAD, CIDA.

Enrollment 1,082 total; 953 undergraduate, 39 graduate, 90 nonprofessional degree.

Art Student Profile 50% females, 50% males, 10% minorities, 1% international.

Art Faculty 45 total (full-time), 129 total (part-time). 56% of full-time faculty have terminal degrees. Graduate students do not teach undergraduate courses.

Student Life Student groups/activities include Industrial Design Society of America, American Society of Interior Designers, Grand Rapids Area Furniture Designers, Society of Illustrators, American Center for Design.

Expenses for 2007–2008 Special program-related fees: $140 per semester for studio lab fee, $205 per semester for technology fee.

Financial Aid Program-specific awards: 250 Kendall Scholarships of Merit for program students ($4000).

Application Procedures Students admitted directly into the professional program freshman year. Deadline for freshmen and transfers: continuous. Required: essay, high school transcript, college transcript(s) for transfer students, minimum 2.0 high school GPA, portfolio, ACT test score only (minimum composite ACT score of 17). Recommended: letter of recommendation. Portfolio reviews held continuously on campus and off campus in various high schools, National Portfolio Days; the submission of slides may be substituted for portfolios.

Web Site http://www.kcad.edu

Contact Sandra Britton, Director of Enrollment Services, Kendall College of Art and Design of Ferris State University, 17 Fountain NW, Grand Rapids, Michigan 49503-2003; 616-451-2787, fax: 616-831-9689.

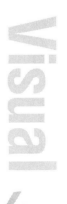

Kent State University

Kent, Ohio

State-supported, coed. Suburban campus. Total enrollment: 22,819. Art program established 1940.

Degrees Bachelor of Fine Arts in the areas of fine arts (drawing, painting, printmaking, sculpture), crafts (ceramics, glass, jewelry/metals, textile arts). Majors and concentrations: ceramics, drawing, glass, jewelry and metalsmithing, painting, printmaking, sculpture, textile arts. Graduate degrees offered: Master of Fine Arts in the areas of ceramics, drawing, glass, jewelry/metals, painting, printmaking, sculpture, textile arts. Program accredited by NASAD.

Enrollment 600 total; 207 undergraduate, 18 graduate, 375 nonprofessional degree.

Art Student Profile 73% females, 27% males, 7% minorities, 1% international.

Art Faculty 21 total (full-time), 43 total (part-time). 86% of full-time faculty have terminal degrees. Graduate students teach a few undergraduate courses. Undergraduate student–faculty ratio: 25:1.

Student Life Student groups/activities include Art Education Club, Fine Arts Clubs, Art History Club. Special housing available for art students.

Expenses for 2008–2009 Application fee: $30. State resident tuition: $8430 full-time. Nonresident tuition: $15,862 full-time. College room and board: $7200. College room only: $4410. Special program-related fees: $10–$240 per semester for art materials and project supplies.

Financial Aid Program-specific awards: 12–14 School of Art Scholarships for program majors ($550–$1000), 12 Creative Arts Awards for program majors ($500–$2000).

Application Procedures Students admitted directly into the professional program freshman year. Deadline for freshmen and transfers: continuous. Required: high school transcript, college transcript(s) for transfer students, minimum 2.0 high school GPA, SAT or ACT test scores (minimum composite ACT score of 21), completion of college preparatory courses. Recommended: minimum 3.0 high school GPA. Portfolio reviews held 5-7 times on campus; the submission of slides may be substituted for portfolios when distance is prohibitive.

Web Site http://dept.kent.edu/art

Undergraduate Contact Dr. Christine Havice, Director, School of Art, Kent State University, PO Box 5190, Kent, Ohio 44242-0001; 330-672-2192, fax: 330-672-4729, e-mail address: chavice@kent.edu

Graduate Contact Prof. Janice Lessman-Moss, Graduate Coordinator, School of Art, Kent State University, PO Box 5190, Kent, Ohio 44242-0001; 330-672-2192, fax: 330-672-4729.

Kutztown University of Pennsylvania

Kutztown, Pennsylvania

State-supported, coed. Rural campus. Total enrollment: 10,295. Art program established 1924.

Web Site http://www.kutztown.edu/

Laguna College of Art & Design

Laguna Beach, California

Independent, coed. Small town campus. Total enrollment: 310. Art program established 1961.

Degrees Bachelor of Fine Arts in the areas of drawing and painting, sculpture, illustration, graphic design, feature animation, hybrid (interdisciplinary art and design). Majors and concentrations: animation, art/fine arts, film animation, graphic design, illustration, painting/drawing, sculpture, visual communication. Graduate degrees offered: Master of Fine Arts in the area of painting. Program accredited by NASAD.

Student Life Student groups/activities include art workshops, gallery exhibitions, American Institute of Graphic Arts.

Expenses for 2008–2009 Application fee: $45. Tuition: $20,600 full-time.

Financial Aid Program-specific awards: merit scholarships ($1000–$9300).

Application Procedures Students admitted directly into the professional program freshman year. Deadline for freshmen and transfers: continuous. Required: high school transcript, college transcript(s) for transfer students, minimum 3.0 high school GPA, letter of recommendation, interview, portfolio, SAT or ACT test scores.

Web Site http://www.lagunacollege.edu

Undergraduate Contact Admissions, Laguna College of Art & Design, 2222 Laguna Canyon Road, Laguna Beach, California 92651; 800-255-0762.

More About the College

Laguna College of Art & Design (LCAD) leads the way in merging the future with the fundamentals. Imagine a student-teacher ratio of no more than ten-to-one in the nation's first totally wireless campus. Then imagine all of that in a pristine wooded canyon nestled against a 70,000-acre nature preserve just minutes from the most beautiful beaches in the world. Students at LCAD learn in the most technologically advanced yet natural environment from the best in their fields.

The College offers Bachelor of Fine Arts programs in drawing and painting, sculpture, illustration, graphic design, and feature animation as well as a number of hybrid programs, which allow students to take classes from two majors to further broaden their area of study.

Laguna College of Art & Design is accredited by the National Association of Schools of Art and Design (NASAD) and the Western Association of Schools and Colleges (WASC). NASAD establishes national standards for visual arts education and accredits only those colleges that meet those standards. WASC sets rigorous academic standards for all universities and colleges in the state of California. As one of only six art and design colleges in California accredited by both NASAD and WASC, Laguna College of Art & Design is committed to maintaining the highest educational standards.

Campus and Surroundings Laguna Beach could not have been designed better than as nature designed it herself. It has hillsides, canyons, sandy beaches with cliffs and dramatic rock formations, the Pacific Ocean, a mild climate, and its world-famous light. These characteristics all make Laguna Beach the idyllic setting for the world's most dynamic artists.

In the early 1900's, artists, intellectuals, and entertainers began making a thriving cultural community of scenic Laguna Beach. Plein air painters like Edgar Payne and Anna Hills founded the Laguna Beach Art Association. The once sleepy little town fast gained a reputation as a vibrant hub of visual arts. Laguna Beach still offers the beauty and tranquility that has inspired artists for over a century. Today, artists of all media gravitate to the city of Laguna Beach to advance in the presence of some of the visual arts' leading players. An hour south of Los Angeles and an hour north of San Diego, Laguna Beach is in a perfect, centralized location to access the major metropolitan art scenes of Southern California.

Faculty, Resident Artists, and Alumni LCAD's faculty of working artists, illustrators, designers, and animators bring experience, reputation, and success to the table. There is no question that these instructors encourage both an individual aesthetic and an uncompromised brand of forward-thinking, market-driven leadership.

Student Exhibit Opportunities Laguna College of Art & Design is an active and energetic environment where there is always something exciting happening. The Laguna College of Art & Design Gallery is open six days a week. Students, faculty members, and visiting artists display their work in this on-campus gallery.

Special Programs From the onset of their education at LCAD, students learn the rules before they are encouraged to break them. The Foundation Program has been ahead of its time for years in how it encourages a forward thinking that is soundly rooted in the mastery of traditional skills. LCAD stays ahead of the curve by consistently acknowledging a future that never forgets its past.

The Foundation Program is the cornerstone of each LCAD student's education. For their first two semesters, students are exposed to painting, drawing, illustration, and graphic design in a unique interdisciplinary curriculum. This program is designed to develop an in-depth understanding of art and life. It draws relevant connections between the social and physical worlds in which the student, the visual artist, will communicate.

LCAD offers a campuswide wireless laptop program, G5 computers in every lab, and over 250 computers on campus. LCAD's entire campus is blanketed by wireless technology. LCAD created the Laptop Program to promote cutting-edge innovation, creative freedom, and unparalleled communication. Requiring all students to own an Apple laptop provides the LCAD community with many advantages, including wireless connectivity on campus and in the greater Laguna Beach community; portability to work on projects at home, campus, or virtually anywhere else; reduced prices through LCAD's partnership with Apple; unprecedented support, including a three-year Apple Care warranty and an on-site, full-time Apple employee; standardized laptop specifications consistent across all curricula; and special workshops free to all students.

Lamar Dodd School of Art

See University of Georgia

La Roche College

Pittsburgh, Pennsylvania

Independent, coed. Suburban campus. Total enrollment: 1,499.

Web Site http://www.laroche.edu/

La Sierra University

Riverside, California

Independent Seventh-day Adventist, coed. Suburban campus. Total enrollment: 1,749. Art program established 1923.

Web Site http://www.lasierra.edu/

Lawrence Technological University

Southfield, Michigan

Independent, coed. Suburban campus. Total enrollment: 4,609. Art program established 1991.

Degrees Bachelor of Fine Arts in the area of imaging; Bachelor of Interior Architecture; Bachelor of Science in the area of transportation design. Majors and concentrations: digital imaging, graphic design, interior architecture, transportation design. Graduate degrees offered: Master of Interior Design. Program accredited by CIDA, NASAD.

Enrollment 150 total; 130 undergraduate, 20 graduate.

Art Student Profile 50% females, 50% males, 10% minorities, 10% international.

Art Faculty 4 undergraduate (full-time), 22 undergraduate (part-time), 2 graduate (full-time). 67% of full-time faculty have terminal degrees. Graduate students do not teach undergraduate courses. Undergraduate student–faculty ratio: 16:1.

Student Life Student groups/activities include International Interior Design Association, American Society of Interior Designers, Illuminating Engineering Society Student Group, American Institute of Graphic Arts.

Expenses for 2007–2008 Application fee: $30. Comprehensive fee: $28,368 includes full-time tuition ($20,176), mandatory fees ($320), and college room and board ($7872). College room only: $5292. Full-time tuition and fees vary according to course level, degree level, location, program, and student level. Room and board charges vary according to board plan and housing facility. Special program-related fees: $100 per studio for studio maintenance.

Financial Aid Program-specific awards: 6–7 LTU Scholarships for incoming freshmen ($8000–$8500), 6–7 Trustee Scholarships for incoming freshmen ($1600–$2000).

Application Procedures Students admitted directly into the professional program freshman year. Deadline for freshmen and transfers: continuous. Required: high school transcript, college transcript(s) for transfer students, minimum 2.5 high school GPA. Recommended: essay, 2 letters of recommendation, interview.

Web Site http://www.ltu.edu

Contact Virginia North, Chair, Department of Art and Design, Lawrence Technological University, 21000 West Ten Mile Road, Southfield, Michigan 48075; 248-204-2848, fax: 248-204-2900, e-mail address: north@ltu.edu

Lehman College of the City University of New York

Bronx, New York

State and locally supported, coed. Urban campus. Total enrollment: 10,922. Art program established 1968.

Degrees Bachelor of Arts; Bachelor of Fine Arts in the areas of printmaking, painting, sculpture, ceramics, photography, computer imaging. Majors and concentrations: art/fine arts, ceramic art and design, computer imaging, painting/drawing, photography, printmaking, sculpture. Graduate degrees offered: Master of Arts in the areas of painting, graphics, sculpture (for secondary school teachers of art); Master of Fine Arts in the areas of painting, graphics, sculpture, computer imaging. Cross-registration with City University of New York System.

Enrollment 115 total; 3 undergraduate, 30 graduate, 82 nonprofessional degree.

Art Student Profile 60% females, 40% males, 75% minorities, 15% international.

Art Faculty 13 total (full-time), 13 total (part-time). 100% of full-time faculty have terminal degrees. Graduate students do not teach undergraduate courses. Undergraduate student–faculty ratio: 8:1.

Student Life Student groups/activities include Meridian (student newspaper), internships in galleries and museums.

Expenses for 2008–2009 Application fee: $65. State resident tuition: $4000 full-time. Nonresident tuition: $10,800 full-time. Mandatory fees: $290 full-time.

Application Procedures Students apply for admission into the professional program by sophomore year. Deadline for freshmen and transfers: continuous. Required: high school transcript, college transcript(s) for transfer students, minimum 3.0 high school GPA, portfolio, SAT or ACT test scores, standing in top third of high school graduating class.

Web Site http://www.lehman.cuny.edu

Undergraduate Contact Mr. Clarence Wilkes, Director of Admissions, 155 Shuster Hall, Lehman College of the City University of New York, 250 Bedford Park Boulevard West, Bronx, New York 10468; 718-960-8706.

Graduate Contact Marilyn Hauser, Coordinator of Graduate Admissions, 155 Shuster Hall, Lehman College of the City University of New York, 250 Bedford Park Boulevard West, Bronx, New York 10468; 718-960-8702.

Leigh Gerdine College of Fine Arts

See Webster University

Lindenwood University

St. Charles, Missouri

Independent Presbyterian, coed. Suburban campus. Total enrollment: 9,633.

Degrees Bachelor of Arts in the areas of arts administration, art education, fashion design, studio art, art history; Bachelor of Fine Arts in the areas of art, fashion design, graphic design, computer art, multimedia. Majors and concentrations: art education, art history, arts administration, ceramics, computer graphics, design, fashion design, graphic design, multimedia, painting/drawing, photography, printmaking, studio art. Graduate degrees offered: Master of Arts in the area of studio art; Master of Fine Arts in the area of studio art. Cross-registration with Maryville University of Saint Louis, Fontbonne University, Missouri Baptist College, Webster University.

Art Faculty 6 undergraduate (full-time), 3 undergraduate (part-time), 6 graduate (full-time), 3 graduate (part-time). 90% of full-time faculty have terminal degrees. Graduate students do not teach undergraduate courses.

Student Life Student groups/activities include juried art shows, The Pride (Lindenwood magazine), scenic painting.

Expenses for 2008–2009 Application fee: $30. Comprehensive fee: $19,500 includes full-time tuition ($12,700), mandatory fees ($300), and college room and board ($6500). College room only: $3400. Special program-related fees: $25–$80 per class for studio lab fees.

Financial Aid Program-specific awards: art scholarships, talent awards for undergraduates and transfers, talent awards and scholarships for high school students.

Application Procedures Students admitted directly into the professional program freshman year. Deadline for freshmen and transfers: continuous. Required: essay, high school transcript, college transcript(s) for transfer students, minimum 2.0 high school GPA, interview, portfolio, ACT test score only. Recommended: letter of recommendation. Portfolio reviews held continuously on campus and off campus in area high schools; community colleges; art exhibitions; the submission of slides may be substituted for portfolios.

Web Site http://www.lindenwood.edu/

Undergraduate Contact Mr. John Troy, Director, Art Department, Lindenwood University, 209 South Kings Highway, St. Charles, Missouri 63301; 636-949-4856, e-mail address: jtroy@lindenwood.edu

Graduate Contact Dr. Elaine C. Tillinger, Chair, Department of Art, Lindenwood University, 209 South Kings Highway, St. Charles, Missouri 63301; 636-949-4862, fax: 636-949-4910, e-mail address: etillinger@lindenwood.edu

Long Island University, C.W. Post Campus

Brookville, New York

Independent, coed. Suburban campus. Total enrollment: 8,361. Art program established 1954.

Degrees Bachelor of Fine Arts in the areas of art education, digital art and design, fine art, photography; Bachelor of Science in the area of art therapy. Majors and concentrations: art education, art therapy, art/fine arts, ceramics, digital art and design, photography. Graduate degrees offered: Master of Arts in the areas of clinical art therapy, art, interactive multimedia; Master of Fine Arts in the area of fine arts and design; Master of Science in the area of art education.

Enrollment 551 total; 364 undergraduate, 174 graduate, 13 nonprofessional degree.

Art Student Profile 65% females, 35% males, 20% minorities, 12% international.

Art Faculty 20 total (full-time), 50 total (part-time). 99% of full-time faculty have terminal degrees. Graduate students do not teach undergraduate courses. Undergraduate student–faculty ratio: 15:1.

Student Life Student groups/activities include American Association for Art Therapists, Art Students League.

Expenses for 2007–2008 Application fee: $30. Comprehensive fee: $35,550 includes full-time tuition ($24,700), mandatory fees ($1250), and college room and board ($9600). College room only: $6320. Room and board charges vary according to board plan and housing facility. Special program-related fees: $75 per course for supplies.

Financial Aid Program-specific awards: 6–8 art scholarships for Art Portfolio Day for freshmen and transfer students ($1000–$5000), 15 O'Malley Scholarship Fund and Posner Awards for continuing program majors ($500–$1000), 1 Harry Siegal Memorial Award for sophomore or junior art majors ($500).

Application Procedures Students admitted directly into the professional program freshman year. Deadline for freshmen and transfers: continuous. Required: high school transcript, college transcript(s) for transfer students, SAT or ACT test scores, minimum verbal SAT score of 430, portfolio for transfer applicants and for scholarship consideration. Recommended: essay, minimum 3.0 high school GPA, 2 letters of recommendation, interview. Portfolio reviews held as needed for transfer applicants on campus; the submission of slides may be substituted for portfolios for large works of art; CD-ROMs also accepted.

Web Site http://www.liu.edu/svpa

Undergraduate Contact Mr. Gary Bergman, Associate Provost for Enrollment Services, Long Island University, C.W. Post Campus, 720 Northern Boulevard, Brookville, New York 11548-1300; 516-299-2900, fax: 516-299-2137, e-mail address: enroll@cwpost.liu.edu

Graduate Contact Ms. Beth Carson, Associate Director of Graduate Admissions, Long Island University, C.W. Post Campus, 720 Northern Boulevard, Brookville, New York 11548-1300; 516-299-2719, fax: 516-299-2137, e-mail address: beth.carson@liu.edu

Longwood University

Farmville, Virginia

State-supported, coed. Total enrollment: 4,727. Art program established 1920.

Web Site http://www.longwood.edu/

Louisiana State University and Agricultural and Mechanical College

Baton Rouge, Louisiana

State-supported, coed. Urban campus. Total enrollment: 28,628. Art program established 1930.

Web Site http://www.lsu.edu/

Louisiana Tech University

Ruston, Louisiana

State-supported, coed. Small town campus. Total enrollment: 10,564. Art program established 1894.

Degrees Bachelor of Fine Arts in the areas of studio art, photography, communication design. Majors and concentrations: art/fine arts, ceramic art and design, commercial art, computer graphics, painting/drawing, photography, printmaking, sculpture. Graduate degrees offered: Master of Fine Arts in the areas of studio art, photography, interior design, communication design. Cross-registration with Grambling State University. Program accredited by NASAD.

Enrollment 394 total; 386 undergraduate, 8 graduate.

Art Student Profile 55% females, 45% males, 5% minorities, 2% international.

Art Faculty 16 total (full-time), 3 total (part-time). 100% of full-time faculty have terminal degrees. Graduate students teach a few undergraduate courses. Undergraduate student–faculty ratio: 24:1.

Student Life Student groups/activities include Art and Architecture Student Association.

Expenses for 2008–2009 Application fee: $20. State resident tuition: $2275 full-time. Nonresident tuition: $6070 full-time. Mandatory fees: $2273 full-time. College room and board: $4740. College room only: $2490. Special program-related fees: $30 per quarter for art and architecture fee and enhancement fee for lecturers, special equipment, and workshops.

Financial Aid Program-specific awards: 8–10 incoming freshmen scholarships for regional high school students ($1000–$2500).

Application Procedures Students admitted directly into the professional program freshman year. Deadline for freshmen and transfers: continuous. Required: high school transcript, college transcript(s) for transfer students, minimum 2.0 high school GPA, SAT or ACT test scores (minimum composite ACT score of 22). Recommended: interview.

Web Site http://www.art.latech.edu

Undergraduate Contact Ms. Katie Wells, Assistant to the Director, School of Art, Louisiana Tech University, PO Box 3175, Ruston, Louisiana 71272; 318-257-3909, fax: 318-257-4890, e-mail address: kwells@latech.edu

Graduate Contact Ms. Marie Bukowski, Graduate Coordinator, School of Art, Louisiana Tech University, PO Box 3175, Ruston, Louisiana 71272; 318-257-3909, fax: 318-257-4890, e-mail address: bukowski@latech.edu

Loyola University New Orleans

New Orleans, Louisiana

Independent Roman Catholic (Jesuit), coed. Urban campus. Total enrollment: 4,360. Art program established 1976.

Degrees Bachelor of Arts in the areas of graphic design, studio art; Bachelor of Fine Arts in the area of studio art. Majors and concentrations: graphic design, studio art.

Enrollment 114 total; all undergraduate.

Art Faculty 10 undergraduate (full-time), 7 undergraduate (part-time). 100% of full-time faculty have terminal degrees. Graduate students do not teach undergraduate courses.

Student Life Student groups/activities include Untitled (art organization), American Institute of Graphic Arts Student Chapter.

Expenses for 2008–2009 Application fee: $20. Comprehensive fee: $37,438 includes full-time tuition ($27,168), mandatory fees ($876), and college room and board ($9394). College room only: $5488. Special program-related fees: $75 per class for lab fee (selected studio courses).

Financial Aid Program-specific awards: 1 Scully Scholarship for upperclassmen ($500–$1000), 1 Visual Arts Scholarship for entering studio art majors, 1 Visual Arts Scholarship for entering graphic design majors ($1000–$3000).

Application Procedures Students admitted directly into the professional program freshman year. Deadline for freshmen: February 15; transfers: continuous. Notification date for freshmen and transfers: March 15. Required: essay, high school transcript, college transcript(s) for transfer students, minimum 2.0 high school GPA, letter of recommendation, portfolio, portfolio for scholarship consideration. Portfolio reviews held twice on campus; the submission of slides may be substituted for portfolios (33mm slide, or Mac compatible c; DVD required).

Web Site http://www.loyno.edu/visualarts/

Undergraduate Contact Georgia McBride, Department of Visual Arts, Loyola University New Orleans, 6363 Saint Charles Avenue, PO Box 008 or 18, New Orleans, Louisiana 70118.

Visual *Arts*

Lyme Academy College of Fine Arts

Old Lyme, Connecticut

Independent, coed. Small town campus. Total enrollment: 160. Art program established 1976.

Degrees Bachelor of Fine Arts. Majors and concentrations: illustration, painting, sculpture. Program accredited by NASAD.

Enrollment 100 undergraduate.

Art Student Profile 52% females, 48% males, 14% minorities, 2% international.

Art Faculty 11 undergraduate (full-time), 10 undergraduate (part-time). Graduate students do not teach undergraduate courses. Undergraduate student–faculty ratio: 14:1.

Student Life Student groups/activities include Student Forum, Student Government.

Expenses for 2008–2009 Application fee: $35. Tuition: $20,245 full-time. Special program-related fees: $1000 for books/art supplies, $1000 for studio fee.

Financial Aid Program-specific awards: Lyme Scholarship for freshmen and transfer students ($500–$7000), merit scholarships for program majors.

Application Procedures Students admitted directly into the professional program freshman year. Deadline for freshmen and transfers: continuous. Required: essay, high school transcript, college transcript(s) for transfer students, minimum 2.0 high school GPA, 2 letters of recommendation, portfolio. Recommended: interview, SAT or ACT test scores. Portfolio reviews held as needed on campus and off campus at National Portfolio Day Conferences; the submission of slides may be substituted for portfolios if a campus visit is impossible.

Web Site http://www.lymeacademy.edu

Undergraduate Contact Debra A. Sigmon, Director of Admissions, Lyme Academy College of Fine Arts, 84 Lyme Street, Old Lyme, Connecticut 06371; 860-434-5232 ext. 119, fax: 860-434-8725.

More About the College

The Lyme Academy College of Fine Arts has the unique mission of supporting a contemporary dialogue with classical sources providing an education in the principles, history, techniques, and critical

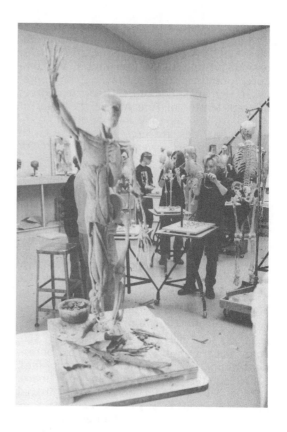

thought processes that have shaped society from the Renaissance to the present.

The College was founded in 1976 by sculptor Elisabeth Gordon Chandler and others dedicated to the belief that serious artists must study the figurative traditions of painting and sculpture, studies that produced the great master artists from Michelangelo to Picasso. The College embraces these disciplines in a rigorous curriculum that places emphasis on life drawing as the foundation for aesthetic development.

Students from across the country seek the College for the education offered, recognizing that their professional future depends on learning the fundamental and basic skills of drawing, painting, and sculpture.

Students and alumni from the College receive honors annually at the Copley Society of Boston, the oldest art association in America. Several have earned the prestigious Robert Brooks Memorial Scholarship. For the past five years, the College's students have earned the four highest awards in the National Arts Club Juried Student Exhibition in New York City. Graduates in the B.F.A. Painting program are eligible to apply for a $5000 Stobart Foundation Fellowship supporting their first year as an emerging artist.

The College offers opportunities for assistantships in area schools and volunteer work for arts groups. The eight-week summer program includes intensive workshops and an eight-week session with a variety of traditional painting, drawing, printmaking, and sculpture courses.

The College's cultural campus extends from New York City to Boston, each just 100 miles away. Additional cultural venues can be found in Connecticut and Rhode Island as well. The College attracts outstanding contemporary, representational, and figurative master teacher/artists to its faculty.

The College encourages its student artists to bring intelligence, passion, and creativity to bear upon each drawing, painting, and sculpture. Emphasizing studio work, the College seeks to create an environment that encourages individual creation and personal responsibility through the profoundly difficult act of making the not-yet-seen and the not-yet-known.

Program Facilities The Lyme Academy College of Fine Arts' studios are located adjacent to the Historic Sill House and feature nine spacious well-lit studios and an art supply/book store. The Art History/seminar room and a classroom are located in the Academic Center. Sill House has a professional gallery, administrative offices, and a student kitchen. Campus facilities doubled in 2003 when the Academic Center was completed, bringing individual senior studios on campus along with additional studios, classrooms, galleries, cafe food service, and administrative offices.

Five drawing and painting studios feature north light, air exchange systems, easels, and large storage racks for oversize paintings. Sculpture facilities include two spacious studios with modeling stands, abundant storage shelves, separate storage rooms for works in progress, a carving studio, and a casting room. Student lockers are in the hallways connecting all studios. The Student Commons provides space for exhibitions and student activities. The Academic Center lecture hall hosts visiting artist's lectures, presentations by art dealers and gallery owners, and additional programming. Conversation and counseling is available in the comfortable Student Services office in the Academic Center.

The Krieble Library features Mission Style chairs, study tables, and large windows overlooking the Lieutenant River. The library has over 13,000 volumes for Fine Arts and Liberal Arts and Sciences and more than 19,000 slides for research and special projects, fifty-six regular periodical subscriptions,

and six computer workstations. The library doubles its size to 46,000 square feet with expansion.

The Art supply/book store has all materials and books necessary for studio and academic programs. Material lists for classes are in the store for reference, which is conveniently open before every class.

Student Exhibit Opportunities Students participate in a Senior Thesis Exhibition before graduation, an annual "All Student Exhibition," and "Faculty Selects Exhibition," and "Student Art Sale" during the holiday season. Freshman-, sophomore-, and junior-level exhibitions are displayed in the Commons and works in progress are shown in the studio hallways. Faculty members recommend students for the National Arts Club Annual Student Exhibition in New York and the Copley Society in Boston. The Academy supports an "Award of Excellence" exhibition fourteen months after graduation.

Special Programs Students may apply for mobility to attend a different college for the first semester of their junior year with an Association of Independent Colleges of Art and Design member school. Frequent trips to New York and Boston take advantage of other cultural opportunities in the area. Precollege life-drawing classes help with portfolio development. The College sponsors a Visiting Artist's Lecture series.

Maharishi University of Management

Fairfield, Iowa

Independent, coed. Small town campus. Total enrollment: 948. Art program established 1983.

Degrees Bachelor of Fine Arts in the area of visual arts. Majors and concentrations: ceramics, digital media, painting/drawing, photography, sculpture, video art.

Enrollment 32 total; 25 undergraduate, 7 nonprofessional degree.

Art Student Profile 50% females, 50% males, 15% minorities, 30% international.

Art Faculty 5 total (full-time), 4 total (part-time). 65% of full-time faculty have terminal degrees. Graduate students do not teach undergraduate courses. Undergraduate student–faculty ratio: 5:1.

Student Life Student groups/activities include Iowa-wide exhibits.

Expenses for 2008–2009 Application fee: $30. Comprehensive fee: $30,430 includes full-time

Maharishi University of Management (continued)

tuition ($24,000), mandatory fees ($430), and college room and board ($6000). Special program-related fees: $10–$100 per course for lab fees, $150 per course for field trips in Art History courses.

Application Procedures Students apply for admission into the professional program by sophomore, junior year. Deadline for freshmen: continuous. Notification date for freshmen: September 15. Required: essay, high school transcript, college transcript(s) for transfer students, 2 letters of recommendation, SAT or ACT test scores, minimum 2.5 high school GPA. Recommended: portfolio. Portfolio reviews held twice on campus; the submission of slides may be substituted for portfolios for transfer applicants.

Web Site http://mum.edu/arts

Undergraduate Contact Barbara Rainbow, Director, Office of Admissions, Maharishi University of Management, 1000 North 4th Street, Fairfield, Iowa 52557; 641-472-1110, fax: 641-472-1179, e-mail address: rainbow@mum.edu

Maine College of Art

Portland, Maine

Independent, coed. Urban campus. Total enrollment: 377. Art program established 1882.

Degrees Bachelor of Fine Arts in the areas of ceramics, graphic design, painting, printmaking, photography, sculpture, metalsmithing and jewelry, self-designed studies, illustration, woodworking and furniture design, new media, art history and curatorial practice. Majors and concentrations: art history and curatorial practice, ceramics, graphic design, illustration, individualized major, metals and jewelry, new media, painting, photography, printmaking, sculpture, woodworking and furniture design. Graduate degrees offered: Master of Fine Arts in the area of self-designed studio concentrations. Cross-registration with Bowdoin College, Greater Portland Alliance of Colleges and Universities. Program accredited by NASAD.

Enrollment 369 total; 340 undergraduate, 29 graduate.

Art Student Profile 63% females, 37% males, 6% minorities, 1% international.

Art Faculty 22 undergraduate (full-time), 30 undergraduate (part-time), 3 graduate (full-time). 12% of full-time faculty have terminal degrees. Graduate students do not teach undergraduate courses. Undergraduate student–faculty ratio: 8:1.

Student Life Student groups/activities include Creative Community Partnerships, Student Representative Association (SRA). Special housing available for art students.

Expenses for 2008–2009 Application fee: $40. Comprehensive fee: $37,140 includes full-time tuition ($26,490), mandatory fees ($1250), and college room and board ($9400). Special program-related fees: $10–$90 per course for studio fees, $150 per year for technology fee.

Financial Aid Program-specific awards: 2 full-tuition scholarships ($26,490), partial-tuition scholarships ($4000–$13,000).

Application Procedures Students admitted directly into the professional program freshman year. Deadline for freshmen and transfers: continuous. Notification date for freshmen and transfers: continuous. Required: essay, high school transcript, college transcript(s) for transfer students, minimum 2.0 high school GPA, 2 letters of recommendation, portfolio, SAT or ACT test scores. Recommended: interview. Portfolio reviews held continuously on campus and off campus at National Portfolio Days; the submission of slides may be substituted for portfolios when distance is prohibitive.

Web Site http://www.meca.edu

Undergraduate Contact Karen Townsend, Director of Admissions, Maine College of Art, 522 Congress Street, Portland, Maine 04101; 207-879-5742 ext. 721, fax: 207-871-1349, e-mail address: ktownsend@meca.edu

Graduate Contact Ms. Katarina Weslien, Director, MFA in Studio Art, Maine College of Art, 522 Congress Street, Portland, Maine 04101; 207-775-5154 ext. 57, fax: 207-871-1349, e-mail address: kweslien@meca.edu

Manhattanville College

Purchase, New York

Independent, coed. Suburban campus. Total enrollment: 3,023. Art program established 1957.

Degrees Bachelor of Fine Arts in the areas of studio art, fine arts, visual arts education, arts and education. Majors and concentrations: ceramics, computer graphics, digital media/ graphic design, graphic communication, illustration, painting, photography, printmaking, sculpture, three-dimensional studies, two-dimensional studies. Graduate degrees offered: Master of Arts in Teaching in the area of visual arts education. Cross-registration with Purchase College-State University of New York.

Enrollment 110 total; 75 undergraduate, 35 nonprofessional degree.

Art Student Profile 68% females, 32% males, 22% minorities, 8% international.

Art Faculty 5 undergraduate (full-time), 27 undergraduate (part-time). 100% of full-time faculty have terminal degrees. Graduate students do not teach undergraduate courses. Undergraduate student–faculty ratio: 5:1.

Student Life Student groups/activities include Art Club, Shakespeare in the Castle, Quad Jam.

Expenses for 2008–2009 Application fee: $65. Comprehensive fee: $44,660 includes full-time tuition ($30,400), mandatory fees ($1220), and college room and board ($13,040). College room only: $7740.

Financial Aid Program-specific awards: merit awards for art for program majors ($5000–$10,000).

Application Procedures Students admitted directly into the professional program freshman year. Deadline for freshmen and transfers: continuous. Required: high school transcript, college transcript(s) for transfer students, minimum 2.0 high school GPA, portfolio, SAT or ACT test scores, high school transcript for transfer applicants with fewer than 45 credits. Recommended: minimum 3.0 high school GPA, 2 letters of recommendation, interview. Portfolio reviews held continuously as needed on campus; the submission of slides may be substituted for portfolios.

Web Site http://www.manhattanville.edu

Undergraduate Contact Mr. Jose Flores, Director of Admissions, Manhattanville College, 2900 Purchase Street, Purchase, New York 10577; 800-328-4553, fax: 914-694-1732, e-mail address: jflores@mville.edu

Marshall University
Huntington, West Virginia

State-supported, coed. Urban campus. Total enrollment: 13,808. Art program established 1984.

Degrees Bachelor of Fine Arts in the area of art studio. Majors and concentrations: ceramics, new media, painting, photography, print media, printmaking, sculpture, weaving. Graduate degrees offered: Master of Arts in the areas of art education, art studio. Program accredited by NCATE.

Enrollment 220 total; 200 undergraduate, 20 graduate.

Art Student Profile 52% females, 48% males, 5% minorities, 1% international.

Art Faculty 15 total (full-time), 15 total (part-time). 100% of full-time faculty have terminal degrees. Graduate students teach a few undergraduate courses. Undergraduate student–faculty ratio: 17:1.

Student Life Student groups/activities include Sculpture Club, Keramos (Ceramics Club), Graphic Design Club-AIGA.

Expenses for 2007–2008 Application fee: $30. State resident tuition: $4360 full-time. Nonresident tuition: $11,264 full-time. Mandatory fees: $200 full-time. Full-time tuition and fees vary according to degree level, location, program, and reciprocity agreements. College room and board: $6818. College room only: $3944. Room and board charges vary according to board plan and housing facility. Special program-related fees: $60 per studio course for art supplies.

Financial Aid Program-specific awards: 4–5 art scholarships for program majors ($500), 10 tuition waivers for program majors ($1000), 1 Garth Brown Memorial Scholarship for program majors ($500), 15 Donald Harper Scholarships for program majors ($4000), 1 College of Fine Arts Gala Scholarship for program majors ($2000), 1 John Q. Hill Memorial Scholarship for minority program majors ($1000), 1 Stewart Smith Scholarship for program majors ($800).

Application Procedures Students admitted directly into the professional program freshman year. Deadline for freshmen and transfers: August 15. Notification date for freshmen and transfers: continuous. Required: high school

Visual

Arts

Marshall University (continued)

transcript, college transcript(s) for transfer students, minimum 2.0 high school GPA, SAT or ACT test scores. Recommended: essay, 3 letters of recommendation, interview, portfolio. Portfolio reviews held twice on campus; the submission of slides may be substituted for portfolios if a campus visit is impossible.

Web Site http://www.marshall.edu/cofa

Undergraduate Contact Byron D. Clercx, Chair, Department of Art, Marshall University, 1 John Marshall Drive, Huntington, West Virginia 25755; 304-696-5451, fax: 304-696-6505.

Graduate Contact Peter Massing, Graduate Coordinator, Department of Art and Design, Marshall University, One John Marshall Drive, Huntington, West Virginia 25755; 304-696-5451, fax: 304-696-6505.

Maryland Institute College of Art

Baltimore, Maryland

Independent, coed. Urban campus. Total enrollment: 1,899. Art program established 1826.

Degrees Bachelor of Fine Arts in the areas of drawing, painting, printmaking, general fine arts, ceramics, fibers, photography, illustration, graphic design, environmental design, experimental animation, video, interactive media, art history, interdisciplinary sculpture; Bachelor of Fine Arts/Master of Arts in the area of digital arts; Bachelor of Fine Arts/Master of Arts in Teaching in the area of art education. Majors and concentrations: animation, art history, art/fine arts, ceramic art and design, drawing, environmental design, fibers, graphic arts, graphic design, illustration, interactive media, interdisciplinary sculpture, painting, photography, printmaking, video art. Graduate degrees offered: Bachelor of Fine Arts/Master of Arts in the area of digital arts; Bachelor of Fine Arts/Master of Arts in Teaching in the area of art education; Master of Arts in the areas of digital arts, art education, community arts; Master of Fine Arts in the areas of painting, sculpture, art education, photography, mixed media, graphic design. Cross-registration with Johns Hopkins University, University of Baltimore, Goucher College, Loyola College, Peabody Conservatory of Mu-

sic, Notre Dame College, Association of Independent Colleges of Art and Design, Institute for American Universities (France), Baltimore Collegetown Network. Program accredited by NASAD.

Enrollment 1,895 total; 1,668 undergraduate, 227 graduate.

Art Student Profile 66% females, 34% males, 21% minorities, 4% international.

Art Faculty 109 undergraduate (full-time), 155 undergraduate (part-time), 21 graduate (full-time), 19 graduate (part-time). 82% of full-time faculty have terminal degrees. Graduate students do not teach undergraduate courses. Undergraduate student–faculty ratio: 10:1.

Student Life Student groups/activities include student-run forum group, National Art Education Association, American Institute of Graphic Arts. Special housing available for art students.

Expenses for 2007–2008 Application fee: $50. One-time mandatory fee: $125. Comprehensive fee: $39,070 includes full-time tuition ($29,700), mandatory fees ($980), and college room and board ($8390). College room only: $6230. Room and board charges vary according to board plan and housing facility.

Financial Aid Program-specific awards: 30 Thalheimer Scholarships for incoming freshmen ($3000–$7500), 15 Academic Excellence Scholarships for incoming freshmen ($5000), 20 C.V. Starr Scholarships for incoming international freshmen or transfers ($2500), 40 Competitive Scholarships for incoming transfers ($1000–$12,000), 150 Competitive Scholarships for incoming freshmen ($1000–$12,000).

Application Procedures Students admitted directly into the professional program freshman year. Deadline for freshmen: February 15; transfers: March 3. Notification date for freshmen: March 15; transfers: April 18. Required: essay, high school transcript, college transcript(s) for transfer students, 3 letters of recommendation, portfolio, SAT or ACT test scores, minimum TOEFL score of 550 for international applicants. Recommended: minimum 3.0 high school GPA, interview, honors and advanced placement level coursework in English and other humanities subjects. Portfolio reviews held continuously on campus and off campus in various cities; the submission of slides may be substituted for portfolios (slides preferred).

Web Site http://www.mica.edu

Undergraduate Contact Ms. Theresa Lynch Bedoya, Vice President and Dean, Admission and Financial Aid, Maryland Institute College of Art, 1300 Mt. Royal Avenue, Baltimore, Maryland 21217; 410-225-2222, fax: 410-225-2337, e-mail address: admissions@mica.edu

Graduate Contact Scott Kelly, Associate Dean of Graduate Admission, Graduate Studies, Maryland Institute College of Art, 1300 Mt. Royal Avenue, Baltimore, Maryland 21217; 410-225-2256, fax: 410-225-2408, e-mail address: graduate@mica.edu

More About the College

For more than 180 years, the top-rated Maryland Institute College of Art (MICA) has assembled some of the most talented and committed students and faculty members from across the nation and around the world in a creatively energized, intellectually stimulating environment. A diverse, 1,900-strong student body comes to this highly selective program from forty-seven states and forty-eight other countries.

Art in the twenty-first century can take the form of object, energy, or expendable materials. The definition of art is expanding. The boundaries among disciplines and mediums are dissolving. MICA's curriculum has been designed to prepare students for these contemporary approaches to art-making and thinking through a wide choice of studio majors. Students can focus on traditional discipline-based processes or they can create art that is interactive, uses multiple mediums, or relies on collaboration with other artists—or scientists, writers, or musicians—for its execution.

MICA has also taken the position that the quality and rigor of its liberal arts program should equal that of its nationally recognized studio program. This commitment is evident in MICA's course offerings

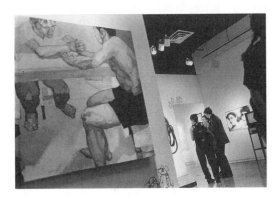

and faculty appointments. Each year students can choose from nearly 200 courses offered in art history, literature, writing, humanities, and sciences taught by an exceptional faculty of scholars who have earned advanced degrees from such institutions as Columbia, Harvard, Oxford, Princeton, and the University of Chicago.

Baltimore, located at the heart of the New York–Washington arts corridor, offers an array of cultural, social, and creative opportunities. MICA's campus of twenty-five buildings is nestled in a charming historic neighborhood in the midst of the city's cultural center. Nearby are world-class museums and galleries, the symphony hall and opera house, experimental and community theaters, cafés, bookstores, shops, and art cinemas. The MICA campus shuttle system provides transportation throughout the city, and weekly trips to New York City and Washington, D.C., are also available.

A highly successful Career Development Center is staffed by dedicated professionals who specialize in developing art and art-related career opportunities. The center provides career counseling and workshops, facilitates connections with the Institute's alumni network, lists 1,000 internship opportunities and 1,130 art-related jobs, hosts dozens of corporate recruiters, and offers reality-based programs and courses in topics ranging from promoting oneself as an artist to developing business skills.

Facilities The twenty-seven buildings on the MICA campus include 430,700 square feet of outstanding instructional facilities dedicated to departments of painting, ceramics, drawing, sculpture, photography, printmaking, fibers, environmental design, graphic design, illustration, video, animation, art education, and liberal arts. There is specialized equipment for work in both traditional and new media in each of these areas. In addition, MICA offers intimately sized liberal arts classrooms; a 550-seat auditorium for film, performance art, theater, poetry readings, and lectures; access to studios seven days a week; independent studio space for seniors; and seven art galleries. The arts-oriented library houses 50,000 volumes, 300 periodicals/media resources, and 250,000 examples of contemporary and historical art in slide, video, CD-ROM, and DVD format. Computers are available for student use in all instructional buildings as well as the twenty-one computer labs and digital classrooms. There are 320 computers for student use; these include Apple G5's Dell Xeon 3-D animation workstations, digital video editing stations, and computer-controlled looms and sewing machines.

Faculty, Resident Artists, and Alumni The faculty of 267 professional artists, designers, and

Maryland Institute College of Art (continued)

scholars are widely published and represented in public and private collections—from MOMA to the Stedelijk. Faculty members' honors include the Fulbright, Guggenheim, and MacArthur Awards. There are also more than 175 visiting artists, designers, critics, poets, art historians, and filmmakers for residencies or lectures each year. Recent visitors included Manthia Diawara, Joan Fontcuberta, David Hickey, Chipp Kidd, Roberta Smith, and William Wegman.

Student Performance/Exhibit Opportunities
MICA has one of the best exhibition programs of art schools in the U.S., with ninety exhibitions per year, many of which are devoted to student work. Students at MICA show their work in the first year. In addition, there are two student-edited and designed publications.

Special Programs MICA offers a five-year, dual-degree Bachelor of Fine Arts/Master of Arts in Teaching (B.F.A./M.A.T.) program, which combines an undergraduate degree in studio art with teaching certification at the master's level. This dual-degree program boasts a 100 percent placement rate. The B.F.A./M.A. degree program in digital arts provides a fifth-year capstone experience. There are study-abroad opportunities in Canada, England, France, Greece, Ireland, Israel, Japan, Mexico, the Netherlands, Scotland, South Korea, and Spain. Students can also participate in MICA's New York studio program, MICA in Tribeca. Cross-enrollment is possible with the Johns Hopkins University and the Peabody Conservatory of Music.

Marylhurst University

Marylhurst, Oregon

Independent Roman Catholic, coed. Suburban campus. Total enrollment: 1,433. Art program established 1982.

Web Site http://www.marylhurst.edu/

Maryville University of Saint Louis

St. Louis, Missouri

Independent, coed. Suburban campus. Total enrollment: 3,422. Art program established 1970.

Degrees Bachelor of Arts in the area of art education K-12; Bachelor of Fine Arts in the areas of studio art, graphic design, interior design. Majors and concentrations: art education, graphic design, interior design, studio art. Cross-registration with Webster University, Fontbonne University, Missouri Baptist University, Lindenwood University. Program accredited by NASAD, NCATE, CIDA.

Enrollment 176 total; 148 undergraduate, 28 nonprofessional degree.

Art Student Profile 86% females, 14% males, 9% minorities, 1% international.

Art Faculty 10 undergraduate (full-time), 22 undergraduate (part-time). 90% of full-time faculty have terminal degrees. Graduate students do not teach undergraduate courses. Undergraduate student–faculty ratio: 11:1.

Student Life Student groups/activities include American Institute of Graphic Arts (AIGA) Student Chapter, Maryville Chapter of American Society of Interior Design/International Designers Association, Student Life Art Club.

Expenses for 2007–2008 Application fee: $25. Comprehensive fee: $26,550 includes full-time tuition ($18,600), mandatory fees ($450), and college room and board ($7500). Full-time tuition and fees vary according to course load. Room and board charges vary according to housing facility. Special program-related fees: $10 per course for audiovisual teaching resources in art history courses, $10–$110 per course for expendable supplies in studio courses.

Financial Aid Program-specific awards: 5–8 art and design scholarships for undergraduates, first time freshmen, and outstanding transfer students ($2500–$4000), 1 The Fine Arts Scholarship for those demonstrating outstanding creative ability in art and design ($1000), 1 The Newman Scholarship for art and design students ($1000).

Application Procedures Deadline for freshmen and transfers: continuous. Required: high school transcript, college transcript(s) for transfer students, minimum 2.0 high school GPA, portfolio, SAT or ACT test scores (minimum composite ACT score of 20). Recommended: letter of recommendation, interview. Portfolio reviews held continuously on campus and off campus in St. Louis, MO; on National Portfolio Days; the submission of slides may be substituted for portfolios if original work is not available, for large works of art, or for three-dimensional pieces.

Web Site http://www.maryville.edu/

Undergraduate Contact Ms. Shani Lenord, Director, Office of Admissions, Maryville University of Saint Louis, 650 Maryville University Drive, St. Louis, Missouri 63141-7299; 314-529-9350, fax: 314-529-9927, e-mail address: admissions@maryville.edu

Rutgers, The State University of New Jersey
Mason Gross School of the Arts

New Brunswick, New Jersey

State-supported, coed. Small town campus. Art program established 1976.

Degrees Bachelor of Fine Arts in the area of visual arts. Majors and concentrations: ceramics, graphic design, painting/drawing, photography, printmaking, sculpture, video production. Graduate degrees offered: Master of Fine Arts in the area of visual arts.

Enrollment 424 total; 300 undergraduate, 44 graduate, 80 nonprofessional degree.

Art Student Profile 57% females, 43% males, 11% minorities, 5% international.

Art Faculty 20 total (full-time), 11 total (part-time). 98% of full-time faculty have terminal degrees. Graduate students teach a few undergraduate courses. Undergraduate student–faculty ratio: 11:1.

Expenses for 2007–2008 Special program-related fees: $20–$50 per class for supplies/materials.

Financial Aid Program-specific awards: 1 James O. Dumont Award for upperclassmen ($2300), 2–3 Betts Scholarships for upperclassmen ($500).

Application Procedures Students admitted directly into the professional program freshman year. Deadline for freshmen: January 15; transfers: March 15. Notification date for freshmen: June 1; transfers: July 1. Required: high school transcript, college transcript(s) for transfer students, minimum 2.0 high school GPA, portfolio, SAT or ACT test scores. Recommended: essay. Portfolio reviews held twice on campus and off campus in various cities at College Art Recruitment Fairs; the submission of slides may be substituted for portfolios for out-of-state applicants.

Web Site http://www.masongross.rutgers.edu

Undergraduate Contact Ms. Diane W. Harris, Associate Director, Undergraduate Admissions, Rutgers, The State University of New Jersey, Mason Gross School of the Arts, 65 Davidson Road, Piscataway, New Jersey 08854-8097; 732-932-INFO, fax: 732-445-0237, e-mail address: admissions@asb-ugadm.rutgers.edu

Graduate Contact Linda Costa, Associate Director, Graduate and Professional Admissions, Rutgers, The State University of New Jersey, Mason Gross School of the Arts, 18 Bishop Place, New Brunswick, New Jersey 08901; 732-932-7711, fax: 732-932-8231, e-mail address: smeds@rci.rutgers.edu

Massachusetts College of Art and Design

Boston, Massachusetts

State-supported, coed. Urban campus. Total enrollment: 2,315. Art program established 1873.

Degrees Bachelor of Fine Arts in the areas of art education, art history, fine arts, design, media and performing arts. Majors and concentrations: animation, architectural design, art education, art history, art/fine arts, ceramic art and design, fashion design and technology, film studies, glass, graphic arts, illustration, industrial design, interrelated media, jewelry and metalsmithing, painting/drawing, photography, printmaking, sculpture, studio art, textile arts. Graduate degrees offered: Master of Fine Arts in the areas of design, fine arts, media and performing arts; Master of Science in the area of art education. Cross-registration with ProArts Consortium, College Academic Program Sharing, Public College Exchange Program, Colleges of the Fenway.

Enrollment 1,682 total; 1,571 undergraduate, 111 graduate.

Art Student Profile 66% females, 34% males, 14% minorities, 3% international.

Art Faculty 85 total (full-time), 134 total (part-time). 78% of full-time faculty have terminal degrees. Graduate students teach a

Massachusetts College of Art and Design (continued)

few undergraduate courses. Undergraduate student–faculty ratio: 13:1.

Student Life Student groups/activities include All School Show, visiting artists and professional exhibitions, Holiday Art Sale and Spring Art Sale.

Expenses for 2007–2008 Application fee: $65. State resident tuition: $7450 full-time. Nonresident tuition: $21,900 full-time. College room and board: $10,900. Room and board charges vary according to housing facility. Special program-related fees: $25–$250 per course for course lab fees.

Financial Aid Program-specific awards: 44 Presidential Awards for outstanding non-Massachusetts residents ($4000–$20,000), 12 Tsongas Scholarships for outstanding Massachusetts residents ($7200).

Application Procedures Students admitted directly into the professional program freshman year. Deadline for freshmen: February 15; transfers: March 15. Notification date for freshmen: April 15; transfers: May 15. Required: essay, high school transcript, college transcript(s) for transfer students, minimum 3.0 high school GPA, 2 letters of recommendation, portfolio, SAT or ACT test scores. Portfolio reviews held continuously on campus.

Web Site http://www.massart.edu/

Undergraduate Contact Ms. Lydia Polanco-Pena, Associate Director of Admissions, Massachusetts College of Art and Design, 621 Huntington Avenue, Boston, Massachusetts 02115-5882; 617-879-7222, fax: 617-879-7250, e-mail address: admissions@massart.edu

Graduate Contact Ms. Nadia Savage, Admissions Assistant, Graduate Programs, Massachusetts College of Art and Design, 621 Huntington Avenue, Boston, Massachusetts 02115-5882; 617-879-7162.

Meadows School of the Arts

See Southern Methodist University

Memphis College of Art

Memphis, Tennessee

Independent, coed. Urban campus. Total enrollment: 341. Art program established 1936.

Degrees Bachelor of Fine Arts in the areas of fine arts, design arts. Majors and concentrations: animation, applied art, ceramic art and design, commercial art, computer graphics, digital film and video, graphic arts, illustration, jewelry and metalsmithing, painting/drawing, photography, printmaking, sculpture, studio art. Graduate degrees offered: Master of Arts in the area of art education; Master of Arts in Teaching in the area of art education with licensure; Master of Fine Arts in the areas of studio art, computer arts. Cross-registration with Rhodes College, Christian Brothers University, Le Moyne-Owen College. Program accredited by NASAD.

Enrollment 341 total; 286 undergraduate, 55 graduate.

Art Student Profile 51% females, 49% males, 27% minorities, 3% international.

Art Faculty 24 undergraduate (full-time), 16 undergraduate (part-time), 2 graduate (full-time), 3 graduate (part-time). 96% of full-time faculty have terminal degrees. Graduate students do not teach undergraduate courses. Undergraduate student–faculty ratio: 10:1.

Student Life Student groups/activities include Student Government, Arteli (Arts in the Schools), children's community art classes. Special housing available for art students.

Expenses for 2008–2009 Application fee: $25. Tuition: $21,000 full-time. Mandatory fees: $560 full-time. College room only: $5760. Special program-related fees: $560 per year for studio/activity.

Financial Aid Program-specific awards: 300 admissions scholarships for program majors ($3500–$20,100), 200 work-study awards for program majors ($1000).

Application Procedures Students admitted directly into the professional program freshman year. Deadline for freshmen and transfers: continuous. Required: high school transcript, college transcript(s) for transfer students, portfolio, SAT or ACT test scores (minimum composite ACT score of 17). Recommended: minimum 2.0 high school GPA, letter of recommendation, interview. Portfolio reviews held weekly on campus and off campus at National Portfolio Days; the submission of slides may be substituted for portfolios whenever needed.

Web Site http://www.mca.edu

Contact Ms. Annette James Moore, Director of Admissions, Memphis College of Art, 1930 Poplar Avenue, Overton Park, Memphis, Tennessee 38104; 800-727-1088, fax: 901-272-5158, e-mail address: info@mca.edu

More About the College

Since 1936, Memphis College of Art (MCA) has been a small, distinctive community of artists. The MCA experience is organized around small classes, independent work, and one-on-one attention and guidance. Currently students from thirty states and seven countries attend MCA, providing a diversity that is often associated with larger schools.

MCA is located in a 342-acre park in midtown Memphis adjacent to the Memphis Brooks Museum of Art and the Memphis Zoo. Nearby student residences provide living space for new and returning students. Suite-style apartments provide each resident a private room with shared kitchen, laundry, and living room areas. Studio spaces are provided. Other residential options include shared apartments or efficiencies. Two roommates share a furnished apartment with hardwood floors, a sun porch, a kitchen, and studio space. A large variety of affordable housing is also available off-campus to suit all lifestyles and budgets.

Memphis is a great place for an aspiring artist. Known for blues, barbecue, and Elvis, Memphis is also home to Fortune 500 companies, the Grizzlies NBA team, a symphony, an opera, a theater, other colleges and universities, museums, galleries, and almost 1 million residents. Annual festivals on Beale Street and the Mississippi River are popular with students.

MCA is a close-knit community where it's easy to make friends. There are plenty of organized activities to keep students busy, such as Friday night movies, exhibition receptions, community dinners, and an annual Talent(less) Show, canoe trip, and Halloween Costume Ball.

Tobey Exhibition Hall hosts numerous shows that expose students to a wide range of contemporary art; the Brode Gallery is a large space dedicated to student art. Students also have the opportunity to learn from visiting artists who provide a constant flow of new creative and intellectual energy. MCA organizes study trips to cities around the world renowned for their culture. In early May, a weeklong workshop is held on Horn Island off the Mississippi coast.

The Career Center offers career assistance for graduating students and part-time job placement for current students. Informative sessions are held to prepare students for career choices and for the job search/interview process. The Job Fair brings regional and national companies to MCA each spring for interviews. Internships and service-learning community projects provide students with professional experience while in school.

Faculty members have been selected for their understanding of the relationship between art and teaching. MCA's Fine Arts faculty members are professional artists who exhibit frequently and regularly execute commissions. The Design Arts faculty members stay on top of the industry through continuing professional design projects. With their knowledge of the job market and galleries at the regional and national levels, faculty members are well qualified to guide students on their career paths. Liberal Studies faculty members are chosen for their impressive credentials and their understanding of the unique nature of MCA students.

MCA is concerned about students whose financial resources are limited. More than 90 percent of the College's students receive some type of financial assistance. Financial aid programs include scholarships, loans, grants, and work-study awards. More than $1 million is awarded by MCA in scholarship and grants each year.

Program Facilities Four fully equipped computer labs feature LCD flat-panel desktop computers with high-speed Internet access, laser printers, large-format color ink jet printers, DVD burners, color scanners, and other high-end multimedia peripherals. All stations have the latest graphic design, video, and multimedia software. MCA's shop has 4,400 square feet, with machines for woodworking, metalworking, plastic molding, glass cutting, shrink wrapping, and stretcher and frame construction. The library has more than 16,000 volumes, 120 art journals and periodicals, 36,000 slides, an extensive reproduction collection, audiovisual equipment, a computer writing lab, and an image file. Students have studio spaces provided in their area of study. Conference rooms allow for slide viewing, critiques, and lectures. Sculpture, small metals, and clay have studios with foundry/welding areas for casting and metal work. Clay has wheels, handbuilding, and glazing space as well as a semi-enclosed firing room. Printmaking, papermaking, and book arts studios provide interaction between these media. Printmaking has facilities

Memphis College of Art (continued)

for lithography, etching, serigraphy, and other processes. Book arts include letter presses and bindery. Papermaking has beaters, hydraulic press, and pulper. Photography has beginning and advanced black-and-white darkrooms to print 35mm through 4x5 formats. Facilities for non-silver and alternative processes and a fully-equipped lighting studio are also available.

Special Programs The New York Studio Program offers students an exciting semester in New York City with artists and students from across the country. The Mobility Program can place a student at another art college for a semester of study. Internships offer experience in fine and design arts fields, such as museum work, art therapy, set design, and advertising. Consortiums with local colleges provide a greater variety of course selection.

Metropolitan State College of Denver

Denver, Colorado

State-supported, coed. Urban campus. Art program established 1965.

Degrees Bachelor of Fine Arts in the area of art. Majors and concentrations: art education, art history, ceramics, communication design, computer imaging, digital art, jewelry and metalsmithing, painting/drawing, photography, printmaking, sculpture. Cross-registration with University of Colorado at Denver, Colorado community colleges. Program accredited by NASAD.

Enrollment 856 total; 837 undergraduate, 19 nonprofessional degree.

Art Student Profile 66% females, 34% males, 27% minorities, 1% international.

Art Faculty 24 undergraduate (full-time), 55 undergraduate (part-time). 96% of full-time faculty have terminal degrees. Graduate students do not teach undergraduate courses. Undergraduate student–faculty ratio: 15:1.

Student Life Student groups/activities include Art Guild and other clubs, Center for Visual Art, Emmanuel Gallery student show.

Expenses for 2007–2008 Application fee: $25. State resident tuition: $2432 full-time. Nonresident tuition: $10,534 full-time. Mandatory fees: $601 full-time. Special program-related fees: $6 per credit hour for expendable materials and modeling fees.

Application Procedures Students admitted directly into the professional program freshman year. Deadline for freshmen and transfers: continuous. Notification date for freshmen and transfers: continuous. Required: high school transcript, college transcript(s) for transfer students, SAT or ACT test scores, minimum college GPA of 2.0 for transfer students.

Web Site http://clem.mscd.edu/~art_cs/

Undergraduate Contact Ms. Patricia Yarrow, Program Assistant, Art Department, Metropolitan State College of Denver, Campus Box 59, PO Box 173362, Denver, Colorado 80217-3362; 303-556-3090, fax: 303-556-4094, e-mail address: yarrowp@mscd.edu

Miami International University of Art & Design

Miami, Florida

Proprietary, coed. Urban campus.

Degrees Bachelor of Fine Arts. Majors and concentrations: audio production, computer animation, fashion design, film and digital production, graphic design, interior design, photography, visual and entertainment arts, visual effects and motion graphics, Web design and interactive media. Graduate degrees offered: Master of Fine Arts in the areas of computer animation, film, graphic design, interior design, visual arts. Program accredited by CIDA.

Expenses for 2007–2008 Contact school for current expenses.

Web Site http://www.artinstitutes.edu/miami

Contact Admissions, Miami International University of Art & Design, 1501 Biscayne Boulevard, Suite 100, Miami, Florida 33132-1418; 800-225-9023, fax: 305-374-5933.

Miami University

Oxford, Ohio

State-related, coed. Small town campus. Total enrollment: 15,922. Art program established 1929.

Degrees Bachelor of Fine Arts in the areas of painting/drawing, jewelry and metalsmithing, printmaking, sculpture, ceramic art and design, graphic arts, photography; Bachelor of Science in the area of art education. Majors and concentrations: art education, art history, ceramic art and design, computer graphics, jewelry and metalsmithing, painting/drawing, photography, printmaking, sculpture. Graduate degrees offered: Master of Arts in the area of art education; Master of Fine Arts in the areas of painting, ceramics, sculpture, jewelry and metalsmithing, printmaking. Cross-registration with John E. Dolibois European Center (Luxembourg). Program accredited by NASAD.

Enrollment 399 total; 380 undergraduate, 19 graduate.

Art Student Profile 68% females, 32% males, 3% minorities.

Art Faculty 12 undergraduate (full-time), 9 undergraduate (part-time), 10 graduate (full-time). 81% of full-time faculty have terminal degrees. Graduate students teach a few undergraduate courses. Undergraduate student–faculty ratio: 15:1.

Student Life Student groups/activities include Art History Association, National Art Education Association Student Chapter, Visual Arts Club. Special housing available for art students.

Expenses for 2007–2008 Application fee: $45. State resident tuition: $9910 full-time. Nonresident tuition: $22,362 full-time. Mandatory fees: $2015 full-time. College room and board: $8600. College room only: $4410. Room and board charges vary according to board plan and housing facility. Special program-related fees: $20–$100 per course for studio supplies.

Financial Aid Program-specific awards: 1 Miami University Scholarship for program majors ($4300), 1 Arthur Damon Art Award for program majors ($1500), 1 School of Fine Arts Award for program majors ($2000), 1 Marston D. Hodgin Award for program majors ($1000), 1 George R. and Galen Glasgow Hoxie Award ($890), 2 Fred and Molly Pye Awards for sophomores and juniors ($475), 1 Barbara Hershey Photo Award for female junior photography majors ($1000), 1 National Woodcarvers Award for upperclass sculpture majors ($1000), 1 Robert Wolfe Printmakers Award for junior and senior printmaking majors ($400).

Application Procedures Students admitted directly into the professional program freshman year. Deadline for freshmen: January 30; transfers: March 1. Notification date for freshmen: March 15. Required: high school transcript, college transcript(s) for transfer students, portfolio, SAT or ACT test scores, essay (art history majors only). Portfolio reviews held twice on campus.

Web Site http://www.fna.muohio.edu/artweb/

Undergraduate Contact Mr. Dennis Tobin, Professor, Department of Art, Miami University, Art Building, Oxford, Ohio 45056; 513-529-1505, fax: 513-529-1532, e-mail address: tobinde@muohio.edu

Graduate Contact Prof. Susan Ewing, Department of Art, Miami University, Art Building, Oxford, Ohio 45056; 513-529-5627, fax: 513-529-1532, e-mail address: ewingsr@muohio.edu

Michigan State University

East Lansing, Michigan

State-supported, coed. Suburban campus. Total enrollment: 46,045. Art program established 1931.

Degrees Bachelor of Fine Arts in the areas of studio art, art education. Majors and concentrations: art education, ceramics, graphic design, painting/drawing, photography, printmaking, sculpture. Graduate degrees offered: Master of Fine Arts in the area of studio art.

Enrollment 340 total; 175 undergraduate, 15 graduate, 150 nonprofessional degree.

Art Faculty 17 total (full-time), 2 total (part-time). 100% of full-time faculty have terminal degrees. Graduate students teach a few undergraduate courses. Undergraduate student–faculty ratio: 13:1.

Student Life Student groups/activities include Saturday Art Program, undergraduate exhibit at Kresge Art Museum, Gallery 114 (student exhibition space).

Expenses for 2007–2008 Application fee: $35. State resident tuition: $8400 full-time. Nonresident tuition: $22,260 full-time. Mandatory fees: $1240 full-time. Full-time tuition and fees vary according to course load, degree level, program, and student level. College room and board: $6676. College room only: $2756. Room

Michigan State University (continued)

and board charges vary according to board plan, housing facility, and student level.

Financial Aid Program-specific awards: 1–4 Creative Arts Scholarships for Michigan resident studio art majors ($500–$3000).

Application Procedures Students admitted directly into the professional program freshman year. Deadline for freshmen and transfers: continuous. Required: high school transcript, college transcript(s) for transfer students, minimum 2.0 high school GPA, SAT or ACT test scores. Recommended: minimum 3.0 high school GPA.

Web Site http://www.art.msu.edu

Undergraduate Contact Cindy Walter, Academic Advisor, Studio Art Undergraduate Program, Michigan State University, 113 Kresge Art Center, East Lansing, Michigan 48824-1119; 517-432-7033, fax: 517-432-3938, e-mail address: walterc2@msu.edu

Graduate Contact Michelle Word, Academic Specialist, Studio Art Graduate Program, Michigan State University, 113 Kresge Art Center, East Lansing, Michigan 48824-1119; 517-355-7610, fax: 517-432-3938, e-mail address: wordmich@msu.edu

Midge Karr Fine Art Department

See New York Institute of Technology

Midwestern State University

Wichita Falls, Texas

State-supported, coed. Urban campus. Total enrollment: 6,027.
Web Site http://www.mwsu.edu/

Millikin University

Decatur, Illinois

Independent, coed. Suburban campus. Total enrollment: 2,376. Art program established 1903.

Degrees Bachelor of Fine Arts. Majors and concentrations: art education, art therapy, art/fine arts, commercial art, computer graphics, studio art.

Enrollment 100 total; all undergraduate.

Art Student Profile 50% females, 50% males, 4% minorities.

Art Faculty 5 undergraduate (full-time), 1 undergraduate (part-time). 100% of full-time faculty have terminal degrees. Graduate students do not teach undergraduate courses. Undergraduate student–faculty ratio: 16:1.

Student Life Student groups/activities include Art Club, AIGA-American Institute of Graphic Arts. Special housing available for art students.

Expenses for 2007–2008 Application fee: $0. Comprehensive fee: $31,055 includes full-time tuition ($23,250), mandatory fees ($595), and college room and board ($7210). College room only: $4010. Full-time tuition and fees vary according to course load. Room and board charges vary according to board plan and housing facility. Special program-related fees: $10–$50 per semester for lab fees.

Financial Aid Program-specific awards: 20–30 talent awards for incoming students ($500–$3000).

Application Procedures Students apply for admission into the professional program by sophomore year. Deadline for freshmen and transfers: continuous. Required: high school transcript, college transcript(s) for transfer students, letter of recommendation, interview, portfolio, SAT or ACT test scores. Portfolio reviews held by appointment on campus and off campus in St. Louis, MO; Indianapolis, IN; the submission of slides may be substituted for portfolios for large works of art.

Web Site http://www.millikin.edu

Undergraduate Contact Mr. Ed Walker, Chairman, Art Department, Millikin University, 1184 West Main Street, Decatur, Illinois 62522; 217-424-6228, fax: 217-424-3993, e-mail address: ewalker@mail.millikin.edu

Milwaukee Institute of Art and Design

Milwaukee, Wisconsin

Independent, coed. Art program established 1974.

Degrees Bachelor of Fine Arts. Majors and concentrations: communication design, computer animation and interactive media, drawing, fine art studio, illustration, industrial design, interior architecture and design, painting, photography, printmaking, sculpture. Cross-registration with Marquette University. Program accredited by NASAD.

Enrollment 646 total; all undergraduate.

Art Student Profile 53% females, 47% males, 16% minorities, 4% international.

Art Faculty 33 undergraduate (full-time), 86 undergraduate (part-time). 70% of full-time faculty have terminal degrees. Graduate students do not teach undergraduate courses. Undergraduate student–faculty ratio: 9:1.

Student Life Student groups/activities include student exhibitions, Student Government, student publication. Special housing available for art students.

Expenses for 2007–2008 Application fee: $25. Comprehensive fee: $31,550 includes full-time tuition ($24,100), mandatory fees ($350), and college room and board ($7100). Room and board charges vary according to board plan. Special program-related fees: $5–$95 per course for supplies/models.

Financial Aid Program-specific awards: 22–35 MIAD Scholarships for continuing students ($2000–$2200), 125 MIAD Admissions Scholarships for incoming students ($5775–$23,100).

Application Procedures Students admitted directly into the professional program freshman year. Deadline for freshmen and transfers: continuous. Required: essay, high school transcript, college transcript(s) for transfer students, minimum 2.0 high school GPA, interview, portfolio. Recommended: minimum 3.0 high school GPA, 2 letters of recommendation, SAT or ACT test scores, minimum 3.0 GPA in high school art classes. Portfolio reviews held continuously on campus and off campus; the submission of slides may be substituted for portfolios when distance is prohibitive.

Web Site http://www.miad.edu

Undergraduate Contact Mr. Mark Fetherston, Director of Admissions, Milwaukee Institute of Art and Design, 273 East Erie Street, Milwaukee, Wisconsin 53202; 414-291-8070, fax: 414-291-8077, e-mail address: miadadm@miad.edu

Minneapolis College of Art and Design

Minneapolis, Minnesota

Independent, coed. Urban campus. Art program established 1886.

Degrees Bachelor of Fine Arts in the areas of design, fine arts, media arts; Bachelor of Science in the area of visualization. Majors and concentrations: advertising, animation, comic art, drawing, filmmaking, furniture design, graphic design, illustration, multimedia, painting, photography, printmaking, sculpture, visualization. Graduate degrees offered: Master of Fine Arts in the area of visual studies. Cross-registration with Macalester College. Program accredited by NASAD.

Enrollment 766 total; 722 undergraduate, 44 graduate.

Art Student Profile 57% females, 43% males, 5% minorities, 3% international.

Art Faculty 41 total (full-time), 81 total (part-time). 75% of full-time faculty have terminal degrees. Graduate students do not teach undergraduate courses. Undergraduate student–faculty ratio: 11:1.

Student Life Student groups/activities include Comic Heads-Comic Book Club, International Association of Graphic Arts Student Chapter (IAGA), Lingo Club. Special housing available for art students.

Expenses for 2007–2008 Application fee: $35. Tuition: $27,000 full-time. Mandatory fees: $200 full-time. College room only: $4160. Special program-related fees: $100 per semester for student activity fee.

Financial Aid Program-specific awards: BFA Trustee Scholarship for new BS/BFA freshmen/BS/BFA transfers ($12,000), BFA Presidential Scholarship for new BS/BFA freshmen/BS/BFA transfers ($10,000), BFA Visual Scholarship for new BS/BFA freshmen/BS/BFA transfers ($8000), BFA Friends of MCAD Award for new BS/BFA freshmen/BS/BFA transfers ($6000), BS Trustee Scholarship for new BS/BFA freshmen/BS/BFA transfers ($12,000), BS Presidential Scholarship for new BS/BFA freshman/BS/BFA transfer ($10,000), BS Emerging Leader Scholarship for new BS/BFA freshmen/BS/BFA transfers ($8000).

Application Procedures Students admitted directly into the professional program freshman

Minneapolis College of Art and Design (continued)

year. Deadline for freshmen and transfers: February 15. Required: essay, high school transcript, college transcript(s) for transfer students, minimum 2.0 high school GPA, letter of recommendation, portfolio, SAT or ACT test scores (minimum combined SAT score of 1100, minimum composite ACT score of 21), statement of interest (BFA and BS applicants), essay for visualization majors (BS applicants only). Recommended: minimum 3.0 high school GPA, interview. Portfolio reviews held as needed by appointment or event on campus and off campus at National Portfolio Days; high school portfolio days; the submission of slides may be substituted for portfolios for large works of art or when distance is prohibitive.

Web Site http://www.mcad.edu/

Contact Mr. William Mullen, Vice President of Enrollment Management, Admissions, Minneapolis College of Art and Design, 2501 Stevens Avenue, Minneapolis, Minnesota 55404; 612-874-3762, fax: 612-874-3701, e-mail address: william_mullen@mcad.edu

Minnesota State University Mankato

Mankato, Minnesota

State-supported, coed. Small town campus. Total enrollment: 14,148.

Degrees Bachelor of Fine Arts in the area of art. Majors and concentrations: ceramics, drawing, fibers, graphic arts, painting, photography, printmaking, sculpture. Graduate degrees offered: Master of Arts in the area of studio art. Cross-registration with Gustavus Adolphus College. Program accredited by NASAD.

Enrollment 312 total; 243 undergraduate, 12 graduate, 57 nonprofessional degree.

Art Student Profile 55% females, 45% males, 2% minorities, 5% international.

Art Faculty 14 undergraduate (full-time), 7 undergraduate (part-time), 14 graduate (full-time). 100% of full-time faculty have terminal degrees. Graduate students teach a few undergraduate courses. Undergraduate student–faculty ratio: 20:1.

Student Life Student groups/activities include Art League, Photography Club, Mudworks Ceramics Student Organization, AIGA-American Institute of Graphic Arts Student Chapter.

Expenses for 2007–2008 Application fee: $20. State resident tuition: $5308 full-time. Nonresident tuition: $11,370 full-time. Mandatory fees: $742 full-time. Full-time tuition and fees vary according to course load and reciprocity agreements. College room and board: $5354. Room and board charges vary according to board plan. Special program-related fees: $15–$90 per semester for art supplies.

Financial Aid Program-specific awards: 6–8 Faculty Nominated Awards for program majors ($500).

Application Procedures Students apply for admission into the professional program by sophomore, junior year. Deadline for freshmen: March 15; transfers: continuous. Notification date for freshmen and transfers: continuous. Required: high school transcript, college transcript(s) for transfer students, SAT or ACT test scores.

Web Site http://www.mnsu.edu/dept/artdept

Contact Mr. James Johnson, Chair, Art Department, Minnesota State University Mankato, Nelson Hall 136, Mankato, Minnesota 56001; 507-389-6412, fax: 507-389-2816, e-mail address: james.johnson@mnsu.edu

Mississippi State University

Mississippi State, Mississippi

State-supported, coed. Total enrollment: 17,039. Art program established 1968.

Degrees Bachelor of Fine Arts in the areas of fine arts, graphic design. Majors and concentrations: ceramics, drawing, graphic design, painting, photography, printmaking, sculpture. Program accredited by NASAD.

Enrollment 1,195 total; 264 undergraduate, 931 nonprofessional degree.

Art Student Profile 41% females, 59% males, 8% minorities, 1% international.

Art Faculty 21 undergraduate (full-time), 1 undergraduate (part-time). 94% of full-time faculty have terminal degrees. Graduate students do not teach undergraduate courses. Undergraduate student–faculty ratio: 13:1.

Student Life Student groups/activities include exhibitions, American Advertising Federation Chapter.

Expenses for 2007–2008 Application fee: $25. State resident tuition: $4978 full-time. Nonresident tuition: $11,469 full-time. College room and board: $6951. College room only: $3716. Room and board charges vary according to board plan, housing facility, and student level. Special program-related fees: $50–$100 per semester for lab fee per class/computer resource access.

Financial Aid Program-specific awards: 10 Gulmon Scholarships for freshmen ($1000), 1 Ferretti/Karnstedt Award for sophomores ($1000), 1 DuBoise Scholarship in Photography for juniors and seniors ($750), 1 Del Rendon Scholarship for freshmen through seniors ($2000), 3 John Richard Scholarships for freshmen through juniors ($1000).

Application Procedures Students admitted directly into the professional program freshman year. Deadline for freshmen and transfers: July 26. Notification date for freshmen and transfers: continuous. Required: high school transcript, college transcript(s) for transfer students, minimum 2.0 high school GPA, SAT or ACT test scores (minimum composite ACT score of 17), portfolio for transfers. Portfolio reviews held twice on campus.

Web Site http://www.msstate.edu/dept/art/index.html

Undergraduate Contact Ms. Kay De Marsche, Head, Department of Art, Mississippi State University, PO Box 5182, Mississippi State, Mississippi 39762; 662-325-3850, fax: 662-325-3850, e-mail address: kdemarsche@caad.msstate.edu

Mississippi University for Women

Columbus, Mississippi

State-supported, coed, primarily women. Small town campus. Total enrollment: 2,379. Art program established 1941.

Web Site http://www.muw.edu/

Missouri State University

Springfield, Missouri

State-supported, coed. Suburban campus. Total enrollment: 19,348. Art program established 1945.

Degrees Bachelor of Fine Arts in the areas of design, art, digital animation; Bachelor of Science in the area of electronic art; Bachelor of Science in Education. Majors and concentrations: art education, ceramics, computer animation, digital art, drawing, electronic arts, graphic design, illustration, jewelry and metalsmithing, painting, photography, printmaking, sculpture. Graduate degrees offered: Master of Science in the area of art education.

Enrollment 572 total; 490 undergraduate, 12 graduate, 70 nonprofessional degree.

Art Faculty 27 total (full-time), 14 total (part-time). 100% of full-time faculty have terminal degrees. Graduate students do not teach undergraduate courses. Undergraduate student–faculty ratio: 15:1.

Student Life Student groups/activities include Design Student Club, Student Artist Association, clubs in various areas of emphasis.

Expenses for 2007–2008 Application fee: $35. State resident tuition: $5988 full-time. Nonresident tuition: $11,088 full-time. Mandatory fees: $618 full-time. Full-time tuition and fees vary according to course load, degree level, location, and program. College room and board: $5312. Room and board charges vary according to board plan and housing facility.

Financial Aid Program-specific awards: 10 departmental awards for program majors ($500–$800).

Application Procedures Students apply for admission into the professional program by sophomore year. Deadline for freshmen and transfers: July 30. Notification date for freshmen and transfers: continuous. Required: high school transcript, college transcript(s) for transfer students, minimum 2.0 high school GPA, portfolio, SAT or ACT test scores. Portfolio reviews held twice on campus; the submission of slides may be substituted for portfolios.

Web Site http://art.missouristate.edu/

Undergraduate Contact Prof. Wade S. Thompson, Department Head, Art and Design Department, Missouri State University, 901 South

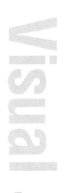

Missouri State University (continued)

National, Springfield, Missouri 65804; 417-836-5110, fax: 417-836-6055, e-mail address: wadethompson@missouristate.edu

Graduate Contact Dr. Steve Willis, Coordinator, Art Education Department, Missouri State University, 901 South National, Springfield, Missouri 65804; 417-836-6693, fax: 417-836-6055, e-mail address: stevewillis@missouristate.edu

Montserrat College of Art

Beverly, Massachusetts

Independent, coed. Suburban campus. Total enrollment: 285. Art program established 1970.

Degrees Bachelor of Fine Arts. Majors and concentrations: animation and interactive media, art education, art history, book arts, graphic design, illustration, painting/drawing, photography and video, printmaking, sculpture. Cross-registration with Northeast Consortium of Colleges and Universities in Massachusetts, Association of Independent Colleges of Art and Design. Program accredited by NASAD.

Enrollment 274 total; all undergraduate.

Art Student Profile 64% females, 36% males, 5% minorities.

Art Faculty 24 undergraduate (full-time), 38 undergraduate (part-time). 67% of full-time faculty have terminal degrees. Graduate students do not teach undergraduate courses. Undergraduate student–faculty ratio: 8:1.

Student Life Student groups/activities include Student Government, Meals-on-the-Cheap Committee, Coffee House Organization. Special housing available for art students.

Expenses for 2007–2008 Application fee: $50. Tuition: $21,500 full-time. Mandatory fees: $800 full-time. Full-time tuition and fees vary according to course load and reciprocity agreements. College room only: $5800. Room charges vary according to housing facility.

Financial Aid Program-specific awards: 208 Montserrat Grants for those demonstrating need ($2940), Presidential Awards for program majors, 188 Portfolio Awards for those demonstrating merit ($1850), 4 Beverly Scholarships for residents of Beverly demonstrating need ($4313), 96 Academic Achievement Awards for those demonstrating merit ($3284), 6 Transfer Scholarships for transfer students demonstrating merit and need ($3750).

Application Procedures Students admitted directly into the professional program freshman year. Deadline for freshmen and transfers: August 1. Notification date for freshmen and transfers: August 15. Required: essay, high school transcript, college transcript(s) for transfer students, minimum 2.0 high school GPA, 2 letters of recommendation, portfolio, minimum TOEFL score of 520 on written test, 190 on computer-based test, and 68 on internet-based test for international students. Recommended: minimum 3.0 high school GPA, interview, SAT or ACT test scores. Portfolio reviews held continuously on campus and off campus in various locations across the country; the submission of slides may be substituted for portfolios if a campus visit is impossible.

Web Site http://www.montserrat.edu

Undergraduate Contact Ms. Jessica Sarin-Perry, Dean of Admissions and Enrollment Management, Montserrat College of Art, 23 Essex Street, Box 26, Beverly, Massachusetts 01915; 800-836-0487, fax: 978-921-4241, e-mail address: jperry@montserrat.edu

More About the College

Montserrat College of Art takes a highly personal approach to teaching, valuing above all else the combination of strong individual support and challenging creative instruction. Located on Boston's North Shore, it is a place where students feel inspired, encouraged, and at home.

Students come to Montserrat to gain professional competence, to develop their own unique abilities, and to engage in new areas of experience in pursuit of their Bachelor of Fine Arts (B.F.A.) degree. With an enrollment of approximately 275 students of diverse cultural and artistic backgrounds, the College is large enough to offer the wide array of courses and concentrations that compose a strong visual arts curriculum, yet small enough to provide the personal attention that is often difficult to find in larger educational environments. Small classes encourage intensive, individualized instruction by a faculty of professional artists and designers and accomplished scholars.

The first year of foundation studies is a carefully crafted sequence of complementary courses emphasizing the visual, technical, written, and verbal skills essential to a successful art college experience. After foundation, a student may choose to major in graphic

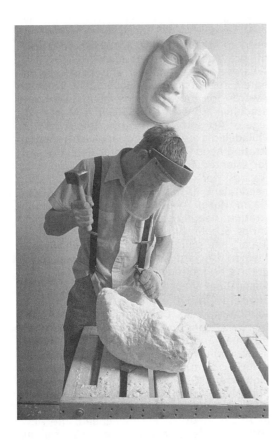

design, illustration, painting and drawing, photography and video, printmaking, or sculpture or do a self-directed study combining elements from different disciplines. Students may also combine any one of the studio concentrations with art education for a dual concentration. The Montserrat curriculum allows students to explore a wide range of studio electives not necessarily related to their concentration, encouraging the development of a truly unique, artistic voice.

Experiential learning provides a unique opportunity for students to gain professional practice. During the junior year, required internships and apprenticeships provide students with opportunities to experience the world of work and to integrate classroom learning with the realities of the workplace.

Entry into the Senior Seminar is determined by a faculty panel. Here, students have the opportunity to delve independently into a significant, coherent body of work and exhibit seminar work. This revelatory experience helps the artist and designer to mature and ultimately make the transition into professional life.

Montserrat is a residential college with apartment-style housing nestled among the homes of downtown Beverly, located on Boston's North Shore. Boston and Cambridge are easily accessible by car or commuter train. World-class museums, such as the Boston Museum of Fine Arts; galleries; libraries; shopping; sports; and a variety of entertainment options provide a stimulating intellectual, cultural, and social environment in which to live and learn.

Program Facilities The Montserrat campus has three galleries that feature exciting exhibitions by professional artists of national and international note and artists within the College community. The Visiting Artist and Lectures Series programs expose students to a wide range of viewpoints and aesthetics.

Montserrat's main building, the historic Hardie Building, houses four floors of studios, classrooms, exhibition spaces, and the Paul Scott Library. Specially equipped studios for printmaking, photography, painting, illustration, and graphic design as well as video and computer labs are located here. The library contains a collection of more than 14,000 books, numerous art and related periodicals, videos, CD-ROMs, and other resources. The library offers Internet access and houses a comprehensive slide collection with more than 60,000 images. The 301 Cabot Studio Building offers facilities for sculpture and semiprivate studios for seniors.

All students are entitled to free admission to Boston's Museum of Fine Arts, which has one of the finest collections of art in the world. The museum houses permanent exhibits of art and artifacts representing virtually all periods and civilizations as well as changing exhibitions of art.

Special Programs Montserrat offers students a variety of opportunities to broaden their horizons and earn credit towards their degree through local, national, and international study. The College is a member of the Northeast Consortium of Colleges and Universities in Massachusetts; students may take classes and use the library facilities of member colleges. Through Montserrat's membership in the Association of Independent Colleges of Art and Design (AICAD), students may spend a semester or year in comparable studies at a member institution. The AICAD New York Studio Program offers third-year students the opportunity to spend a summer in New York City.

Students may spend a month in the walled, papal city of Viterbo in Italy while attending Montserrat's summer, residential program. Intensive courses in painting, drawing, photography, art history, and writing are offered. A two-week trip to Mali, Africa, is also offered during the winter break.

Montserrat College of Art (continued)

High school students can experience life at Montserrat through the summer Pre-College program, which takes place in July on the College's campus. This four-week program is primarily for students entering their sophomore, junior, or senior year of high school and is designed to help young artists evaluate a career in the arts and develop a portfolio suitable for college admission. Students participate in assignments and critiques led by top instructors from Montserrat and other Boston-area colleges and, upon completion of the program, earn 3 college credits.

Moore College of Art & Design

Philadelphia, Pennsylvania

Independent, women only. Urban campus. Total enrollment: 557. Art program established 1848.

Degrees Bachelor of Fine Arts in the areas of art education, art history, fine arts, fashion design, illustration, interior design, graphic design, textile design, curatorial studies, photography, digital arts. Majors and concentrations: art education, art history, curatorial studies, fashion design, graphic design, illustration, interior design, photography/digital arts, textile arts, three-dimensional studies, two-dimensional studies. Program accredited by NASAD, CIDA.

Enrollment 557 total; 525 undergraduate, 32 graduate.

Art Student Profile 100% females, 22% minorities, 2% international.

Art Faculty 30 undergraduate (full-time), 114 undergraduate (part-time). 70% of full-time faculty have terminal degrees. Graduate students do not teach undergraduate courses. Undergraduate student–faculty ratio: 8:1.

Student Life Student groups/activities include senior show/student show, fashion show, Moore Magazine. Special housing available for art students.

Expenses for 2008–2009 Application fee: $40. Comprehensive fee: $38,350 includes full-time tuition ($26,800), mandatory fees ($1048), and college room and board ($10,502). College room only: $6322.

Financial Aid Program-specific awards: 1 Evelyn A. Whittaker Award for those demonstrating need and talent ($15,000), 100 Moore College of Art and Design Presidential and Merit Awards for academically and artistically talented students ($500–$4000), 10 W. W. Smith Awards for those demonstrating talent and academic achievement ($2000), 1 Moore College of Art and Design Partnership Award for Philadelphia public school applicants demonstrating need ($15,000), 8 Sarah Peters Awards for talented freshmen ($500), 2–4 Appleman Awards for adult students demonstrating need/talent ($10,000–$12,500), 8 Fred and Naomi Hazell Awards for oil painters demonstrating need/talent ($16,000), 1 Charming Shops Scholarship for fashion/textile design juniors and seniors ($2000), 1 Kristen McCabe Memorial Award for talented junior or senior graphic design majors ($500).

Application Procedures Students apply for admission into the professional program by sophomore year. Deadline for freshmen and transfers: continuous. Notification date for freshmen and transfers: August 15. Required: essay, high school transcript, college transcript(s) for transfer students, minimum 2.0 high school GPA, letter of recommendation, portfolio, SAT or ACT test scores (minimum combined SAT score of 850, minimum composite ACT score of 18). Recommended: interview. Portfolio reviews held continuously on campus and off campus at National Portfolio Days; the submission of slides may be substituted for portfolios when distance is prohibitive.

Web Site http://www.moore.edu

Undergraduate Contact Ms. Heeseung Lee, Director of Admissions, Admissions, Moore College of Art & Design, 20th and The Parkway, Philadelphia, Pennsylvania 19103-1179; 215-568-4515 ext. 1107, fax: 215-568-3547, e-mail address: admiss@moore.edu

More About the College

Moore College of Art & Design sets the standard of excellence in educating women for careers in art and design. As the first and only women's college of the visual arts in the nation, founded in 1848, Moore students enjoy an accessible, supportive small college community and learn from a dedicated faculty of award-winning artists, designers, and scholars.

With 515 students and an 8:1 student-to-faculty member ratio, Moore offers ten Bachelor of Fine Arts majors in art education, art history, curatorial studies, fashion design, fine arts (with 2-D and/or 3-D emphasis), graphic design, illustration, interior design, photography and digital arts, and textile design. Career and leadership skills are emphasized throughout the academic programs, with each major providing extensive career preparation for their respective fields.

The Locks Career Center for Women in the Arts facilitates internships for students to gain practical professional experience. The Locks Career Center also provides a broad range of career resources for students and alumnae, such as one-on-one career counseling, mentoring, job bulletins, and workshops on topics from networking to resume writing.

On-campus leadership organizations provide the chance to learn about and utilize leadership skills, and to develop self-confidence. Leadership fellowship opportunities provide financial support for students to work, either with an individual leader in the arts community or within an innovative organization. Other experiences are available through community service or study abroad.

Moore's size creates a community experience where students live and learn in a supportive, comfortable environment—one where students from different majors, backgrounds, cultures, and lifestyles can learn from each other. The campus includes Sarah Peter Hall, Wilson Hall, Stahl Residence Hall, and Sartain Hall. The main campus includes expansive studios and classrooms, technology centers, two auditoriums, Fox Commons, MAC and PC computer labs, a professional woodshop, ferrous and nonferrous metal workshops, ceramic studios with indoor and outdoor kilns, abundant student exhibition space, two contemporary art galleries, several outdoor courtyards, and the dining café. The Connolly Library's holdings feature 40,000 monographs, Internet access, 185 art journals, a slide collection of more than 123,000 images, and picture files of 300,000 images.

The support system and friendships formed by living in college housing often help ease first-year students' transition into the college setting. Approximately 70 percent of first-year students live in College housing, which includes Stahl Residence Hall and Sartain Hall. Other students choose to live off campus. There are numerous apartments in Philadelphia's neighboring residential areas.

Moore graduates become part of and have access to a broad network of fellow alumnae of accomplished artists, designers, and creative leaders in a wide variety of industries. Among Moore's notable graduates are fashion designer and business icon Adrienne Vittadini; renowned twentieth-century portraitist Alice Neel; award-winning interior designer Karen Daroff; and Pulitzer Prize-winning photojournalist Sharon J. Wohlmuth.

Moore College of Art & Design is accredited by the Commission on Higher Education of the Middle States Association of Colleges and Schools, 3624 Market Street, Philadelphia, Pennsylvania 19104-2680, 215-662-5606. The Commission on Higher Education is an institutional accrediting agency recognized by the U.S. Secretary of Education and the Commission on Recognition of Postsecondary Accreditation; by the National Association of Schools of Art and Design, 11250 Roger Bacon Drive, Suite 21, Reston, Virginia 20190, 703-437-0700; by the Commonwealth of Pennsylvania, Department of Education, 333 Market Street, Harrisburg, Pennsylvania 17126-0333, 717-787-5820; and by the Council for Interior Design Accreditation (formerly FIDER), 146 Monroe Center NW, #1318, Grand Rapids, Michigan 49503-2822, 616-458-0400.

Mount Allison University

Sackville, New Brunswick, Canada

Province-supported, coed. Small town campus. Total enrollment: 2,170. Art program established 1941.

Degrees Bachelor of Fine Arts. Majors and concentrations: open media, painting/drawing, photography, printmaking, sculpture. Cross-registration with Université de Strasbourg (France), Universitöt Tubingen (Germany).

Enrollment 127 total; all undergraduate.

Art Student Profile 95% females, 5% males, 16% international.

Art Faculty 7 undergraduate (full-time), 3 undergraduate (part-time). 86% of full-time faculty have terminal degrees. Graduate students do not teach undergraduate courses. Undergraduate student–faculty ratio: 18:1.

Student Life Student groups/activities include Fine Arts Society.

Expenses for 2007–2008 Application fee: $50 Canadian dollars. Tuition, fee, and room and board charges are reported in Canadian dollars. Province resident tuition: $6720 full-time. Mandatory fees: $257 full-time. Full-time tuition and fees vary according to course load. College room and board: $6795. College room only: $3530. Room and board charges vary according to board plan. International student tuition: $13,440 full-time.

Mount Allison University (continued)

Financial Aid Program-specific awards: 1 Pulford Award for freshmen program majors ($1000), 1–2 Chang Awards for senior program majors ($500–$1000), 1 Crake Award for graduating students ($500), 2 Gairdner Awards for top program majors ($1000), University Scholarships for those in top 10% of program ($750).

Application Procedures Students admitted directly into the professional program freshman year. Deadline for freshmen: April 1; transfers: July 5. Notification date for freshmen and transfers: continuous. Required: high school transcript, college transcript(s) for transfer students, minimum 3.0 high school GPA, 2 letters of recommendation, portfolio. Portfolio reviews held once on campus; the submission of slides may be substituted for portfolios at student's discretion, (CD/DVD also accepted).

Web Site http://www.mta.ca/faculty/arts-letters/finearts/

Undergraduate Contact Mr. Matt Sheridan-Jonah, Manager of Admissions, Scholarships and Financial Aid, Student Services, Mount Allison University, 65 York Street, Sackville, New Brunswick E4L 1E4, Canada; 506-364-3294, fax: 506-364-2272, e-mail address: mjonah@mta.ca

Murray State University

Murray, Kentucky

State-supported, coed. Small town campus. Total enrollment: 10,149. Art program established 1926.

Degrees Bachelor of Fine Arts in the areas of studio art, art education. Majors and concentrations: art education, ceramics, graphic design, jewelry and metalsmithing, painting/drawing, photography, printmaking, sculpture, wood. Program accredited by NASAD, NCATE.

Enrollment 178 total; 89 undergraduate, 89 nonprofessional degree.

Art Student Profile 65% females, 35% males, 8% minorities, 3% international.

Art Faculty 14 undergraduate (full-time), 2 undergraduate (part-time). 100% of full-time faculty have terminal degrees. Graduate students do not teach undergraduate courses. Undergraduate student–faculty ratio: 14:1.

Student Life Student groups/activities include Organization of Murray Art Students.

Expenses for 2008–2009 Application fee: $30. State resident tuition: $4932 full-time. Nonresident tuition: $7426 full-time. Mandatory fees: $816 full-time. College room and board: $6004. College room only: $3278. Special program-related fees: $14 per credit hour for supplies and equipment.

Financial Aid Program-specific awards: 15–20 Department of Art Scholarships for program majors ($500–$2500).

Application Procedures Students admitted directly into the professional program freshman year. Deadline for freshmen and transfers: continuous. Required: high school transcript, college transcript(s) for transfer students, ACT test score only.

Web Site http://www.murraystate.edu

Undergraduate Contact Mr. Dick Dougherty, Chair, Department of Art, Murray State University, 604 Fine Arts Building, Murray, Kentucky 42071-3342; 270-809-3784, fax: 270-809-3920, e-mail address: dick.dougherty@murraystate.edu

Myers School of Art

See The University of Akron

The New England School of Art & Design

See Suffolk University

New Hampshire Institute of Art

Manchester, New Hampshire

Proprietary, coed. Urban campus. Art program established 1997.

Degrees Bachelor of Fine Arts. Majors and concentrations: ceramics, illustration, interdisciplinary studies, painting, photography. Program accredited by NASAD.

Enrollment 286 undergraduate.

Art Student Profile 70% females, 30% males, 3% minorities, 1% international.

Art Faculty 16 undergraduate (full-time), 42 undergraduate (part-time). 85% of full-time faculty have terminal degrees. Graduate students do not teach undergraduate courses. Undergraduate student–faculty ratio: 10:1.

Student Life Student groups/activities include Gallery Committee, Student Council, student reviews/exhibition. Special housing available for art students.

Expenses for 2007–2008 Application fee: $25. Tuition: $12,960 full-time. Mandatory fees: $1440 full-time. College room only: $6300. Room charges vary according to housing facility. Special program-related fees: $30 per semester for registration fee, $40 per semester for student activity fee, $50 per semester for technology fee, $175 per semester for supplemental lab fee, $600 per semester for studio fee.

Financial Aid Program-specific awards: Founders Award for outstanding applicants, Fuller Merit Award for students with outstanding portfolios, Gakidis Award for current, nontraditional students, Housing Award for students with financial need, NHIA Scholastic Art Awards Top Portfolio, Presidential Award for students with outstanding portfolio and GPA, Transfer Award for students with a minimum of 24 college credits, Paul and Anne Harvey Award for nominated current students, John Hubenthal Award for nominated junior/senior students.

Application Procedures Students admitted directly into the professional program freshman year. Deadline for freshmen and transfers: continuous. Required: essay, high school transcript, college transcript(s) for transfer students, 2 letters of recommendation, interview, portfolio. Recommended: minimum 2.0 high school GPA, SAT or ACT test scores. Portfolio reviews held ongoing on campus and off campus in several locations; the submission of slides may be substituted for portfolios applicant is unable to visit campus for a portfolio review.

Web Site http://www.nhia.edu

Undergraduate Contact Amanda Abbott, Admissions Administrator, Admissions, New Hampshire Institute of Art, 148 Concord Street, Manchester, New Hampshire 03104; 603-836-2576, fax: 603-647-0658, e-mail address: aabbott@nhia.edu

New Mexico Highlands University

Las Vegas, New Mexico

State-supported, coed. Small town campus. Total enrollment: 3,457.

Degrees Bachelor of Fine Arts. Majors and concentrations: ceramics, drawing, foundry, jewelry, metals, painting, photography, printmaking, sculpture, studio art, visual communication.

Art Faculty 2 undergraduate (full-time), 5 undergraduate (part-time). 100% of full-time faculty have terminal degrees. Graduate students do not teach undergraduate courses.

Student Life Student groups/activities include Crossroads Art Club.

Expenses for 2007–2008 Application fee: $15. State resident tuition: $2516 full-time. Nonresident tuition: $3775 full-time. Full-time tuition varies according to course load and location. College room and board: $3431. College room only: $1826. Room and board charges vary according to board plan and housing facility. Special program-related fees: $25–$45 per course for specific studio courses.

Financial Aid Program-specific awards: Lorraine Schula Outstanding Art Student Award for junior/senior program majors.

Application Procedures Students admitted directly into the professional program freshman year. Deadline for freshmen and transfers: May 15. Notification date for freshmen and transfers: continuous. Required: high school transcript, college transcript(s) for transfer students, minimum 2.0 high school GPA, portfolio, SAT or ACT test scores. Portfolio reviews held twice on campus.

Web Site http://www.nmhu.edu

Undergraduate Contact Ms. Melissa A. Williamson, Administrative Secretary, Department of Communication and Fine Arts, New Mexico Highlands University, Burris Hall, Las Vegas, New Mexico 87701; 505-454-3024, fax: 505-454-3241, e-mail address: mawilliamson@nmhu.edu

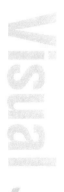

New Mexico State University

Las Cruces, New Mexico

State-supported, coed. Suburban campus. Total enrollment: 16,726. Art program established 1948.

Degrees Bachelor of Fine Arts in the area of studio art. Majors and concentrations: ceramic art and design, graphic design, jewelry and metalsmithing, painting/drawing, photography, printmaking, sculpture. Graduate degrees offered: Master of Arts in the areas of studio art, art history; Master of Fine Arts in the area of studio art.

Enrollment 302 total; 272 undergraduate, 30 graduate.

Art Student Profile 55% females, 45% males, 30% minorities.

Art Faculty 12 total (full-time), 4 total (part-time). 100% of full-time faculty have terminal degrees. Graduate students teach a few undergraduate courses. Undergraduate student–faculty ratio: 15:1.

Student Life Special housing available for art students.

Expenses for 2007–2008 Application fee: $20. State resident tuition: $3274 full-time. Nonresident tuition: $13,002 full-time. Mandatory fees: $1178 full-time. College room and board: $5766. College room only: $3322. Room and board charges vary according to board plan and gender.

Financial Aid Program-specific awards: 1 Jose Cisneros Student Travel Award for art students ($400), 2 Mary Lawbaugh Awards for art students ($400), 10 Janet Swenson Memorial Awards for art students ($500), 6 Dodier Awards for art students ($2000).

Application Procedures Students admitted directly into the professional program freshman year. Deadline for freshmen and transfers: August 14. Required: high school transcript, college transcript(s) for transfer students, minimum 2.0 high school GPA, SAT or ACT test scores.

Web Site http://www.nmsu.edu/~artdept

Contact Mr. Spencer Fidler, Head, Art Department, New Mexico State University, Box 30001, Department 3572, Las Cruces, New Mexico 88003-0001; 505-646-1705, fax: 505-646-8036, e-mail address: artdept@nmsu.edu

The New School

See Parsons The New School for Design

New World School of the Arts

Miami, Florida

State-supported, coed. Urban campus. Total enrollment: 416. Art program established 1988.

Degrees Bachelor of Fine Arts in the area of visual art. Majors and concentrations: drawing, electronic intermedia, graphic design, painting, photography, printmaking, sculpture. Mandatory cross-registration with University of Florida, Miami Dade College. Program accredited by NASAD.

Enrollment 174 total; all undergraduate.

Art Student Profile 54% females, 46% males, 76% minorities, 2% international.

Art Faculty 5 undergraduate (full-time), 13 undergraduate (part-time). 100% of full-time faculty have terminal degrees. Graduate students do not teach undergraduate courses. Undergraduate student–faculty ratio: 11:1.

Student Life Student groups/activities include juried art shows.

Expenses for 2007–2008 Application fee: $0. State resident tuition: $3000 full-time. Nonresident tuition: $10,000 full-time.

Financial Aid Program-specific awards: 4 Nation's Bank Merit Scholarships for program majors ($2000), 6 Ronnie Bogaev Merit Scholarships for female in-state program majors ($2000), 18 Frances Wolfson Merit Scholarships for program majors ($2000), 15 Miami-Dade College Scholarships for program majors ($1000).

Application Procedures Students admitted directly into the professional program freshman year. Deadline for freshmen and transfers: continuous. Notification date for freshmen and transfers: continuous. Required: essay, high school transcript, college transcript(s) for transfer students, 2 letters of recommendation, portfolio. Recommended: minimum 2.0

high school GPA, interview, SAT or ACT test scores. Portfolio reviews held continuously on campus and off campus in various locations in Florida; the submission of slides may be substituted for portfolios when distance is prohibitive.

Web Site http://www.mdc.edu/nwsa

Undergraduate Contact Pamela Neumann, Recruitment and Admissions Coordinator, Student Services, New World School of the Arts, 300 NE 2nd Avenue, Miami, Florida 33132; 305-237-7007, fax: 305-237-3794, e-mail address: nwsaadm@mdc.edu

Midge Karr Fine Art Department
New York Institute of Technology

Old Westbury, New York

Independent, coed. Suburban campus. Total enrollment: 11,126. Art program established 1960.

Degrees Bachelor of Fine Arts in the areas of computer graphics, graphic design, art education. Majors and concentrations: art education, computer graphics, graphic design. Graduate degrees offered: Master of Fine Arts in the areas of computer graphics, fine art, graphic design.

Enrollment 250 undergraduate, 30 graduate.

Art Student Profile 55% females, 45% males, 25% minorities, 20% international.

Art Faculty 8 undergraduate (full-time), 30 undergraduate (part-time). 100% of full-time faculty have terminal degrees. Graduate students do not teach undergraduate courses. Undergraduate student–faculty ratio: 7:1.

Student Life Student groups/activities include American Society of Interior Designers, Digital Sculpture Club, Computer Graphics Club.

Expenses for 2007–2008 Application fee: $50. Comprehensive fee: $31,512 includes full-time tuition ($20,908), mandatory fees ($590), and college room and board ($10,014). Full-time tuition and fees vary according to course load and program. Room and board charges vary according to board plan, housing facility, and location. Special program-related fees: $10–$40 per course for studio supplies.

Financial Aid Program-specific awards: Presidential Awards for academically qualified applicants ($2200–$2600), Academic Achievement Awards for academically qualified applicants ($1200–$1800), Academic Incentive Awards for academically qualified applicants ($600).

Application Procedures Students admitted directly into the professional program freshman year. Deadline for freshmen and transfers: continuous. Required: essay, high school transcript, college transcript(s) for transfer students, minimum 2.0 high school GPA, interview, portfolio, SAT or ACT test scores. Recommended: 2 letters of recommendation. Portfolio reviews held continuously on campus and off campus in New York, NY; the submission of slides may be substituted for portfolios for out-of-state applicants.

Web Site http://www.nyit.edu

Undergraduate Contact Mr. Emanuel Saladino, Administrative Assistant, Midge Karr Fine Art Department, New York Institute of Technology, PO Box 8000, Old Westbury, New York 11568-8000; 516-686-7542, fax: 516-686-7428, e-mail address: esaladin@nyit.edu

New York School of Interior Design

New York, New York

Independent, coed, primarily women. Urban campus. Total enrollment: 703. Art program established 1916.

Degrees Bachelor of Fine Arts in the area of interior design. Majors and concentrations: interior design. Graduate degrees offered: Master of Fine Arts in the area of interior design. Program accredited by NASAD, CIDA.

Enrollment 685 total; 141 undergraduate, 18 graduate, 526 nonprofessional degree.

Art Student Profile 82% females, 18% males, 22% minorities, 10% international.

Art Faculty 2 total (full-time), 71 total (part-time). 35% of full-time faculty have terminal degrees. Graduate students do not teach undergraduate courses. Undergraduate student–faculty ratio: 10:1.

Student Life Student groups/activities include American Society of Interior Designers Student Chapter.

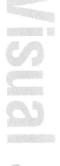

New York School of Interior Design
(continued)

Expenses for 2008–2009 Application fee: $50. Tuition: $19,500 full-time. Mandatory fees: $290 full-time.

Financial Aid Program-specific awards: 50 Institutional and Endowed Scholarships for program majors ($1000–$10,000).

Application Procedures Students admitted directly into the professional program freshman year. Deadline for freshmen and transfers: continuous. Required: essay, high school transcript, college transcript(s) for transfer students, minimum 2.0 high school GPA, 2 letters of recommendation, portfolio, SAT or ACT test scores (minimum combined SAT score of 1500, minimum composite ACT score of 20). Recommended: minimum 3.0 high school GPA, interview. Portfolio reviews held continuously on campus and off campus in various college fairs; the submission of slides may be substituted for portfolios when distance is prohibitive.

Web Site http://www.nysid.edu

Contact Mr. David T. Sprouls, Director of Admissions, New York School of Interior Design, 170 East 70th Street, New York, New York 10021; 212-472-1500 ext. 202, fax: 212-472-1867, e-mail address: admissions@nysid.edu

More About the School

Throughout its history, the New York School of Interior Design (NYSID) has devoted all of its resources to a single field of study—interior design. NYSID is specifically designed for those who wish to pursue a career in one or more of the various fields of interior design and wish to do so under the guidance of a faculty consisting of practicing designers, architects, and art and architectural historians. The various academic programs comprise an integrated curriculum covering architecture, design problem solving, history of art, interior design concepts, interiors and furniture, materials and methods, philosophy and theory, professional design procedures, and technical and communication skills.

Because of its select faculty and established reputation, the School continues to maintain a close relationship with the interior design industry. This provides an excellent means for students to develop associations that offer opportunities to move into the profession after completing their degree program at NYSID.

Many of the world's most important museums, galleries, and showrooms are within walking distance. The city is world-renowned for its cultural activities, architecture, historic districts, and cosmopolitan urban experience.

NYSID is located on a quiet, tree-lined street in Manhattan's landmark Upper East Side Historic District. The School has two auditorium spaces, light-filled studios and classrooms, a CAD lab, and a lighting design lab. NYSID also has a library containing a comprehensive collection of books, journals, periodicals, and trade and auction catalogs specifically devoted to the interior design field and related fine arts; a materials library; an atelier; two galleries; a rooftop terrace; and a café, bookstore, and student lounge.

NYSID has an active student chapter of the American Society of Interior Designers (ASID). ASID organizes lectures, tours, workshops, and other events throughout the school year, providing an inside view of the interior design industry.

One of the strengths of NYSID is its gallery exhibitions relating to architecture and design. Open to both students and the public, the gallery has mounted such acclaimed shows as *Designers Salute Edith Wharton and The Mount; Albert Hadley: Drawings and the Design Process;* and *Bob the Roman: Heroic Antiquity and the Architecture of Robert Adam.* The School also sponsors lectures and symposia. Guest lecturers have included Mario Buatta, Charlotte Moss, Albert Hadley, Eric Cohler, John Saladino, Clodagh, and David Garrard Lowe. Students are encouraged to attend the lecture series.

The School maintains an active placement service for graduates and current students. Many students find work while still at NYSID. Because of its reputation in the design field, many NYSID graduates are employed in the best design, architectural, and industry-related firms in New York City, across the United States, and around the world.

Steinhardt School of Culture, Education, and Human Development, Department of Art and Art Professions

New York University

New York, New York

Independent, coed. Urban campus. Total enrollment: 41,783.

Degrees Bachelor of Fine Arts in the area of studio art. Majors and concentrations: studio art. Graduate degrees offered: Master of Arts in the areas of studio art (3-summer program), visual culture: theory, visual culture: costume studies, art education, visual arts administration, art therapy; Master of Fine Arts in the area of studio art. Doctor of Philosophy in the area of visual culture and education.

Enrollment 475 total; 229 undergraduate, 246 graduate.

Art Student Profile 81% females, 19% males, 22% minorities, 12% international.

Art Faculty 16 total (full-time), 89 total (part-time). 81% of full-time faculty have terminal degrees. Graduate students teach a few undergraduate courses. Undergraduate student–faculty ratio: 2:1.

Student Life Student groups/activities include gallery exhibitions, lectures, performances, panels, symposia with visiting artists and scholars, courses in partnership with the International Center for Photography and others.

Expenses for 2007–2008 Application fee: $65. Comprehensive fee: $47,490 includes full-time tuition ($33,268), mandatory fees ($2022), and college room and board ($12,200). Full-time tuition and fees vary according to course load and program. Room and board charges vary according to board plan and housing facility. Special program-related fees: $250 per semester for lab fees.

Financial Aid Program-specific awards: Art Talent Scholarships for BFA candidates.

Application Procedures Students admitted directly into the professional program freshman year. Deadline for freshmen: January 15; transfers: April 1. Notification date for freshmen: April 1; transfers: September 1. Required: essay, high school transcript, college transcript(s) for transfer students, 3 letters of recommendation, portfolio, SAT or ACT test scores, TOEFL score for non-native English speakers, strong high school GPA. Portfolio reviews held on campus and off campus in venues in New York State; the submission of slides may be substituted for portfolios.

Web Site http://www.steinhardt.nyu.edu/arts2008

Undergraduate Contact Ms. Candice MacLusky, Assistant Director of Undergraduate Admissions, New York University, 22 Washington Square North, New York, New York 10011-9191; 212-998-4500, fax: 212-995-4902.

Graduate Contact Mr. John Myers, Director of Enrollment Services, Office of Graduate Admissions, New York University, 82 Washington Square East, 3rd Floor, New York, New York 10003-6680; 212-998-5030, fax: 212-995-4328, e-mail address: steinhardt.gradadmissions@nyu.edu

More About the University

NYU's Steinhardt School of Culture, Education, and Human Development offers a diverse range of undergraduate and graduate programs in applied psychology, art, communication, education, health, and music. Our School has a long history of connecting theory to applied learning experiences through dozens of affiliations and partnerships with urban institutions, building communities within and beyond our classrooms and nurturing the human spirit. Our faculty members are intellectually adventurous and socially conscious. Our students study in the expansive environment of a great research university, and use the urban neighborhoods of New York City and countries around the world as their laboratories. Now in our 118th year of educating artists, professionals, scholars, and researchers, we are applying our creativity and knowledge where it is needed most.

Located in the heart of downtown New York, NYU Steinhardt's Department of Art and Art Professions is shaped by the intensity and innovation of the international art world. A home for artists who are celebrated for their dedication, creativity, and skill in exploring unconventional ideas, New York City has long been a place where art truly matters. The city's galleries, museums, schools, studios, and performance spaces are an integral part of our department, as are the University's vast intellectual and academic resources.

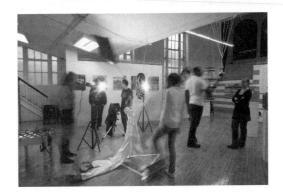

Visual Arts

New York University (continued)

The department's Barney Building, a six-story complex of studios, classrooms, and exhibition spaces—as well as facilities for painting, drawing, sculpture, craft media, printmaking, photography, video, and digital art—pays homage to the visionary and iconoclastic artists of its legendary East Village neighborhood. Enriched by this legacy, the department's interdisciplinary approach to art, with its commitment to individual insight and experimentation as well as collaboration and community practice, underscores the central role of contemporary art in translating social and historical change into human experience. We seek to nurture and empower our students and artists to find a visual language through which they can respond to current culture on their own terms.

The B.F.A. combines an ambitious series of interdisciplinary studio courses with art history, seminar, and liberal arts classes to expose students to a wide range of ideas and practices. Many participate in internships during the junior and senior years, and one or two semesters of study abroad is encouraged. In the senior year, students take the course Art, Culture, and Society, which culminates in a written thesis. With special permission, students may also enroll in a senior honors studio course in which they participate in group critiques and meet independently in their studio workspace with two senior mentors and visiting artists. Over the course of the senior year, all students develop a cohesive body of work as well as a written thesis outlining the ideas and contexts that drive their creative process. In the spring, students participate in formal exhibitions.

The M.F.A. and M.A. programs bring exceptional students together with artists, educators, therapists, administrators, and visual culture innovators who influence the visual arts at local, national, and international levels. The department offers top graduate-level internship and field placement experiences with unparalleled networking potential. Recent internships have included the Metropolitan Museum of Art, the Museum of Modern Art, the Whitney Museum of American Art, the New Museum, P.S. 1, Art in General, Percent for Art, Creative Time, Christie's, Sotheby's, and prominent galleries and artists' studios.

The department is a work in progress, bringing exceptional students together with internationally renowned artists, critics, educators, and art professionals in a shared exploration of the issues, forms, and ideas that continually redefine contemporary art.

Faculty, Resident Artists, and Alumni Faculty members are artists, educators, and professionals who are recognized nationally and internationally for their expertise and accomplishments. Faculty artists show extensively worldwide and represent broadly diverse approaches to content and media. Faculty arts professionals influence arts policy and practice. The department is supported by a strong network of alumni who exhibit, educate, curate, publish, manage, and consult all over the world.

Student Exhibition Opportunities Undergraduate and graduate students have many exhibition opportunities throughout the department and can submit proposals to participate as curators and exhibitors in the Rosenberg Gallery and the Commons. Barney Building open houses and open studios are organized twice a year, and all students are encouraged to participate. The department's 80 Washington Square East Galleries provide excellent professional exhibition space in the heart of the campus.

Special Programs Undergraduates are encouraged to enroll in one of several excellent University-based study-abroad programs in Berlin, Buenos Aires, Florence, Ghana, London, Madrid, Paris, Prague, and Shanghai. Graduate summer-study-abroad programs include studio art in Venice; photography in China; visual arts culture in Cape Town and Pretoria, South Africa; and arts administration in the Netherlands and Berlin. A high school residential summer art intensive allows young artists ages 16 to 18 the opportunity to explore their ideas in the heart of the international art world.

Tisch School of the Arts - Department of Photography and Imaging

New York University

New York, New York

Independent, coed. Urban campus. Total enrollment: 41,783. Art program established 1965.

Degrees Bachelor of Fine Arts. Majors and concentrations: photography and imaging.

Enrollment 130 total; all undergraduate.

Art Student Profile 63% females, 37% males, 20% minorities, 5% international.

Art Faculty 10 undergraduate (full-time), 20 undergraduate (part-time). 50% of full-time faculty have terminal degrees. Graduate students do not teach undergraduate courses. Undergraduate student–faculty ratio: 4:1.

Student Life Student groups/activities include Community Connections, The Collective, Tisch Talent Guild.

Expenses for 2007–2008 Application fee: $65. Comprehensive fee: $47,490 includes full-time tuition ($33,268), mandatory fees ($2022), and college room and board ($12,200). Full-time tuition and fees vary according to course load and program. Room and board charges vary according to board plan and housing facility. Special program-related fees: $255 per course for photo lab fee.

Application Procedures Students admitted directly into the professional program freshman year. Deadline for freshmen: January 15; transfers: April 1. Notification date for freshmen: April 1; transfers: May 15. Required: essay, high school transcript, college transcript(s) for transfer students, 2 letters of recommendation, portfolio, SAT or ACT test scores, resumé, department questionnaire. Recommended: minimum 3.0 high school GPA.

Web Site http://photo.tisch.nyu.edu

Undergraduate Contact Ms. Patricia A. Decker, Director of Recruitment, Tisch School of the Arts, New York University, 721 Broadway, 8th Floor, New York, New York 10003-6807; 212-998-1900, fax: 212-995-4060.

North Carolina School of the Arts

Winston-Salem, North Carolina

State-supported, coed. Urban campus. Total enrollment: 864. Art program established 1990.

Degrees Bachelor of Fine Arts in the area of filmmaking. Majors and concentrations: cinematography, directing, editing and sound, production, production/design, screenwriting.

Enrollment 243 total; 204 undergraduate, 39 nonprofessional degree.

Art Student Profile 29% females, 71% males, 17% minorities, 2% international.

Art Faculty 25 undergraduate (full-time), 2 undergraduate (part-time), 2 graduate (full-time). 14% of full-time faculty have terminal degrees. Graduate students do not teach undergraduate courses. Undergraduate student–faculty ratio: 10:1.

Student Life Special housing available for art students.

Expenses for 2007–2008 Application fee: $50. State resident tuition: $3224 full-time. Nonresident tuition: $14,654 full-time. Mandatory fees: $1837 full-time. Full-time tuition and fees vary according to program. College room and board: $6431. College room only: $3289. Room and board charges vary according to board plan and housing facility. Special program-related fees: $750 per year for supplies.

Financial Aid Program-specific awards: 100 talent/need scholarships ($1879).

Application Procedures Students admitted directly into the professional program freshman year. Deadline for freshmen and transfers: March 1. Required: essay, high school transcript, college transcript(s) for transfer students, 2 letters of recommendation, interview, audition, on-site writing exercise. Recommended: SAT or ACT test scores.

Web Site http://www.ncarts.edu

Undergraduate Contact Ms. Sheeler Lawson, Director of Admissions, North Carolina School of the Arts, 1533 South Main Street, Winston-Salem, North Carolina 27117; 336-770-3291, fax: 336-770-3370, e-mail address: admissions@ncarts.edu

Northern Illinois University

De Kalb, Illinois

State-supported, coed. Small town campus. Total enrollment: 25,254.

Degrees Bachelor of Arts in the areas of art history, art; Bachelor of Fine Arts in the area of studio and design; Bachelor of Science in the area of art education. Majors and concentrations: art education, art history, art/fine arts, ceramics, fibers, illustration, metals and jewelry, painting/drawing, photography, printmaking, sculpture, time arts, visual communication. Graduate degrees offered: Master of Arts in the area of studio art and design; Master of Fine Arts in the area of studio and design; Master of Science in Education in the area of art education. Cross-registration with twelve Illinois community colleges. Program accredited by NASAD.

Northern Illinois University (continued)

Enrollment 690 undergraduate, 124 graduate, 109 nonprofessional degree.

Art Student Profile 59% females, 41% males, 6% minorities, 1% international.

Art Faculty 41 total (full-time), 21 total (part-time). 90% of full-time faculty have terminal degrees. Graduate students teach a few undergraduate courses. Undergraduate student–faculty ratio: 16:1.

Student Life Student groups/activities include National Art Education Association Student Chapter, American Institute of Graphic Arts Student Chapter, Ars Nova Student Group. Special housing available for art students.

Expenses for 2007–2008 State resident tuition: $5940 full-time. Nonresident tuition: $12,500 full-time. Mandatory fees: $1515 full-time. College room and board: $7568. Room and board charges vary according to board plan and housing facility. Special program-related fees: $5–$126 per course for lab/materials fees/visiting artists and scholars/technology.

Financial Aid Program-specific awards: 6–12 tuition scholarships for entering first year students ($2362–$3148).

Application Procedures Students admitted directly into the professional program freshman year. Deadline for freshmen and transfers: continuous. Notification date for freshmen and transfers: continuous. Required: high school transcript, college transcript(s) for transfer students, minimum 2.0 high school GPA, SAT or ACT test scores (minimum composite ACT score of 19), standing in top half of graduating class, completion of college preparatory courses.

Web Site http://www.vpa.niu.edu/art/

Undergraduate Contact Office of Admissions, Northern Illinois University, Williston Hall Room 101, De Kalb, Illinois 60115; 815-753-0446, fax: 815-753-1783, e-mail address: admissions-info@niu.edu

Graduate Contact Yale Factor, Coordinator of Graduate Program, School of Art, Northern Illinois University, De Kalb, Illinois 60115-2883; 815-753-0292.

Northern Kentucky University

Highland Heights, Kentucky

State-supported, coed. Suburban campus. Total enrollment: 14,785. Art program established 1968.

Degrees Bachelor of Fine Arts in the areas of graphic design, intermedia, art history with studio. Majors and concentrations: applied photography, art education, art history, ceramics, graphic design, intermedia, painting/drawing, photography, printmaking, sculpture. Cross-registration with Northern Kentucky/Greater Cincinnati Consortium of Colleges and Universities.

Enrollment 410 total; 60 undergraduate, 350 nonprofessional degree.

Art Student Profile 60% females, 40% males, 2% minorities, 1% international.

Art Faculty 19 undergraduate (full-time), 7 undergraduate (part-time). 90% of full-time faculty have terminal degrees. Graduate students do not teach undergraduate courses. Undergraduate student–faculty ratio: 17:1.

Student Life Student groups/activities include Students in Design, Mudd Club, Photography Club.

Expenses for 2008–2009 Application fee: $40. State resident tuition: $6528 full-time. Nonresident tuition: $11,952 full-time. College room and board: $6560. Special program-related fees: $20–$200 per semester for incidental fee, technology fee, and support of learning surcharge.

Financial Aid Program-specific awards: 1–2 Friends of Fine Arts Awards for continuing students ($2500), 6 University Art Awards for continuing students ($2500), 1 Schiff Scholarship for continuing students ($2500).

Application Procedures Students apply for admission into the professional program by sophomore, junior year. Deadline for freshmen and transfers: August 1. Required: high school transcript, college transcript(s) for transfer students, minimum 2.0 high school GPA, ACT test score only, minimum 2.5 college GPA with a 3.0 art major GPA.

Web Site http://www.nku.edu/~art

Undergraduate Contact Thomas McGovern, Office of Admissions, Northern Kentucky University, Lucas Administrative Center, Highland Heights, Kentucky 41099; 859-572-5220, fax: 859-572-6665, e-mail address: admitnku@nku.edu

Northwestern State University of Louisiana

Natchitoches, Louisiana

State-supported, coed. Small town campus. Total enrollment: 9,037.

Degrees Bachelor of Fine Arts in the area of fine and graphic arts. Majors and concentrations: graphic communication, studio art. Program accredited by NASAD.

Enrollment 112 total; all undergraduate.

Art Student Profile 60% females, 40% males, 20% minorities, 5% international.

Art Faculty 7 total (full-time), 1 total (part-time). 83% of full-time faculty have terminal degrees. Graduate students teach a few undergraduate courses. Undergraduate student–faculty ratio: 16:1.

Student Life Student groups/activities include Kappa Pi International Art Fraternity (Gamma Mu Chapter), Student Art Show. Special housing available for art students.

Expenses for 2007–2008 Application fee: $20. State resident tuition: $2240 full-time. Nonresident tuition: $8318 full-time. Mandatory fees: $1288 full-time. Full-time tuition and fees vary according to course load. College room and board: $5850. College room only: $3700. Room and board charges vary according to board plan, housing facility, and location. Special program-related fees: $25–$50 for supplies, models.

Financial Aid Program-specific awards: 10 art scholarships ($500).

Application Procedures Students admitted directly into the professional program freshman year. Deadline for freshmen and transfers: continuous. Required: high school transcript, college transcript(s) for transfer students, minimum 2.0 high school GPA, SAT or ACT test scores (minimum composite ACT score of 20), 16.5 units of Regents' High School core curriculum (T.O.P.S.). Recommended: minimum 3.0 high school GPA, letter of recommendation, portfolio. Portfolio reviews held continu-

ously on campus; the submission of slides may be substituted for portfolios.

Web Site http://www.nsula.edu/capa

Undergraduate Contact Dr. Roger A. Chandler, Associate Professor/Coordinator of Fine and Graphic Art, Fine and Graphic Arts, Northwestern State University of Louisiana, NSU College Avenue, Natchitoches, Louisiana 71497; 318-357-6176, fax: 318-357-5906, e-mail address: chandlerr@nsula.edu

Notre Dame de Namur University

Belmont, California

Independent Roman Catholic, coed. Suburban campus. Total enrollment: 1,491. Art program established 1851.

Degrees Bachelor of Arts; Bachelor of Fine Arts. Majors and concentrations: art, art history, graphic design, painting/drawing, printmaking, studio art. Cross-registration with Trinity College, Emmanuel College.

Enrollment 35 total; all undergraduate.

Art Student Profile 70% females, 30% males, 40% minorities, 10% international.

Art Faculty 2 undergraduate (full-time), 7 undergraduate (part-time). 100% of full-time faculty have terminal degrees. Graduate students do not teach undergraduate courses. Undergraduate student–faculty ratio: 7:1.

Student Life Student groups/activities include College Art Association, American Institute of Graphic Arts.

Expenses for 2008–2009 Application fee: $50. Comprehensive fee: $36,250 includes full-time tuition ($25,300), mandatory fees ($270), and college room and board ($10,680). College room only: $7000.

Financial Aid Program-specific awards: 8 Emerging Artist Talent Scholarships for program students ($7500–$9500).

Application Procedures Students admitted directly into the professional program freshman year. Deadline for freshmen and transfers: continuous. Notification date for freshmen and transfers: continuous. Required: essay, high school transcript, college transcript(s) for transfer students, letter of recommendation, SAT or ACT test scores, minimum 2.0 college

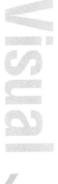

Notre Dame de Namur University (continued)

GPA for transfers. Recommended: portfolio. Portfolio reviews held 24 times on campus; the submission of slides may be substituted for portfolios.

Web Site http://www.ndnu.edu

Undergraduate Contact Betty Friedman, Chair, Department of Art, Notre Dame de Namur University, 1500 Ralston Avenue, Belmont, California 94002-1997; 650-508-3631, fax: 650-508-3488, e-mail address: bfriedman@ndnu.edu

NSCAD University

Halifax, Nova Scotia, Canada

Province-supported, coed. Urban campus. Art program established 1887.

Degrees Bachelor of Arts in the area of art history; Bachelor of Design; Bachelor of Fine Arts in the area of fine arts. Majors and concentrations: art history, art/fine arts, ceramics, film, interdisciplinary design, jewelry and metalsmithing, media arts, photography, textiles. Graduate degrees offered: Master of Arts in the area of art education; Master of Fine Arts in the areas of fine arts, design, craft. Cross-registration with Dalhousie University, St. Mary's University, Mount St. Vincent University, University of King's College.

Enrollment 1,106 total; 1,088 undergraduate, 18 graduate.

Art Student Profile 70% females, 30% males, 6% international.

Art Faculty 42 total (full-time), 38 total (part-time). 95% of full-time faculty have terminal degrees. Graduate students teach a few undergraduate courses. Undergraduate student–faculty ratio: 12:1.

Student Life Student groups/activities include "SOTA" (college publication), Women's Collective, Mosaic (minority ethnic group).

Expenses for 2007–2008 Application fee: $35 Canadian dollars. Tuition and fee charges are reported in Canadian dollars. Province resident tuition: $5500 full-time. Mandatory fees: $375 full-time. International student tuition: $12,125 full-time.

Financial Aid Program-specific awards: 85 merit scholarships for those demonstrating talent and academic achievement ($800), 6 Joseph Beuys Memorial Scholarships for those demonstrating talent and academic achievement ($1500), 5 Harrison McCain Scholarships for those demonstrating talent and academic achievement ($13,500).

Application Procedures Students admitted directly into the professional program freshman year. Deadline for freshmen: March 15; transfers: February 15. Notification date for freshmen and transfers: June 20. Required: essay, high school transcript, college transcript(s) for transfer students, portfolio, minimum TOEFL score of 577 for non-English speaking applicants, 2 letters of recommendation for mature applicants. Recommended: interview. Portfolio reviews held twice on campus; the submission of slides may be substituted for portfolios for all portfolio submissions.

Web Site http://www.nscad.ns.ca

Contact Mr. Terrence Bailey, Director of Admissions and Enrollment Services, Office of Student and Academic Services, NSCAD University, 5163 Duke Street, Halifax, Nova Scotia B3J 3J6, Canada; 902-494-8129, fax: 902-425-2987, e-mail address: admissions@nscad.ca

Ohio Northern University

Ada, Ohio

Independent, coed. Small town campus. Total enrollment: 3,603. Art program established 1961.

Degrees Bachelor of Fine Arts. Majors and concentrations: advertising design, graphic design, studio art. Cross-registration with University of Ulster (UK), Burren College of Art (Ireland), Studio Art Centers International (Italy).

Enrollment 30 total; all undergraduate.

Art Student Profile 50% females, 50% males, 3% minorities, 1% international.

Art Faculty 4 undergraduate (full-time), 5 undergraduate (part-time). 100% of full-time faculty have terminal degrees. Graduate students do not teach undergraduate courses. Undergraduate student–faculty ratio: 5:1.

Student Life Student groups/activities include Kappa Pi/Alpha Epsilon Rho, Theta Alpha Phi, American Institute of Graphic Arts.

Expenses for 2008–2009 Application fee: $30. Comprehensive fee: $38,655 includes full-time tuition ($30,555), mandatory fees ($210), and college room and board ($7890). College room only: $3945.

Financial Aid Program-specific awards: art talent awards for art majors ($2500–$8000).

Application Procedures Students admitted directly into the professional program freshman year. Deadline for freshmen and transfers: continuous. Notification date for freshmen and transfers: August 15. Required: high school transcript, college transcript(s) for transfer students, minimum 2.0 high school GPA, SAT or ACT test scores, minimum 2.5 high school GPA, portfolio for scholarship consideration. Recommended: essay, minimum 3.0 high school GPA, interview, portfolio. Portfolio reviews held by request on campus; the submission of slides may be substituted for portfolios with approval from the department.

Web Site http://www.onu.edu

Undergraduate Contact Ms. Karen Condeni, Vice President and Dean of Admissions, Ohio Northern University, 525 South Main Street, Ada, Ohio 45810; 419-772-2260, fax: 419-772-2313, e-mail address: admissions-ug@onu.edu

The Ohio State University

Columbus, Ohio

State-supported, coed. Total enrollment: 52,568.

Degrees Bachelor of Fine Arts. Majors and concentrations: art and technology, ceramics, glass, painting/drawing, photography, printmaking, sculpture. Graduate degrees offered: Master of Fine Arts in the areas of ceramics, glass, sculpture, painting/drawing, printmaking, photography, art and technology. Program accredited by NASAD.

Enrollment 345 total; 158 undergraduate, 54 graduate, 133 nonprofessional degree.

Art Student Profile 60% females, 40% males, 3% minorities, 20% international.

Art Faculty 22 total (full-time), 15 total (part-time). 100% of full-time faculty have terminal degrees. Graduate students teach more than half of undergraduate courses. Undergraduate student–faculty ratio: 7:1.

Student Life Student groups/activities include Student League of Independent Potters, Student Printmakers Association, Undergraduate Student Art League. Special housing available for art students.

Expenses for 2007–2008 Application fee: $40. State resident tuition: $8406 full-time. Nonresident tuition: $21,015 full-time. Mandatory fees: $270 full-time. Full-time tuition and fees vary according to course load, program, reciprocity agreements, and student level. College room and board: $7365. College room only: $4605. Room and board charges vary according to board plan and housing facility. Special program-related fees: $50 per quarter for technology fee.

Financial Aid Program-specific awards: 1 Hoylt L. Sherman Scholarship for art majors ($1500), 2–5 Arthur E. Baggs Memorial Scholarships for ceramic majors ($750), 1–3 Robert and Marion Gatrell Scholarships for art majors ($900), 1–5 Edith Fergus Gilmore Awards for art majors ($400).

Application Procedures Students apply for admission into the professional program by sophomore, junior year. Deadline for freshmen and transfers: continuous. Required: high school transcript, college transcript(s) for transfer students, SAT or ACT test scores, portfolio upon completion of foundation courses. Portfolio reviews held twice a year on campus; the submission of slides may be substituted for portfolios for transfer applicants when original work is no longer available or for large works of art and three-dimensional pieces.

Web Site http://art.osu.edu

Undergraduate Contact University Admissions, The Ohio State University, 1800 Cannon Drive, 3rd Floor Lincoln Tower, Columbus, Ohio 43210; 614-292-3980, fax: 614-292-4818.

Graduate Contact Ms. Stephanie Hall, Assistant to Chair, Department of Art, The Ohio State University, 146 Hopkins Hall, 128 North Oval Mall, Columbus, Ohio 43210; 614-292-5072, fax: 614-292-1674, e-mail address: hall.1084@osu.edu

Oklahoma Baptist University

Shawnee, Oklahoma

Independent Southern Baptist, coed. Art program established 1980.

Oklahoma Baptist University (continued)

Degrees Bachelor of Fine Arts.

Enrollment 40 total; 6 undergraduate, 34 nonprofessional degree.

Art Student Profile 75% females, 25% males, 13% minorities.

Art Faculty 3 undergraduate (full-time), 3 undergraduate (part-time). 33% of full-time faculty have terminal degrees. Graduate students do not teach undergraduate courses. Undergraduate student–faculty ratio: 13:1.

Student Life Student groups/activities include Art Club.

Expenses for 2008–2009 Application fee: $25. One-time mandatory fee: $25. Comprehensive fee: $20,668 includes full-time tuition ($15,468) and college room and board ($5200). Special program-related fees: $25 per course for material fees.

Financial Aid Program-specific awards: 24 art scholarships for program majors ($1117).

Application Procedures Students admitted directly into the professional program freshman year. Deadline for freshmen and transfers: continuous. Required: high school transcript, college transcript(s) for transfer students, minimum 2.0 high school GPA, SAT or ACT test scores. Recommended: portfolio. Portfolio reviews held continuously on campus; the submission of slides may be substituted for portfolios when distance is prohibitive.

Web Site http://www.okbu.edu

Undergraduate Contact Mr. Bruce Perkins, Director of Admissions, Oklahoma Baptist University, Box 61174, 500 West University, Shawnee, Oklahoma 74804; 800-654-3285, fax: 405-878-2046, e-mail address: bruce.perkins@okbu.edu

Oklahoma State University

Stillwater, Oklahoma

State-supported, coed. Small town campus. Total enrollment: 23,005. Art program established 1924.

Web Site http://osu.okstate.edu/

Old Dominion University

Norfolk, Virginia

State-supported, coed. Urban campus. Total enrollment: 22,287. Art program established 1963.

Degrees Bachelor of Fine Arts in the area of studio art. Majors and concentrations: art education, drawing, fibers, graphic design, jewelry and metalsmithing, painting, photography, printmaking, sculpture, studio art. Graduate degrees offered: Master of Fine Arts in the area of visual studies. Cross-registration with Tidewater Community College, Norfolk State University. Program accredited by NASAD.

Enrollment 340 total; 300 undergraduate, 15 graduate, 25 nonprofessional degree.

Art Student Profile 52% females, 48% males, 15% minorities, 10% international.

Art Faculty 14 undergraduate (full-time), 27 undergraduate (part-time), 12 graduate (full-time), 6 graduate (part-time). 92% of full-time faculty have terminal degrees. Graduate students teach a few undergraduate courses. Undergraduate student–faculty ratio: 18:1.

Student Life Student groups/activities include Student Art League, Art Education Club.

Expenses for 2008–2009 Application fee: $40. Special program-related fees: $20–$30 per course for lab fees.

Financial Aid Program-specific awards: 3 Sibley Scholarships for enrolled program students by portfolio competition ($1000), 2 Margolious Scholarships for enrolled program students by portfolio competition ($700), 1–2 Gorlinsky Scholarships for enrolled program students by portfolio competition ($300–$500).

Application Procedures Students admitted directly into the professional program freshman year. Deadline for freshmen: March 15; transfers: July 1. Required: high school transcript, college transcript(s) for transfer students, minimum 2.0 high school GPA, SAT or ACT test scores, portfolio for transfer students. Recommended: interview, portfolio. Portfolio reviews held on a case-by-case basis on campus; the submission of slides may be substituted for portfolios at student's discretion.

Web Site http://www.odu.edu/al/art

Undergraduate Contact Mr. Ken Daley, Chief Departmental Advisor, Art Department, Old Dominion University, Visual Arts Building, 49th

Street, Norfolk, Virginia 23529; 757-683-4047, fax: 757-683-5923, e-mail address: kdaley@odu.edu

Graduate Contact Mr. Elliott Jones, Graduate Program Director, Visual Studies Department, Old Dominion University, Visual Arts Building, 49th Street, Norfolk, Virginia 23529; 757-683-4047, fax: 757-683-5923, e-mail address: ejones@odu.edu

O'More College of Design

Franklin, Tennessee

Independent, coed, primarily women. Small town campus. Total enrollment: 219. Art program established 1970.

Web Site http://www.omorecollege.edu/

Oregon College of Art & Craft

Portland, Oregon

Independent, coed. Urban campus. Total enrollment: 153 (2007). Art program established 1994.

Degrees Bachelor of Fine Arts in the area of crafts. Majors and concentrations: book arts, ceramics, fibers, metals, painting/drawing, photography, wood. Cross-registration with All Oregon Independent Colleges. Program accredited by NASAD.

Enrollment 139 total; 134 undergraduate, 5 nonprofessional degree.

Art Student Profile 65% females, 35% males, 8% minorities, 2% international.

Art Faculty 10 undergraduate (full-time), 15 undergraduate (part-time). 90% of full-time faculty have terminal degrees. Graduate students do not teach undergraduate courses. Undergraduate student–faculty ratio: 9:1.

Student Life Student groups/activities include teaching summer children's classes, Annual Juried Student Show, Student Lecture Series. Special housing available for art students.

Expenses for 2007–2008 Application fee: $35. Comprehensive fee: $26,585 includes full-time tuition ($17,745), mandatory fees ($1340), and college room and board ($7500). College room only: $3600. Room and board charges vary

according to location. Special program-related fees: $1000 per year for studio fees.

Financial Aid Program-specific awards: 85 tuition grants for those demonstrating need ($1500), 52 tuition work-study awards for those demonstrating need ($2300), 5 merit scholarships for talented incoming students ($5000), 2 May Georges Fibers Scholarships for first, second, and third-year students ($500–$3000), 1 Jean Vollum Metals Scholarship for first, second, and third-year students ($500–$1000), 2 Oregon Guild of Woodworkers Scholarships for first, second, and third-year students ($250).

Application Procedures Students admitted directly into the professional program freshman year. Deadline for freshmen and transfers: continuous. Required: essay, high school transcript, college transcript(s) for transfer students, 2 letters of recommendation, interview, portfolio, minimum 2.5 high school GPA for applicants direct from high school, minimum 2.0 college GPA for transfer students. Recommended: minimum 3.0 high school GPA, SAT or ACT test scores. Portfolio reviews held as needed on campus and off campus at National Portfolio Days; the submission of slides may be substituted for portfolios (slides preferred).

Web Site http://www.ocac.edu

Undergraduate Contact Debrah J. Spencer, Interim Director of Admissions, Oregon College of Art & Craft, 8245 Southwest Barnes Road, Portland, Oregon 97225; 800-390-0632 ext. 129, fax: 503-297-9651, e-mail address: admissions@ocac.edu

Otis College of Art and Design

Los Angeles, California

Independent, coed. Urban campus. Total enrollment: 1,177. Art program established 1918.

Degrees Bachelor of Fine Arts in the areas of fine arts, architecture/landscape/interiors, communication arts, digital media, fashion design, interactive product design, toy design. Majors and concentrations: advertising design, architecture, art/fine arts, digital multi-media, drawing, fashion design and technology, graphic design, illustration, interior design, landscape architecture, new genres, painting, photogra-

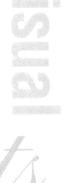

Otis College of Art and Design (continued)

phy, printmaking, product design, sculpture, toy design, video art. Graduate degrees offered: Master of Fine Arts in the areas of painting, photography, sculpture, new media, writing, public practice, graphic design. Program accredited by NASAD.

Enrollment 1,177 total; 1,121 undergraduate, 56 graduate.

Art Student Profile 66% females, 34% males, 55% minorities, 12% international.

Art Faculty 59 total (full-time), 212 total (part-time). 71% of full-time faculty have terminal degrees. Graduate students teach a few undergraduate courses. Undergraduate student–faculty ratio: 9:1.

Student Life Student groups/activities include Wash Magazine, SIGGRAPH, Cultural and Social Network Groups. Special housing available for art students.

Expenses for 2007–2008 Application fee: $50. Tuition: $28,346 full-time. Mandatory fees: $600 full-time. Special program-related fees: $150 per semester for general college materials fee, $200 per semester for registration fee.

Financial Aid Program-specific awards: 805 Otis Institutional Grants for program students ($7734), 24 international student scholarships for international students ($5244), 99 transfer student scholarships for transfer students ($2878).

Application Procedures Students admitted directly into the professional program freshman year. Deadline for freshmen and transfers: continuous. Notification date for freshmen and transfers: continuous. Required: essay, high school transcript, college transcript(s) for transfer students, portfolio, SAT or ACT test scores, minimum TOEFL score of 550 (paper-based), 79 (internet), 213 (computer-based) for international applicants 79/internet, minimum 2.5 high school GPA/college GPA. Recommended: minimum 3.0 high school GPA, 2 letters of recommendation, interview. Portfolio reviews held continuously on campus and off campus at National Portfolio Days; the submission of slides may be substituted for portfolios (slides or CDs/DVDs preferred).

Web Site http://www.otis.edu

Undergraduate Contact Mr. Marc D. Meredith, Dean of Admissions, Admissions Office, Otis College of Art and Design, 9045 Lincoln Boulevard, Los Angeles, California 90045; 310-665-6820, fax: 310-665-6821, e-mail address: admissions@otis.edu

Graduate Contact Graduate Studies, Otis College of Art and Design, 9045 Lincoln Boulevard, Los Angeles, California 90045; 310-665-6892, fax: 310-665-6890, e-mail address: grads@otis.edu

More About the School

Otis prepares diverse students of art and design to enrich the world through their creativity, their skills, and their vision.

A four-year education at Otis begins with Foundation year, during which students from all majors take core studio classes: drawing and composition, figure-drawing, and two- and three-dimensional design. The philosophy is that all artists and designers need well-developed hand-eye skills and sophisticated creative-thinking skills in order to succeed. As they move into the second year, students begin to make their skills more specialized according to their intended major. Top-level studio training in all disciplines is enhanced by a liberal arts and sciences curriculum (LAS) that emphasizes cultural curiosity and intellectual rigor. The LAS classes are intended to complement and expand students' critical thinking as they prepare for the workplaces of the future.

Faculty members who are working professionals, along with visiting artists, designers, lecturers, and writers, share a wealth of expertise and new perspectives with the diverse student population. Lectures, hands-on instruction, studio visits, and personal critiques facilitate dynamic teacher/student and student/student interactions. As part of the commitment to giving students every opportunity to

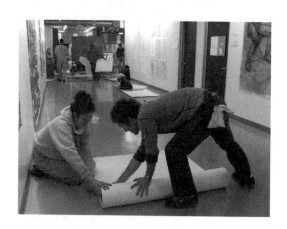

succeed, Otis offers a new Learning Resource Center. Otis also offers an Honors program in liberal studies and art history.

A network of alumni includes individuals who have created such cultural icons as the first Walt Disney animated cartoons; the Academy Award–winning special effects for *Lord of the Rings;* products and promotional materials for Columbia, A&M, and Virgin Records; editorial illustrations and cover art for the *Los Angeles Times, Time, Omni, The New Yorker, Buzz,* and *American Film*; costumes for the *Titanic,* Bram Stoker's *Dracula,* and *Harry Potter* and numerous Academy Award–winning films costumed by alumna Edith Head; production design for Spike Lee; and the fashion-forward imagery of such industry leaders as NIKE, Guess?, Richard Tyler, Isaac Mizrahi, Mossimo, and Anne Cole. Otis alumni are featured in major museums, such as the Whitney Museum of American Art; Museum of Modern Art, New York; Guggenheim Museum; Art Institute of Chicago; Corcoran Gallery of Art; Los Angeles County Museum of Art; and Museum of Contemporary Art, Los Angeles, and in galleries around the world.

Otis College of Art and Design, founded in 1918, stands as one of LA's oldest and most important cultural institutions. Otis is proud of its long traditions. Its growth and dynamic character demonstrate the long-term commitment of the College, its faculty members, and its administration as well as the solid support of the art, design, and philanthropic communities. Today's Otis students are artists and designers dedicated to developing technical, critical, and creative skills that can lead them into the future.

Program Facilities The new Galef Center for Fine Arts houses painting and sculpture studios, photo/video studios, and individual student spaces. Other facilities include wood/metal/plastic shops; expanded industry-standard Mac/Windows lab and scanning, large-scale output, and 3-D laser modeling; video/sound editing; lithography/etching presses; the city's oldest, most renowned college fine arts press; extensive library holdings in fine art, design, art history, humanities, critical studies, and periodicals; visual resources center; and Graduate Studios.

Faculty and Visiting Artists Professional faculty members include fashion, toy, digital, and product designers; architects; photographers; and fine artists, among them Roy Dowell, Annette Kapon, Suzanne Lacy, Linda Pollari, Harry Mott, Martin Caveza, Steve McAdam, Ave Pildas, Rosemary Brantley, Scott Grieger, Holly Tempo, Carole Caroompas, Linda Burnham, Judie Bamber, Meg Cranston, Dana Duff, Linda Hudson, Larry Johnson, Debra Ballard, Parme Giutini, Heather Joseph-Witham, and Paul Vangelisti. Guest lecturers and visiting artists/designers include Dave Hickey, Alexis Smith, Barbara Kruger, Dan Graham, Rod Beatty, Bob Mackie, Jeremy Scott, Eduardo Lucero, and Isabel Toldeo.

Student Exhibit Opportunities Students have the opportunity to exhibit their work at numerous locations and functions, such as the Abe and Helen Bolsky Gallery, extensive informal exhibit space in the Galef Center, the annual senior show in all departments, the MFA exhibition, local and national competitions, juried fashion shows, the annual literary magazine, and the Otis Design and Illustration Groups.

Special Programs Special Programs include the Summer of Art precollege program; summer study in Pont-Aven, France; the Spring Paris trip for Foundation students; internship opportunities in all departments; OTIS-LA, an intensive language and acculturation program designed for incoming international students; and community outreach through Otis Evening College. A new fine arts program, ACT (Artists, Community, and Teaching), gives students an introduction to teaching art as a social practice and as a career path.

Housing The College recently added Otis Housing, which is based in a nearby luxury apartment complex and overseen by the Student Affairs Office. Geared toward first-year students, the apartments are two-bedroom/two-bath units that are shared by 4 students. Paid utilities, secure parking, T1 access, and full kitchens, along with a pool, spa, and recreation facilities, make Otis Housing attractive and comfortable. Residence Life staff members live in the complex.

Campuses Otis College of Art and Design's Goldsmith Campus consists of the Galef Center for Fine Arts (housing the School of Fine Arts) and Kathleen Ahmanson Hall (housing Architecture/Landscape/Interiors, Communication Arts, Digital Media, Interactive Product Design, and Toy Design). The campus is located on Los Angeles' Westside. Nearby are the communities of Venice and Santa Monica, home to many prominent fine arts studios and galleries. The location of the Goldsmith campus and the nearby Graduate Studios places students in the center of the vital, international artistic/design community that fuels the Los Angeles fine arts, toy, digital media, and product design worlds.

Otis School of Fashion is located in LA's downtown fashion district within the California Mart Center that is headquarters for many fashion collections and vendors. This places students' day-to-

Otis College of Art and Design (continued)

day activities in a unique relationship to an industry that is in need of talented and well-educated designers. The program's structure brings in top designers to work as mentors with junior and senior students on projects from children's sports and swimwear categories to finely tailored men's and glamorous women's evening wear. The annual Otis Scholarship Benefit Fashion Show is an important fashion industry and celebrity event that showcases the best work created by students.

Pacific Northwest College of Art

Portland, Oregon

Independent, coed. Urban campus. Total enrollment: 432. Art program established 1909.
Web Site http://www.pnca.edu/

Paier College of Art, Inc.

Hamden, Connecticut

Proprietary, coed. Suburban campus. Total enrollment: 249. Art program established 1946.

Degrees Bachelor of Fine Arts. Majors and concentrations: art/fine arts, graphic design, illustration, interior design, photography.

Enrollment 226 total; all undergraduate.

Art Student Profile 71% females, 29% males, 1% minorities, 1% international.

Art Faculty 10 undergraduate (full-time), 36 undergraduate (part-time). 79% of full-time faculty have terminal degrees. Graduate students do not teach undergraduate courses. Undergraduate student–faculty ratio: 7:1.

Expenses for 2008–2009 Application fee: $25. Tuition: $12,000 full-time. Mandatory fees: $385 full-time. Special program-related fees: $100–$250 per course for lab and model fees.

Financial Aid Program-specific awards: Paier Minority Scholarship for minority students, PCA tuition reductions for those demonstrating need.

Application Procedures Students admitted directly into the professional program freshman year. Deadline for freshmen and transfers: continuous. Required: high school transcript,

college transcript(s) for transfer students, 2 letters of recommendation, interview, portfolio, SAT or ACT test scores. Portfolio reviews held twice and by appointment on campus; the submission of slides may be substituted for portfolios for large works of art.

Web Site http://www.paiercollegeofart.edu

Undergraduate Contact Ms. Lynn Pascale, Secretary, Admissions Department, Paier College of Art, Inc., 20 Gorham Avenue, Hamden, Connecticut 06514-3902; 203-287-3031, fax: 203-287-3021, e-mail address: paier.admin@snet.net

The New School
Parsons The New School for Design

New York, New York

Independent, coed. Urban campus. Total enrollment: 3,948. Art program established 1896.

Degrees Bachelor of Fine Arts in the areas of fine art, illustration, communication design, fashion design, product design, architectural design, interior design, photography, integrated design curriculum, design and technology, environmental studies; Bachelor of Business Administration in the area of design and management. Majors and concentrations: architectural design, architecture, art/fine arts, communication design, design and management, design technology, environmental studies, fashion design, fashion merchandising, graphic arts, history of decorative arts, illustration, integrated design curriculum, interior design, lighting design, photography, product design. Graduate degrees offered: Master of Arts in the area of history of decorative arts; Master of Fine Arts in the areas of design and technology, fine arts, lighting design, photography; Master of Architecture. Cross-registration with Eugene Lange College The New School for Liberal Arts. Program accredited by NASAD.

Enrollment 3,948 total; 3,537 undergraduate, 411 graduate.

Art Student Profile 77% females, 23% males, 44% minorities, 32% international.

Art Faculty 132 total (full-time), 860 total (part-time). 60% of full-time faculty have terminal degrees. Graduate students do not teach undergraduate courses. Undergraduate student–faculty ratio: 9:1.

Student Life Student groups/activities include Student Gallery, Student Government.

Expenses for 2007–2008 Application fee: $50. Comprehensive fee: $44,390 includes full-time tuition ($31,940), mandatory fees ($700), and college room and board ($11,750). College room only: $8750. Room and board charges vary according to board plan and housing facility.

Financial Aid Program-specific awards: Parsons Scholarships for those demonstrating need, University Scholars Scholarships for African-American and Latino students demonstrating need, Parsons Restricted Scholarships for those demonstrating need and academic achievement.

Application Procedures Students admitted directly into the professional program freshman year. Deadline for freshmen and transfers: continuous. Notification date for freshmen and transfers: July 1. Required: high school transcript, college transcript(s) for transfer students, minimum 2.0 high school GPA, portfolio, SAT or ACT test scores, home examination, minimum TOEFL score of 550 (paper-based) for all non-native speakers of English. Recommended: minimum 3.0 high school GPA, interview. Portfolio reviews held continuously by appointment on campus; the submission of slides may be substituted for portfolios when distance is prohibitive.

Web Site http://www.parsons.edu

Contact Terence Peavy, Assistant Vice President for Admissions, Parsons The New School for Design, 66 Fifth Avenue, New York, New York 10011-8878; 212-229-5150, fax: 212-229-8975, e-mail address: parsadm@newschool.edu

More About the School

At Parsons The New School for Design in New York City, students not only learn about art and design—they redefine it. They explore new ways to use art and design to address society's evolving needs, including using green technology in architecture projects, developing educational video games, and building portable, low-cost dwellings. The faculty members, many of whom are working artists and designers in New York City, bring their professional expertise into the classroom, challenging and encouraging students to realize their artistic and professional goals.

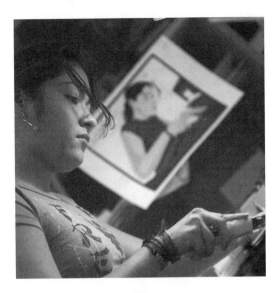

Parsons' undergraduate programs include architectural design, design and management, design and technology, fashion design, fashion marketing, fine arts, graphic design, illustration, integrated design, interior design, photography, product design, and an innovative new program in environmental studies (submitted for New York State approval).

Campus and Surroundings Parsons' New York City location provides students with perhaps their most important resource. An international center for art, entertainment, and commerce, the city is an exceptional place to study design. The School's main campus is located in Greenwich Village, and the Fashion Design Department is located in midtown, in the heart of the Fashion District. For Parsons' students, New York City becomes their home, campus, and source of ideas and inspiration. What else would someone expect from a city that is home to the Metropolitan Museum of Art, Cooper-Hewitt National Design Museum, the Museum of Modern Art, and about eighty other museums? Parsons' faculty members use New York City as an urban design laboratory, and Parsons students have the opportunity to show their work in some of the major galleries and design fairs in New York. In the past, student work has appeared in Chelsea galleries and museums, the International Contemporary Furniture Fair, the Art Director's Club, and Saks Fifth Avenue, among other notable venues.

Program Facilities Parsons The New School for Design is part of The New School, a major urban university, and students benefit from being part of a diverse university community. Campuswide liberal

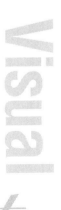

Visual Arts

Parsons The New School for Design (continued)

arts programs give Parsons students the opportunity to study with other New School faculty members and share classes with students in liberal studies, social and political science, and performing arts programs. Taking full advantage of the university setting, Parsons and Eugene Lang College The New School for Liberal Arts offer a five-year dual-degree program in which students simultaneously complete a fine arts or design B.F.A. and a liberal arts B.A. (http://www.newschool.edu/babfa) The New School offers students access to more than 1,000 computer workstations and several libraries. The Adam & Sophie Gimbel Design Library includes new and rare books and special collections books on art and design as well as mounted plates, slide collections, periodicals, and a digital image collection accessible online. A citywide consortium links the libraries of Parsons, The New School, New York University, and Cooper Union, providing unparalleled access to information. The new Angelo Donghia Materials Library and Study Center houses a computer lab, gallery, lecture hall, and library that put state-of-the-art materials at students' fingertips.

Plans unveiled the 25,000-square-foot Shelia C. Johnson Design Center at Fifth Avenue and 13th Street. This innovative "urban quad" features state-of-the-art galleries, lecture and meeting spaces, and the Anna-Maria and Stephen Kellen Archives Center, a major collection of drawings, photographs, letters, and objects documenting twentieth-century design.

Faculty, Resident Artists, and Alumni Parsons' alumni appear on the short list of outstanding practitioners in every realm of art and design. Alumni are an important part of the Parsons community and make up an unparalleled network of designers and artists. Notable graduates include Mark Badgley and James Mischka, fashion designers; Sheila Bridges, interior designer; Bridget de Socio, graphic designer; Peter de Seve, illustrator; Sue de Beer, artist; Angelo Donghia, interior designer; Jamie Drake, interior designer; Bea Feitler, graphic designer; Tom Ford, fashion designer; Albert Hadley, interior designer; Edward Hopper, artist; Marc Jacobs, fashion designer; Jasper Johns, artist; Donna Karan, fashion designer; Reed Krakoff, CEO of Coach; Alex Lee, product designer and president of OXO; Ryan McGinley, photographer; Lazaro Hernandez and Jack McCollough, fashion designers (Proenza Schouler); Norman Rockwell, illustrator; Joel Schumacher, filmmaker; Richard Silverstein, graphic designer; Anna Sui, fashion designer; and Brian Tolle, artist.

Student Performance Opportunities As a prominent member of New York City's art and design community, Parsons provides students with extraordinary opportunities to participate in public exhibitions and programs on campus and around the city. Supplementing studio and classwork, university-sponsored panel discussions and lectures offer interaction with top professionals from all areas of art and design. Past guests include Chuck Close, Frank Gehry, and Parsons alumna Donna Karan.

Special Programs Parsons has been an innovator in the field of art and design since the school's founding in 1896, and it was the first art and design school in America to found a campus abroad. Today, Parsons has affiliate schools in Paris; Kanazawa, Japan; Seoul, South Korea; and Altos de Chavon in the Dominican Republic.

Parsons' outstanding career services program helps connect students to internships while they are in school and exciting professional opportunities with top firms after they graduate. Current and past internships include Marc Jacobs, Polo–Ralph Lauren, HBO, MTV, the *New York Times, Rolling Stone* magazine, Marvel Comics, and the Museum of Modern Art.

Peck School of the Arts
See University of Wisconsin–Milwaukee

Pennsylvania Academy of the Fine Arts
Philadelphia, Pennsylvania

Independent, coed. Urban campus. Art program established 1805.

Degrees Bachelor of Fine Arts in the areas of painting, printmaking, sculpture, drawing. Majors and concentrations: drawing, painting, printmaking, sculpture. Graduate degrees offered: Master of Fine Arts in the areas of painting, sculpture, printmaking, drawing. Cross-registration with University of Pennsylvania. Program accredited by NASAD.

Enrollment 322 total; 226 undergraduate, 96 graduate.

Art Student Profile 50% females, 50% males, 16% minorities, 5% international.

Art Faculty 31 total (full-time), 32 total (part-time). 40% of full-time faculty have terminal degrees. Graduate students do not teach undergraduate courses. Undergraduate student–faculty ratio: 6:1.

Student Life Student groups/activities include visiting artists lectures, sculpture competitions, drawing marathon. Special housing available for art students.

Expenses for 2007–2008 Special program-related fees: $20 for locker fee, $20 for technology fee, $40 for student activity fee, $175 for general fee, $200 for studio deposit (3rd and 4th year).

Financial Aid Program-specific awards: travel scholarships for juniors and seniors, Institutional Scholarships for those demonstrating need and merit.

Application Procedures Students admitted directly into the professional program freshman year. Deadline for freshmen and transfers: March 1. Required: essay, high school transcript, college transcript(s) for transfer students, 2 letters of recommendation, portfolio, TOEFL score and affidavit of support for international applicants. Recommended: minimum 3.0 high school GPA, interview. Portfolio reviews held as needed on campus; the submission of slides may be substituted for portfolios for large works of art or when distance is prohibitive.

Web Site http://www.pafa.edu

Contact Stan Greidus, Vice President of Admissions and Financial Aid, Pennsylvania Academy of the Fine Arts, 128 North Broad Street, Philadelphia, Pennsylvania 19102; 215-972-7625, fax: 215-569-0153, e-mail address: admissions@pafa.edu

More About the Academy

The Pennsylvania Academy has been training America's best artists for more than 200 years. Steeped in history, the Academy has a long list of famous alumni and a current faculty of working professional artists who form a continuous tradition of excellence in the studio arts of painting, drawing, sculpture, and printmaking. Students at the Academy are passionate about their craft and their future as artists. The Academy teaches technique and imparts knowledge and skills to enable students to become the artists they want to be. The Academy is a unique community of working artists combined with a world-class collection of American art, located in one of the largest and liveliest art communities in the country.

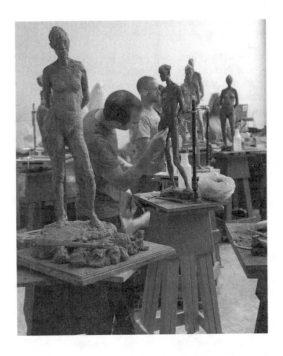

The Academy offers a two-year Master of Fine Arts (M.F.A.) Program, a one-year Post-Baccalaureate Certificate in Graduate Studies, a four-year Certificate Program, the Academy Bachelor of Fine Arts (B.F.A.), and a coordinated Bachelor of Fine Arts (B.F.A.) program with the University of Pennsylvania. The Academy focuses exclusively on the fine arts, with majors in painting, drawing, printmaking, and sculpture. Students receive individual attention and work closely with a large faculty of resident and visiting artist-critics. The range of styles and approaches represented by both students and faculty members is diverse and supportive of the many directions in contemporary art making. Students at the Academy come from all walks of life, age groups, and widely varying backgrounds. This creates a high-energy community, bound together by a passion for making art and being artists.

The four-year Certificate Program is the most historic of the academic programs at the Pennsylvania Academy. In the first two years, students receive a thorough training in traditional and contemporary techniques of painting, drawing, sculpture, and printmaking. Under the mentorship of master artists, students take classes in cast drawing, life drawing and painting, anatomy, color, still life, figure modeling, perspective, etching, woodcut, and art history. In their second year, students choose to focus their study in the majors of drawing, painting, sculpture, or

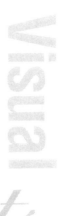

*Pennsylvania Academy of the Fine Arts
(continued)*

printmaking. Third- and fourth-year students receive private studios while continuing an intensive mentoring relationship with critics chosen from a large faculty of professional working artists who represent a wide range of aesthetic viewpoints.

The Academy B.F.A. is the School of Fine Art's newest degree program, enrolling its first class in 2008. The Academy B.F.A. is a 126-credit program that combines the Academy's strong studio courses with the liberal arts coursework offered exclusively at the Academy. The Academy B.F.A. is the ideal program for transfer students from both community colleges and other four-year institutions.

Academy students can also obtain a Bachelor of Fine Arts (B.F.A.) degree through the coordinated program with the University of Pennsylvania. Since 1929, the Pennsylvania Academy of the Fine Arts and the University of Pennsylvania have cooperatively offered a unique educational combination of nationally renowned studio art training and Ivy League academics.

Students admitted to the coordinated B.F.A. program may begin studies at Penn after completing their first year of study at the Academy. This self-paced program offers students maximum flexibility in their academic pursuits.

The Master of Fine Arts (M.F.A.) program is an intensive, two-year studio art–making experience that involves daily interaction with an outstanding faculty of resident and visiting artists, regular private and group critiques, seminars in critical readings, a written thesis component, exposure to an outstanding visiting-artist program, and participation in graduate drawing and painting—reflecting the Pennsylvania Academy's emphasis on achieving a high degree of skill in drawing and studio art–making practice. Students are expected to possess an unusually strong work ethic and to be highly productive and able to work independently.

The master's degree program is centered in the studio arts of painting, drawing, printmaking, and sculpture, but within these disciplines, it displays considerable diversity in its approach. All students are provided a private studio in the new Samuel M.V. Hamilton Building, with proper ventilation and 24-hour secure access to facilities.

During both years of study, every M.F.A. student must enroll in drawing and seminar classes that meet once a week at scheduled times. Students may also elect to take classes within the Academy's Certificate Program, with its emphasis on working from life and the acquisition of traditional art-making skills. This,

in conjunction with extensive access to the private studio, provides an open schedule that allows flexibility within the program. The Studio Critique system allows the student to choose three faculty critics from a large faculty representing a wide range of studio practice.

The Post-Baccalaureate Certificated in Graduate Studies is designed to address the needs of a wide range of students: those with an undergraduate degree who have substantial studio experience but need an additional year of studio work to develop a strong, cohesive, and competitive body of work; students requiring a year of intensive studio work prior to beginning a graduate-level program, or individuals with a degree in art who wish to pursue work in a different medium. It combines an advanced academic program of foundation and techniques with an upper-level, independent studio/critique system and seminars designed to develop personal vision through exposure to trends in contemporary art issues.

Pennsylvania College of Art & Design

Lancaster, Pennsylvania

Independent, coed. Urban campus. Art program established 1982.

Degrees Bachelor of Fine Arts in the areas of communication arts, fine art, photography. Majors and concentrations: art/fine arts, graphic design, illustration, photography. Program accredited by NASAD.

Enrollment 255 total; all undergraduate.

Art Student Profile 60% females, 40% males, 14% minorities.

Art Faculty 11 undergraduate (full-time), 40 undergraduate (part-time). 70% of full-time faculty have terminal degrees. Graduate students do not teach undergraduate courses. Undergraduate student–faculty ratio: 9:1.

Student Life Student groups/activities include Society of Illustrators Student Competition, Lancaster Museum of Art Annual Open Art Award Exhibition, client-based projects resulting in printed work (for designers and illustrators).

Expenses for 2007–2008 Application fee: $40. Tuition: $14,425 full-time. Mandatory fees: $780 full-time.

Financial Aid Program-specific awards: 3 PCAD Foundation Scholarships for incoming foundation students demonstrating artistic merit and academic achievement ($3500), 1 Brenda Swain Memorial Scholarship for juniors demonstrating academic and artistic achievement ($500), 1 UPS Scholarship for current students demonstrating academic achievement ($1425), 1 UPS Minority Scholarship for current students of Hispanic or African-American descent demonstrating academic achievement ($1425).

Application Procedures Students admitted directly into the professional program freshman year. Deadline for freshmen and transfers: continuous. Required: essay, high school transcript, college transcript(s) for transfer students, interview, portfolio. Recommended: minimum 2.0 high school GPA, 2 letters of recommendation. Portfolio reviews held on campus and off campus in Baltimore, MD; Philadelphia, PA; the submission of slides may be substituted for portfolios when distance is prohibitive.

Web Site http://www.pcad.edu

Undergraduate Contact Rebeca Adey, Senior Admissions Counselor, Pennsylvania College of Art & Design, 204 North Prince Street, Lancaster, Pennsylvania 17608-0059; 717-396-7833, fax: 717-396-1339, e-mail address: admissions@pcad.edu

More About the College

Pennsylvania College of Art and Design (PCA&D) began as the dream of a handful of dedicated artists and their supporters in the spring of 1982. More than two decades later, PCA&D has grown into a professional art college recognized as a leader in Central Pennsylvania's visual arts community. While the school has grown and the curriculum has been enhanced, PCA&D's mission has remained the same—to be a leading professional art college offering B.F.A. degrees, certificates, credentials, and course work so students of all ages can pursue art as their life's work.

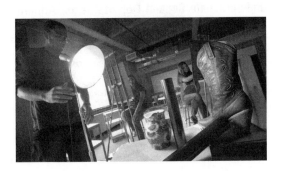

Accredited by the National Association of Schools of Art and Design, and a candidate for accreditation by the Middle States Association of Colleges and Schools, PCA&D offers four-year Bachelor of Fine Arts (B.F.A.) degree programs in fine arts, graphic design, illustration, and photography. The College also offers continuing education opportunities with certificate programs in print design, Web design, home interiors, and mural painting. In addition, a wide variety of credit and noncredit studio and computer courses for adults and youths are available.

Providing a complementary balance to the program's studio work, the College has carefully developed specific liberal arts requirements and electives with a relevance to the education and life of an artist. Another feature of the curriculum is the required internship program for all B.F.A. students, which provides them with professional experiences and opportunities. PCA&D students have produced work for or interned at numerous companies on the East Coast, including advertising agencies, design studios, art galleries, publishing companies, and museums.

PCA&D prides itself on maintaining a professionally relevant curriculum and providing students with a good educational value. The College is pleased to offer its program at a tuition that is considerably less expensive than other professional art colleges. Coupling that with the fact that PCA&D is located in historic downtown Lancaster, Pennsylvania, a city where living expenses are much lower than its metropolitan counterparts, further alleviates the impact of financing a college education.

Another attribute of PCA&D's programs is the low teacher-student ratio (1:9). With individualized attention from faculty members, who are all working artists and designers, PCA&D students have a first-hand view of an artist's lifestyle, challenges, and rewards. Gaining such insight is critical to sustaining a career in the visual arts.

PCA&D salutes its alumni who are making their mark in the field of art and design. Whether they are exhibiting fine artists, creative directors in advertising agencies, designers for international corporations, or illustrators for national publications, the College's graduates are sharing their talents with industry giants. These successes are evidence of the high-quality education and invaluable real-life experiences the College provides its students.

The College facility has more than 62,000 square feet of well-maintained and highly-functional work and study space, with numerous art and design

Pennsylvania College of Art & Design (continued)

studios, computer imaging labs, printmaking studios, darkrooms, woodshop, photo labs, plug-n-play labs, and galleries. The College also houses its own library on-site, with Access Pennsylvania (AccessPA) privileges.

Pennsylvania College of Art & Design's Lancaster, Pennsylvania, location offers both the advantages of a city and the comfort and safety of a small town. The city's tree-lined streets provide a beautiful setting for many galleries, shops, restaurants, and clubs. In addition, Lancaster is centrally located and only a few hours from some of the East Coast's most important cultural centers—Baltimore, New York City, Philadelphia, and Washington, D.C.

PCA&D is proud of the quality and strength of its programs, curriculum, and faculty, and encourages prospective students to visit the College and learn more about the PCA&D experience.

For more information, students should contact: Pennsylvania College of Art and Design, 204 N. Prince Street, P.O. Box 59, Lancaster, Pennsylvania 17608-0059; Phone: (717) 396-7833; E-mail: admissions@pcad.edu; Web site: http://www.pcad.edu.

Penn State University Park

University Park, Pennsylvania

State-related, coed. Small town campus. Total enrollment: 43,252. Art program established 1964.

Web Site http://www.psu.edu/

Pittsburg State University

Pittsburg, Kansas

State-supported, coed. Small town campus. Total enrollment: 7,087.

Web Site http://www.pittstate.edu/

Plymouth State University

Plymouth, New Hampshire

State-supported, coed. Total enrollment: 6,290. Art program established 1960.

Degrees Bachelor of Arts in the areas of fine arts, studio art, graphic design, art history; Bachelor of Fine Arts in the area of studio and graphic design; Bachelor of Science in the area of art education. Majors and concentrations: art education, art history, ceramics, drawing, graphic design, interdisciplinary studies, painting, printmaking, sculpture. Graduate degrees offered: Master of Arts in Teaching in the area of art education. Program accredited by NCATE.

Enrollment 372 undergraduate, 15 graduate.

Art Student Profile 50% females, 50% males, 2% minorities, 5% international.

Art Faculty 12 undergraduate (full-time), 17 undergraduate (part-time), 2 graduate (full-time), 2 graduate (part-time). 100% of full-time faculty have terminal degrees. Graduate students do not teach undergraduate courses. Undergraduate student–faculty ratio: 15:1.

Student Life Student groups/activities include exhibition program, Art Education Mentor Network, Art and Art History Club.

Expenses for 2008–2009 Application fee: $35. State resident tuition: $6600 full-time. Nonresident tuition: $14,450 full-time. Mandatory fees: $1824 full-time. College room and board: $8150. College room only: $5850.

Financial Aid Program-specific awards: 1 Karl Drerup Scholarship for program students ($500), 2 Art Department Scholarships for program students ($700).

Application Procedures Students admitted directly into the professional program freshman year. Deadline for freshmen: May 30. Required: high school transcript, 2 letters of recommendation, portfolio, SAT or ACT test scores, extracurricular activities. Portfolio reviews held 8-10 times on campus; the submission of slides may be substituted for portfolios.

Web Site http://www.plymouth.edu/psc/artdept

Undergraduate Contact Deb Stalnaker, Administrative Assistant, Art Department, Plymouth State University, 17 High Street, Plymouth, New Hampshire 03264-1595; 603-535-2201, fax: 603-535-2938, e-mail address: dstalnaker@plymouth.edu

Graduate Contact Dennise Maslakowski, Associate Vice President, College of Graduate Studies, Plymouth State University, MSC 11, 23 Avery Street, Plymouth, New Hampshire 03264; 603-535-2286, fax: 603-535-2648, e-mail address: dmmaslakowski@plymouth.edu

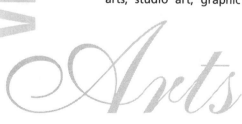

Point Park University

Pittsburgh, Pennsylvania

Independent, coed. Urban campus. Total enrollment: 3,592. Art program established 2003.

Degrees Bachelor of Arts in the area of cinema and digital arts. Majors and concentrations: cinema and digital arts. Cross-registration with Carnegie Mellon University, University of Pittsburgh, Chatham College, Robert Morris University, Duquesne University, Carlow University.

Enrollment 176 total; all undergraduate.

Art Student Profile 29% females, 71% males, 8% minorities, 2% international.

Art Faculty 4 undergraduate (full-time), 10 undergraduate (part-time). 90% of full-time faculty have terminal degrees. Graduate students do not teach undergraduate courses. Undergraduate student–faculty ratio: 18:1.

Student Life Student groups/activities include John P. Harris Film Club.

Expenses for 2007–2008 Application fee: $40. Comprehensive fee: $27,430 includes full-time tuition ($18,460), mandatory fees ($530), and college room and board ($8440). College room only: $3980. Full-time tuition and fees vary according to program. Room and board charges vary according to board plan and housing facility.

Financial Aid Program-specific awards: Cinema Scholarship for those demonstrating talent and academic achievement ($1500–$5000), Cinema Apprenticeship for those demonstrating talent ($1500–$5000), Academic Scholarship for those demonstrating talent and academic achievement ($1000–$5000).

Application Procedures Students admitted directly into the professional program freshman year. Deadline for freshmen and transfers: May 1. Required: essay, high school transcript, minimum 2.0 high school GPA, 2 letters of recommendation, interview, portfolio, SAT or ACT test scores. Portfolio reviews held 10 times on campus and off campus in by telephone.

Web Site http://www.pointpark.edu

Undergraduate Contact Ms. Bonnie Sampson, Administrative Assistant, Cinema & Digital Arts, Conservatory of Performing Arts, Point Park University, 201 Wood Street, Pittsburgh, Pennsylvania 15222-1988; 412-392-4313.

More About the University

Point Park University offers students real-world experiences in an exciting campus environment, the chance to meet and learn with students from thirty-five states and fifty countries, and the excitement and culture of the vibrant city surrounding the University.

The Cinema and Digital Arts Program is offered through the Media Production Program, which is part of the Conservatory of Performing Arts. As one of the top programs of its kind in the nation, the Conservatory of Performing Arts combines hands-on experience and rigorous training with internationally recognized master teachers, so students develop their craft working with professional artists who are involved in their professions outside of the University as well as in the classroom.

Cinema and Digital Arts is an innovatively designed program, with an emphasis on professional education and liberal arts, both in theory and in practice. Exploring the integration of media and the arts in society as well as the impact of technology on culture, the curriculum provides practical, professional training while developing a sound foundation in the arts and humanities. Theory and aesthetics are taught as an integral part of developing communication and production skills. The degree offered is a four-year, 120-credit Bachelor of Arts (B.A.).

The program consists of a combination of courses, workshops, productions, and crew assignments, and students have opportunities to earn credit for real-world experience through the internship program. There is a strong emphasis on collaboration. While the teachers demand professionalism and discipline, they go out of their way to mentor and evaluate the students as they develop as artists.

During the first two years, students are trained in all the fundamental crafts of cinema production. Then, in the junior and senior years, students select a concentration in producing, directing, editing, screenwriting, or cinematography for advanced study and practice. Each year, students make films using professional digital video cameras and nonlinear editing systems. This approach allows each student to develop a specific set of skills and to produce a reel that showcases their talents in their specializations. Furthermore, by shooting primarily on digital formats, students do not have the extra expense of film, processing, and video transfers. So, instead of worrying about the budget, they can focus on the creative challenges of bringing their stories to the screen. Students graduate with several great pieces and all the technical skills they need to take the world by storm.

Point Park University (continued)

The University's downtown location provides convenient access to numerous theaters, restaurants, parks, sports venues, museums, and movie theaters. Through the philanthropic efforts of such financial entrepreneurs as Carnegie and Frick, Pittsburgh has had a long tradition as a cultural center. The city has an excellent symphony and ballet company, and the Pittsburgh Opera gives performances regularly. Theaters, ethnic festivals, and club attractions fill out the entertainment spectrum. In addition, the nation's first educational television station, WQED, provides a wealth of stimulating offerings. PNC Park, Heinz Field, and Mellon Arena are homes of Pittsburgh's professional sports teams, which also host concerts and other special events and are within walking distance of the University. A short bus ride away is the Oakland section of Pittsburgh, the location of several renowned museums.

Program Facilities The Cinema and Digital Arts Program has new, state-of-the-art facilities, including ten nonlinear editing suites, a sound mixing studio, a Foley/audio recording studio, and a professionally equipped soundstage. With Western Pennsylvania as its back lot, the creative possibilities are limitless.

The recent construction of the television studio in the University Center marks the start of a two-year period of exciting capital projects. The state-of-the-art television studio and editing suites, together with the GRW Theater that is already there, will provide cutting-edge experiences for students in the Cinema and Digital Arts Program.

Exhibit Opportunities The campus offers a student-run cinema society, the Sprocket Guild, and frequent movie screenings that include open showings of student work. The Cinema and Digital Arts Program culminates with the annual Point Park Digital Film Festival, which is presented to showcase graduating senior thesis production projects.

Special Programs Characterized by a willingness to innovate, the University has been active since its inception in establishing internship possibilities with the many resources for career preparation in Pittsburgh, including internship programs with local broadcasting stations.

Pratt Institute

Brooklyn, New York

Independent, coed. Urban campus. Total enrollment: 4,668. Art program established 1887.

Degrees Bachelor of Arts in the areas of critical and visual studies, art history; Bachelor of Architecture; Bachelor of Fine Arts in the areas of communications design, fine arts, fashion design, interior design, art and design education, criticism and history of art, media arts, writing, digital arts; Bachelor of Industrial Design; Bachelor of Science in the area of construction management; Bachelor of Professional Studies in the area of construction management. Majors and concentrations: animation, architecture, art direction, art education, art history, ceramic art and design, construction management, digital art, drawing, fashion design, film, graphic design, illustration, industrial design, interior design, jewelry and metalsmithing, painting/drawing, photography, printmaking, sculpture, visual and critical studies, writing. Graduate degrees offered: Master of Architecture; Master of Fine Arts in the areas of fine arts, digital arts, art history; Master of Industrial Design; Master of Professional Studies in the areas of art therapy, design management, arts and cultural management, art therapy-special education; Master of Science in the areas of interior design, art and design education, art history and criticism, urban design, library science, industrial design, architecture, historic preservation, city/regional planning, environmental systems management, facilities management. Program accredited by NASAD, CIDA, NAAB.

Enrollment 3,040 undergraduate, 1,587 graduate.

Art Student Profile 64% females, 36% males, 24% minorities, 15% international.

Art Faculty 119 total (full-time), 820 total (part-time). Graduate students do not teach undergraduate courses. Undergraduate student–faculty ratio: 11:1.

Student Life Student groups/activities include Industrial Design Society of America, American Society of Interior Designers, American Institute of Graphic Arts. Special housing available for art students.

Expenses for 2008–2009 Application fee: $50. Comprehensive fee: $42,466 includes full-time tuition ($31,700), mandatory fees ($1290), and college room and board ($9476). College room only: $5976. Special program-related fees: $240 per year for student activities fee, $450 per year for technology fee, $600 per year for academic facilities fee.

photography, printmaking, sculpture, watercolors. Graduate degrees offered: Master of Fine Arts in the area of art.

Enrollment 236 total; 49 undergraduate, 27 graduate, 160 nonprofessional degree.

Art Student Profile 65% females, 35% males, 7% minorities, 1% international.

Art Faculty 14 total (full-time), 6 total (part-time). 87% of full-time faculty have terminal degrees. Graduate students teach a few undergraduate courses. Undergraduate student–faculty ratio: 14:1.

Student Life Student groups/activities include Student Art Guild, Jewelry Guild, Ceramic Guild. Special housing available for art students.

Expenses for 2007–2008 Application fee: $50. State resident tuition: $4026 full-time. Nonresident tuition: $12,360 full-time. Mandatory fees: $2150 full-time. College room and board: $6490. College room only: $3452. Room and board charges vary according to board plan and housing facility.

Financial Aid Program-specific awards: 5 Arts Society Scholarships for program students ($600–$1100), 2 De la Burdé Scholarships for program students ($600–$1100), 1 Fran Carson Scholarship for program students ($600–$1100), 1 Zheng Liang Feng Scholarship for international art program students ($750).

Application Procedures Students apply for admission into the professional program by freshman, sophomore, junior year. Deadline for freshmen: April 1; transfers: June 1. Notification date for freshmen and transfers: continuous. Required: high school transcript, college transcript(s) for transfer students, minimum 2.0 high school GPA, SAT or ACT test scores, minimum 2.0 college GPA for transfer students. Portfolio reviews held once on campus.

Web Site http://www.radford.edu/~art-web/

Undergraduate Contact Admissions, Radford University, Box 6903, Radford, Virginia 24142; 540-831-5371, fax: 540-831-5038, e-mail address: ruadmiss@radford.edu

Graduate Contact College of Graduate and Extended Education, Radford University, Box 6928, Radford, Virginia 24142; 540-831-5724, e-mail address: gradcoll@radford.edu

Rhode Island College

Providence, Rhode Island

State-supported, coed. Suburban campus. Total enrollment: 9,042.
Web Site http://www.ric.edu/

Rhode Island School of Design

Providence, Rhode Island

Independent, coed. Urban campus. Art program established 1877.

Degrees Bachelor of Graphic Design; Bachelor of Fine Arts; Bachelor of Industrial Design. Majors and concentrations: apparel design, architecture, ceramics, film/animation/video, furniture design, glass, graphic design, illustration, industrial design, interior architecture, jewelry and metalsmithing, painting, photography, printmaking, sculpture, textiles. Graduate degrees offered: Master of Arts in the area of art education; Master of Architecture; Master of Arts in Teaching in the area of art education; Master of Fine Arts in the areas of ceramics, furniture design, graphic design, glass, jewelry and metals, painting, printmaking, photography, sculpture, textiles, digital media; Master of Interior Architecture; Master of Industrial Design; Master of Landscape Architecture. Cross-registration with Brown University. Program accredited by NASAD, ASLA, NAAB.

Enrollment 2,337 total; 1,927 undergraduate, 410 graduate.

Art Student Profile 66% females, 34% males, 22% minorities, 17% international.

Art Faculty 144 total (full-time), 375 total (part-time). 73% of full-time faculty have terminal degrees. Graduate students teach a few undergraduate courses. Undergraduate student–faculty ratio: 9:1.

Student Life Student groups/activities include Film Society, Performance Club. Special housing available for art students.

Expenses for 2007–2008 Application fee: $50. Comprehensive fee: $42,978 includes full-time tuition ($32,858), mandatory fees ($260), and college room and board ($9860). College room

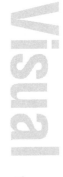

Rhode Island School of Design (continued)

only: $5630. Special program-related fees: $10–$100 per course for lab fees for certain courses.

Financial Aid Program-specific awards: 600 RISD Scholarships for those demonstrating financial need ($12,141), 5–7 Trustees Scholarships for above-average students with exceptional artistic ability ($5000).

Application Procedures Students admitted directly into the professional program freshman year. Deadline for freshmen: February 15; transfers: March 15. Notification date for freshmen: April 1; transfers: April 25. Required: essay, high school transcript, college transcript(s) for transfer students, portfolio, SAT or ACT test scores, 3 original drawings. Recommended: minimum 3.0 high school GPA, 3 letters of recommendation. the submission of slides may be substituted for portfolios (slides, prints, or digital files required).

Web Site http://www.risd.edu

Contact Admissions Office, Rhode Island School of Design, 2 College Street, Providence, Rhode Island 02903; 401-454-6300, fax: 401-454-6309, e-mail address: admissions@risd.edu

More About the School

Students who come to Rhode Island School of Design (RISD, pronounced riz-dee) join an intense creative artists' community that has been internationally respected for its excellent education for more than 130 years. This dynamic atmosphere—created among people with similar interests, talents, and focus—is frequently noted by many sources as a distinguishing feature of RISD, which has been cited consistently as a leading visual arts college in numerous college guides and surveys.

RISD's 2,260 students, coming from more than forty-five nations around the world, find an extensive range of sixteen majors in areas of architecture, design, and the fine arts. This diverse choice of disciplines creates an enriched environment of ideas and personal directions. Students find balance in the curriculum between focus on their major interest, experimentation in related studios, and innovative cross-disciplinary study. It is a frequent happening at RISD for a student in one studio major to work jointly with a classmate from another department on a single project, broadening understanding of the creative opportunities between disciplines. Digital technology continues to expand the range of tools available to artists and designers, and RISD now has more than 400 computer systems and related equipment available in twenty departmental and specialized labs. A number of departments now assign each student a powerful laptop computer with specialized software, running on a wireless campus network. There are a number of real-world connections to industry at RISD, involving research design studios sponsored by NASA, Sikorsky, Rubbermaid, and Nissan and innovative courses taught jointly with other colleges, such as the product development collaboration between RISD's Industrial Design Department and M.B.A. students from MIT.

The environment of the college is greatly enhanced by the advanced projects and research undertaken by 400 graduate students in seventeen graduate programs. RISD's graduate programs are widely respected and frequently cited in surveys as leaders in their visual disciplines.

RISD's 400 studio faculty members are among the leaders in the visual arts, passionate about the fulfillment that the arts bring to the individual and the role of the arts and design in society. They include designers of products found in most homes, award-winning authors and illustrators, painters and sculptors whose work can be seen in major museums and galleries, and acclaimed architects, filmmakers, and textile artists.

Liberal arts form an important component of each student's study as well, and RISD invests notably in the quality of its academic course offerings. There are 28 full-time faculty members in liberal arts departments, all holding the highest degree in their discipline, and 55 part-time faculty members who specialize in certain areas; this number and quality of academic faculty members is unusual for a visual arts college and results in a varied selection of more than 210 courses yearly. Students may choose to enrich the basic liberal arts requirements by pursuing a concentration in art history; English; or history, philosophy, and social sciences. RISD students may also enroll for courses at our neighbor, Brown University.

RISD is located in Providence, described in numerous media stories as a "Renaissance City" and chronicled recently in *Money* magazine as "the best place to live in the eastern United States." Home to students from a number of colleges, Providence offers numerous social and cultural opportunities and an active visual and performing arts community.

Comprehensive career planning support is available to all students and alumni in the Alumni and Career Services Office. Seminars on a wide array of topics that are critical to artists and their career development, individual career counseling, on-campus recruiting, and online listings of available jobs, internships, and fellowships are among the services available. Students are encouraged to participate in professional internships and, on average, more than 60 percent of graduates have experienced at least one internship opportunity. Students have interned recently at WGBE, Cannondale, Walt Disney, Pixar, and Pentagram. RISD surveys all graduates one year after the completion of their studies and, consistently, about 91 percent are employed in their discipline or a related art or design field.

RISD alumni consistently win major competitions, prestigious awards, and recognition for their works in the arts, industry, and education. David Weisner and Chris van Allsburg have won the nationally acclaimed Caldecott Medal for their children's books. Designer Nicole Miller is noted for her collections of women's apparel and men's accessories. Roz Chast's books of her own cartoons (featured often in *The New Yorker*) and Henry Horenstein's photography books have won numerous awards. Seth MacFarlane is the creator of the animated sitcom, *Family Guy*. Architect Deborah Berke is recognized for her work in a variety of residential and commercial settings. Glass artists Toots Zynsky and Howard Ben Tre, painter Kara Walker, and filmmakers Martha Coolidge and Gus van Sant are but a few of the successes among RISD's 16,000 alumni. In 2007, four RISD alums were awarded a MacArthur Fellowship, bringing the total to eight RISE recipients of this prestigious award over the last ten years. Profiles of many others are available on RISD's Web site at http://www.risd.edu.

Program Facilities RISD's facilities consist of forty buildings with more than 1,000,000 square feet of space, including specialized studio spaces and equipment; access to studio spaces, with upperclass students often having a private studio space; sixteen residence halls offering a variety of living environments; the Museum of Art, with more than 85,000 objects frequently used for study purposes by faculty members and students; a library with more than 130,000 volumes, including artist's and rare books, an image research collection of 470,000 clippings and photographs and 160,000 slides; and the Nature Lab with 80,000 objects available for study and research.

Faculty and Resident Artists RISD has 480 faculty members, 145 of them full-time and readily available to students on campus. More than 200 artists and guest critics visit the campus on average each year. Among recent visitors were Janine Antoni, sculptor; Philip Glass, composer/musician; Pat Olezko, performance artist; David Byrne, musician; Todd Oldham, designer; David Hickey, art critic; James Rosenquist, painter; Gore Vidal, author; and Dale Chihuly, glass artist.

Student Exhibit Opportunities Exhibition opportunities for students include two college-wide galleries and eight departmental exhibition spaces on campus, with an average of 125 shows staged each year.

Special Programs The European Honors Program allows students to study in Rome for their junior or senior year. Study-abroad exchange agreements are in place with fifty other art and design colleges around the world. Wintersession term provides unique study opportunities each year, including travel-abroad courses (recently to Italy, Switzerland, Paris, Cuba, Ghana, New Zealand, and Mexico). Mobility program are available with thirty-two other arts colleges. RISD also offers a Summer Studies Program, with courses designed to meet the needs of beginning to advanced students. These courses run from two to six weeks, many offer college credit, and all are taught by distinguished teachers drawn from the School's regular faculty members or visiting experts. Summer Studies also offers a study-abroad option.

Rider University

See Westminster College of the Arts of Rider University

Ringling College of Art and Design

Sarasota, Florida

Independent, coed. Small town campus. Total enrollment: 1,199. Art program established 1931.

Degrees Bachelor of Arts in the area of business of art and design; Bachelor of Fine Arts in the areas of advertising design, painting, printmaking, sculpture. Majors and concentrations: advertising design, art/fine arts, business of art and design, computer animation, digital film and video, game art and design, graphic and interactive communication, illustration, interior design, painting, photography and digital imaging, printmaking, sculpture. Cross-registration with members of Association of Independent Colleges of Art and Design. Program accredited by NASAD, CIDA.

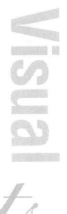

Ringling College of Art and Design (continued)

Enrollment 1,199 total; all undergraduate.

Art Student Profile 54% females, 46% males, 21% minorities, 4% international.

Art Faculty 71 undergraduate (full-time), 65 undergraduate (part-time). 61% of full-time faculty have terminal degrees. Graduate students do not teach undergraduate courses. Undergraduate student–faculty ratio: 13:1.

Student Life Student groups/activities include Campus Activities Board, Phi Delta Theta/ Sigma Sigma Sigma, preprofessional organizations. Special housing available for art students.

Expenses for 2007–2008 Application fee: $40. Comprehensive fee: $34,725 includes full-time tuition ($24,100), mandatory fees ($625), and college room and board ($10,000). College room only: $5500. Full-time tuition and fees vary according to course load, program, and student level. Room and board charges vary according to board plan and housing facility. Special program-related fees: $900 per year for fine arts technology fee, $1300 per year for illustration technology fee, $1300 per year for core studio program technology fee, $1400 per year for photography and digital imaging technology fee, $1500 per year for interior design technology fee, $1800 per year for graphic and interactive communication technology fee, $2600 per year for computer animation technology fee.

Financial Aid Program-specific awards: 7 Dean's Scholarships for incoming students ($6429), 7 Trustee Scholarships for seniors ($3000), 5 Presidential Scholarships for incoming students ($10,000), 96 need/merit scholarships for incoming students ($2438).

Application Procedures Students admitted directly into the professional program freshman year. Deadline for freshmen and transfers: continuous. Notification date for freshmen and transfers: continuous. Required: essay, high school transcript, college transcript(s) for transfer students, minimum 2.0 high school GPA, 2 letters of recommendation, portfolio. Recommended: interview, SAT or ACT test scores. Portfolio reviews held continuously on campus and off campus at National Portfolio Days; the submission of slides may be substituted for portfolios.

Web Site http://www.ringling.edu

Undergraduate Contact Mr. James H. Dean, Interim Executive Director for Admissions, Marketing and Communications, Ringling College of Art and Design, 2700 North Tamiami Trail, Sarasota, Florida 34234; 941-351-5100 ext. 7523, fax: 941-359-7517, e-mail address: admissions@ringling.edu

More About the College

For nearly 75 years, Ringling College of Art and Design has cultivated the creative spirit in art and design students from around the globe . . . transforming our visual world. Founded in 1931 by noted art collector, real estate magnate, and circus impresario John Ringling, the private, not-for-profit college is fully accredited by the National Association of Schools of Art and Design (NASAD; http://nasad. arts-accredit.org) and the Southern Association of Colleges and Schools (SACS; http://www.sacscoc.org).

Located on the Gulf Coast of Florida, the picturesque 35-acre campus today includes ninety buildings and enrolls more than 1,100 students from forty-three states and twenty-eight other countries— more than half of whom reside on the pedestrian-friendly residential campus. The College's 130 faculty members are all professional artists, designers, and scholars who actively pursue their own work outside the classroom.

The College's rigorous curriculum engages innovation and tradition through a strong, well-rounded first-year Core Studio Program and a deep focus on the liberal arts. Students pursue one of fourteen majors leading to their B.F.A. degrees: advertising design, broadcast design/motion graphics, business of art and design, computer animation, digital film, fine

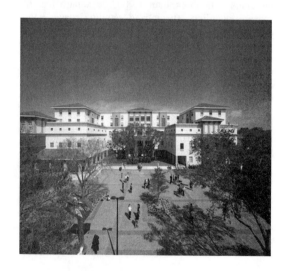

arts, game art and design, graphic and interactive communication, illustration, interior design, painting, photography and digital imaging, printmaking, or sculpture.

The academic emphasis on professional portfolio development and career preparation provides students with a well-rounded education. This is backed up by the extensive career-related services available during a student's time at the College and throughout their professional life.

The Center for Career Services lists nearly 1,000 employment opportunities and internships each year, available 24 hours a day at http://www.collegecentral. com/ringling. The center offers workshops and seminars on professional skills, such as portfolio preparation, resume writing, and interviewing, and can assist students in researching opportunities for additional training and graduate education. Nearly four dozen nationally recognized recruiters visit Ringling College's campus each year to interview students and to make employment and internship offers. Among the most outstanding organizations recruiting at Ringling College are Hallmark Cards, CNN, Target, Headline News, Sony Pictures ImageWorks, DreamWorks Animation SKG, Disney, Electronic Arts (EA), American Greetings, and even the Central Intelligence Agency (CIA).

The College believes passionately in the development and support of the whole student by preparing each graduate to be successful in their chosen careers as well as socially responsible artist-citizens. As a testament to the educational principles instilled in them, students donate hours upon hours of their personal time to volunteering on myriad local community public service projects and participating in student organizations. Clubs on campus provide a well-balanced calendar of cocurricular events, leadership opportunities, and social activities. Organizations include the Student Government Association and many diverse clubs focusing on artistic development, recreation, special interests, theater and dance, social and community service, Greek and spiritual life, and more. Students are recognized for their contributions through awards and honors and a comprehensive cocurricular transcript reflecting their participation in these areas.

Ringling College traditions include Family Weekend, Latino Heritage Month, National Collegiate Alcohol Awareness Week, National Coming Out Day, Black History Month, and Women's History Month. Other celebrations include beach parties, holiday parties, and a President's reception for graduates and their families.

More than half of Ringling College students live on campus in one of ten different, modern, and well-equipped residence halls and apartments. In addition to the convenience of campus living, residents benefit from a variety of programs, residence hall support staff, and campus food service. To enhance the campus experience and create a hub for student activities, a dynamic, 80,000-square-foot five-story Student Center opened in fall 2006. The building includes a fitness center and exercise studio, student activity center and meeting spaces, Outtakes Café, classrooms, an exhibition hall, and two floors of student residences.

To begin the school year, a New Student Orientation program is held for all new students and their parents during the week prior to the start of the fall semester. Orientation includes opportunities to meet other students, hear from key faculty members and administrators, attend presentations on academic expectations and campus resources, and to enjoy a number of relaxing, social activities with family members and classmates.

Ringling College of Art and Design welcomes applications from students with a serious commitment to the visual arts. Admission is based on a review of the student's portfolio, academic record, essay, and teacher recommendations. All applicants are reviewed individually, with special consideration given to creative ability and potential for success in college-level studies.

Program/Academic Facilities At Ringling College, facilities include the Verman Kimbrough Memorial Library, with 55,000 volumes, including more than 6,100 videos, CDs, and DVDs, 350 periodical subscriptions, hand-made artist's books, and a separate collection of more than 127,000 slides; Selby Gallery, with international and nationally recognized shows, annual juried student and faculty exhibitions; specialized studios for painting, printmaking, sculpture, wood, graphic design, computer animation, illustration, figure drawing, interior design, and CAD; and the Deborah M. Cooley Photography Center, with studios, darkrooms, and digital labs.

The computer-student ratio is greater than 1:2. Computer facilities include four high-end visual 3-D workstation laboratories, twelve high-end Macintosh workstation laboratories, three Intel-Xeon-based class workstation laboratories, three audio and video editing laboratories, and several digital photography labs. Labs are equipped with high-end workstations, peripherals (scanners, printers, etc.), and numerous general-purpose software packages and tools, including desktop publishing, editors, file-transfer tools, spreadsheets, Web tools, imaging tools, utility applications, and graphics-generation equipment. All

Ringling College of Art and Design
(continued)

personal computers, workstations, and printers are connected to the campus network.

A rich collection of discipline-specific software packages is also available in the computer labs, including Alias Maya; 2d3 Boujou; Shake; Pixar Rendering Tools; Apple Computer: Compressor, Cinema Tools, FinalCut Pro, DVD Studio Pro, iDVD, iPhoto, iMovie, iTunes, LiveType, Safari, Soundtrack, Pro Kit, and Ableton; Crater: CTP; Reel Smart: Motion Blur and Stop Motion Pro; Maxon: Body Paint 3D, Auto*des*sys, and FormZ; AutoDesk: Architectural Desktop, AutoCAD, and Autodesk VIZ; Adobe Creative Suite; Acrobat Pro; After Effects; Audition; GoLive; Encore; ImageReady; FontFolio; Premiere; Dreamweaver and Flash; Microsoft: Office, Front Page, Access, Project, and Implementation Tools; and Corel: Painter, BareBones, and BBEdit.

All on-campus residence halls allow students direct access to on-campus computing resources and the Internet with a blazing DS3 speed from the comfort and convenience of their own rooms.

Rockford College

Rockford, Illinois

Independent, coed. Suburban campus. Total enrollment: 1,566.

Degrees Bachelor of Fine Arts in the area of art. Majors and concentrations: ceramics, drawing, painting, photography, printmaking, sculpture.

Art Student Profile 60% females, 40% males, 16% minorities, 1% international.

Art Faculty 4 undergraduate (full-time), 1 undergraduate (part-time). 100% of full-time faculty have terminal degrees. Graduate students do not teach undergraduate courses. Undergraduate student–faculty ratio: 10:1.

Student Life Student groups/activities include Art Club, SOAP (Society of Artsy People).

Expenses for 2008–2009 Application fee: $35. Comprehensive fee: $30,250 includes full-time tuition ($23,500) and college room and board ($6750). College room only: $3850.

Financial Aid Program-specific awards: Margaret Schuh Des Pland Scholarship for senior women art students.

Application Procedures Students apply for admission into the professional program by

sophomore year. Deadline for freshmen and transfers: continuous. Required: high school transcript, college transcript(s) for transfer students, portfolio, SAT or ACT test scores (minimum composite ACT score of 19), minimum 2.65 high school GPA, minimum 2.3 cumulative college GPA for transfer students, top 1/2 of graduating class for first-years. Recommended: 2 letters of recommendation, interview. Portfolio reviews held once each semester on campus.

Web Site http://www.rockford.edu

Undergraduate Contact Cassie Swanson, Assistant Director of Admission, Rockford College, Burpee Center, 5050 East State Street, Rockford, Illinois 61108-2393; 800-892-2984, fax: 815-226-2822, e-mail address: rcadmission@rockford.edu

Rocky Mountain College of Art & Design

Denver, Colorado

Proprietary, coed. Suburban campus. Total enrollment: 498. Art program established 1963.

Degrees Bachelor of Fine Arts. Majors and concentrations: animation, art education, art/fine arts, graphic design and interactive media, illustration, interior design. Program accredited by NASAD, CIDA.

Enrollment 455 total; all undergraduate.

Art Student Profile 58% females, 42% males, 5% minorities, 4% international.

Art Faculty 24 undergraduate (full-time), 48 undergraduate (part-time). 80% of full-time faculty have terminal degrees. Graduate students do not teach undergraduate courses. Undergraduate student–faculty ratio: 19:1.

Student Life Student groups/activities include ASIFA (International Animated Film Association), American Society of Interior Designers, American Institute of Graphic Arts.

Expenses for 2007–2008 Application fee: $50. Comprehensive fee: $28,192 includes full-time tuition ($19,752) and college room and board ($8440).

Financial Aid Program-specific awards: admissions merit award for incoming students ($15,000), RMCAD Portfolio Merit Award for incoming students ($12,000).

Application Procedures Students admitted directly into the professional program freshman year. Deadline for freshmen and transfers: continuous. Notification date for freshmen and transfers: continuous. Required: essay, high school transcript, college transcript(s) for transfer students, minimum 2.0 high school GPA, interview, portfolio, SAT or ACT test scores. Portfolio reviews held continuously on campus; the submission of slides may be substituted for portfolios.

Web Site http://www.rmcad.edu

Undergraduate Contact Ms. Angela Carlson, Director of Admissions, Rocky Mountain College of Art & Design, 1600 Pierce Street, Denver, Colorado 80214; 800-888-2787, fax: 303-759-4970, e-mail address: admissions@rmcad.edu

Roger Williams University

Bristol, Rhode Island

Independent, coed. Total enrollment: 5,166. Art program established 1972.

Degrees Bachelor of Arts in the area of visual art studies. Majors and concentrations: art, ceramics, drawing, painting, photography.

Enrollment 20 total; all undergraduate.

Art Student Profile 72% females, 28% males, 5% minorities.

Art Faculty 5 undergraduate (full-time), 14 undergraduate (part-time). 5% of full-time faculty have terminal degrees. Graduate students do not teach undergraduate courses. Undergraduate student–faculty ratio: 3:1.

Student Life Student groups/activities include Art Society.

Expenses for 2007–2008 Application fee: $50. Comprehensive fee: $37,432 includes full-time tuition ($24,312), mandatory fees ($1630), and college room and board ($11,490). College room only: $5990.

Application Procedures Students admitted directly into the professional program freshman year. Deadline for freshmen and transfers: continuous. Required: essay, high school transcript, college transcript(s) for transfer students, 2 letters of recommendation, portfolio, SAT or ACT test scores. Portfolio reviews held

on campus; the submission of slides may be substituted for portfolios.

Web Site http://www.rwu.edu

Undergraduate Contact Didier Bouvet-Marechal, Executive Director of Undergraduate Admissions, Roger Williams University, 1 Old Ferry Road, Bristol, Rhode Island 02809; 401-254-3500, fax: 401-254-3557, e-mail address: dbouvet@rwu.edu

Rosemont College

Rosemont, Pennsylvania

Independent Roman Catholic, Suburban campus. Total enrollment: 940. Art program established 1969.

Degrees Bachelor of Fine Arts. Majors and concentrations: art education, art therapy, art/fine arts, fashion design, graphic design, interior design. Cross-registration with Cabrini College, Villanova University, Eastern College, Arcadia University.

Enrollment 50 undergraduate.

Art Student Profile 100% females.

Art Faculty 4 undergraduate (full-time), 10 undergraduate (part-time). 100% of full-time faculty have terminal degrees. Graduate students do not teach undergraduate courses. Undergraduate student–faculty ratio: 10:1.

Student Life Student groups/activities include Studio Art Club.

Expenses for 2007–2008 Application fee: $35. Comprehensive fee: $32,035 includes full-time tuition ($21,630), mandatory fees ($1205), and college room and board ($9200). Room and board charges vary according to housing facility. Special program-related fees: $50 per course for supply fees.

Financial Aid Program-specific awards: 1 Sister Stella Kelly Scholarship for high school senior art students ($13,480).

Application Procedures Deadline for freshmen and transfers: continuous. Required: essay, high school transcript, college transcript(s) for transfer students, letter of recommendation, interview, portfolio, SAT or ACT test scores. Portfolio reviews held twice on campus; the submission of slides may be substituted for portfolios when distance is prohibitive.

Web Site http://www.rosemont.edu/

Rosemont College (continued)

Undergraduate Contact Amy Orr, Department Chair, Arts Division, Rosemont College, 1400 Montgomery Avenue, Rosemont, Pennsylvania 19010-1699; 610-527-0200 ext. 2311, fax: 610-527-0341, e-mail address: a.orr@rosemont.edu

Roski School of Fine Arts

See University of Southern California

Roy H. Park School of Communications

See Ithaca College

Russell Sage College

Troy, New York

Independent, Urban campus. Total enrollment: 682. Art program established 1916.

Degrees Bachelor of Arts. Majors and concentrations: creative arts and therapy. Program accredited by NASAD.

Enrollment 29 total; all undergraduate.

Art Student Profile 100% females, 10% minorities.

Art Faculty 4 undergraduate (full-time), 2 undergraduate (part-time). 81% of full-time faculty have terminal degrees. Graduate students do not teach undergraduate courses. Undergraduate student–faculty ratio: 11:1.

Expenses for 2007–2008 Application fee: $30. Comprehensive fee: $34,790 includes full-time tuition ($25,000), mandatory fees ($990), and college room and board ($8800). College room only: $4500.

Application Procedures Students admitted directly into the professional program freshman year. Deadline for freshmen: August 1; transfers: continuous. Required: essay, high school transcript, college transcript(s) for transfer students, minimum 2.0 high school GPA, 2 letters of recommendation, SAT or ACT test scores. Recommended: interview, portfolio. Portfolio reviews held on an individual basis on campus; the submission of slides may be substituted for portfolios.

Web Site http://www.sage.edu

Undergraduate Contact Kathy Rusch, Director of Admissions, Admissions, Russell Sage College, 45 Ferry Street, Troy, New York 12180; 518-244-2217, fax: 518-244-6880, e-mail address: ruschk@sage.edu

Rutgers, The State University of New Jersey

See Mason Gross School of the Arts

St. Cloud State University

St. Cloud, Minnesota

State-supported, coed. Suburban campus. Total enrollment: 15,808. Art program established 1973.

Degrees Bachelor of Fine Arts in the areas of studio art, graphic design. Majors and concentrations: ceramics, drawing, graphic design, painting, photography, printmaking, sculpture. Program accredited by NASAD.

Enrollment 365 total; 175 undergraduate, 190 nonprofessional degree.

Art Student Profile 50% females, 50% males, 1% minorities, 10% international.

Art Faculty 16 undergraduate (full-time), 7 undergraduate (part-time). 100% of full-time faculty have terminal degrees. Graduate students do not teach undergraduate courses. Undergraduate student–faculty ratio: 20:1.

Student Life Student groups/activities include Art Student Union, Graphic Design Association, Future Art Educators.

Expenses for 2007–2008 Application fee: $20. State resident tuition: $5247 full-time. Nonresident tuition: $11,389 full-time. Mandatory fees: $708 full-time. Full-time tuition and fees vary according to course load and reciprocity agreements. College room and board: $5592. College room only: $3596. Room and board charges vary according to board plan and housing facility. Special program-related fees for course supplies.

Financial Aid Program-specific awards: 2–3 Bill Ellingson Awards for program majors ($300), 1 May Bowle Award for program majors ($300).

Application Procedures Students apply for admission into the professional program by sophomore year. Deadline for freshmen and transfers: June 1. Required: high school transcript, college transcript(s) for transfer students, minimum 2.0 high school GPA, ACT test score only, portfolio for scholarship consideration, portfolio for admission to majors upon completion of foundation classes. Portfolio reviews held twice on campus; the submission of slides may be substituted for portfolios whenever needed.

Web Site http://www.stcloudstate.edu/~art

Undergraduate Contact Dr. David Sebberson, Chair, Art Department, St. Cloud State University, Kiehle Visual Arts Building, St. Cloud, Minnesota 56301; 320-255-4283, fax: 320-255-2232.

St. John's University

Jamaica, New York

Independent, coed. Urban campus. Total enrollment: 20,086.

Degrees Bachelor of Fine Arts in the areas of fine arts, graphic design, photography, illustration. Majors and concentrations: graphic design, illustration, painting, photography, printmaking. Mandatory cross-registration with International Center of Photography (for photography majors). Program accredited by NASAD.

Enrollment 100 total; all undergraduate.

Art Student Profile 40% females, 60% males, 30% minorities, 10% international.

Art Faculty 13 undergraduate (full-time), 17 undergraduate (part-time). 100% of full-time faculty have terminal degrees. Graduate students do not teach undergraduate courses. Undergraduate student–faculty ratio: 15:1.

Student Life Student groups/activities include New Vision Art Society, art exhibits in University Gallery, Torch/University Newspaper, Sequoya/University Literary Magazine. Special housing available for art students.

Expenses for 2007–2008 Application fee: $50. Comprehensive fee: $38,960 includes full-time tuition ($26,200), mandatory fees ($690), and college room and board ($12,070). College room only: $7600. Full-time tuition and fees vary according to class time, course load, program, and student level. Room and board charges vary according to board plan and housing facility. Special program-related fees: $30 per course per semester for studio lab fee.

Financial Aid Program-specific awards: 2 Fine Arts Scholarships for incoming freshmen ($13,000), 1 Fine Arts Scholarship for incoming freshmen ($26,000), 3 Visual Arts Awards for incoming freshmen ($1000).

Application Procedures Students admitted directly into the professional program freshman year. Deadline for freshmen and transfers: continuous. Required: high school transcript, college transcript(s) for transfer students, 2 letters of recommendation, portfolio, SAT test score only (minimum combined SAT score of 1050). Recommended: essay, minimum 3.0 high school GPA, interview. Portfolio reviews held continuously by appointment on campus; the submission of slides may be substituted for portfolios for international students and U.S. students from a great distance.

Web Site http://www.stjohns.edu/

Undergraduate Contact Mr. Andrew Ippolito, Director, Admissions, St. John's University, 8000 Utopia Parkway, Jamaica, New York 11439; 718-990-5579, fax: 718-990-1677, e-mail address: ippolita@stjohns.edu

Saint Mary's College

Notre Dame, Indiana

Independent Roman Catholic, women only. Suburban campus. Total enrollment: 1,604.

Degrees Bachelor of Arts in the area of art; Bachelor of Fine Arts in the area of art. Majors and concentrations: art history, art/fine arts, ceramic art and design, fibers, painting/drawing, photography, printmaking, sculpture, studio art. Cross-registration with University of Notre Dame, Indiana Technical College, Indiana University South Bend, Goshen College, Bethel College. Program accredited by NASAD.

Enrollment 58 total; all undergraduate.

Art Student Profile 100% females, 10% minorities, 10% international.

Art Faculty 6 undergraduate (full-time), 3 undergraduate (part-time). 100% of full-time faculty have terminal degrees. Graduate students do not teach undergraduate courses. Undergraduate student–faculty ratio: 10:1.

Student Life Student groups/activities include Art Club, National Association of Schools of Art and Design.

Saint Mary's College (continued)

Expenses for 2007–2008 Application fee: $30. Comprehensive fee: $35,550 includes full-time tuition ($26,285), mandatory fees ($590), and college room and board ($8675). College room only: $5343.

Financial Aid Program-specific awards: art talent awards for art majors demonstrating need ($500), 5 Theresa McLaughlin Awards for freshmen art majors demonstrating need ($1000).

Application Procedures Students admitted directly into the professional program freshman year. Deadline for freshmen: March 1; transfers: April 15. Notification date for freshmen and transfers: continuous. Required: essay, high school transcript, college transcript(s) for transfer students, minimum 3.0 high school GPA, letter of recommendation, SAT or ACT test scores. Recommended: interview, portfolio. Portfolio reviews held twice on campus; the submission of slides may be substituted for portfolios for large works of art and three-dimensional pieces.

Web Site http://www.saintmarys.edu

Undergraduate Contact Admissions Office, Saint Mary's College, Notre Dame, Indiana 46556; 574-284-4587, fax: 219-284-4716.

Salisbury University

Salisbury, Maryland

State-supported, coed. Small town campus. Total enrollment: 7,581.

Degrees Bachelor of Fine Arts in the area of art. Majors and concentrations: art/fine arts, ceramics, glass, graphic design, new media, painting/drawing, photography, sculpture, three-dimensional studies, two-dimensional studies. Cross-registration with University of Maryland System, The Art Institute of Philadelphia, Art Institute of Atlanta.

Enrollment 250 total; all undergraduate.

Art Student Profile 60% females, 40% males, 10% minorities, 2% international.

Art Faculty 15 undergraduate (full-time), 12 undergraduate (part-time). 93% of full-time faculty have terminal degrees. Graduate students do not teach undergraduate courses. Undergraduate student–faculty ratio: 15:1.

Student Life Student groups/activities include Glass Club, Art Club. Special housing available for art students.

Expenses for 2007–2008 Application fee: $45. State resident tuition: $4814 full-time. Nonresident tuition: $12,902 full-time. Mandatory fees: $1598 full-time. College room and board: $7601. College room only: $3880. Room and board charges vary according to board plan and housing facility. Special program-related fees: $60 per year for supplies for studio courses.

Financial Aid Program-specific awards: 1 3-D Scholarship for 3-D majors in sculpture, glass, or ceramics ($500), 3 art scholarships for program majors ($500), 2–4 Art Department Meritorious Awards for program students ($50), 1 Photography Award for photography majors ($500), 1 Student Assistantship Award for program majors ($250).

Application Procedures Students admitted directly into the professional program freshman year. Deadline for freshmen: February 1; transfers: March 1. Required: high school transcript, college transcript(s) for transfer students, minimum 2.0 high school GPA, SAT or ACT test scores, portfolio for scholarship consideration. Recommended: essay. Portfolio reviews held once and as needed on campus; the submission of slides may be substituted for portfolios when distance is prohibitive (may submit CD digital images).

Web Site http://www.salisbury.edu/ArtDept/

Undergraduate Contact Admissions Department, Salisbury University, 1101 Camden Avenue, Salisbury, Maryland 21801; 410-543-6000, fax: 410-546-6016.

San Francisco Art Institute

San Francisco, California

Independent, coed. Urban campus. Art program established 1871.

Degrees Bachelor of Arts in the areas of history and theory of contemporary art, urban studies; Bachelor of Fine Arts in the areas of design and technology, film, new genres, painting, photography, printmaking, sculpture, ceramics. Majors and concentrations: ceramics, design and technology, film, history and theory of contemporary art, new genres, painting, photography, printmaking, sculpture, urban studies. Graduate degrees offered: Master of Arts in the areas of exhibition and museum studies, history and theory of contemporary art, urban studies; Master of Fine Arts in the areas of design and technology, film, new genres, painting, photography, printmaking, sculpture, ceramics. Cross-registration with International exchange program with 15+ institutions. Program accredited by NASAD.

Enrollment 658 total; 399 undergraduate, 259 graduate.

Art Student Profile 55% females, 45% males, 29% minorities, 9% international.

Art Faculty 48 total (full-time), 99 total (part-time). 99% of full-time faculty have terminal degrees. Graduate students do not teach undergraduate courses. Undergraduate student–faculty ratio: 3:1.

Student Life Student groups/activities include student-run galleries, exhibitions, and lectures, Student Union events, internships. Special housing available for art students.

Financial Aid Program-specific awards: 153 merit-based scholarships for all undergraduate students ($6515), 50 partnership scholarships for BFA candidates recommended by partner high school or community colleges ($8500), 307 competitive scholarships for all undergraduate students ($5717).

Application Procedures Students admitted directly into the professional program freshman year. Deadline for freshmen and transfers: continuous. Required: essay, high school transcript, college transcript(s) for transfer students, 2 letters of recommendation, portfolio, SAT or ACT test scores, TOEFL score of 550 for international students, English translation of transcripts for international students, WES evaluation for international students. Recommended: minimum 2.0 high school GPA, interview. Portfolio reviews held continuously on campus and off campus in locations nationwide, see www.npda.org; the submission of slides may be substituted for portfolios for out-of-state or international applicants.

Web Site http://www.sfai.edu

Contact Director of Admissions, San Francisco Art Institute, 800 Chestnut Street, San Francisco, California 94133; 415-749-4500, fax: 415-749-4592, e-mail address: admissions@sfai.edu

More About the College

San Francisco Art Institute (SFAI) consists of two schools: the School of Studio Practice and the School of Interdisciplinary Studies. The School of Studio Practice offers B.F.A., M.F.A., and Low-residency Summer M.F.A. degree programs and postbaccalaureate certificates in design+technology, film, new genres, painting, photography, printmaking, and sculpture. The School of Interdisciplinary Studies offers degree programs in exhibition and museum studies (M.A.), history and theory of contemporary art (B.A., M.A.), and urban studies (B.A., M.A.). Students at SFAI receive a broad education that informs and enhances their primary area of study, choosing electives and fulfilling curriculum requirements from both schools. The high percentage of electives in the curriculum allows for an individualized education that is as well-rounded as it is focused. SFAI prepares students to be creative leaders in whatever professions they pursue.

Students at SFAI build on a rich legacy of the kind of questioning that encourages the experimentation necessary for independent and collaborative invention. Students work closely with peers and faculty members from a wide variety of backgrounds and fields; studio courses and seminars have a maximum of fifteen students. Students also participate in projects that allow them to move beyond the classroom and into the world. These programs combine SFAI's historical ways of teaching—through critique seminars, studio courses, and tutorials—with forms of research that emphasize the independent and collaborative nature of both teaching and learning. Internships, independent study, travel courses, and international exchange programs give students practical and professional experience.

Program Facilities SFAI's main campus is located at 800 Chestnut Street in San Francisco's Russian Hill

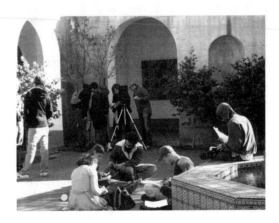

San Francisco Art Institute (continued)

neighborhood, overlooking the bay. The campus provides 24-hour access to light-filled painting, drawing, sculpture, photography, and printmaking studios; black-box studios for film, video, and performance; galleries; and lecture hall/theater and seminar rooms. Postproduction facilities include darkrooms, mural printing, and large-scale digital photo output; Super 8 and 16mm film processing and editing; digital video and Final Cut Pro editing; an HDcam- and DVCam-equipped video finishing suite; and sound studios. SFAI's Anne Bremer Memorial Library holds over 30,000 volumes, subscriptions to more than 200 periodicals, and collections of slides, audiotapes, videotapes, films, and DVDs.

The Graduate Center is a large industrial loft building along the San Francisco Bay. The facility houses individual and group studios, a digital lab, film and sound studios, darkrooms, a wood shop, seminar classrooms, a gallery, and installation critique rooms and provides 24-hour access and convenience to public transportation. Graduate students also have access to all of the facilities on the main campus.

Faculty, Resident Artists, and Alumni With a faculty of more than 130, SFAI enjoys an extraordinary student-faculty ratio of 5:1. Students work closely with faculty members and develop important and lasting relationships that continue beyond graduation.

SFAI's faculty includes artists, curators, writers, historians, theorists, activists, critics, urbanists, architects, designers, performers, philosophers, musicians, and scientists. Okwui Enwezor, Dean of Academic Affairs, is a curator and writer and was the Artistic Director of the 2006 Bienal Internacional de Arte Contemporaneo in Seville, Spain. Renée Green is Dean of Graduate Studies at SFAI, and her work has been seen throughout the world in museums, galleries, biennials, and festivals. Hou Hanru, Chair of SFAI's graduate program in exhibitions and museum studies, is the curator of the Chinese pavilion at the 2007 Venice Biennale and director of the 2007 Istanbul Biennial. Trisha Donnelly's work was included in the 2004 and 2006 Whitney Biennials. Caitlin Mitchell-Dayton's paintings were used in the film "Art School Confidential." Henry Wessel's photographs were recently published as a five-volume boxed set by Steidl. Jon Phillips is an open-source programmer for Creative Commons. Mark Van Proyen is one of the editors of *AfterBurn: Reflections on Burning Man.* Amy Franceschini is the founder of FutureFarmers and has been involved in numerous projects aimed at raising public awareness of critical ecological issues. Thomas Humphrey is a nuclear physicist and director of exhibitions at the Exploratorium.

In addition to working with SFAI's esteemed full- and part-time faculty, students are introduced to a spectrum of visiting artists and scholars. SFAI provides students direct access to an exhibition program showcasing the work of regional and international artists as well as SFAI students; an extensive roster of lectures that brings over 60 artists, designers, curators, and writers to campus every year; and film screenings, symposia, and panel discussions that engage in contemporary issues and ideas.

The accomplishments of SFAI's alumni can be found in museums and galleries around the world, in libraries and bookstores, in movie theaters, on the Web, on television, on the streets, and elsewhere. A partial list includes Annie Leibovitz, who began photographing for Rolling Stone while a student; Molly Katzen's vegetarian *Moosewood Cookbook,* which she wrote and illustrated; Don Ed Hardy's over 20 books on the art of tattooing; Karen Finley, whose performances challenge notions of femininity and political power; the music of the Tubes, Romeo Void, Mutants, and Avengers, all pioneers of Punk; the work of Lance Acord, cinematographer for *Adaptation, Lost in Translation,* and *Marie Antoinette;* Peter Strietmann and Christopher Seguine, editors and cinematographers for Mathew Barney's *Cremaster"* cycle; painter Kehinde Wiley's commissioned portraits of VH1's 2005 honorees; environmental activist Roxanne Quimby's Burt's Bees products; Robert Gamblin's eco-friendly oil paint; Devendra Banhart's music and drawings; Rob Reger's Emily the Strange; and many more.

Exhibition Opportunities Two large student-run galleries show weekly exhibitions of student work; each department has its own exhibition space; the lecture hall is open for student film and video screenings as well as performances; large exterior walls are designated for mural projects; outdoor terraces and the meadow are used for large sculpture and installation work; and weekly noon concerts by student musicians and DJs are held in the Quad. The annual Winter Sale is both an exhibition and opportunity to sell work open to all students. The M.F.A. Graduate exhibition, attracting over 5,000 visitors each year, occupies 4,000 square feet at Fort Mason. The B.F.A. exhibition takes over the entire Chestnut Street campus each May.

San Jose State University

San Jose, California

State-supported, coed. Urban campus. Total enrollment: 29,604 (2007). Art program established 1911.

Web Site http://www.sjsu.edu/

Savannah College of Art and Design

Savannah, Georgia

Independent, coed. Urban campus. Total enrollment: 8,966. Art program established 1978.

Degrees Bachelor of Fine Arts. Majors and concentrations: advertising design, animation, architectural history, architecture, art history, broadcast design and motion graphics, dramatic writing, fashion design, fibers, film and television, furniture design, graphic design, historical preservation, illustration, industrial design, interactive design and game development, interior design, metals and jewelry, painting, performing arts, photography, printmaking, production/design, professional writing, sculpture, sequential art, sound design, urban design, visual effects. Graduate degrees offered: Master of Arts; Master of Arts in Teaching; Master of Fine Arts; Master of Architecture; Master of Urban Design. Cross-registration with nineteen area colleges and universities (Atlanta Regional Consortium member schools). Program accredited by NAAB.

Enrollment 8,866 total; 7,423 undergraduate, 1,443 graduate.

Art Student Profile 55% females, 45% males, 12% minorities, 9% international.

Art Faculty 423 total (full-time), 100 total (part-time). 75% of full-time faculty have terminal degrees. Graduate students do not teach undergraduate courses. Undergraduate student–faculty ratio: 17:1.

Student Life Student groups/activities include Industrial Design Society of America, American Institute of Graphic Arts, American Institute of Architecture Students.

Expenses for 2008–2009 Application fee: $50. Comprehensive fee: $36,480 includes full-time tuition ($25,965), mandatory fees ($500), and college room and board ($10,015). College room only: $6460.

Financial Aid Program-specific awards: various scholarships for entering freshmen and transfer students (specific criteria vary by award) ($500–$25,965), May and Paul Poetter Scholarships for entering students with 4.0 GPA and perfect score on SAT or ACT ($25,965), Frances Larkin McCommon Scholarship for talented freshman or transfer student, Transfer Scholars Awards for talented transfer students who have completed at least 27 semester hours of college coursework ($15,000), Atlanta College of Art Scholars Award for artistically talented students with minimum 3.5 high school GPA, and minimum SAT/ACT score of 1220/27 or International Baccalaureate diploma ($15,000).

Application Procedures Students admitted directly into the professional program freshman year. Deadline for freshmen and transfers: continuous. Notification date for freshmen and transfers: continuous. Required: essay, high school transcript, college transcript(s) for transfer students, 3 letters of recommendation, SAT or ACT test scores, portfolio for some studio majors. Recommended: interview, portfolio. Portfolio reviews held monthly on campus and off campus in various cities; the submission of slides may be substituted for portfolios when distance is prohibitive and for international applicants.

Web Site http://www.scad.edu

Undergraduate Contact Ginger Hansen, Executive Director of Recruitment, Admission, Savannah College of Art and Design, PO Box 2072, Savannah, Georgia 31402-3146; 912-525-5964, fax: 912-525-5983, e-mail address: ghunt@scad.edu

Graduate Contact Darrell Tutchton, Director of Graduate Enrollment, Admission, Savannah College of Art and Design, PO Box 2072, Savannah, Georgia 31402-3146; 912-525-5961, fax: 912-525-5985, e-mail address: dtutchto@scad.edu

More About the College

The Savannah College of Art and Design exists to prepare talented students for professional careers, emphasizing learning through individual attention in a positively oriented university environment. The goal of the college is to nurture and cultivate the unique qualities of each student through an interest-

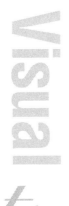

Savannah College of Art and Design (continued)

ing curriculum, in an inspiring environment, under the leadership of involved professors. A balanced fine arts and liberal arts curriculum has attracted students from every state and more than ninety countries, making SCAD one of the largest art and design colleges in the United States; current enrollment is approximately more than 8,000 students.

The Savannah College of Art and Design is a private, nonprofit institution accredited by the Commission on Colleges of the Southern Association of Colleges and Schools (1866 Southern Lane, Decatur, Georgia 30033-4097; phone: 404-679-4501) to award bachelor's and master's degrees. The College offers Bachelor of Arts, Bachelor of Fine Arts, Master of Architecture, Master of Arts, Master of Arts in Teaching, Master of Fine Arts, and Master of Urban Design degrees as well as undergraduate and graduate certificates. The five-year professional M.Arch. degree is accredited by the National Architectural Accrediting Board. Online programs are available through SCAD-eLearning.

Degrees are offered in advertising design, animation, architectural history, architecture (professional and postprofessional), art history, arts administration, broadcast design and motion graphics, cinema studies, design management, fashion, fibers, film and television, furniture design, graphic design, historic preservation, illustration (and illustration design), industrial design, interactive design and game development, interior design, metals and jewelry, painting, performing arts (and dramatic writing), photography (commercial, digital, documentary), printmaking, production design, professional writing, sculpture, sequential art, sound design, teaching (art or design), urban design, and visual effects.

SCAD has locations in Atlanta and Savannah, Georgia. The Savannah campus offers a full university experience in one of the largest National Historic Landmark districts in the United States. The state-of-the-art Atlanta facility is situated in a major metropolitan hub for business, the arts, and transportation.

Attractive residence hall accommodations, with meal plans, are provided for on a first-come, first-served basis. Furnishings include drafting tables, and the housing fee covers utilities.

SCAD offers men's and women's basketball, cross-country, equestrian, golf, soccer, swimming, and tennis; women's softball and volleyball; and men's baseball and men's and women's lacrosse. Fencing and cheerleading are offered as club sports.

Campus events such as concerts, lectures, plays, film screenings, and other entertainment, as well as cultural, recreational, and social programs, are planned and produced by the Student Activities Council.

Program Facilities Architecture, interior design, and historic preservation facilities include an intranet of PCs configured with electronic-design software including AutoCAD, Bentley Microstation V8, Adobe Photoshop, form-Z, 3D Studio VIZ, SURFCAM, and Autodesk Maya and Revit. A video microscope, as well as architectural conservation, metals conservation, and paint-analysis labs, also are available in the School of Building Arts.

Animation, broadcast design, interactive design and game development, and visual effects facilities offer ready access to high-end industry-standard equipment and software, including an intranet of Macintosh G4, Pentium IV, and SGI workstations configured with a diverse range of graphics software; high-end 2-D, 3-D, interactive, and compositing tools, including the Adobe product line; Flipbook, Autodesk Maya, Anime Studio, Side Effects' Houdini products; Pixar's Renderman; Discreet 3ds max; the Unreal game engine; and Z-Brush and Shake. Other tools include Lightwave and Macromedia products. SCAD's cutting-edge computer systems are combined with two green-screen stages, HD cameras, and a Vicon motion capture studio to provide visual effects students with a complete digital production facility.

Fashion and fibers students use computer-aided design workstations and scanners; Juki industrial sewing machines and sergers; a heat transfer press; customized dress forms; weaving facilities, including a variety of four- and eight-shaft floor looms, two AVL CompuDobby looms, and an AVL electronic Jacquard loom; a digital fabric printer and a dye lab; and a screenprinting studio. Fibers students use NedGraphics, an industry-standard software program.

The Gulfstream Center for Furniture and Industrial Design in Savannah is a 43,000-square-foot facility with a woodworking and metals and plastics fabrication lab, bench rooms and design studios, a plastic working area, a welding facility, a three-axis computer numeric controlled vertical milling machine, spray booths and a finishing room, and state-of-the-art electronic design studios configured with the latest versions of design and visualization software, such as Auto CAD, Autodesk Studio, Rhino 3-D, SolidWorks, and Maya. The computer lab has two 3-D printers with capabilities to print polycarbonate or ABS 3-D models of computer-generated designs.

Visual

Arts

Advertising design, graphic design, and illustration facilities include Macintosh computers with CD and DVD burners, scanners, black-and-white laser printers, light tables, and digital cameras. The Adobe product line; Macromedia Director, Dreamweaver, Flash, and FreeHand; Quark XPress; and other graphics packages are available.

Photography students have access to Macintosh digital imaging labs with extensive peripherals, wide-format inkjet printers, a Durst Theta printer, Imacon scanners, professional RA-4 color print processing machines for both negative and reversal papers, E-6 and C-41 color film processing machines, an alternative processes lab, studios, lighting equipment, view camera systems, medium-format camera systems, and digital SLR systems. Some labs are graduate-only.

Metals and jewelry studios include an FDM Prodigy Plus rapid prototyping 3-D printer with capabilities for ABS or wax models of CAD prototypes, and four-axis CNC milling machines.

Film and television facilities include the Steadicam EFP and Super Panther Dolly, a chroma key/green screen studio, and a sound stage. The department houses Avid Adrenaline, Symphony, and Xpress DV workstations; MiniDV and DVC Pro cameras; Sony digital high-definition television cameras; 16mm, Super 16mm, and 35mm cameras; and an all-digital studio. Sound design equipment and software includes ten DH Pro Tools labs, two dedicated surround sound mix/mastering rooms, a MIDI lab, a recording studio for music production and Foley, two suites for dialog recording and editing, and a professionally equipped location sound cart for film production.

Located next to the High Museum of Art in Midtown Atlanta, the sculpture facility is one of the finest in the Southeast. Designed by architect Renzo Piano, the facility contains a comprehensive wood and metal shop, a foundry for bronze and stainless steel, and studios and support equipment as well as exhibition space.

Performing Arts facilities include the 1,200-seat historic Lucas Theatre for the Arts, the 1,100-seet Trustees Theater, the 90-seat Afifi Amphitheater at the Pei Ling Chan Garden for the Arts, and the 150-seat black box Mondanaro Theater.

Student Performance/Exhibit Opportunities

The College is enlivened by a full calendar of gallery exhibitions, lectures, festivals, workshops, performances, and conferences each year. The College holds exhibitions of a variety of work (including student work) in several on-campus galleries, hosts a spring fashion show and an internationally renowned film festival, and features year-round student theater performances on campus. The College also hosts exhibitions in New York City, Paris, and elsewhere.

Faculty, Visiting Artists, and Alumni During the academic year, each major field of study may sponsor lectures and workshops, providing students the opportunity to meet and talk with working artists, architects, and designers. Special on-campus programming has included exhibits of work by renowned artists such as Robert Rauschenberg, Jasper Johns, Helen Frankenthaler, Romare Bearden, Andy Warhol, and Miriam Schapiro. Recently, Christo and Jeanne-Claude, Audrey Flack, Betye Saar, Benny Andrews, Sandy Skoglund, Judy Pfaff, Maya Lin, Danny Glover, Robert Redford, and Gregory Hines have lectured at SCAD.

Special Programs The College offers professional and faculty academic counseling, with special programs for first-year students and tutors available at no charge. SCAD also provides an English as a Second Language program for students whose native language is not English. Writing assistance, drawing assistance, and other learning assistance is provided for students as needed.

Internships are available and highly recommended for undergraduate and graduate students in a wide variety of programs. The federal work-study program is also available.

Study trips to major centers of artistic activity provide further opportunities for enrichment. SCAD faculty members direct off-campus studies in locations throughout the world.

Career Planning and Placement The office of career planning and placement provides career development and professional job search assistance to students and alumni through individual career counseling and exploration of career opportunities in art and design. The office also provides instruction in writing resumes and cover letters, making portfolio presentations, self- promotion, honing interviewing skills, and developing networking techniques to prepare students for the job market. The College routinely attracts major art and design corporate recruiters from companies such as Industrial Light and Magic, Pixar, Sony Pictures Imageworks, Nike, Michelin, Hallmark, and many others.

School of the Art Institute of Chicago
Chicago, Illinois

Independent, coed. Urban campus. Art program established 1866.

School of the Art Institute of Chicago (continued)

Degrees Bachelor of Arts in the area of visual and critical studies; Bachelor of Fine Arts in the areas of studio with emphasis in art history, theory and criticism; art education; writing; Bachelor of Interior Architecture. Majors and concentrations: architecture, art and technology, art education, art history, ceramic art and design, designed objects, fashion design and technology, fiber arts, film/video/new media, graphic arts/visual communication, interior architecture, painting/drawing, performance art, photography, print media, sculpture, sound design, textile arts, theory and criticism, video art, visual and critical studies, writing. Graduate degrees offered: Master of Arts in the areas of art education, modern art history and criticism, art therapy, teaching, visual and critical studies, arts administration and policy, new arts journalism; Master of Design in the areas of fashion, body, and garment; Master of Fine Arts in the areas of studio, writing; Master of Science in the area of historic preservation; Master of Architecture; Master of Design in Designed Objects; Master of Interior Architecture. Cross-registration with Roosevelt University, member schools of Association of Independent Colleges of Art and Design. Program accredited by NASAD.

Enrollment 3,028 total; 2,330 undergraduate, 602 graduate, 96 nonprofessional degree.

Art Student Profile 64% females, 36% males, 24% minorities, 18% international.

Art Faculty 135 total (full-time), 533 total (part-time). 88% of full-time faculty have terminal degrees. Graduate students teach a few undergraduate courses. Undergraduate student–faculty ratio: 11:1.

Student Life Student groups/activities include Student Government, "F" Student Newspaper, Student Union Galleries. Special housing available for art students.

Expenses for 2007–2008 Application fee: $65. Tuition: $30,750 full-time. Mandatory fees: $270 full-time. College room only: $8900. Special program-related fees: $290 for technology fee.

Financial Aid Program-specific awards: Chairman's Awards (full tuition) for qualified applicants, Distinguished Scholar Grants for qualified applicants ($8000), New Artist Society Presidential Awards for qualified applicants ($15,000), Recognition Scholarships for qualified applicants ($6000), Incentive Awards for qualified applicants ($4000), Scholar's Enrichment Awards for qualified applicants ($2000).

Application Procedures Students admitted directly into the professional program freshman year. Deadline for freshmen: June 1; transfers: continuous. Required: essay, high school transcript, college transcript(s) for transfer students, letter of recommendation, portfolio, SAT or ACT test scores. Recommended: minimum 3.0 high school GPA, interview. Portfolio reviews held continuously on campus and off campus; the submission of slides may be substituted for portfolios required for transfer credit evaluation.

Web Site http://www.saic.edu

Undergraduate Contact Scott Ramon, Director, Undergraduate Admissions, School of the Art Institute of Chicago, 36 South Wabash Avenue, Chicago, Illinois 60603; 312-629-6100, fax: 312-629-6101, e-mail address: admiss@saic.edu

Graduate Contact Andre Van De Putte, Associate Director, Graduate Admissions, School of the Art Institute of Chicago, 36 South Wabash Avenue, Suite 1201, Chicago, Illinois 60603; 312-629-6100, fax: 312-629-6101, e-mail address: admiss@saic.edu

More About the School

Since its founding in 1866, the School of the Art Institute of Chicago (SAIC) has been providing a leading global vision for the education of artists, designers, and others who shape contemporary art practice. SAIC's primary purpose is to foster the conceptual and technical education of artists, designers, and scholars in a highly professional, studio-oriented, and academically rigorous environment, encouraging excellence, critical inquiry, and experimentation. In 2002, the School was recognized as "the most influential art school in the nation" by a poll conducted by Columbia University and a panel of national art critics. *U.S. News & World Report* has consistently ranked SAIC's Master of Fine Arts program as number one in the nation.

Some 2,300 undergraduates, over 600 graduate students, and a faculty consisting of artists, designers, and scholars work in an environment that facilitates the exchange of ideas, the sharing of resources, and the critiquing and refining of technical abilities and conceptual issues.

SAIC is distinguished from other art and design schools in the breadth and depth of its curriculum, with more than 900 courses offered each semester. SAIC is committed to interdisciplinary exploration and the awareness that the boundaries between artistic fields are not always easily defined. Students do not declare a major but are free to design a path of study that best suits their creative development. A student may choose to do all their course work in one area of study or amongst multiple department areas. SAIC's credit/no-credit grading system encourages students to think creatively and to develop the self-motivation necessary for life as a practicing artist, designer, and scholar. SAIC enriches its strong studio program with a first-rate, nationally and regionally accredited liberal arts education, and it has one of the largest art history departments in the nation. SAIC is the only college in the country that offers a systematic series of courses on the history, theory, and philosophical bases of art criticism.

SAIC is located in the heart of downtown Chicago, home to the nation's second-largest art scene that includes world-class museums, galleries, alternative spaces, and arts organizations. Chicago itself is a vital part of SAIC, as a source of social and cultural activities and the stimulus for ideas and attitudes ultimately expressed through art. Peter Frank, art critic and curator says, "Of all American cities, Chicago has contributed the most solid and distinctive artwork and art thinking. The School of the Art Institute of Chicago is at the nucleus of this longstanding distinction."

Millennium Park, located across the street from SAIC, is a twenty-first-century marvel, and SAIC, its faculty members, and its students played a key role in its realization. One of the signature pieces of public art in the park, the Crown Fountain by Spanish artist Jaume Plensa, was created with the assistance of both SAIC students and faculty members, who collaborated with Plensa in producing the 1,000 video portraits that are screened continuously on the fountain's twin video towers. The park, with its unique mix of art, architecture, and nature, has become an urban oasis for SAIC students.

SAIC maintains two distinctive residence halls with loft-style rooms—each with their own bathroom, kitchen, voicemail, and Internet access. The residence halls offer 24-hour security and controlled access as well as spacious, well-lit studios; lounge rooms with big screen TVs; computer labs; and laundry facilities. Students can immerse themselves in a community of fellow artists, live in the heart of Chicago's loop, and enjoy conveniences unavailable in most student apartments.

SAIC offers a wide variety of unique resources, beginning with the collection of its sister institution, the Art Institute of Chicago, and its Ryerson Library and Burnham Library of Architecture, the largest art and architecture research libraries in the country. The Gene Siskel Film Center presents significant programs of world cinema and presentations by an international array of film and video artists. SAIC's Video Data Bank houses more than 1,600 titles and is the leading resource in the country for videotapes by and about contemporary artists. The Poetry Center brings renowned poets and writers to Chicago to share their work with the public.

Additional services include an international student office, a multicultural affairs office, health and counseling services, a learning center (offering support services for students with learning disabilities), and an extensive program for academic advising. SAIC is home to the largest and most successful arts-related Cooperative Education program in the country, providing employment opportunities worldwide. The Career Development Center assists in researching job and grant opportunities, preparing portfolios and artist statements, exploring exhibition possibilities, and understanding the legal aspects of entrepreneurship. The center maintains an online database that lists local and national positions, including freelance, part-time, and full-time employment.

Program Facilities SAIC's campus encompasses seven buildings in downtown Chicago, including a 40,000-square-foot permanent exhibition space. There are fully equipped studios for each area of concentration, and the School's policy allows 24-hour access to facilities.

The Painting and Drawing department has many well-lit studio classrooms, individual space for select undergraduate and graduate students, and space for critiques. Facilities in the sculpture department include a complete woodshop, a welding shop, a bronze and aluminum foundry, a plaster room, and both indoor and outdoor exhibition spaces. A well-equipped metals shop allows for forging, forming, joining, and casting of nonferrous metals. The Printmedia department has a digital platemaker and two-color high-speed offset press and bookbinding facilities.

The Art and Technology department maintains a multimedia authoring suite, an electronics construction shop, a microcontroller development and programming area, a kinetics shop, neon and holography studios, installation space, and MIDI and digital sound systems. The Film, Video, and New Media department has equipment ranging from a unique

School of the Art Institute of Chicago (continued)

hand-built image processor to the latest prosumer, professional, and industrial video equipment. Equipment available to students includes digital cameras, projectors, switchers, light kits, and microphones. Professional quality film/video and sound mixing suites, traditional and 3-D animation facilities, and HD video and film production equipment are also available.

The Photography department has a Lambda digital photographic printer; traditional photographic process facilities, including non-silver, color, and black and white printing; and loans of digital, medium-format, and large-format cameras and lighting equipment. The Sound department offers studios and workstations equipped with digital editing systems, multitracks and digital recorders, and several digital and rare vintage analog synthesizers and samplers. A larger configurable space is equipped with a multichannel sound system and ceiling grid that makes it suitable for performances and installations.

The Ceramics department's facilities include clay mixers, an extruder, a slab roller, complete moldmaking and casting facilities, and several styles of wheels. Diverse firing options in various kiln styles include high- and low-fire oxidation and reduction, soda, and raku. The Visual Communication department's facilities include state-of-the-art computer labs with color scanners, a copy stand, and spacious studios. Students in the Fashion Design department study design and construction in a spacious facility with industrial-grade equipment. The department houses a Fashion Resource Center, with a collection of worldwide designer garments and a research library with rare books, videotapes, and international publications. The Fiber and Material Studies department has AVL computer looms, more than thirty traditional looms, a large area for hand construction, full facilities for screenprinting on fabric that includes a darkroom for photo-screeners, a computer lab, and a kitchen with industrial washers and dryers used for the setting of dyes.

Architecture, interior architecture, and designed objects equipment and facilities include an advanced output center with ABS plastic rapid prototyper, laser cutter, and large format printers; complete wood and plastic shop with heavy machine tools and a CNC router; separate highly ventilated mold-making room with paint hood, wax and fume hood, and vacuformer; graduate and undergraduate studios with desks, pin up areas, and complete built-in digital audio visual support; the GFRY display studio funded by Motorola Corporation; several critique and exhibition spaces; a materials library; 2-D/slide scanner and projectors; digital copy stand; small model tools; and lecture room. In the new AIADO Design Shop, students can work with both analog fabrication/modeling equipment and digitally controlled (CNC) tools.

Three general-access Media Centers lend thousands of pieces of audiovisual equipment to students. General-access computer labs are equipped with the latest model Apple computers installed with the latest versions of digital video, desktop publishing, 3-D rendering, Web-site authoring, animation, multimedia, graphic, and audio software applications. The workstations are equipped with various flatbed, negative, and slide scanners and Imacon high-end scanners. The lab offers 24-hour access and weekly instructional workshops on specialized equipment. SAIC also has a full-service color digital output Service Bureau equipped with laser cutting and 3-D printing.

The John M. Flaxman Library collections include 60,000 volumes on art and the liberal arts and sciences, 360 periodical subscriptions, films, videos, audiotapes, CDs, microforms, and picture files. The Joan Flasch Artists' Book Collection contains more than 3,000 artists' books, along with a research collection of exhibition catalogs and other related material. The MacLean Visual Resource Center maintains a noncirculating collection of more than 500,000 slides.

Faculty, Resident Artists, and Alumni Faculty members are selected for their skills, insight, and dedication as teachers and for their professional accomplishments as artists, designers, and scholars. There are currently over 600 full- and part-time faculty members, among them NEA grant recipients, Louis Comfort Tiffany Foundation Fellowship recipients, and Rockefeller Foundation grant recipients. SAIC faculty members have their work exhibited in museums, galleries, and festivals nationally and internationally. They publish books, plays, poetry, and criticism; organize and curate exhibitions; and design, build, and preserve buildings throughout the world. Each year, 100 or more well-known visiting artists, including poets, political activists, designers, and visual artists, present workshops and provide individual student critiques through the Visiting Artists Program. Notable alumni include Claes Oldenburg, Ivan Albright, Georgia O'Keefe, David Sedaris, Cynthia Rowley, and Vincente Minnelli.

Student Performance/Exhibit Opportunities

The School's exhibition spaces include the Betty Rymer Gallery, which highlights work from departments and presents special exhibitions, and Gallery 2,

Visual

Arts

with exhibition space, a performance space, and a space designed for site-specific installations. In addition, Gallery X and the Lounge Gallery, sponsored by the Student Union Galleries, provide exhibition space for currently enrolled students. The Fashion department hosts a fashion show in late spring for students in their second, third, and fourth year. The First-Year Program sponsors ArtBash in the spring of each year, highlighting the work produced in its program.

Off-Campus Arrangements SAIC's Mobility Program allows students to attend partner schools within the United States and Canada and includes the New York Studio semester. The School also maintains semester exchange agreements with more than twenty schools in Europe, Asia, and South America, and students may develop their own individual programs. SAIC faculty members also lead study trips during each summer and winter interim to such destinations as Cuba, Czech Republic, Italy, Japan, Los Angeles, Puerto Rico, and Vietnam.

School of the Museum of Fine Arts, Boston

Boston, Massachusetts

Independent, coed. Urban campus. Total enrollment: 797. Art program established 1876.

Degrees Bachelor of Fine Arts. Majors and concentrations: animation, art education, art/fine arts, ceramics, drawing, film, graphic design, illustration, interdisciplinary studies, jewelry and metalsmithing, painting, papermaking, performance, photography, printmaking, screenprinting, sculpture, self-designed art, sound art, stained glass, studio art, text and image art, video art. Graduate degrees offered: Master of Arts in Teaching; Master of Fine Arts. Cross-registration with Colleges in the ProArts Consortium, Tufts University, Wheaton College, Massachusetts Institute of Technology. Program accredited by NASAD.

Enrollment 797 total; 640 undergraduate, 87 graduate, 70 nonprofessional degree.

Art Student Profile 69% females, 31% males, 15% minorities, 7% international.

Art Faculty 49 total (full-time), 34 total (part-time). 73% of full-time faculty have terminal degrees. Graduate students teach a

few undergraduate courses. Undergraduate student–faculty ratio: 9:1.

Student Life Student groups/activities include student exhibitions, Infrasculpture, Gay/Lesbian/Transgender and Supporters (Outloud!). Special housing available for art students.

Expenses for 2007–2008 Application fee: $65. One-time mandatory fee: $125. Tuition: $26,950 full-time. Mandatory fees: $1020 full-time. Full-time tuition and fees vary according to course load, degree level, and program. College room only: $11,600. Special program-related fees: $510 per semester for comprehensive fee, $1790 per year for health insurance fee.

Financial Aid Program-specific awards: 125 art merit scholarships ($8500), 416 School of the Museum of Fine Arts Grants for those demonstrating need ($17,500).

Application Procedures Students admitted directly into the professional program freshman year. Deadline for freshmen: February 1; transfers: March 1. Notification date for freshmen and transfers: continuous. Required: essay, high school transcript, college transcript(s) for transfer students, 2 letters of recommendation, portfolio, SAT or ACT test scores. Recommended: interview. Portfolio reviews held weekly on campus and off campus at National Portfolio Days; the submission of slides may be substituted for portfolios.

Web Site http://www.smfa.edu

Undergraduate Contact Ms. Susan Clain, Dean of Admissions, School of the Museum of Fine Arts, Boston, 230 The Fenway, Boston, Massachusetts 02115; 617-369-3626, fax: 617-369-4264, e-mail address: admissions@smfa.edu

Graduate Contact Mr. Jesse Tarantino, Assistant Dean of Admissions, School of the Museum of Fine Arts, Boston, 230 The Fenway, Boston, Massachusetts 02115; 617-369-3626, fax: 617-369-4264, e-mail address: admissions@smfa.edu

More About the School

The School of the Museum of Fine Arts, Boston (SMFA), is a unique institution dedicated to educating artists and focused on fostering creative investigation, risk-taking, and individual vision. Everyone at the SMFA recognizes that disciplines converge and influence each other and that contemporary art is truly interdisciplinary. All students are encouraged to build solid foundations and acquire

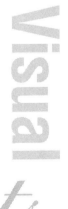

Visual Arts

School of the Museum of Fine Arts, Boston (continued)

skill sets in numerous disciplines in order to create new possibilities and forms of artmaking rather than majoring in one studio area. Students are given the freedom to design a program of study that best suits their needs and goals. This freedom comes with strong support and guidance from faculty advisers.

In partnership with Tufts University, the School offers the following degree programs: the Bachelor of Fine Arts (B.F.A.), the Bachelor of Fine Arts Plus Master of Arts in Teaching (M.A.T.) in Art Education, the five-year combined-degree program (B.A./B.F.A. or B.S./B.F.A.), the Master of Fine Arts (M.F.A.), and the Master of Arts in Teaching (M.A.T.) in art education. In partnership with Northeastern, the School offers a Bachelor of Fine Arts and a Master of Fine Arts in studio art. All students in degree programs are fully enrolled at the School of the Museum of Fine Arts and Tufts or Northeastern University and graduate with a Tufts or Northeastern degree. The School also offers the Diploma Program, the one-year Fifth Year Certificate Program, and the Post-Baccalaureate Certificate Program. The School is a division of the Museum of Fine Arts, Boston, which is located across the street from the School.

The diversity of the faculty members and the range of facilities allow the student to develop a very personal and individual means of expression. Course teaching methods range from structured classes, with regular attendance, to individual instruction for work done independently outside the School. Class sizes are generally small, and every area of study is supported by accomplished, professional faculty members; extensive programs with visiting artists; and an energetic schedule of exhibitions. At the end of each semester, the student presents a body of art work to a review board consisting of faculty members and students. There is a discussion of the total semester experience, and suggestions are made for future study. A block of credits is awarded, appropriate to the term's accomplishments, and a written evaluation is made.

Boston is home to many educational and cultural institutions. The Museum School is a vital member of the art community, presenting a dynamic schedule of exhibitions, lectures, and panel discussions throughout the academic year. As a division of the Museum of Fine Arts, students also have special access to the educational resources, collections, curatorial departments, and special programs of one of the most comprehensive and outstanding collections of art in the world.

Program Facilities The SMFA campus features several buildings with 24-hour security and extensive access for students. The two main buildings house classrooms, studios, state-of-the-art equipment, exhibition spaces, computer and video labs, the Writing Center, the W. Van Alan Clark Jr. Library, and Café des Arts, which serves breakfast, lunch, and dinner.

The School provides a limited number of individual studio spaces for undergraduate degree students and diploma students. Students have 24-hour access to most studio spaces and facilities. Students may apply for studio space in the summer months.

There is a limited amount of residential housing in the Artists' Residence Hall at Massachusetts College of Art. The majority of students choose to live in nearby off-campus apartments, and the SMFA Student Affairs Office can help find the right location and the right roommate.

Faculty, Visiting Artists, and Alumni All studio faculty members are practicing professional artists with regional, national, and international reputations. The Visiting Artists and Curators program encourages students to interact with prominent artists.

Exhibition Opportunities The Museum School provides students with more than 8,000 square feet of exhibition space in six galleries. These excellent sites are in addition to contemporary gallery space at the Museum of Fine Arts, Boston, where winners of the prestigious Traveling Scholarship awards exhibit every year. Student-curated exhibitions are also on view at the Museum throughout the year. The School also sponsors a number of special prize funds, offering students the chance to win travel grants, cash awards, and exhibition opportunities.

Special Programs The School is a member of the Pro Arts Consortium in Boston, which allows students to take classes on a space-available basis at Berklee College of Music, the Boston Architectural Center, Emerson College, the Boston Conservatory, and Massachusetts College of Art. The School also offers selective cross-registration with MIT. As a member of the Association of Independent Colleges of Art and Design (AICAD), students also have the opportunity to study at colleges throughout the United States and abroad.

School of Visual Arts
New York, New York

Proprietary, coed. Urban campus. Total enrollment: 3,946. Art program established 1947.

Degrees Bachelor of Fine Arts in the areas of advertising, animation, cartooning, computer art/computer animation/visual effects, film and video, fine arts, graphic design, illustration, interior design, photography, visual and critical studies. Majors and concentrations: advertising design, animation, art/fine arts, cartooning, computer art/animation/visual effects, film and video production, graphic design, illustration, interior design, photography, visual studies. Graduate degrees offered: Master of Arts in Teaching in the area of art education; Master of Fine Arts in the areas of computer art, design, fine arts, illustration as visual essay, art criticism and writing, photography, video and related media, interaction design, social documentary film; Master of Professional Studies in the areas of art therapy, digital photography. Program accredited by NASAD.

Enrollment 3,747 total; 3,323 undergraduate, 424 graduate.

Art Student Profile 55% females, 45% males, 14% minorities, 15% international.

Art Faculty 830 total (part-time). Graduate students do not teach undergraduate courses. Undergraduate student–faculty ratio: 4:1.

Student Life Student groups/activities include Visual Arts Students Association, Visual Opinion (campus literary magazine), WSVA campus radio station.

Expenses for 2007–2008 Application fee: $50. Tuition: $23,520 full-time. Full-time tuition varies according to program. College room only: $11,350. Room charges vary according to gender, housing facility, and location. Special program-related fees: $200–$1200 per semester for departmental fee.

Financial Aid Program-specific awards: Silas H. Rhodes Scholarship ($10,000).

Application Procedures Students admitted directly into the professional program freshman year. Deadline for freshmen and transfers: continuous. Required: essay, high school transcript, college transcript(s) for transfer students, portfolio, SAT or ACT test scores, 2-part essay for film applicants, TOEFL score for applicants whose primary language is not English. Portfolio reviews held by appointment year-round on campus and off campus in various locations throughout the U.S. on National Portfolio Days; the submission of slides may be substituted for portfolios (required for transfers, scholarship applicants, and students not attending an in-person portfolio review).

Web Site http://www.sva.edu

Contact Adam Rogers, Director of Admissions, School of Visual Arts, 209 East 23rd Street, New York, New York 10010; 212-592-2100, fax: 212-592-2116, e-mail address: admissions@sva.edu

More About the School

The School of Visual Arts (SVA) in New York City is an established leader and innovator in the education of artists. From its inception in 1947, the faculty has consisted of professionals working in the arts and art-related fields. SVA provides an environment that nurtures creativity, inventiveness, and experimentation—enabling students to develop a strong sense of identity and a clear direction of purpose.

The four-year curriculum remains responsive to the needs and demands of the industry and is designed to allow students a greater freedom of choice in electives and requirements with each succeeding year. The first year of each program, a foundation year, ensures the mastery of basic skills in each chosen discipline as well as in writing and art history. After the first year, students focus on specific areas of concentration and, under the guidance of academic advisers and faculty members, pursue their own individual goals.

In addition, SVA's Internship for Credit Program gives students the chance to work alongside top art directors, photographers, painters, and illustrators as well as in film and animation studios. SVA has a very high job placement rate—approximately 88 percent of SVA's students are employed within a year of graduation.

Program Facilities SVA provides students with studios that continually mirror the standards of the professional art world. Studio space and equipment are offered in different departments, varying in availability depending on such factors as the student's class seniority and major of study. The SVA library's holdings include distinctive multimedia collections, over 65,000 books, more than 260 periodicals subscriptions, and special collections of pictures, color slides, film scripts, comics, videotapes, exhibition catalogs, CD-ROMs, and recordings.

Faculty, Resident Artists, and Alumni The School of Visual Arts is proud of its illustrious faculty of more than 700 professional artists and designers who represent an array of fields in the fine and

School of Visual Arts (continued)

applied arts. Each faculty member has chosen to commit to the professional art world as well as to teaching the next generation of artists. The SVA community is enthusiastic about the faculty's ability to balance the life of a dynamic artist with the vivaciousness that only a dedicated teacher can provide to his or her students. SVA has some of the world's greatest artists among its alumni. Many of them live and work in New York City; others can be found throughout the United States and in more than thirty countries around the world. They work at advertising agencies, television networks, publishing houses, film studios, recording companies, design firms, art galleries, and major museums. Others do freelance work or run their own start-up companies.

Exhibit Opportunities The College operates two campus galleries as well as a Chelsea gallery space, affording SVA students the opportunity to exhibit their work twelve months a year. Students are encouraged to show their work outside of SVA by participating in exhibits and competitions held in New York City and throughout the United States.

Special Programs SVA students have the opportunity to participate in art programs abroad during the summer semester. SVA offers Painting in Barcelona, Painting in Florence, Digital Photography in Florence, Art History in Southern France, Cinema in Italy, and the Myths and History of Ancient Greece in Greece. For more information, students should contact the Office of International Studies at 212-592-2543.

Seton Hall University

South Orange, New Jersey

Independent Roman Catholic, coed. Suburban campus. Total enrollment: 9,637 (2006). Art program established 1968.

Degrees Bachelor of Arts in the areas of art history, fine arts, graphic interactive and advertising design; Bachelor of Science in the area of art education. Majors and concentrations: advertising, art education, art history, art/fine arts, graphic design, interactive design. Graduate degrees offered: Master of Arts in the area of museum professions.

Enrollment 130 total; 60 undergraduate, 70 graduate.

Art Student Profile 60% females, 40% males, 15% minorities, 5% international.

Art Faculty 9 undergraduate (full-time), 8 undergraduate (part-time), 3 graduate (full-

time), 4 graduate (part-time). 100% of full-time faculty have terminal degrees. Graduate students do not teach undergraduate courses. Undergraduate student–faculty ratio: 15:1.

Student Life Student groups/activities include student exhibitions, gallery exhibitions.

Expenses for 2007–2008 Application fee: $55. One-time mandatory fee: $300. Comprehensive fee: $38,678 includes full-time tuition ($25,900), mandatory fees ($1950), and college room and board ($10,828). College room only: $6914. Full-time tuition and fees vary according to course load. Room and board charges vary according to board plan and housing facility. Special program-related fees: $50 per graphic design for computer fees.

Financial Aid Program-specific awards: 1 Henry Gasser Scholarship for art majors demonstrating talent and/or academic achievement ($1800).

Application Procedures Students admitted directly into the professional program freshman year. Deadline for freshmen and transfers: continuous. Required: essay, high school transcript, college transcript(s) for transfer students, minimum 2.0 high school GPA, 3 letters of recommendation, SAT or ACT test scores. Recommended: minimum 3.0 high school GPA, interview, portfolio. Portfolio reviews held as needed on campus; the submission of slides may be substituted for portfolios for large works of art.

Web Site http://www.shu.edu

Undergraduate Contact Admissions Office, Seton Hall University, 400 South Orange Avenue, South Orange, New Jersey 07079-2696; 973-761-9000 ext. 9332.

Graduate Contact Dr. Petra Chu, Director, MA Program in Museum Professions, Department of Art and Music, Seton Hall University, 400 South Orange Avenue, South Orange, New Jersey 07079-2696; 973-761-7966, fax: 973-275-2368, e-mail address: chupetra@shu.edu

Seton Hill University

Greensburg, Pennsylvania

Independent Roman Catholic, coed. Small town campus. Total enrollment: 1,967. Art program established 1955.

Degrees Bachelor of Fine Arts in the areas of graphic design, 2-D media, 3-D media, art and technology. Majors and concentrations: art and technology, graphic design, three-dimensional studies, two-dimensional studies. Graduate degrees offered: Master of Arts in the area of art therapy. Cross-registration with Pittsburgh Filmmakers, St. Vincent College, University of Pittsburgh at Greensburg, Westmoreland County Community College.

Enrollment 141 total; 53 undergraduate, 27 graduate, 61 nonprofessional degree.

Art Student Profile 80% females, 20% males, 10% minorities, 10% international.

Art Faculty 6 undergraduate (full-time), 5 undergraduate (part-time), 1 graduate (full-time), 2 graduate (part-time). 85% of full-time faculty have terminal degrees. Graduate students do not teach undergraduate courses. Undergraduate student–faculty ratio: 8:1.

Student Life Student groups/activities include Student In The Arts (SITA), Graphic Design Club, Student Art Therapy Association.

Expenses for 2007–2008 Application fee: $35. Comprehensive fee: $32,746 includes full-time tuition ($24,806), mandatory fees ($200), and college room and board ($7740). Room and board charges vary according to board plan and housing facility. Special program-related fees: $120 per course for supplies.

Financial Aid Program-specific awards: Division of Visual and Performing Arts Scholarships for incoming freshmen ($3000), 1 Josefa Filkosky Scholarship for juniors ($700).

Application Procedures Students admitted directly into the professional program freshman year. Deadline for freshmen and transfers: August 15. Notification date for freshmen and transfers: continuous. Required: essay, high school transcript, college transcript(s) for transfer students, minimum 2.0 high school GPA, 3 letters of recommendation, portfolio, SAT or ACT test scores. Recommended: minimum 3.0 high school GPA, interview. Portfolio reviews held continuously on campus; the submission of slides may be substituted for portfolios when distance is prohibitive.

Web Site http://www.setonhill.edu

Undergraduate Contact Sherri Bett, Director, Admissions Office, Seton Hill University, 1 Seton Hill Drive, Greensburg, Pennsylvania 15601; 724-838-4255, fax: 724-830-4611, e-mail address: bett@setonhill.edu

Graduate Contact Ms. Nina Denninger, Director, Graduate Program in Art Therapy, Seton Hill University, Seton Hill Drive, Greensburg, Pennsylvania 15601; 724-830-1047, fax: 724-830-4611, e-mail address: denninger@setonhill.edu

Shepherd University

Shepherdstown, West Virginia

State-supported, coed. Small town campus. Total enrollment: 4,119. Art program established 1950.

Degrees Bachelor of Fine Arts in the areas of graphic design, photography/computer digital imagery, painting, printmaking, sculpture. Majors and concentrations: art/fine arts, digital imaging, graphic design, illustration, painting/drawing, photography, printmaking, sculpture.

Enrollment 275 total; 225 undergraduate, 50 nonprofessional degree.

Art Student Profile 55% females, 45% males, 9% minorities, 5% international.

Art Faculty 10 undergraduate (full-time), 10 undergraduate (part-time). 100% of full-time faculty have terminal degrees. Graduate students do not teach undergraduate courses. Undergraduate student–faculty ratio: 15:1.

Student Life Student groups/activities include Art Alliance Exhibits, Performing and Visual Arts Series, American Institute of Graphic Arts.

Expenses for 2007–2008 Application fee: $35. State resident tuition: $4564 full-time. Nonresident tuition: $12,036 full-time. Full-time tuition varies according to program and reciprocity agreements. College room and board: $6714. Room and board charges vary according to board plan and housing facility. Special program-related fees: $30 per course for studio fee.

Financial Aid Program-specific awards: 12 art scholarships for West Virginia resident program majors ($2000), 2 Blundell Awards for first-year students ($700), 2 Bridgeforth Awards for photography/computer imaging students ($500–$1000), 2 Hendricks Scholarships for art majors ($600), 1 Jeffrey Miller Scholarship for non-traditional design majors ($500).

Application Procedures Students admitted directly into the professional program freshman year. Deadline for freshmen and transfers: February 1. Notification date for freshmen and transfers: April 1. Required: high school transcript, college transcript(s) for transfer stu-

Shepherd University (continued)

dents, minimum 2.0 high school GPA, interview, portfolio, SAT or ACT test scores. Portfolio reviews held 6 times on campus; the submission of slides may be substituted for portfolios (slides/CD preferred).

Web Site http://www.shepherd.edu

Undergraduate Contact Ms. Kimberly Scranage, Director of Admissions, Shepherd University, PO Box 3210, Shepherdstown, West Virginia 25443; 304-876-5212, fax: 304-876-3101, e-mail address: kscranag@shepherd.edu

Shorter College

Rome, Georgia

Independent Baptist, coed. Small town campus. Total enrollment: 1,394. Art program established 1994.

Degrees Bachelor of Fine Arts in the area of art. Majors and concentrations: ceramics, painting/drawing, sculpture. Cross-registration with Berry College.

Enrollment 46 total; 40 undergraduate, 6 nonprofessional degree.

Art Student Profile 60% females, 40% males, 2% minorities, 5% international.

Art Faculty 2 undergraduate (full-time), 2 undergraduate (part-time). 100% of full-time faculty have terminal degrees. Graduate students do not teach undergraduate courses. Undergraduate student–faculty ratio: 15:1.

Student Life Student groups/activities include Art Student League.

Expenses for 2007–2008 Application fee: $25. Comprehensive fee: $22,160 includes full-time tuition ($14,850), mandatory fees ($310), and college room and board ($7000). College room only: $3800. Full-time tuition and fees vary according to course load. Room and board charges vary according to board plan and housing facility.

Financial Aid Program-specific awards: 10 art scholarships for art majors ($500–$3000).

Application Procedures Students admitted directly into the professional program freshman year. Deadline for freshmen and transfers: continuous. Required: essay, high school transcript, college transcript(s) for transfer students, minimum 2.0 high school GPA, letter of recommendation, interview, portfolio, SAT or ACT test scores. Portfolio reviews held 4 times on campus.

Web Site http://www.shorter.edu

Undergraduate Contact Dr. Alan B. Wingard, Dean, School of the Arts, Shorter College, 315 Shorter Avenue, Rome, Georgia 30165; 706-233-7248, fax: 706-236-1517, e-mail address: awingard@shorter.edu

Simon Fraser University

Burnaby, British Columbia, Canada

Province-supported, coed. Suburban campus. Total enrollment: 26,128. Art program established 1992.

Web Site http://www.sfu.ca/

Sonoma State University

Rohnert Park, California

State-supported, coed. Small town campus. Total enrollment: 8,586. Art program established 1967.

Degrees Bachelor of Fine Arts in the areas of painting, printmaking, sculpture, photography. Majors and concentrations: art history, art/fine arts, painting, photography, printmaking, sculpture, works on paper. Cross-registration with San Francisco State University. Program accredited by NASAD.

Enrollment 198 total; 18 undergraduate, 180 nonprofessional degree.

Art Student Profile 60% females, 40% males, 30% minorities.

Art Faculty 6 undergraduate (full-time), 3 undergraduate (part-time). 100% of full-time faculty have terminal degrees. Graduate students do not teach undergraduate courses. Undergraduate student–faculty ratio: 15:1.

Student Life Student groups/activities include BFA Student Exhibition, Student Art Exhibition, Ceramics Guild.

Expenses for 2007–2008 Application fee: $55. State resident tuition: $0 full-time. Nonresident tuition: $8136 full-time. Mandatory fees: $3946 full-time. Full-time tuition and fees vary according to course load and degree level. College room and board: $8820. Room and board charges vary according to housing facility. Special program-related fees: $10–$68 per course for supplies.

Financial Aid Program-specific awards: 1 William Smith Award for ceramics majors ($500), 1 William Smith Award for studio art majors ($500), 1 Brooks Award for art history majors ($400), 1 John Bolles Scholarship for program majors ($750), 2 Art Department Scholarships for program majors ($300), 2 Edward Boyle Scholarships for program majors ($250), 1 Hendrickson Family Scholarship for painting majors ($750).

Application Procedures Students apply for admission into the professional program by sophomore, junior year. Deadline for freshmen and transfers: May 31. Required: essay, college transcript(s) for transfer students, minimum 3.0 high school GPA, 2 letters of recommendation, portfolio, completion of lower division studio requirements. Portfolio reviews held twice on campus; the submission of slides may be substituted for portfolios (slides preferred).

Web Site http://www.sonoma.edu/art/

Undergraduate Contact Mr. Stephen Galloway, Department of Art and Art History, Sonoma State University, 1801 East Cotati Avenue, Rohnert Park, California 94928; 707-664-2364, fax: 707-664-4333, e-mail address: stephen.galloway@sonoma.edu

Southern California Institute of Architecture

Los Angeles, California

Independent, coed. Urban campus. Total enrollment: 438 (2007).

Degrees Bachelor of Architecture in the area of architecture. Majors and concentrations: architecture. Graduate degrees offered: Master of Architecture in the area of architecture. Program accredited by NAAB.

Enrollment 422 total; 201 undergraduate, 221 graduate.

Art Student Profile 35% females, 65% males, 35% minorities, 23% international.

Art Faculty 28 total (full-time), 50 total (part-time). Graduate students do not teach undergraduate courses. Undergraduate student–faculty ratio: 15:1.

Student Life Student groups/activities include Sci-Arc Public Programs (Lecture Series) and Gallery Installations and Exhibits, Student Union and Academic Council.

Expenses for 2007–2008 Application fee: $60. Tuition: $10,772 full-time. Mandatory fees: $60 full-time.

Financial Aid Program-specific awards: 28 Undergraduate Admissions Awards for undergraduate students ($3260), 14 Undergrad Financial Aid awards for undergraduate F.A. students ($2692).

Application Procedures Students admitted directly into the professional program freshman year. Deadline for freshmen: February 1; transfers: May 1. Notification date for freshmen and transfers: August 1. Required: essay, high school transcript, college transcript(s) for transfer students, minimum 2.0 high school GPA, 3 letters of recommendation, portfolio, SAT or ACT test scores, TOEFL scores for international applicants, $60 processing fee. Recommended: minimum 3.0 high school GPA, interview. Portfolio reviews held continuously March-July on campus.

Web Site http://www.sciarc.edu/

Contact Mr. J. J. Jackman, Director, Admissions, Southern California Institute of Architecture, 960 East 3rd Street, Los Angeles, California 90013; 213-356-5321, fax: 213-613-2260, e-mail address: jj@sciarc.edu

Southern Illinois University Carbondale

Carbondale, Illinois

State-supported, coed. Rural campus. Total enrollment: 20,983. Art program established 1931.

Degrees Bachelor of Fine Arts in the area of art. Majors and concentrations: art education, ceramic art and design, communication design, glass, industrial design, jewelry and metalsmithing, painting/drawing, printmaking, sculpture. Graduate degrees offered: Master of Fine Arts in the area of art. Program accredited by NASAD.

Enrollment 509 total; 159 undergraduate, 55 graduate, 295 nonprofessional degree.

Art Student Profile 46% females, 54% males, 17% minorities, 4% international.

Southern Illinois University Carbondale (continued)

Art Faculty 20 total (full-time), 9 total (part-time). 100% of full-time faculty have terminal degrees. Graduate students teach about a quarter of undergraduate courses. Undergraduate student–faculty ratio: 5:1.

Student Life Student groups/activities include League of Art and Design, Industrial Design Society of America Student Chapter, American Center for Design. Special housing available for art students.

Expenses for 2007–2008 Application fee: $30. State resident tuition: $6348 full-time. Nonresident tuition: $15,870 full-time. Mandatory fees: $2551 full-time. Full-time tuition and fees vary according to course load. College room and board: $6666. College room only: $3650. Room and board charges vary according to board plan and housing facility. Special program-related fees: $3–$75 per course for studio materials, $70 per course for model fees.

Financial Aid Program-specific awards: 5–7 talent scholarships for incoming students ($1000), 2 Mitchell Scholarships for incoming students from southern Illinois ($1000), 2–4 Celine A. Chu Memorial Scholarships for junior and senior painting, drawing, printmaking majors ($500), 2–10 Rickert Ziebold Trust Awards for graduating seniors ($2000–$10,000).

Application Procedures Students apply for admission into the professional program by sophomore year. Deadline for freshmen and transfers: continuous. Notification date for freshmen and transfers: continuous. Required: high school transcript, college transcript(s) for transfer students, portfolio, SAT or ACT test scores (minimum composite ACT score of 20), minimum 2.0 college GPA for transfer students. Portfolio reviews held twice on campus.

Web Site http://www.artanddesign.siu.edu

Undergraduate Contact Ms. Valerie L. Brooks, Academic Advisor, School of Art and Design, Southern Illinois University Carbondale, 1100 South Normal Avenue, MC 4301, Carbondale, Illinois 62901; 618-453-4313, fax: 618-453-7710, e-mail address: vlbrooks@siu.edu

Graduate Contact Mr. Chris Wildrick, Graduate Program Head, School of Art and Design, Southern Illinois University Carbondale, 1100 South Normal Avenue, MC 4301, Carbondale, Illinois 62901; 618-453-7760, fax: 618-453-7710, e-mail address: wildrick@siu.edu

Southern Illinois University Edwardsville

Edwardsville, Illinois

State-supported, coed. Suburban campus. Total enrollment: 13,298. Art program established 1958.

Degrees Bachelor of Fine Arts in the area of art studio; Bachelor of Science in the area of art education. Majors and concentrations: art education, art history, ceramic art and design, computer graphics, jewelry and metalsmithing, painting/drawing, photography, printmaking, sculpture, textile arts. Graduate degrees offered: Master of Arts in the area of art therapy; Master of Fine Arts in the area of art studio.

Enrollment 310 total; 238 undergraduate, 52 graduate, 20 nonprofessional degree.

Art Student Profile 55% females, 45% males, 20% minorities, 10% international.

Art Faculty 16 undergraduate (full-time), 10 undergraduate (part-time), 3 graduate (full-time), 2 graduate (part-time). 100% of full-time faculty have terminal degrees. Graduate students teach a few undergraduate courses. Undergraduate student–faculty ratio: 16:1.

Student Life Student groups/activities include Student Sculpture on Campus Program, Mexico Foreign Study Program, New York and Washington D.C. study program. Special housing available for art students.

Expenses for 2007–2008 Application fee: $30. Area resident tuition: $5228 full-time. State resident tuition: $5938 full-time. Nonresident tuition: $13,069 full-time. Mandatory fees: $1180 full-time. College room and board: $6750. College room only: $3970. Special program-related fees: $12–$75 per course for studio fee.

Financial Aid Program-specific awards: 10 Chancellor's Scholarships for art majors ($3000).

Application Procedures Students apply for admission into the professional program by sophomore, junior year. Deadline for freshmen and transfers: continuous. Notification date for freshmen and transfers: continuous. Required: essay, high school transcript, college transcript(s) for transfer students, minimum 3.0 high school GPA, SAT or ACT test scores (minimum combined SAT score of 810, minimum composite ACT score of 17). Portfolio reviews held twice on campus; the submission of slides may be substituted for portfolios (slides preferred).

Web Site http://www.siue.edu/ART/

Undergraduate Contact Dr. Todd Burrell, Director of Admission, Southern Illinois University Edwardsville, Campus Box 1047, Edwardsville, Illinois 62026; 618-650-2937, fax: 618-650-5013, e-mail address: tburrel@siue.edu

Graduate Contact Paul A. Dresang, Graduate Advisor, Art and Design Department, Southern Illinois University Edwardsville, Campus Box 1774, Edwardsville, Illinois 62026; 618-650-3071, fax: 618-650-3096.

Meadows School of the Arts
Southern Methodist University

Dallas, Texas

Independent, coed. Suburban campus. Total enrollment: 10,829. Art program established 1939.

Degrees Bachelor of Fine Arts in the area of art. Majors and concentrations: ceramics, drawing, painting, photography, printmaking, sculpture. Graduate degrees offered: Master of Fine Arts in the area of art. Program accredited by NASAD.

Enrollment 87 total; 75 undergraduate, 12 graduate.

Art Student Profile 59% females, 41% males, 22% minorities, 5% international.

Art Faculty 12 total (full-time), 4 total (part-time). 90% of full-time faculty have terminal degrees. Graduate students do not teach undergraduate courses. Undergraduate student–faculty ratio: 6:1.

Student Life Student groups/activities include Student Art Association, Meadows Graduate Council, Pollock Gallery. Special housing available for art students.

Expenses for 2008–2009 Application fee: $60. Comprehensive fee: $45,073 includes full-time tuition ($29,430), mandatory fees ($3768), and college room and board ($11,875). College room only: $7655. Special program-related fees: $30 per credit hour for model and supply fees.

Financial Aid Program-specific awards: 10–15 Meadows Artistic Scholarships for talented program majors ($1000–$6000).

Application Procedures Students apply for admission into the professional program by sophomore year. Deadline for freshmen and transfers: continuous. Required: essay, high school transcript, college transcript(s) for transfer students, letter of recommendation, SAT or ACT test scores. Recommended: interview, portfolio. Portfolio reviews held once on campus and off campus in digital format by uploading to Web site: smu.slideshow.com.

Web Site http://smu.edu/meadows/art/

Undergraduate Contact Tommy Newton, Director of Recruitment, Meadows School of the Arts, Southern Methodist University, PO Box 750275-0356, Dallas, Texas 75275-0356; 214-768-4067, fax: 214-768-3272, e-mail address: tnewton@smu.edu

Graduate Contact Ms. Jean Cherry, Director of Graduate Admissions, Meadows School of the Arts, Southern Methodist University, PO Box 750356, Dallas, Texas 75275-0356; 214-768-3765, fax: 214-768-3272, e-mail address: jcherry@smu.edu

Southern Oregon University

Ashland, Oregon

State-supported, coed. Small town campus. Total enrollment: 4,801. Art program established 1983.

Degrees Bachelor of Fine Arts. Majors and concentrations: ceramics, digital art and design, painting/drawing, photography, printmaking, sculpture. Cross-registration with members of the National Student Exchange Program, Rogue Community College.

Enrollment 271 total; 21 undergraduate, 250 nonprofessional degree.

Art Student Profile 50% females, 50% males, 10% minorities, 10% international.

Art Faculty 10 undergraduate (full-time). 90% of full-time faculty have terminal degrees.

Southern Oregon University (continued)

Graduate students do not teach undergraduate courses. Undergraduate student–faculty ratio: 2:1.

Student Life Student groups/activities include Schneider Museum of Art, student gallery management programs, Southern Oregon Fine Art Students.

Expenses for 2007–2008 Application fee: $50. State resident tuition: $5409 full-time. Nonresident tuition: $17,988 full-time. Full-time tuition varies according to course load, location, and reciprocity agreements. College room and board: $7941. Room and board charges vary according to board plan and housing facility. Special program-related fees: $5–$100 per course for lab/materials fees, $50 per quarter for resource fee.

Financial Aid Program-specific awards: 1 Mulling Award in Art for art majors demonstrating artistic ability ($500), 1 Schneider Merit Award in Art for art majors demonstrating artistic ability ($1000), 1–4 John Humbird Dickey Memorial Scholarships for art majors demonstrating artistic ability and financial need ($1000), 1 Sam and Helen Bernstein Award for artistically talented students ($200), 4 Leon Mulling Awards for art majors demonstrating academic excellence ($3000).

Application Procedures Students apply for admission into the professional program by sophomore year. Deadline for freshmen and transfers: continuous. Notification date for freshmen and transfers: continuous. Required: high school transcript, college transcript(s) for transfer students, minimum 3.0 high school GPA, portfolio, SAT or ACT test scores, artist statement. Portfolio reviews held twice on campus; the submission of slides may be substituted for portfolios for transfer applicants.

Web Site http://www.sou.edu/art/

Undergraduate Contact Mara Affre, Director, Admissions and Records Department, Southern Oregon University, 1250 Siskiyou Boulevard, Ashland, Oregon 97520; 541-552-6411, fax: 541-552-6614.

State University of New York at Fredonia

Fredonia, New York

State-supported, coed. Small town campus. Total enrollment: 5,404. Art program established 1968.

Degrees Bachelor of Fine Arts in the areas of drawing and painting, sculpture, ceramics, animation and illustration, photography, graphic design, media arts. Majors and concentrations: animation and illustration, ceramics, graphic design, media arts, painting, painting/drawing, photography, sculpture.

Enrollment 240 total; 30 undergraduate, 210 nonprofessional degree.

Art Student Profile 55% females, 45% males, 1% minorities, 2% international.

Art Faculty 14 undergraduate (full-time), 6 undergraduate (part-time). 100% of full-time faculty have terminal degrees. Graduate students do not teach undergraduate courses. Undergraduate student–faculty ratio: 14:1.

Student Life Student groups/activities include Art Forum, AIGA-American Institute of Graphic Arts, Media Arts.

Expenses for 2007–2008 Application fee: $40. State resident tuition: $4350 full-time. Nonresident tuition: $10,610 full-time. Mandatory fees: $1192 full-time. College room and board: $8380. College room only: $5050. Room and board charges vary according to board plan and housing facility. Special program-related fees: $10–$75 per course for lab fees.

Financial Aid Program-specific awards: 6 departmental scholarships for talented students ($500), 1 George W. Booth Award for incoming freshmen ($2000).

Application Procedures Students apply for admission into the professional program by junior year. Deadline for freshmen and transfers: continuous. Required: essay, high school transcript, college transcript(s) for transfer students, portfolio, SAT or ACT test scores (minimum combined SAT score of 1000). Recommended: minimum 3.0 high school GPA, 3 letters of recommendation, interview. Portfolio reviews held by appointment on campus; the submission of slides may be substituted for portfolios (slides or CD/DVD preferred).

Web Site http://www.fredonia.edu/department/art/

Undergraduate Contact Ms. Elizabeth Lee, Chair, Department of Visual Arts and New Media, State University of New York at Fredonia, Rockefeller Center, Fredonia, New York 14063; 716-673-3537, fax: 716-673-4990, e-mail address: elizabeth.lee@fredonia.edu

State University of New York at Plattsburgh

Plattsburgh, New York

State-supported, coed. Small town campus. Total enrollment: 6,259.

Degrees Bachelor of Fine Arts in the area of art. Majors and concentrations: studio art. Cross-registration with Clinton Community College, State University of New York Empire State College.

Enrollment 242 total; all undergraduate.

Art Student Profile 66% females, 34% males, 7% minorities, 7% international.

Art Faculty 10 undergraduate (full-time), 5 undergraduate (part-time). 100% of full-time faculty have terminal degrees. Graduate students do not teach undergraduate courses. Undergraduate student–faculty ratio: 20:1.

Student Life Student groups/activities include campus student exhibits, on-campus workshops presented by renowned artists, critics, and historians, off-campus field trips.

Expenses for 2007–2008 Application fee: $40. State resident tuition: $4350 full-time. Nonresident tuition: $10,610 full-time. Mandatory fees: $1066 full-time. College room and board: $7970. Room and board charges vary according to board plan. Special program-related fees: $15–$35 per studio course for specialized lab/equipment fees.

Financial Aid Program-specific awards: 15 Winkel Awards for art students ($200–$1000), 1 Glauhinger Award for sculpture students ($3400), 1 Parnass Award for photography students ($2000).

Application Procedures Students admitted directly into the professional program freshman year. Deadline for freshmen and transfers: continuous. Required: high school transcript, college transcript(s) for transfer students, minimum 3.0 high school GPA, portfolio, SAT or ACT test scores (minimum composite ACT score of 19). Recommended: essay, interview, 2-3 letters of recommendation. Portfolio reviews held continuously on campus; the submission of slides may be substituted for portfolios.

Web Site http://www.plattsburgh.edu/art

Undergraduate Contact Richard J. Higgins, Director, Admissions, State University of New York at Plattsburgh, 101 Broad Street, Kehoe Administration Building, Plattsburgh, New York 12901; 518-564-2040, e-mail address: higginrj@plattsburgh.edu

Steinhardt School of Culture, Education, and Human Development, Department of Art and Art Professions

See New York University

Stephen F. Austin State University

Nacogdoches, Texas

State-supported, coed. Small town campus. Total enrollment: 11,607. Art program established 1923.

Web Site http://www.sfasu.edu/

Stephens College

Columbia, Missouri

Independent, Urban campus. Total enrollment: 1,050. Art program established 1954.

Degrees Bachelor of Fine Arts in the areas of graphic design, fashion design, interior design. Majors and concentrations: fashion design, graphic design, interior design. Cross-registration with Mid-Missouri Associated Colleges and Universities.

Enrollment 155 total; all undergraduate.

Art Student Profile 100% females, 17% minorities.

Art Faculty 8 undergraduate (full-time), 19 undergraduate (part-time). 80% of full-time

Visual

Arts

Stephens College (continued)

faculty have terminal degrees. Graduate students do not teach undergraduate courses. Undergraduate student–faculty ratio: 12:1.

Student Life Student groups/activities include Pi Phi Rho (fashion honorary society), Innovative Fashion Association (all fashion majors), Interior Design Club.

Expenses for 2008–2009 Application fee: $25. Comprehensive fee: $31,730 includes full-time tuition ($23,000) and college room and board ($8730). College room only: $5080. Special program-related fees: $20–$150 per course for lab fee.

Financial Aid Program-specific awards: 1–3 Gardner Nettleton Endowed Scholarships for outstanding art and graphic students ($3500), 1–2 Carolyn Jill Kasten Scholarships for outstanding fashion design students ($3000).

Application Procedures Students admitted directly into the professional program freshman year. Deadline for freshmen and transfers: July 31. Notification date for freshmen and transfers: continuous. Required: essay, high school transcript, college transcript(s) for transfer students, minimum 2.0 high school GPA, letter of recommendation, SAT or ACT test scores (minimum composite ACT score of 21). Recommended: minimum 3.0 high school GPA, interview, portfolio. Portfolio reviews held as needed for advanced placement on campus; the submission of slides may be substituted for portfolios if original work is not available.

Web Site http://www.stephens.edu

Undergraduate Contact Office of Admission, Stephens College, Campus Box 2121, Columbia, Missouri 65215; 800-876-7207, fax: 573-876-7237, e-mail address: apply@stephens.edu

The New England School of Art & Design

Suffolk University

Boston, Massachusetts

Independent, coed. Urban campus. Total enrollment: 9,083. Art program established 1923.

Degrees Bachelor of Fine Arts in the areas of fine arts, graphic design, interior design. Majors and concentrations: art/fine arts, graphic design, interior design. Graduate degrees offered: Master of Arts in the areas of interior design, graphic design. Program accredited by NASAD, CIDA.

Enrollment 344 total; 214 undergraduate, 118 graduate, 12 nonprofessional degree.

Art Student Profile 72% females, 28% males, 5% minorities, 18% international.

Art Faculty 17 undergraduate (full-time), 48 undergraduate (part-time), 3 graduate (full-time), 6 graduate (part-time). 91% of full-time faculty have terminal degrees. Graduate students do not teach undergraduate courses. Undergraduate student–faculty ratio: 8:1.

Student Life Student groups/activities include American Society of Interior Designers Student Chapter, International Interior Design Association Student Chapter, American Institute of Graphic Arts (AIGA).

Expenses for 2007–2008 Application fee: $50. Comprehensive fee: $37,550 includes full-time tuition ($24,170), mandatory fees ($80), and college room and board ($13,300). College room only: $11,120. Room and board charges vary according to board plan and housing facility. Special program-related fees: $140 per course for studio fee.

Financial Aid Program-specific awards: 2–4 J.W.S. Cox Scholarships for those demonstrating talent ($1000–$2000), 1–2 Peter and Gretchen Paige Scholarships for those demonstrating talent ($4000–$5000), 2–4 Schrafft Scholarships Program for Boston residents ($2000–$3000).

Application Procedures Students admitted directly into the professional program freshman year. Deadline for freshmen and transfers: continuous. Required: essay, high school transcript, college transcript(s) for transfer students, minimum 2.0 high school GPA, 2 letters of recommendation, portfolio, SAT or ACT test scores. Recommended: interview. Portfolio reviews held continuously on campus and off campus at National Portfolio Days; the submission of slides may be substituted for portfolios whenever needed.

Web Site http://www.suffolk.edu/nesad

Undergraduate Contact Ms. Kristen Cahalane, Admissions Counselor, Undergraduate Admission, Suffolk University, 8 Ashburton Place, Boston, Massachusetts 02108; 617-573-8460, fax: 617-742-4291, e-mail address: kcahalan@suffolk.edu

Visual

Arts

Graduate Contact Ms. Terry Bishop, Director of Admission, Graduate Admission, Suffolk University, 8 Ashburton Place, Boston, Massachusetts 02108; 617-573-8302, fax: 617-523-0116, e-mail address: tbishop@suffolk.edu

Sul Ross State University

Alpine, Texas

State-supported, coed. Small town campus. Total enrollment: 1,954 (2007). Art program established 1923.

Web Site http://www.sulross.edu/

Syracuse University

Syracuse, New York

Independent, coed. Urban campus. Total enrollment: 17,677. Art program established 1873.

Degrees Bachelor of Fine Arts in the areas of advertising design, art education, ceramics, computer art, communication design, fiber art/material studies, history of art, interior design, jewelry/metalsmithing, painting, photography, printmaking, sculpture, surface pattern design, illustration, film; Bachelor of Industrial Design in the area of industrial and interaction design; Bachelor of Science in the area of environmental design. Majors and concentrations: advertising design, art education, art history, ceramics, communication design, computer art, environmental design, fashion design, fibers, film, illustration, industrial design, interior design, jewelry and metalsmithing, painting/drawing, photography, printmaking, sculpture, surface design, textile design, video art. Graduate degrees offered: Master of Fine Arts in the areas of art education, ceramics, computer arts, fiber arts/ material studies, film, illustration, jewelry and metalsmithing, museum studies, painting, photography, printmaking, sculpture, surface pattern design, video; Master of Industrial Design. Program accredited by NASAD, CIDA.

Enrollment 1,403 total; 1,259 undergraduate, 144 graduate.

Art Student Profile 66% females, 34% males, 13% minorities.

Art Faculty 67 total (full-time), 43 total (part-time). 88% of full-time faculty have terminal degrees. Graduate students teach a few undergraduate courses. Undergraduate student–faculty ratio: 18:1.

Student Life Student groups/activities include American Society of Interior Designers, Industrial Design Society of America, New York Society of Illustrators.

Expenses for 2007–2008 Application fee: $70. Comprehensive fee: $42,626 includes full-time tuition ($30,470), mandatory fees ($1216), and college room and board ($10,940). College room only: $5660. Room and board charges vary according to board plan and housing facility. Special program-related fees: $10–$150 per semester for lab fees to cover costs of models and special supplies.

Financial Aid Program-specific awards: art merit scholarships for incoming freshmen ($4000), 1 National Scholastic Award for Art National Scholarship winners ($2000).

Application Procedures Students admitted directly into the professional program freshman year. Deadline for freshmen and transfers: January 1. Notification date for freshmen: March 1; transfers: August 15. Required: essay, high school transcript, college transcript(s) for transfer students, minimum 3.0 high school GPA, 2 letters of recommendation, portfolio, SAT or ACT test scores, high school counselor evaluation. Recommended: interview. Portfolio reviews held continuously on campus and off campus in New York, NY; Boston, MA; Philadelphia, PA; Baltimore, MD; Hartford, CT; Chicago, IL; the submission of slides may be substituted for portfolios when distance is prohibitive.

Web Site http://vpa.syr.edu/

Undergraduate Contact Director, CVPA Recruitment and Admissions, College of Visual and Performing Arts, Syracuse University, 202 Crouse College, Syracuse, New York 13244-1010; 315-443-2769, fax: 315-443-1935, e-mail address: admissu@syr.edu

Graduate Contact Graduate School, Syracuse University, Suite 303 Bowne Hall, Syracuse, New York 13244; 315-443-3028, fax: 315-443-3423, e-mail address: gradschl@syr.edu

Temple University, Tyler School of Art

See Tyler School of Art of Temple University

Tennessee Technological University

See Appalachian Center for Craft

Texas A&M University–Commerce

Commerce, Texas

State-supported, coed. Small town campus. Total enrollment: 8,882.

Degrees Bachelor of Arts in the area of photography; Bachelor of Fine Arts in the areas of design communications, new media, art direction, studio art; Bachelor of Science in the area of photography. Majors and concentrations: art, art direction, art education, ceramics, design communication, experimental studies, illustration, new media, painting, photography, sculpture. Graduate degrees offered: Master of Fine Arts in the areas of sculpture, painting, ceramics, illustration, experimental studies, photography, design communication. Cross-registration with University of North Texas, Texas Woman's University.

Enrollment 280 total; 261 undergraduate, 19 graduate.

Art Student Profile 51% females, 49% males, 21% minorities, 3% international.

Art Faculty 18 undergraduate (part-time), 9 graduate (full-time). 100% of full-time faculty have terminal degrees. Graduate students do not teach undergraduate courses. Undergraduate student–faculty ratio: 14:1.

Student Life Student groups/activities include Student Art Association, Photo Society, Clay Club.

Expenses for 2008–2009 Application fee: $25. State resident tuition: $5126 full-time. Nonresident tuition: $13,466 full-time. College room and board: $6484. Special program-related fees: $5–$50 per semester for instruction and curriculum fee.

Financial Aid Program-specific awards: 7–12 endowed scholarships for program majors ($200–$1000).

Application Procedures Students apply for admission into the professional program by sophomore year. Deadline for freshmen: August 15; transfers: August 19. Required: high school transcript, college transcript(s) for transfer students, SAT or ACT test scores, portfolio for transfer students in communication arts and photography. Portfolio reviews held by request on campus; the submission of slides may be substituted for portfolios if of good quality.

Web Site http://www.tamu-commerce.edu/art

Undergraduate Contact Michael Odom, Head, Department of Art, Texas A&M University–Commerce, PO Box 3011, Commerce, Texas 75429-3011; 903-886-5234, fax: 903-886-5987, e-mail address: michael-odom@tamu-commerce.edu

Graduate Contact Mr. Michael Miller, Graduate Coordinator, Department of Art, Texas A&M University–Commerce, PO Box 3011, Commerce, Texas 75429-3011; 903-886-5208, fax: 903-886-5987, e-mail address: michael_miller@tamu-commerce.edu

Texas A&M University–Corpus Christi

Corpus Christi, Texas

State-supported, coed. Suburban campus. Total enrollment: 8,585 (2007).

Degrees Bachelor of Fine Arts. Majors and concentrations: art education, studio art. Graduate degrees offered: Master of Fine Arts in the area of studio art.

Enrollment 163 total; 26 undergraduate, 8 graduate, 129 nonprofessional degree.

Art Student Profile 67% females, 33% males, 31% minorities, 2% international.

Art Faculty 9 total (full-time), 1 total (part-time). 90% of full-time faculty have terminal degrees. Graduate students do not teach undergraduate courses.

Student Life Student groups/activities include Student Art Association.

Expenses for 2007–2008 Application fee: $30. State resident tuition: $4020 full-time. Nonresident tuition: $12,360 full-time. Mandatory fees: $1620 full-time. College room and board: $9971. College room only: $7398. Room and board charges vary according to location. Special program-related fees: $25–$65 per course for art material fees.

Financial Aid Program-specific awards: Fine Arts Studio Scholarships for program majors ($500–$2000).

Application Procedures Students apply for admission into the professional program by junior year. Required: essay, high school transcript, college transcript(s) for transfer students, minimum 2.0 high school GPA, portfolio, SAT or ACT test scores, completion of college preparatory courses. Recommended: minimum 3.0 high school GPA, letter of recommendation. Portfolio reviews held twice on campus; the submission of slides may be substituted for portfolios if accompanied by a slide list and descriptions.

Web Site http://www.tamucc.edu

Undergraduate Contact Prof. Jack Gron, Chair, Department of Art, Texas A&M University–Corpus Christi, 6300 Ocean Drive, Unit 5721, Corpus Christi, Texas 78412-5721; 361-825-3473, fax: 361-825-6097, e-mail address: jack.gron@tamucc.edu

Graduate Contact Prof. Jack Gron, Graduate Program Coordinator, Professor, Department of Art, Texas A&M University–Corpus Christi, 6300 Ocean Drive, Unit 5721, Corpus Christi, Texas 78412-5721; 361-825-3473, fax: 361-825-6097, e-mail address: jack.gron@tamucc.edu

Texas Christian University

Fort Worth, Texas

Independent, coed. Suburban campus. Total enrollment: 8,668. Art program established 1884.

Degrees Bachelor of Fine Arts in the areas of art education, graphic design, studio art. Majors and concentrations: art education, ceramics, graphic design, painting/drawing, photography, printmaking, sculpture. Graduate degrees offered: Master of Arts in the area of art history; Master of Fine Arts in the areas of painting, printmaking, sculpture. Cross-registration with Universidad de las Américas (Mexico).

Enrollment 165 total; 126 undergraduate, 12 graduate, 27 nonprofessional degree.

Art Student Profile 72% females, 28% males, 14% minorities, 2% international.

Art Faculty 16 total (full-time), 14 total (part-time). 100% of full-time faculty have terminal degrees. Graduate students do not teach undergraduate courses. Undergraduate student–faculty ratio: 10:1.

Student Life Student groups/activities include Visual Arts Committee of the Student Programming Council, Design Focus.

Expenses for 2007–2008 Application fee: $40. Comprehensive fee: $33,068 includes full-time tuition ($24,820), mandatory fees ($48), and college room and board ($8200). College room only: $5000. Room and board charges vary according to board plan and housing facility.

Financial Aid Program-specific awards: 2 Nordan Scholarships for freshmen ($7000).

Application Procedures Students admitted directly into the professional program freshman year. Deadline for freshmen and transfers: April 15. Required: essay, high school transcript, college transcript(s) for transfer students, minimum 3.0 high school GPA, 3 letters of recommendation, SAT or ACT test scores. Recommended: interview.

Web Site http://www.artandarthistory.tcu.edu

Contact Mr. Ronald Watson, Chairman, Department of Art and Art History, Texas Christian University, 2805 S. University, TCU Box 298000, Fort Worth, Texas 76129; 817-257-7643, fax: 817-257-7399, e-mail address: r.watson@tcu.edu

Texas State University–San Marcos

San Marcos, Texas

State-supported, coed. Suburban campus. Total enrollment: 28,121. Art program established 1940.

Web Site http://www.txstate.edu/

Texas Tech University

Lubbock, Texas

State-supported, coed. Urban campus. Total enrollment: 28,257. Art program established 1967.

Degrees Bachelor of Fine Arts in the areas of studio art, design communication, visual studies. Majors and concentrations: ceramics, communication design, jewelry and metalsmithing, painting/drawing, photography, printmaking, sculpture, visual studies. Graduate degrees

Texas Tech University (continued)

offered: Master of Fine Arts in the area of art. Doctor of Arts in the area of fine arts. Program accredited by NASAD.

Enrollment 452 total; 400 undergraduate, 32 graduate, 20 nonprofessional degree.

Art Student Profile 54% females, 46% males, 18% minorities, 1% international.

Art Faculty 29 total (full-time), 14 total (part-time). 93% of full-time faculty have terminal degrees. Graduate students teach a few undergraduate courses. Undergraduate student–faculty ratio: 11:1.

Student Life Student groups/activities include National Art Education Association Student Chapter, Design Communication Association, Metalsmithing Club.

Expenses for 2007–2008 Application fee: $50. State resident tuition: $4310 full-time. Nonresident tuition: $12,650 full-time. Mandatory fees: $2473 full-time. Full-time tuition and fees vary according to course load, program, and reciprocity agreements. College room and board: $7460. College room only: $3980. Room and board charges vary according to board plan and housing facility. Special program-related fees: $8–$150 per course for art supplies.

Financial Aid Program-specific awards: 20–25 art scholarships for program students ($200–$500), 3–5 H.Y. Price Scholarships for program students ($3000).

Application Procedures Students admitted directly into the professional program freshman year. Deadline for freshmen and transfers: continuous. Notification date for freshmen and transfers: continuous. Required: essay, high school transcript, minimum 2.0 high school GPA, SAT or ACT test scores, minimum TOEFL score of 550 for international applicants, slides or videotape of portfolio. Portfolio reviews held 4 times on campus and off campus in Junction, TX.

Web Site http://www.art.ttu.edu

Undergraduate Contact Djuana Young, Director, Undergraduate Admissions, Texas Tech University, Box 45005, Lubbock, Texas 79409-5005; 806-742-1482.

Graduate Contact Ann McGlynn, Assistant Dean, Graduate Admissions, Texas Tech University, Box 41030, Lubbock, Texas 79409-1030; 806-742-2787, fax: 806-742-4038.

Texas Woman's University

Denton, Texas

State-supported, coed, primarily women. Suburban campus. Total enrollment: 12,168. Art program established 1903.

Degrees Bachelor of Fine Arts in the areas of painting, photography, ceramics, sculpture, graphic design. Majors and concentrations: art history, clay, graphic design, painting/drawing, photography, sculpture. Graduate degrees offered: Master of Arts in the areas of art education, graphic design, art history; Master of Fine Arts in the areas of painting, photography, ceramics, sculpture. Cross-registration with University of North Texas, Texas A&M University-Commerce.

Enrollment 230 total; 150 undergraduate, 50 graduate, 30 nonprofessional degree.

Art Student Profile 90% females, 10% males, 25% minorities, 10% international.

Art Faculty 9 total (full-time), 4 total (part-time). 100% of full-time faculty have terminal degrees. Graduate students teach a few undergraduate courses. Undergraduate student–faculty ratio: 13:1.

Student Life Student groups/activities include Delta Phi Delta, Clay Underground, Art Teachers Network, Sculpture-No Boundaries, Photographic Artists Coalition, Painters At Large, Pioneers in Design, Homecoming, Open House Studios, Denton Arts and Jazz Festival. Special housing available for art students.

Expenses for 2008–2009 Application fee: $30. State resident tuition: $4740 full-time. Nonresident tuition: $13,080 full-time. Mandatory fees: $1800 full-time. College room and board: $5846. College room only: $2828. Special program-related fees: $12–$90 per semester for studio courses.

Financial Aid Program-specific awards: 2–5 Marie Delleney Awards for art majors ($200–$500), 2 Helen Thomas Perry Awards for junior or senior art majors ($1000), 1–3 Hazel Snodgrass Awards for art majors ($200–$300), 1–2 Ludie Clark Thompson Awards for art majors ($200–$300), 2–4 Noreen Kitsinger Awards for art education majors ($200–$300), 2–5 Sue Comer Awards for art majors ($200–$300), 1–3 Dorothy Laselle Awards for freshmen or sophomore art majors ($300–$400),

6–12 Coreen Spellman Awards for Delta Phi Delta members ($100–$200), 1 J. Brough Miller Scholarship for art majors ($400), 1–2 Rowena Caldwell Elkin Scholarships for art majors ($500–$1000), 6 Delta Phi Delta Awards for art majors ($200–$300).

Application Procedures Students admitted directly into the professional program freshman year. Deadline for freshmen and transfers: July 15. Required: high school transcript, college transcript(s) for transfer students, minimum 2.0 high school GPA, SAT or ACT test scores. Recommended: 3 letters of recommendation, interview, portfolio. Portfolio reviews held twice on campus; the submission of slides may be substituted for portfolios (or electronic disk portfolio).

Web Site http://www.twu.edu/as/va

Contact Mr. John Weinkein, Chair, Department of Visual Arts, Texas Woman's University, PO Box 425469, TWU Station, Denton, Texas 76204; 940-898-2530, fax: 940-898-2496, e-mail address: visualarts@twu.edu

Tisch School of the Arts - Department of Photography and Imaging

See New York University

Truman State University

Kirksville, Missouri

State-supported, coed. Small town campus. Total enrollment: 5,866. Art program established 1985.

Degrees Bachelor of Fine Arts in the areas of studio art, visual communications. Majors and concentrations: ceramic art and design, fibers, painting, printmaking, sculpture, visual communication. Graduate degrees offered: Master of Art Education.

Enrollment 205 total; 173 undergraduate, 5 graduate, 27 nonprofessional degree.

Art Student Profile 70% females, 30% males, 1% minorities.

Art Faculty 13 total (full-time). 100% of full-time faculty have terminal degrees. Graduate students do not teach undergraduate courses. Undergraduate student–faculty ratio: 14:1.

Student Life Student groups/activities include Student Art History Society, Missouri Art Education Association, American Institute of Graphic Arts.

Expenses for 2007–2008 Application fee: $0. One-time mandatory fee: $250. State resident tuition: $6210 full-time. Nonresident tuition: $10,820 full-time. Mandatory fees: $222 full-time. College room and board: $5815. Room and board charges vary according to housing facility. Special program-related fees: $10–$30 per semester for art supplies.

Financial Aid Program-specific awards: 8 endowed scholarships for outstanding program majors ($500–$1500), 14 service scholarships for program majors ($400–$700).

Application Procedures Students admitted directly into the professional program freshman year. Deadline for freshmen and transfers: May 1. Notification date for freshmen: December 15. Required: essay, high school transcript, college transcript(s) for transfer students, minimum 3.0 high school GPA, portfolio, SAT or ACT test scores. Portfolio reviews held twice on campus; the submission of slides may be substituted for portfolios when distance is prohibitive.

Web Site http://www.truman.edu

Undergraduate Contact Mr. Russell Nelson, Chair, Art, Truman State University, 100 East Normal, Ophelia Parrish 1101, Kirksville, Missouri 63501; 660-785-4417, fax: 660-785-7463, e-mail address: art@truman.edu

Graduate Contact Prof. Wynne Wilbur, MAE Program Coordinator, Art, Truman State University, 100 East Normal, Ophelia Parrish 1101, Kirksville, Missouri 63501; 660-785-4417, fax: 660-785-7463, e-mail address: wwilbur@truman.edu

Temple University, Tyler School of Art

Tyler School of Art of Temple University

Philadelphia, Pennsylvania

State-related, coed. Urban campus. Total enrollment: 34,696. Art program established 1935.

Degrees Bachelor of Architecture in the area of architecture; Bachelor of Fine Arts in the areas of ceramics/glass, fibers, graphic and interactive design, painting/drawing, photography, printmaking, sculpture, art education, metals/jewelry/CAD-CAM. Majors and concentrations: architecture, art education, art history, CAD/CAM, ceramic art and design, commercial art, computer graphics, digital imaging, fibers, glass, graphic arts, graphic design, illustration, jewelry and metalsmithing, painting/drawing, photography, printmaking, sculpture, visual studies. Graduate degrees offered: Master of Arts in the area of art history; Master of Education in the area of art education; Master of Fine Arts in the areas of ceramics/glass, fibers, jewelry/metals, painting/drawing, photography, printmaking, sculpture, graphic and interactive design. Doctor of Philosophy in the area of art history. Program accredited by NASAD, NAAB.

Enrollment 1,449 total; 760 undergraduate, 81 graduate, 608 nonprofessional degree.

Art Student Profile 60% females, 40% males, 14% minorities, 4% international.

Art Faculty 70 total (full-time), 32 total (part-time). 95% of full-time faculty have terminal degrees. Graduate students teach a few undergraduate courses. Undergraduate student–faculty ratio: 11:1.

Student Life Student groups/activities include Student Alliance, Intellectual Heritage Society, Art Honor Society. Special housing available for art students.

Expenses for 2007–2008 Application fee: $50. State resident tuition: $10,252 full-time. Non-resident tuition: $18,770 full-time. Mandatory fees: $550 full-time. Full-time tuition and fees vary according to course load, program, and reciprocity agreements. College room and board: $8518. College room only: $5604. Room

and board charges vary according to board plan and housing facility. Special program-related fees: $25–$300 per course for lab fees.

Financial Aid Program-specific awards: 10–25 merit scholarships for program students ($1000–$12,500), academic scholarships for program students ($1000–$12,500).

Application Procedures Students admitted directly into the professional program freshman year. Deadline for freshmen: April 1; transfers: June 1. Notification date for freshmen and transfers: continuous. Required: essay, high school transcript, college transcript(s) for transfer students, portfolio, SAT or ACT test scores (minimum composite ACT score of 23), slides for transfer applicants (or CD ROM), self-portrait. Recommended: minimum 3.0 high school GPA, interview. Portfolio reviews held 27 times on campus and off campus at National Portfolio Day Association venues and selected high schools; the submission of slides may be substituted for portfolios for freshmen applicants, for large works of art, or if distance is prohibitive.

Web Site http://www.temple.edu/tyler

Undergraduate Contact Ms. Carmina Cianciulli, Assistant Dean for Admissions, Tyler School of Art, Temple University, 7725 Penrose Avenue, Elkins Park, Pennsylvania 19027; 215-782-2875, fax: 215-782-2711, e-mail address: tylerart@temple.edu

Graduate Contact Ms. Carmina Cianciulli, Assistant Dean for Admissions, Tyler School of Art of Temple University, Temple University, 7725 Penrose Avenue, Elkins Park, Pennsylvania 19027; 215-782-2875, fax: 215-782-2711, e-mail address: tylerart@temple.edu

University at Buffalo, the State University of New York

Buffalo, New York

State-supported, coed. Total enrollment: 28,054. Art program established 1954.

Degrees Bachelor of Fine Arts in the area of fine art. Majors and concentrations: communication design, painting/drawing, photography, printmaking, sculpture, studio art/

emerging practices, visual studies. Graduate degrees offered: Master of Fine Arts in the area of fine art. Cross-registration with State University of New York College at Buffalo. Program accredited by NASAD.

Enrollment 273 total; 171 undergraduate, 22 graduate, 80 nonprofessional degree.

Art Student Profile 61% females, 39% males, 18% minorities, 6% international.

Art Faculty 15 total (full-time), 14 total (part-time). 93% of full-time faculty have terminal degrees. Graduate students teach a few undergraduate courses. Undergraduate student–faculty ratio: 12:1.

Student Life Student groups/activities include university gallery exhibits, Student Visual Art Organization, Visual Studies Department Gallery exhibits.

Expenses for 2007–2008 Application fee: $40. State resident tuition: $4350 full-time. Nonresident tuition: $10,610 full-time. Mandatory fees: $1867 full-time. College room and board: $8620. College room only: $5360. Room and board charges vary according to board plan and housing facility. Special program-related fees: $20–$100 per course for lab fees, supplies, models.

Financial Aid Program-specific awards: 1 Julius Bloom Memorial Scholarship for graphic arts or graphic design students ($350), 1 Dennis Domkowski Memorial Scholarship for communication design program students ($350), 1 Rumsey Summer Scholarship for junior art majors ($2000), 8 Morrison Scholarships for art majors demonstrating financial need ($1500), 1 Elliott Painting Scholarship for painting juniors ($500–$600), 1 Sentz Award for art majors ($450), 2 Eugene L. Gaier Excellence in Printmaking Awards for students in printmaking ($250), 1 Eugene L. Gaier Excellence in Drawing Award for drawing students ($500), 1 Sentz Award for art majors ($450), 1 Cober Award for drawing students ($500), 1 Townsend Award for photo students ($500).

Application Procedures Students admitted directly into the professional program freshman year. Deadline for freshmen: April 15; transfers: October 30. Notification date for freshmen: May 1; transfers: November 15. Required: high school transcript, college transcript(s) for transfer students, SAT or ACT test scores, portfolio review after freshman year for admission to department. Recom-

mended: essay, portfolio. Portfolio reviews held 5 times on campus and off campus at National Portfolio Days; Rochester or Syracuse NY; Toronto, CAN; Cleveland, OH; Sarasota, FL; the submission of slides may be substituted for portfolios if a campus visit is impossible.

Web Site http://www.visualstudies.buffalo.edu

Undergraduate Contact Mr. Kim James Yarwood, Academic Advisor, Department of Visual Studies, University at Buffalo, the State University of New York, 202 Center for the Arts, Buffalo, New York 14260-6010; 716-645-6000 ext. 1351, fax: 716-645-6970, e-mail address: yarwood@buffalo.edu

Graduate Contact Ms. Adele Henderson, Director of Graduate Studies, Department of Visual Studies, University at Buffalo, the State University of New York, 202 Center for the Arts, Buffalo, New York 14260-6010; 716-645-6878 ext. 1353, fax: 716-645-6970, e-mail address: adeleh@buffalo.edu

Myers School of Art
The University of Akron
Akron, Ohio

State-supported, coed. Urban campus. Total enrollment: 23,007. Art program established 1970.

Degrees Bachelor of Arts in the areas of art studio, art history, art education; Bachelor of Fine Arts in the areas of photography, printmaking, metalsmithing, graphics, sculpture, ceramics, painting and drawing. Majors and concentrations: art education, art history, ceramic art and design, graphic design, jewelry and metalsmithing, painting/drawing, photography, printmaking, sculpture, studio art. Program accredited by NASAD.

Enrollment 852 total; 490 undergraduate, 362 nonprofessional degree.

Art Student Profile 50% females, 50% males, 8% minorities, 1% international.

Art Faculty 23 undergraduate (full-time), 23 undergraduate (part-time). 100% of full-time faculty have terminal degrees. Graduate students do not teach undergraduate courses. Undergraduate student–faculty ratio: 14:1.

Student Life Student groups/activities include Student Art League.

The University of Akron (continued)

Expenses for 2007–2008 Application fee: $30. State resident tuition: $7218 full-time. Nonresident tuition: $16,467 full-time. Mandatory fees: $1164 full-time. Full-time tuition and fees vary according to course load, degree level, and location. College room and board: $8003. College room only: $4955. Room and board charges vary according to board plan and housing facility. Special program-related fees: $35 per semester for metalsmithing materials, $35 per semester for printmaking materials, $35 per semester for photography supplies, $50 per semester for computer materials, $65 per semester for ceramics supplies.

Financial Aid Program-specific awards: 1–4 Scholastics Art and Writing Awards for incoming freshmen program majors ($2000), 1–4 Governor's Art Youth Awards for Ohio resident program majors ($1000), 3–7 incoming freshmen awards for incoming freshmen program majors ($1200), 13–20 School of Art Scholarships for continuing program majors based on portfolio and GPA ($2000), 25 funded travel awards for current students ($1000), 10 tools and materials awards for current students ($500).

Application Procedures Required: high school transcript, college transcript(s) for transfer students, minimum 2.0 high school GPA, SAT or ACT test scores, portfolio for transfer students, minimum 3.0 college GPA in art courses for transfer students, letters of recommendation and portfolio for scholarship consideration. Recommended: minimum 3.0 high school GPA, letter of recommendation, interview, portfolio.

Web Site http://www.uakron.edu/art/

Undergraduate Contact Office of Admissions, The University of Akron, 381 Buchtel Common, Akron, Ohio 44325-2001; 330-972-7100, fax: 330-972-7022, e-mail address: admissions@uakron.edu

The University of Alabama

Tuscaloosa, Alabama

State-supported, coed. Suburban campus. Total enrollment: 25,544. Art program established 1946.

Degrees Bachelor of Fine Arts in the area of studio art. Majors and concentrations: art/fine arts, ceramic art and design, digital media, painting/drawing, photography, printmaking, sculpture. Graduate degrees offered: Master of Arts in the areas of studio art, art history; Master of Fine Arts in the areas of painting, printmaking, ceramics, sculpture, photography, studio art. Program accredited by NASAD.

Enrollment 270 total; 42 undergraduate, 25 graduate, 203 nonprofessional degree.

Art Student Profile 63% females, 37% males, 13% minorities, 2% international.

Art Faculty 14 total (full-time), 4 total (part-time). 93% of full-time faculty have terminal degrees. Graduate students teach a few undergraduate courses. Undergraduate student–faculty ratio: 2:1.

Student Life Student groups/activities include Art Student League, Crimson Ceramics Society, College of Arts and Sciences Undergraduate Research Competition.

Expenses for 2007–2008 Application fee: $35. State resident tuition: $5700 full-time. Nonresident tuition: $16,518 full-time. Full-time tuition varies according to course load. College room and board: $5868. College room only: $3750. Room and board charges vary according to board plan and housing facility. Special program-related fees: $25–$55 per semester for studio fees for classes.

Financial Aid Program-specific awards: 3 Mary M. Morgan Scholarships for program students ($9000), 3 Bradley Endowed Scholarships for program students ($4330), 1 Ruth K. Larcom Society for the Fine Arts Scholarship for students based on competition ($4400), 5 Julie Peake Holaday Memorial Scholarships for program students ($7228), 2 Art Students Endowed Scholarships for program students ($1462), 1 Richard Zollner Scholarship for program students ($1542), 2 Alvin C. Sella and Joseph Sella Endowed Scholarships for program students ($1338).

Application Procedures Students admitted directly into the professional program freshman year. Deadline for freshmen and transfers: continuous. Required: high school transcript, college transcript(s) for transfer students, minimum 2.0 high school GPA, SAT or ACT test scores (minimum composite ACT score of 22), high school transcript for transfer applicants with fewer than 24 semester hours. Portfolio

Visual

Arts

reviews held twice on campus; the submission of slides may be substituted for portfolios contact department for details.

Web Site http://www.as.ua.edu/art

Undergraduate Contact Ms. Mary K. Spiegel, Director, Undergraduate Admissions, The University of Alabama, Box 870132, Tuscaloosa, Alabama 35487; 205-348-8197, fax: 205-348-9046, e-mail address: mary.spiegel@ua.edu

Graduate Contact Dr. Carl F. Williams, Director, Graduate Admissions and Recruitment, The University of Alabama, PO Box 870118, Tuscaloosa, Alabama 35487; 205-348-5921, fax: 205-348-0400, e-mail address: cwilliam@aalan.ua.edu

The University of Arizona

Tucson, Arizona

State-supported, coed. Urban campus. Total enrollment: 37,217.

Degrees Bachelor of Fine Arts in the areas of art education, studio art. Majors and concentrations: art education, art history, ceramic art and design, computer graphics, painting/drawing, photography, printmaking, sculpture, studio art, textile arts, visual communication. Graduate degrees offered: Master of Arts in the areas of art education, art history; Master of Fine Arts in the area of studio art. Doctor of Philosophy in the area of history and theory of art. Program accredited by NASAD.

Enrollment 831 total; 274 undergraduate, 54 graduate, 503 nonprofessional degree.

Art Student Profile 67% females, 33% males, 17% minorities.

Art Faculty 39 total (full-time), 6 total (part-time). 97% of full-time faculty have terminal degrees. Graduate students teach about a quarter of undergraduate courses. Undergraduate student–faculty ratio: 17:1.

Student Life Student groups/activities include AHGSA-Art History Graduate Student Association, Art Club/Photo Club, SAGA-School of Art Graduate Association, American Institute of Graphic Arts Student Chapter, Clay Club, National Art Education Association Student Chapter.

Expenses for 2007–2008 Application fee: $25. State resident tuition: $4824 full-time. Nonresident tuition: $16,058 full-time. Mandatory fees: $224 full-time. Full-time tuition and fees vary according to course load. College room and board: $7370. College room only: $4670. Room and board charges vary according to board plan and housing facility. Special program-related fees: $10–$50 per semester for supplies for some studio courses.

Financial Aid Program-specific awards: 1 Robert C. Brown Memorial Scholarship for program majors ($750), Edward Francis Dunn Scholarships for program majors ($4600), Albert and Kathryn Haldeman Scholarships for program majors ($3600), 1 Hudson Foundation Scholarship for program majors ($1200), Samuel Latta Kingan Scholarships for program majors ($2300), 1 Stephen Langmade Scholarship for program majors ($950), 8 Regents In-State Registration Scholarships for state resident program majors ($1700), 5 Regents In-State Registration Scholarships for state resident program majors demonstrating need ($1700), 36 Regents Non-Resident Tuition Scholarships for out-of-state program majors ($4000), 1 Sandy Truett Memorial Scholarship for program majors ($1050).

Application Procedures Students admitted directly into the professional program freshman year. Deadline for freshmen and transfers: May 1. Required: high school transcript, college transcript(s) for transfer students, 2 letters of recommendation, portfolio, SAT or ACT test scores (minimum composite ACT score of 22), minimum 2.0 high school GPA for state residents, minimum 2.5 high school GPA for out-of-state residents. Portfolio reviews held twice on campus; the submission of slides may be substituted for portfolios.

Web Site http://www.arts.arizona.edu/art

Undergraduate Contact Martina Shenal, Assistant Director, School of Art, The University of Arizona, Art Building, Room 101D, PO Box 210002, Tucson, Arizona 85721-0002; 520-621-7570, fax: 520-621-2353, e-mail address: mshenal@email.arizona.edu

Graduate Contact Brooke Grucella, Graduate Program Coordinator, School of Art, The University of Arizona, Art Building, Room 101D, PO Box 210002, Tucson, Arizona 85721-0002; 520-621-8518, fax: 520-621-2955, e-mail address: brookeg@email.arizona.edu

Visual

Arts

J. William Fulbright College of Arts and Sciences

University of Arkansas

Fayetteville, Arkansas

State-supported, coed. Suburban campus. Total enrollment: 18,648. Art program established 1874.

Degrees Bachelor of Fine Arts in the areas of studio art, art education. Majors and concentrations: art education, ceramics, graphic design, painting, photography, printmaking, sculpture, visual design. Graduate degrees offered: Master of Fine Arts in the area of art.

Enrollment 212 total; 40 undergraduate, 12 graduate, 160 nonprofessional degree.

Art Faculty 12 total (full-time), 4 total (part-time). 98% of full-time faculty have terminal degrees. Graduate students do not teach undergraduate courses.

Student Life Student groups/activities include Fine Arts League, University Union Programs Fine Arts Committee.

Expenses for 2007–2008 Application fee: $40. State resident tuition: $4772 full-time. Nonresident tuition: $13,226 full-time. Mandatory fees: $1266 full-time. Full-time tuition and fees vary according to program. College room and board: $7017. College room only: $4387. Room and board charges vary according to board plan and housing facility. Special program-related fees: $4 per credit hour for teaching equipment.

Financial Aid Program-specific awards: David Durst Award for program students, Blanche Elliot Awards for sophomores, juniors, and seniors, Tom Turpin Award for freshmen, Neppie Conner Award for sophomores, Collier Photo Award for juniors and seniors, Bedford Camera Award for juniors and seniors, Charles Okerbloom Scholarships for program majors, Mountain Lake Estates Photography Award for program majors, Nina Erikson Awards for program majors.

Application Procedures Students apply for admission into the professional program by sophomore year. Deadline for freshmen: February 15. Notification date for freshmen and transfers: August 15. Required: essay, high school transcript, college transcript(s) for transfer students, SAT or ACT test scores (minimum composite ACT score of 30), minimum 2.0 college GPA for transfers.

Web Site http://www.uark.edu/~artinfo/art.html

Undergraduate Contact Chair, Art Department, University of Arkansas, 116 Fine Arts Center, Fayetteville, Arkansas 72701; 479-575-5202, fax: 479-575-2062.

Graduate Contact Prof. Michael Peven, MFA Coordinator, Art Department, University of Arkansas, 116 Fine Arts Center, Fayetteville, Arkansas 72701; 479-575-5202, fax: 479-575-2062, e-mail address: mpeven@uark.edu

University of Bridgeport

Bridgeport, Connecticut

Independent, coed. Urban campus. Total enrollment: 4,752.

Degrees Bachelor of Arts in the areas of graphic design, illustration; Bachelor of Fine Arts in the areas of graphic design, illustration; Bachelor of Science in the areas of interior design, industrial design, graphic design, illustration. Majors and concentrations: graphic design, illustration, industrial design, interior design. Program accredited by NASAD.

Enrollment 123 total; all undergraduate.

Art Student Profile 51% females, 49% males, 35% minorities, 15% international.

Art Faculty 5 undergraduate (full-time), 14 undergraduate (part-time). 100% of full-time faculty have terminal degrees. Graduate students do not teach undergraduate courses. Undergraduate student–faculty ratio: 10:1.

Student Life Student groups/activities include art shows.

Expenses for 2007–2008 Application fee: $25. Comprehensive fee: $32,860 includes full-time tuition ($21,150), mandatory fees ($1710), and college room and board ($10,000). College room only: $5200. Full-time tuition and fees vary according to program. Room and board charges vary according to board plan and student level.

Application Procedures Students admitted directly into the professional program freshman year. Deadline for freshmen and transfers: continuous. Required: essay, high school tran-

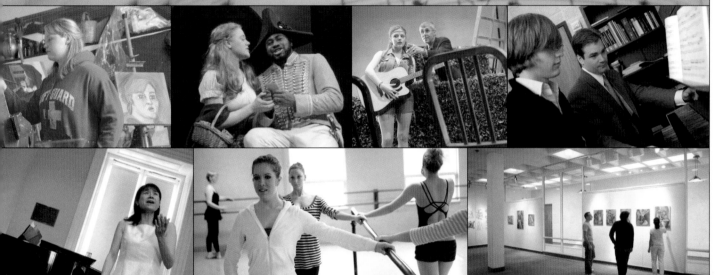
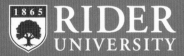

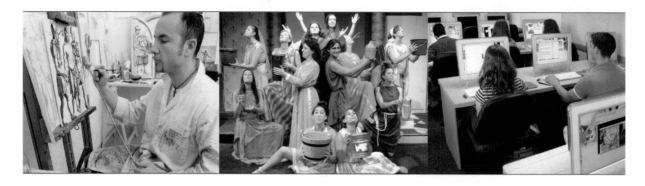

Our world can be your stage.

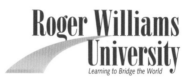

Learning to Bridge the World

Office of Undergraduate Admission
One Old Ferry Road
Bristol, RI 02809-2921

1-866-570-8173
admit@rwu.edu
www.rwu.edu

Creativity flourishes at Roger Williams University, a leading liberal arts university in New England.

Refine your writing and visual arts skills as well as your performance techniques, energized by our beautiful 140-acre waterfront campus in historic Bristol, Rhode Island – easily accessible from Boston and New York.

Accredited by the New England Association of Schools and Colleges, Roger Williams University draws 3,800 full-time undergraduates who benefit from a dedicated faculty and an ideal academic setting with excellent facilities, recreation, athletics and social opportunities. The Roger Williams education produces well-rounded students who successfully bridge transitions to a rewarding career and gratifying life.

The Theatre Program
The Roger Williams Theatre Program is unique in the range and breadth of its areas of study, leading to a Bachelor of Arts degree.

Creative Writing Program
Roger Williams University is one of the few colleges and universities in the United States to offer an undergraduate major in Creative Writing, leading to a Bachelor of Fine Arts degree.

Dance Performance Studies
The University offers courses in technique, choreography, history, pedagogy, movement analysis, performance techniques and movement theatre (we are the only dance-based university program in the country to offer this training).

Graphic Design Communications
This program consists of a contemporary blend of a liberal arts education and applied technology. Students draw on their complete educational experience to create images and visual messages that are thought-provoking, well-researched and technically excellent.

Visual Arts Studies
Our School of Architecture, Art and Historic Preservation offers the Bachelor of Arts degree in Visual Arts Studies. You can develop your talents in one of the following disciplines: Painting/Drawing/Printmaking, Sculpture or Photography/Digital Media.

script, college transcript(s) for transfer students, portfolio, SAT or ACT test scores. Recommended: minimum 2.0 high school GPA, 2 letters of recommendation, interview. Portfolio reviews held as needed on campus; the submission of slides may be substituted for portfolios for international applicants.

Web Site http://www.bridgeport.edu

Undergraduate Contact Ms. Audrey Ashton Savage, Vice President Enrollment Management, University of Bridgeport, 126 Park Avenue, Bridgeport, Connecticut 06604; 800-EXCEL-UB, fax: 203-576-4941, e-mail address: admit@bridgeport.edu

The University of British Columbia

Vancouver, British Columbia, Canada

Province-supported, coed. Urban campus. Total enrollment: 43,720. Art program established 1955.

Web Site http://www.ubc.ca/

University of Calgary

Calgary, Alberta, Canada

Province-supported, coed. Urban campus. Art program established 1967.

Degrees Bachelor of Fine Arts in the area of visual studies (studio concentration and developmental art concentration). Majors and concentrations: developmental art, painting/drawing, photography, printmaking, sculpture. Graduate degrees offered: Master of Fine Arts in the area of art.

Enrollment 249 total; 162 undergraduate, 12 graduate, 75 nonprofessional degree.

Art Student Profile 66% females, 34% males, 4% international.

Art Faculty 12 total (full-time), 9 total (part-time). 100% of full-time faculty have terminal degrees. Graduate students teach a few undergraduate courses. Undergraduate student–faculty ratio: 14:1.

Student Life Student groups/activities include on-campus exhibitions in two venues, BFA and MFA shows, Art Students Society.

Expenses for 2007–2008 Application fee: $130 Canadian dollars. Tuition, fee, and room and board charges are reported in Canadian dollars. Province resident tuition: $2370 full-time. Mandatory fees: $300 full-time. Full-time tuition and fees vary according to course load, degree level, and program. College room and board: $6178. College room only: $3102. Room and board charges vary according to board plan, housing facility, and student level. International student tuition: $8070.00 full-time.

Financial Aid Program-specific awards: 1 Alberta Printmakers Society Award for printmakers ($100), 1 Continuing Arts Association Travel Scholarship for those demonstrating academic achievement ($900), 1 Bow Fort Chapter I.O.D.E. Bursary for those demonstrating academic achievement ($250), 2 Heinz Jordan Memorial Scholarships for those demonstrating academic achievement ($500), 2 Santo Mignosa Awards for printmakers ($500), 1 Sadie M. Nelson Bursary in Art for those demonstrating need and academic merit ($500), 1 Western Silk Screen Prize for silk screen majors ($300), 1 BFA Graduation Committee Prize for those entering final year in visual arts program ($250), 1 Jack Wise Award for Excellence in Painting for continuing students who have completed Art 451 and 453 ($300), 2 25th Anniversary Scholarships for those demonstrating academic merit ($1000), 1 Stadelbauer Award for developmental art students ($1250).

Application Procedures Students admitted directly into the professional program freshman year. Deadline for freshmen and transfers: April 1. Required: high school transcript, portfolio, standing in top 75% of graduating class. Recommended: SAT test score only. Portfolio reviews held once on campus; the submission of slides may be substituted for portfolios (CD or DVD only).

Web Site http://www.ucalgary.ca

Contact Ms. Karen Lyons, Student Advisor, Faculty of Fine Arts Student Success Team (FASST), University of Calgary, 2500 University Drive, NW, Calgary, Alberta T2N 1N4, Canada; 403-220-5384, fax: 403-282-6925, e-mail address: lyons@ucalgary.ca

University of Central Arkansas

Conway, Arkansas

State-supported, coed. Small town campus. Total enrollment: 12,619. Art program established 1927.

Degrees Bachelor of Fine Arts. Majors and concentrations: studio art. Program accredited by NASAD.

Enrollment 220 total; 19 undergraduate, 201 nonprofessional degree.

Art Student Profile 66% females, 34% males, 15% minorities, 3% international.

Art Faculty 13 undergraduate (full-time), 6 undergraduate (part-time). 100% of full-time faculty have terminal degrees. Graduate students do not teach undergraduate courses. Undergraduate student–faculty ratio: 15:1.

Student Life Student groups/activities include American Institute of Graphic Arts Student Chapter, National Art Education Association Student Chapter, Student Art History Association, Clay Club.

Expenses for 2007–2008 Application fee: $0. State resident tuition: $4830 full-time. Nonresident tuition: $9660 full-time. Mandatory fees: $1375 full-time. College room and board: $4600. College room only: $2680. Room and board charges vary according to board plan and housing facility.

Financial Aid Program-specific awards: 1 Windgate Scholarship for art majors ($10,000), 15 Performance in Art Scholarships for art majors ($1000–$2000), 1 Disterheft Scholarship for art majors ($1200), 1 Curtis Scholarship for art majors ($600).

Application Procedures Students apply for admission into the professional program by sophomore year. Deadline for freshmen and transfers: continuous. Required: high school transcript, college transcript(s) for transfer students, ACT test score only, portfolio review for transfer students. Recommended: minimum 3.0 high school GPA.

Web Site http://www.uca.edu/cfac/art

Undergraduate Contact Dr. Jeffry R. Young, Chair, Department of Art, University of Central Arkansas, Conway, Arkansas 72035; 501-450-3113, fax: 501-450-5788, e-mail address: jyoung@uca.edu

University of Central Florida

Orlando, Florida

State-supported, coed. Suburban campus. Total enrollment: 48,497.
Web Site http://www.ucf.edu/

University of Central Missouri

Warrensburg, Missouri

State-supported, coed. Small town campus. Total enrollment: 10,918. Art program established 1871.
Web Site http://www.ucmo.edu/

University of Cincinnati

Cincinnati, Ohio

State-supported, coed. Urban campus. Total enrollment: 29,319. Art program established 1967.

Degrees Bachelor of Fine Arts in the area of fine arts. Majors and concentrations: media arts, three-dimensional studies, two-dimensional studies. Graduate degrees offered: Master of Arts in the areas of art history, art education; Master of Fine Arts in the area of fine arts. Cross-registration with The Ohio Valley Consortium of Colleges and Universities. Program accredited by NASAD.

Enrollment 500 total; 380 undergraduate, 120 graduate.

Art Student Profile 55% females, 45% males, 2% minorities, 5% international.

Art Faculty 26 total (full-time), 9 total (part-time). 100% of full-time faculty have terminal degrees. Graduate students teach a few undergraduate courses. Undergraduate student–faculty ratio: 13:1.

Student Life Student groups/activities include Fine Arts Association, National Art Education Association Student Chapter, Graduate Student Association-Fine Arts Chapter.

Expenses for 2007–2008 Application fee: $40. State resident tuition: $7896 full-time. Nonresident tuition: $22,419 full-time. Mandatory

Visual

Arts

fees: $1503 full-time. Full-time tuition and fees vary according to course load, degree level, location, program, and reciprocity agreements. College room and board: $8799. College room only: $5259. Room and board charges vary according to board plan and housing facility. Special program-related fees: $45 per course for lab fee-art supplies.

Financial Aid Program-specific awards: 3–7 Wolf Stein Travel Fellowships for upper-level undergraduates ($1500–$2500), 1 Rockwood Production Grant for electronic art majors ($1000), 1 Dean Tatgenhorst Conrad Scholarship for art/art history majors ($1000), 6 art scholarships for art majors ($1500).

Application Procedures Students admitted directly into the professional program freshman year. Deadline for freshmen and transfers: continuous. Notification date for freshmen: September 20. Required: essay, high school transcript, college transcript(s) for transfer students, minimum 3.0 high school GPA, portfolio, SAT or ACT test scores (minimum combined SAT score of 1020, minimum composite ACT score of 22), minimum 2.5 college GPA for transfer students. Recommended: interview. Portfolio reviews held 6 times on campus and off campus in Cincinnati, OH; Louisville, KY; the submission of slides may be substituted for portfolios if the applicant cannot come personally.

Web Site http://daap.uc.edu/art

Undergraduate Contact Prof. Denise Burge, Undergraduate Advisor, School of Art, University of Cincinnati, Mail Location 0016, Cincinnati, Ohio 45221; 513-556-2426, fax: 513-556-2887, e-mail address: dburge@cinci.rr.com

Graduate Contact Ms. Kimberly Burleigh, Director of Graduate Studies in Fine Arts, School of Art, University of Cincinnati, Mail Location 0016, Cincinnati, Ohio 45221; 513-556-2075, fax: 513-556-2887, e-mail address: kimberly.burleigh@uc.edu

University of Colorado at Boulder

Boulder, Colorado

State-supported, coed. Suburban campus. Total enrollment: 31,470. Art program established 1932.

Degrees Bachelor of Arts in the area of art history; Bachelor of Fine Arts in the area of studio art; Bachelor of Arts in Studio Arts. Majors and concentrations: art history, studio art. Graduate degrees offered: Master of Arts in the area of art history; Master of Fine Arts in the area of studio art.

Enrollment 1,157 total; 1,100 undergraduate, 57 graduate.

Art Student Profile 69% females, 31% males, 7% minorities, 4% international.

Art Faculty 31 total (full-time), 10 total (part-time). 100% of full-time faculty have terminal degrees. Graduate students teach about a quarter of undergraduate courses. Undergraduate student–faculty ratio: 35:1.

Student Life Student groups/activities include Art Student League.

Expenses for 2008–2009 Application fee: $50. One-time mandatory fee: $112. State resident tuition: $5922 full-time. Nonresident tuition: $25,400 full-time. Mandatory fees: $1356 full-time. College room and board: $9860. Special program-related fees: $50 per course for non-studio course, $50 per credit hour for studio course.

Financial Aid Program-specific awards: 20 scholarships for program majors ($500–$2000).

Application Procedures Deadline for freshmen and transfers: continuous. Required: high school transcript, college transcript(s) for transfer students, minimum 2.0 high school GPA, SAT or ACT test scores, portfolio upon completion of foundation courses (slides permissible) for BFA. Portfolio reviews held once on campus; the submission of slides may be substituted for portfolios.

Web Site http://www.colorado.edu/arts

Undergraduate Contact Admissions, University of Colorado at Boulder, Campus Box 552, Boulder, Colorado 80309; 303-492-6301.

Graduate Contact Alexei Bogdanov, Graduate Coordinator, Department of Fine Arts, University of Colorado at Boulder, Campus Box 318, Boulder, Colorado 80309-0318; 303-492-2419, fax: 303-492-4886, e-mail address: alexei.bogdanov@colorado.edu

University of Connecticut

Storrs, Connecticut

State-supported, coed. Rural campus. Total enrollment: 23,692.

Visual

Arts

University of Connecticut (continued)

Degrees Bachelor of Fine Arts in the area of art. Majors and concentrations: art history, art/fine arts, communication design, illustration, painting/drawing, photography, printmaking, sculpture. Graduate degrees offered: Master of Fine Arts in the area of art. Program accredited by NASAD.

Enrollment 260 total; 240 undergraduate, 20 graduate.

Art Student Profile 58% females, 42% males, 7% minorities, 3% international.

Art Faculty 24 total (full-time), 14 total (part-time). 100% of full-time faculty have terminal degrees. Graduate students teach a few undergraduate courses. Undergraduate student–faculty ratio: 14:1.

Student Life Special housing available for art students.

Expenses for 2008–2009 Application fee: $70. State resident tuition: $7200 full-time. Nonresident tuition: $21,912 full-time. Mandatory fees: $2138 full-time. College room and board: $9300. College room only: $4210. Special program-related fees: $15–$75 per course for expendable supplies in studio courses.

Financial Aid Program-specific awards: 1 Victor Borge Scholarship for incoming freshmen ($1000), 8 Fine Arts Talent Scholarships for program students ($3000), 1 Anniversary Scholarship for program students ($1400), 1 Alaimo Scholarship for program students ($1000), 2 Fine Arts Talent Scholarships for incoming freshmen ($3000), 1 Fine Arts Talent Scholarship for incoming freshmen ($1000).

Application Procedures Students admitted directly into the professional program freshman year. Deadline for freshmen: April 1; transfers: May 1. Required: essay, high school transcript, college transcript(s) for transfer students, minimum 2.0 high school GPA, portfolio, SAT or ACT test scores. Recommended: minimum 3.0 high school GPA, 3 letters of recommendation, interview. Portfolio reviews held 3 times on campus and off campus in Boston, MA; Hartford, CT; the submission of slides may be substituted for portfolios at student's discretion.

Web Site http://www.art.uconn.edu

Undergraduate Contact Ray DiCapua, Associate Head and Associate Professor, Department of Art and Art History, University of Connecticut,

830 Bolton Road, U-1099, Storrs, Connecticut 06269-1099; 860-486-3930, fax: 860-486-3869, e-mail address: ralph.dicapua@uconn.edu

Graduate Contact Monica Bock, Graduate Program Coordinator and Associate Professor, Department of Art and Art History, University of Connecticut, 830 Bolton Road, U-1099, Storrs, Connecticut 06269-1099; 860-486-3930, fax: 860-486-3869.

University of Dayton
Dayton, Ohio

Independent Roman Catholic, coed. Suburban campus. Total enrollment: 10,395. Art program established 1960.

Degrees Bachelor of Fine Arts in the areas of art education, studio art, visual communication design, photography. Majors and concentrations: art education, art/fine arts, computer graphics, graphic arts, illustration, photography, studio art. Cross-registration with Miami Valley Consortium. Program accredited by NASAD.

Enrollment 209 total; 149 undergraduate, 60 nonprofessional degree.

Art Student Profile 73% females, 27% males, 5% minorities, 1% international.

Art Faculty 13 undergraduate (full-time), 19 undergraduate (part-time). 100% of full-time faculty have terminal degrees. Graduate students do not teach undergraduate courses. Undergraduate student–faculty ratio: 6:1.

Student Life Student groups/activities include Horvath Student Art Show, Stander Symposium, student organization in design, fine art, and photography.

Expenses for 2007–2008 Application fee: $50. Comprehensive fee: $33,670 includes full-time tuition ($24,880), mandatory fees ($1070), and college room and board ($7720). College room only: $4550. Full-time tuition and fees vary according to program. Room and board charges vary according to board plan, housing facility, and student level. Special program-related fees: $20–$75 per semester for studio/lab fees.

Financial Aid Program-specific awards: 5–10 Visual Arts Scholarships for freshmen ($4000), 1 Gordon Richardson Scholarship for juniors ($2000), 3 Horvath Scholarships for sophomores ($1000), 1 Anne Perman Scholarship for upperclassmen ($2000).

Application Procedures Required: essay, high school transcript, college transcript(s) for transfer students, minimum 2.0 high school GPA, letter of recommendation, SAT or ACT test scores, record of leadership and service. Recommended: interview, portfolio.

Web Site http://www.as.udayton.edu/visualarts/

Undergraduate Contact Office of Admission, University of Dayton, 300 College Park, Dayton, Ohio 45469-1611; 937-229-4411.

University of Denver

Denver, Colorado

Independent, coed. Total enrollment: 11,053. Art program established 1929.

Degrees Bachelor of Fine Arts in the areas of electronic media arts design, art education, studio art, pre-art-conservation. Majors and concentrations: ceramics, painting/drawing, photography, printmaking, sculpture. Graduate degrees offered: Master of Arts in the area of art history/museum studies; Master of Fine Arts in the area of electronic media arts design. Program accredited by NASAD.

Enrollment 192 total; 27 undergraduate, 46 graduate, 119 nonprofessional degree.

Art Student Profile 77% females, 23% males, 15% minorities, 10% international.

Art Faculty 17 total (full-time), 5 total (part-time). 100% of full-time faculty have terminal degrees. Graduate students teach a few undergraduate courses. Undergraduate student–faculty ratio: 12:1.

Student Life Student groups/activities include ...isms (student art organization), Gallery 023 (student run exhibition space), American Institute of Graphic Arts (AIGA) Student Chapter.

Expenses for 2007–2008 Application fee: $50. Comprehensive fee: $41,910 includes full-time tuition ($31,428), mandatory fees ($804), and college room and board ($9678). College room only: $6015. Full-time tuition and fees vary according to class time, course load, and program. Room and board charges vary according to board plan and housing facility. Special program-related fees: $10–$80 per course for lab fees, course materials.

Financial Aid Program-specific awards: 5 Harrison Scholarships for those demonstrating talent and need ($5000–$20,000), 20 art scholarships for those demonstrating talent and academic achievement ($4000–$20,000).

Application Procedures Students admitted directly into the professional program freshman year. Deadline for freshmen: February 1; transfers: continuous. Notification date for freshmen and transfers: continuous. Required: essay, high school transcript, college transcript(s) for transfer students, 2 letters of recommendation, interview, portfolio, SAT or ACT test scores. Portfolio reviews held as needed on campus; the submission of slides may be substituted for portfolios (slides or URL or CD-ROM preferred).

Web Site http://www.du.edu/art/

Undergraduate Contact Ms. Margret Korzus, Associate Dean, Office of Admissions, University of Denver, University Hall, 2197 South University Boulevard, Denver, Colorado 80208; 303-871-2794, fax: 303-871-3301, e-mail address: mkorzus@du.edu

Graduate Contact Dr. Elizabeth Owen, School of Art and Art History, University of Denver, 2121 East Asbury Avenue, Denver, Colorado 80208; 303-871-2846, fax: 303-871-4112, e-mail address: eowen@du.edu

University of Evansville

Evansville, Indiana

Independent, coed. Urban campus. Total enrollment: 2,898. Art program established 1960.

Degrees Bachelor of Fine Arts. Majors and concentrations: ceramics, painting, sculpture.

Enrollment 80 total; all undergraduate.

Art Student Profile 62% females, 38% males, 1% minorities, 15% international.

Art Faculty 3 undergraduate (full-time), 6 undergraduate (part-time). 100% of full-time faculty have terminal degrees. Graduate students do not teach undergraduate courses. Undergraduate student–faculty ratio: 11:1.

Student Life Student groups/activities include Clay Club, Kappa Pi.

Expenses for 2007–2008 Application fee: $35. Comprehensive fee: $31,990 includes full-time tuition ($23,710), mandatory fees ($630), and college room and board ($7650). College room

University of Evansville (continued)

only: $3890. Room and board charges vary according to board plan and housing facility. Special program-related fees: $25–$50 per semester for ceramics, photography, printmaking, metals, sculpture.

Financial Aid Program-specific awards: 25 art and academic scholarships for freshmen program majors ($500–$10,000), art and academic scholarships for transfer program majors.

Application Procedures Students apply for admission into the professional program by sophomore, junior year. Deadline for freshmen: May 1; transfers: June 1. Notification date for freshmen and transfers: continuous. Required: essay, high school transcript, college transcript(s) for transfer students, minimum 2.0 high school GPA, SAT or ACT test scores (minimum composite ACT score of 19). Recommended: minimum 3.0 high school GPA, 2 letters of recommendation, interview, portfolio. Portfolio reviews held continuously on campus and off campus in Louisville, KY; the submission of slides may be substituted for portfolios whenever needed.

Web Site http://www.evansville.edu

Undergraduate Contact Mr. William F. Brown, Chairman, Department of Art, University of Evansville, 1800 Lincoln Avenue, Evansville, Indiana 47722; 812-479-2043, fax: 812-479-2320, e-mail address: bb32@evansville.edu

University of Florida

Gainesville, Florida

State-supported, coed. Suburban campus. Total enrollment: 51,725. Art program established 1929.

Degrees Bachelor of Arts in the areas of art history, art education, general visual art studies; Bachelor of Fine Arts in the areas of ceramics, drawing, graphic design, painting, creative photography, printmaking, sculpture, digital media. Majors and concentrations: art education, art history, ceramics, digital media, general visual arts studies, graphic design, painting/drawing, photography, printmaking, sculpture. Graduate degrees offered: Master of Arts in the areas of museum studies, art education, art history; Master of Fine Arts in the areas of ceramics, drawing, graphic design, painting, creative photography, printmaking, sculpture, digital media. Doctor of Philosophy in the area of art history. Cross-registration with Penland School of Crafts, New World School for the Arts. Program accredited by NASAD, NCATE.

Enrollment 552 total; 450 undergraduate, 102 graduate.

Art Student Profile 68% females, 32% males, 30% minorities, 2% international.

Art Faculty 27 total (full-time), 2 total (part-time). 97% of full-time faculty have terminal degrees. Graduate students teach about a quarter of undergraduate courses. Undergraduate student–faculty ratio: 17:1.

Student Life Student groups/activities include Departure: GNV publication, Fine Arts College Council, Annual Juried Student Exhibition. Special housing available for art students.

Expenses for 2007–2008 Application fee: $30. State resident tuition: $3257 full-time. Nonresident tuition: $17,841 full-time. College room and board: $7020. College room only: $4530. Room and board charges vary according to board plan. Special program-related fees: $8–$65 per course for lab fee for studio courses.

Financial Aid Program-specific awards: 2 Amy DeGrove Scholarships for freshmen and juniors ($2500), 2 James J. Rizzi Scholarships for studio majors ($3000).

Application Procedures Students apply for admission into the professional program by sophomore year. Deadline for freshmen: January 30; transfers: February 15. Notification date for freshmen: continuous; transfers: March 29. Required: essay, high school transcript, college transcript(s) for transfer students, minimum 3.0 high school GPA, letter of recommendation, SAT or ACT test scores (minimum composite ACT score of 20), completion of pre-professional courses Drawing I and II, Design I and II, Survey Art History I and II, portfolio for transfers. Portfolio reviews held twice on campus; the submission of slides may be substituted for portfolios.

Web Site http://www.arts.ufl.edu/art

Undergraduate Contact Dana Myers, Undergraduate Coordinator/Academic Advisor, School of Art and Art History, University of Florida, FAC 101, PO Box 115801, Gainesville, Florida 32611-5801; 352-392-0201, fax: 352-392-8453, e-mail address: dmyers@arts.ufl.edu

Graduate Contact Kristin Flierl, Graduate Program Assistant, School of Art and Art History, University of Florida, FAC 101, PO Box 115801, Gainesville, Florida 32611-5801; 352-392-0201 ext. 201, fax: 352-392-8453, e-mail address: kflierl@ufl.edu

Lamar Dodd School of Art
University of Georgia
Athens, Georgia

State-supported, coed. Suburban campus. Total enrollment: 33,831. Art program established 1937.

Degrees Bachelor of Fine Arts in the area of art. Majors and concentrations: art education, art history, ceramics, digital media, fabric design, graphic design, interior design, jewelry and metalsmithing, painting/drawing, photography, printmaking, scientific illustration, sculpture. Graduate degrees offered: Master of Arts in the areas of art history, art education; Master of Fine Arts in the area of art. Doctor of Education in the area of art education; Doctor of Philosophy in the areas of art history, art education. Cross-registration with 19 area institutions. Program accredited by NASAD, CIDA.

Enrollment 1,072 total; 296 undergraduate, 96 graduate, 680 nonprofessional degree.

Art Student Profile 68% females, 32% males, 12% minorities, 4% international.

Art Faculty 57 total (full-time), 20 total (part-time). 98% of full-time faculty have terminal degrees. Graduate students teach a few undergraduate courses. Undergraduate student–faculty ratio: 15:1.

Student Life Student groups/activities include American Society of Interior Designers Student Chapter, National Art Education Association Student Chapter.

Expenses for 2007–2008 Application fee: $50. State resident tuition: $4496 full-time. Nonresident tuition: $19,600 full-time. Mandatory fees: $1126 full-time. Full-time tuition and fees vary according to course load, location, program, and student level. College room and board: $7292. College room only: $4010. Room and board charges vary according to board plan and housing facility. Special program-related fees: $10–$100 per course for supplies.

Financial Aid Program-specific awards: 30 art awards for program students ($500–$1000).

Application Procedures Students apply for admission into the professional program by freshman year. Deadline for freshmen: March 1; transfers: July 1. Notification date for freshmen: March 31. Required: high school transcript, minimum 3.0 high school GPA, SAT or ACT test scores, portfolio after the first semester.

Web Site http://www.art.uga.edu

Undergraduate Contact Dr. Nancy G. McDuff, Director of Admissions, University of Georgia, 114 Academic Building, Athens, Georgia 30602; 706-542-8776, fax: 706-542-1466.

Graduate Contact Ms. Kate Gearity, Degree Program Specialist, Lamar Dodd School of Art, University of Georgia, Visual Arts Building, Athens, Georgia 30602; 706-542-1636, fax: 706-542-0226.

Hartford Art School
University of Hartford
West Hartford, Connecticut

Independent, coed. Suburban campus. Total enrollment: 7,290. Art program established 1877.

Degrees Bachelor of Fine Arts in the area of art. Majors and concentrations: ceramics, drawing, illustration, media arts, painting, photography, printmaking, sculpture, visual communication design. Graduate degrees offered: Master of Fine Arts in the area of art. Cross-registration with Trinity College, Saint Joseph College, Hartford Seminary, Central Connecticut University, University of Connecticut-Hartford, Capital Community College. Program accredited by NASAD.

Enrollment 387 total; 340 undergraduate, 47 graduate.

Art Student Profile 55% females, 45% males, 5% minorities, 2% international.

Art Faculty 20 undergraduate (full-time), 22 undergraduate (part-time), 1 graduate (full-time), 9 graduate (part-time). 86% of full-time faculty have terminal degrees. Graduate students do not teach undergraduate courses. Undergraduate student–faculty ratio: 14:1.

Student Life Student groups/activities include Student Association, student newspaper and

University of Hartford (continued)

yearbook staff, professional fraternities and sororities. Special housing available for art students.

Expenses for 2008–2009 Application fee: $35. Comprehensive fee: $39,048 includes full-time tuition ($26,942), mandatory fees ($1230), and college room and board ($10,876). College room only: $6706.

Financial Aid Program-specific awards: 45 endowed scholarships for those demonstrating need ($2500), 15–20 artistic merit awards for artistically talented students ($5000–$17,000), 15–25 academic talent awards for those with high SAT scores, high GPA, in top 10% of class ($9000–$15,000).

Application Procedures Students admitted directly into the professional program freshman year. Deadline for freshmen and transfers: continuous. Notification date for freshmen and transfers: continuous. Required: high school transcript, college transcript(s) for transfer students, minimum 2.0 high school GPA, 2 letters of recommendation, portfolio, SAT or ACT test scores. Recommended: essay, interview. Portfolio reviews held by appointment on campus and off campus in Hartford, CT; Philadelphia, PA; Miami, FL; New York, NY; Boston, MA; Syracuse, NY; Baltimore, MD; the submission of slides may be substituted for portfolios when distance is prohibitive.

Web Site http://www.hartfordartschool.org

Undergraduate Contact Mr. Robert Calafiore, Assistant Dean, Hartford Art School, University of Hartford, 200 Bloomfield Avenue, West Hartford, Connecticut 06117; 860-768-4827, fax: 860-768-5296.

Graduate Contact Ms. Mary Frey, Professor, Graduate Director, Hartford Art School, University of Hartford, 200 Bloomfield Avenue, West Hartford, Connecticut 06117; 860-768-4393, fax: 860-768-5296.

University of Houston

Houston, Texas

State-supported, coed. Urban campus. Total enrollment: 34,663. Art program established 1962.

Degrees Bachelor of Fine Arts in the areas of graphic communication, photography/digital media, sculpture, painting. Majors and concentrations: graphic design, painting/drawing, photography/digital media, sculpture. Graduate degrees offered: Master of Fine Arts in the areas of graphic communication, photography/digital media, painting, sculpture.

Enrollment 1,151 total; 830 undergraduate, 39 graduate, 282 nonprofessional degree.

Art Student Profile 68% females, 32% males, 50% minorities, 3% international.

Art Faculty 22 total (full-time), 11 total (part-time). 100% of full-time faculty have terminal degrees. Graduate students teach a few undergraduate courses. Undergraduate student–faculty ratio: 25:1.

Student Life Student groups/activities include Graphic Communication Student Association, Clayworks (ceramics student association).

Expenses for 2007–2008 Application fee: $50. State resident tuition: $4826 full-time. Nonresident tuition: $13,166 full-time. Mandatory fees: $2624 full-time. Full-time tuition and fees vary according to course level, course load, degree level, location, program, reciprocity agreements, and student level. College room and board: $6651. College room only: $3778. Room and board charges vary according to board plan and housing facility. Special program-related fees: $20–$100 per course for equipment maintenance and supplies fee.

Financial Aid Program-specific awards: 10–25 Flaxman Scholarships for seniors ($500–$1500), 2–4 George Bunker Scholarships for program majors ($1500–$2000), 1–4 Choate/Palmer Scholarships for program majors demonstrating need ($700–$1000), 1 Swails Fine ARts Scholarship for program majors with financial need ($500).

Application Procedures Students admitted directly into the professional program freshman year. Deadline for freshmen: April 1; transfers: May 1. Notification date for freshmen and transfers: continuous. Required: high school transcript, college transcript(s) for transfer students, SAT or ACT test scores, GPA (minimum varies according to test scores and class rank).

Web Site http://www.art.uh.edu/

Undergraduate Contact Admission Office, University of Houston, 129 Ezekiel Cullen Building, Houston, Texas 77204-2023; 713-743-1010.

Graduate Contact Cathy Hunt, Graduate Advisor, School of Art, University of Houston, Fine

Arts Building, Room 100, Houston, Texas 77204-4019; 713-743-2830, fax: 713-743-2823, e-mail address: chunt@uh.edu

University of Illinois at Chicago

Chicago, Illinois

State-supported, coed. Total enrollment: 25,747. Art program established 1966.

Degrees Bachelor of Fine Arts in the areas of studio arts, graphic design, industrial design, photo/film/electronic media, art education. Majors and concentrations: art education, electronic arts, film, graphic arts, industrial design, painting/drawing, photography, sculpture, studio art, video art. Graduate degrees offered: Master of Fine Arts in the areas of studio arts, photography, graphic design, industrial design, film/animation/video, electronic visualization. Program accredited by NASAD.

Enrollment 697 total; 607 undergraduate, 90 graduate.

Art Student Profile 60% females, 40% males, 20% minorities, 10% international.

Art Faculty 27 total (full-time), 9 total (part-time). 100% of full-time faculty have terminal degrees. Graduate students teach a few undergraduate courses. Undergraduate student–faculty ratio: 25:1.

Student Life Student groups/activities include American Center for Design Student Chapter, Industrial Design Society of America Student Chapter.

Expenses for 2007–2008 Application fee: $40. State resident tuition: $7424 full-time. Nonresident tuition: $19,814 full-time. Mandatory fees: $3122 full-time. Full-time tuition and fees vary according to program. College room and board: $7818. Room and board charges vary according to board plan and housing facility. Special program-related fees: $15–$150 per class for models, equipment, darkroom facilities.

Financial Aid Program-specific awards: 10–12 talent/tuition waivers for academically qualified program majors ($2722–$6052).

Application Procedures Students apply for admission into the professional program by sophomore year. Deadline for freshmen: May 1; transfers: June 1. Notification date for freshmen and transfers: continuous. Required: high school transcript, college transcript(s) for transfer students, minimum 2.0 high school GPA, SAT or ACT test scores (minimum composite ACT score of 21), minimum TOEFL score of 520 for international applicants, minimum 2.5 (4.0 scale) or 3.75 (5.0 scale) college GPA for transfer students, portfolio for graphic design and art education majors and transfers in certain areas, standing in upper 50% of graduating class. Recommended: essay, letter of recommendation, interview. Portfolio reviews held by arrangement on campus; the submission of slides may be substituted for portfolios (slides preferred).

Web Site http://www.uic.edu/aa/artd/

Undergraduate Contact Erin Brady, Academic Advisor, Undergraduate, School of Art and Design, University of Illinois at Chicago, 929 West Harrison Street, 106 Jefferson Hall, M/C 036, Chicago, Illinois 60607-7038; 312-996-3337, fax: 312-413-2333, e-mail address: ebrady@uic.edu

Graduate Contact Mara Kruger, Academic Advisor, Graduate, School of Art and Design, University of Illinois at Chicago, 929 West Harrison Street, 106 Jefferson Hall M/C 036, Chicago, Illinois 60607-7038; 312-996-3337, fax: 312-413-2333, e-mail address: marak@uic.edu

University of Illinois at Urbana–Champaign

Champaign, Illinois

State-supported, coed. Urban campus. Total enrollment: 42,326. Art program established 1877.

Degrees Bachelor of Fine Arts in the areas of ceramics, GD, ID, metals, painting, photography, art history, art education, sculpture, new media. Majors and concentrations: art education, art history, ceramics, graphic design, industrial design, metals, new media, painting, photography, sculpture. Graduate degrees offered: Master of Arts in the areas of art education, art history; Master of Fine Arts in the areas of ceramics, graphic design, industrial design, metals, painting, photography, sculpture, new media. Doctor of Educa-

University of Illinois at Urbana–Champaign (continued)

tion; Doctor of Philosophy in the areas of art history, art education. Program accredited by NASAD.

Enrollment 620 total; 520 undergraduate, 100 graduate.

Art Student Profile 64% females, 36% males, 1% minorities, 2% international.

Art Faculty 7 undergraduate (part-time), 49 graduate (full-time). 98% of full-time faculty have terminal degrees. Graduate students teach a few undergraduate courses. Undergraduate student–faculty ratio: 10:1.

Student Life Student groups/activities include organizations for all major areas, Industrial Design Society of America, National Art Education Association Student Chapter.

Expenses for 2007–2008 Application fee: $40. State resident tuition: $8440 full-time. Nonresident tuition: $22,526 full-time. Mandatory fees: $2690 full-time. Full-time tuition and fees vary according to course load, program, and student level. College room and board: $8196. Room and board charges vary according to board plan and housing facility. Entering degree-seeking students are guaranteed the same tuition rates for 4 years. Special program-related fees: $200–$300 per semester for equipment and materials fees.

Financial Aid Program-specific awards: 60–70 tuition support awards for program majors ($3000–$4000).

Application Procedures Students apply for admission into the professional program by freshman year. Deadline for freshmen: January 1; transfers: March 1. Notification date for freshmen: March 15. Required: essay, high school transcript, college transcript(s) for transfer students, SAT or ACT test scores, CD or slide portfolio for all studio programs, writing sample for art history transfers, ITBS for transfer into art education. Recommended: minimum 3.0 high school GPA. Portfolio reviews held on campus by committee only, off campus at National Portfolio days on campus and off campus in Chicago, IL; St. Louis, MO; and Indianapolis, IN; the submission of slides may be substituted for portfolios (CD or slides also permissible).

Web Site http://www.art.uiuc.edu

Undergraduate Contact Mark Avery, Undergraduate Specialist in Academic Affairs, School of Art and Design, University of Illinois at Urbana–Champaign, 408 East Peabody Drive, Champaign, Illinois 61820; 217-333-6632, fax: 217-244-7688.

Graduate Contact Ms. Marsha Biddle, Graduate Specialist in Academic Affairs, School of Art and Design, University of Illinois at Urbana–Champaign, 408 East Peabody Drive, Champaign, Illinois 61820; 217-333-0642, fax: 217-244-7688.

University of Indianapolis

Indianapolis, Indiana

Independent, coed. Urban campus. Total enrollment: 4,598. Art program established 1904.

Degrees Bachelor of Fine Arts in the areas of studio art, visual communication design. Majors and concentrations: ceramics, painting/drawing, visual communication design, works on paper. Cross-registration with Consortium for Urban Education. Program accredited by NASAD.

Enrollment 107 total; 13 undergraduate, 94 nonprofessional degree.

Art Student Profile 60% females, 40% males, 5% minorities, 15% international.

Art Faculty 6 undergraduate (full-time), 6 total (part-time). 100% of full-time faculty have terminal degrees. Graduate students do not teach undergraduate courses. Undergraduate student–faculty ratio: 6:1.

Student Life Student groups/activities include Indianapolis Student Art Association.

Expenses for 2007–2008 Application fee: $25. Comprehensive fee: $27,290 includes full-time tuition ($19,540), mandatory fees ($190), and college room and board ($7560). College room only: $3590. Room and board charges vary according to board plan and housing facility.

Financial Aid Program-specific awards: 1 Gerald Boyce Scholarship for art majors ($3000), 6–8 departmental scholarships for incoming freshmen ($3000), 1 A. E. Gott Award for art majors ($1000), 1 M. E. Gott Award for art majors ($600).

Application Procedures Students apply for admission into the professional program by sophomore year. Deadline for freshmen and transfers: continuous. Required: essay, high school transcript, college transcript(s) for transfer students, minimum 2.0 high school GPA,

Visual *Arts*

SAT or ACT test scores, interview and portfolio for scholarship consideration. Portfolio reviews held once in January, February, and June on campus; the submission of slides may be substituted for portfolios when distance in prohibitive.

Web Site http://art.uindy.edu

Undergraduate Contact Ronald Wilks, Director of Admissions, University of Indianapolis, 1400 East Hanna Avenue, Indianapolis, Indiana 46227-3697; 317-788-3216, fax: 317-788-6105, e-mail address: cambridge@uindy.edu

The University of Iowa

Iowa City, Iowa

State-supported, coed. Small town campus. Total enrollment: 29,117. Art program established 1936.

Degrees Bachelor of Fine Arts in the area of studio arts. Majors and concentrations: art education, art history, ceramics, design, intermedia, jewelry and metalsmithing, painting/drawing, photography, printmaking, sculpture, studio art. Graduate degrees offered: Master of Arts in the areas of art history, studio arts; Master of Fine Arts in the area of studio arts. Doctor of Philosophy in the area of art history.

Enrollment 753 undergraduate, 124 graduate.

Art Student Profile 60% females, 40% males, 8% minorities, 4% international.

Art Faculty 31 total (full-time), 13 total (part-time). 100% of full-time faculty have terminal degrees. Graduate students teach a few undergraduate courses. Undergraduate student–faculty ratio: 17:1.

Student Life Student groups/activities include Art History Society, College Art Association, art exhibitions.

Expenses for 2008–2009 Application fee: $40. State resident tuition: $5548 full-time. Nonresident tuition: $19,662 full-time. Mandatory fees: $996 full-time. College room and board: $7673. Special program-related fees: $10–$200 per course for model/lab fees/materials.

Financial Aid Program-specific awards: 1 Iowa Center for Art Scholarship for freshmen program majors, 1–2 Mary Sue Miller Memorial Awards for freshmen program majors ($600–$1000), 1–2 Emma McAllister Novel Awards for minority program majors ($1000), 1–3

Schumacher Awards for program majors ($1600–$1800), 1–3 Paula Patton Grahame Award for upperclass students in sculpture, studio art, 1 Glenn C. Nelson Scholarship for upperclass students in ceramics ($1000), 1–3 Louise Losten Scholarships for upperclass students in metals and jewelry, 1 Luanda Mendenhalle Wilde Scholarship for upperclass undergraduates ($600), 1 Orton and Eugenia Hamby Scholarship for studio art majors.

Application Procedures Students admitted directly into the professional program freshman year. Deadline for freshmen and transfers: continuous. Required: high school transcript, college transcript(s) for transfer students, SAT or ACT test scores, minimum 2.25 high school GPA. Recommended: interview, portfolio for transfer students. Portfolio reviews held twice on campus; the submission of slides may be substituted for portfolios for three-dimensional works of art.

Web Site http://www.uiowa.edu/~art/

Undergraduate Contact Evelyn Acosta-Weirich, Undergraduate Advisor, School of Art and Art History, The University of Iowa, 120 Art Building West, Iowa City, Iowa 52242; 319-335-1779, fax: 319-335-1774, e-mail address: evelyn-weirich@uiowa.edu

Graduate Contact Ms. Laura Jorgensen, Graduate Secretary, School of Art and Art History, The University of Iowa, 122 Art Building West, Iowa City, Iowa 52242; 319-335-1758, fax: 319-335-1774, e-mail address: laura-jorgensen@uiowa.edu

University of Kansas

Lawrence, Kansas

State-supported, coed. Suburban campus. Total enrollment: 28,569.

Degrees Bachelor of Fine Arts in the areas of painting, sculpture, printmaking, expanded media. Majors and concentrations: expanded media, painting, printmaking, sculpture. Graduate degrees offered: Master of Fine Arts in the areas of painting, sculpture, printmaking, expanded media. Program accredited by NASAD.

Enrollment 174 total; 156 undergraduate, 17 graduate, 1 nonprofessional degree.

Art Faculty 15 total (full-time), 5 total (part-time). 100% of full-time faculty have terminal

University of Kansas (continued)

degrees. Graduate students teach a few undergraduate courses. Undergraduate student–faculty ratio: 9:1.

Student Life Special housing available for art students.

Expenses for 2007–2008 Application fee: $30. State resident tuition: $6390 full-time. Nonresident tuition: $16,800 full-time. Mandatory fees: $756 full-time. Full-time tuition and fees vary according to program, reciprocity agreements, and student level. College room and board: $6144. College room only: $3224. Room and board charges vary according to board plan and housing facility.

Financial Aid Program-specific awards: 7 Creative and Performing Arts Scholarships for incoming freshmen ($4100), 6 Foundations Scholarships for sophomores ($1500), 50 departmental scholarships and awards for program majors ($3100), 13 Hollander Foundation Scholarships and Awards for program majors ($2700).

Application Procedures Students apply for admission into the professional program by freshman year. Deadline for freshmen: April 1; transfers: June 1. Notification date for freshmen and transfers: January 19. Required: high school transcript, SAT or ACT test scores. Recommended: portfolio for transfer applicants. Portfolio reviews held 3 times in Chicago, IL; St. Louis, MO; Kansas City, MO; the submission of slides may be substituted for portfolios for large works of art.

Web Site http://www.ku.edu/~sfa/

Undergraduate Contact Ms. Dawn Marie Guernsey, Chair, Department of Art, University of Kansas, 1467 Jayhawk Boulevard, Lawrence, Kansas 66045-7531; 785-864-4401, fax: 785-864-4404, e-mail address: guernsey@ku.edu

Graduate Contact Gina Westergard, Graduate Director, Department of Art, University of Kansas, 1467 Jayhawk Boulevard, Lawrence, Kansas 66045-7531; 785-864-4401, fax: 785-864-4404, e-mail address: ginaw@ku.edu

University of Louisiana at Lafayette

Lafayette, Louisiana

State-supported, coed. Urban campus. Total enrollment: 16,345. Art program established 1957.

Web Site http://www.louisiana.edu/

Allen R. Hite Art Institute
University of Louisville

Louisville, Kentucky

State-supported, coed. Urban campus. Total enrollment: 20,592. Art program established 1936.

Degrees Bachelor of Fine Arts in the areas of interior architecture, communication arts and design, 2-D studios, 3-D studios. Majors and concentrations: graphic arts, interior design, three-dimensional studies, two-dimensional studies. Graduate degrees offered: Master of Arts in the areas of art, art history, critical and curatorial studies; Master of Arts in Teaching in the area of art education. Doctor of Philosophy in the area of art history. Cross-registration with Metroversity/University Exchange Consortium. Program accredited by CIDA.

Enrollment 557 total; 149 undergraduate, 67 graduate, 341 nonprofessional degree.

Art Student Profile 69% females, 31% males, 9% minorities, 2% international.

Art Faculty 23 total (full-time), 12 total (part-time). 100% of full-time faculty have terminal degrees. Graduate students do not teach undergraduate courses. Undergraduate student–faculty ratio: 7:1.

Student Life Student groups/activities include Student Art League, American Society of Interior Designers, Louisville Graphic Design Association.

Expenses for 2008–2009 Application fee: $40. State resident tuition: $7564 full-time. Nonresident tuition: $18,354 full-time. College room and board: $6058. College room only: $4068. Special program-related fees: $13–$25 per course for supplies.

Financial Aid Program-specific awards: 24 Hite Scholarships for enrolled students ($1000–$5500), 4 Hendershot Scholarships for incoming freshmen ($6000), 1 Nay Scholarship for incoming freshmen ($5500), 1 Kaden Scholarship for enrolled students ($1000–$3000).

Application Procedures Students apply for admission into the professional program by sophomore year. Deadline for freshmen and transfers: continuous. Required: essay, high school transcript, college transcript(s) for transfer students, minimum 2.0 high school GPA, portfolio, SAT or ACT test scores (minimum composite ACT score of 21). Recommended: interview, minimum 3.0 high school GPA in major area. Portfolio reviews held as needed on campus; the submission of slides may be substituted for portfolios (slides or digital images preferred).

Web Site http://art.louisville.edu

Undergraduate Contact Theresa Berbet, Administrative Assistant, Fine Arts Department, University of Louisville, 104 Schneider Hall, Louisville, Kentucky 40292; 502-852-6794, fax: 502-852-6791.

Graduate Contact Ms. Janice Blair, Program Assistant, Fine Arts Department, University of Louisville, Lutz Hall, Louisville, Kentucky 40292; 502-852-5914, fax: 502-852-6791, e-mail address: janice.blair@louisville.edu

University of Massachusetts Amherst

Amherst, Massachusetts

State-supported, coed. Total enrollment: 25,873. Art program established 1958.
Web Site http://www.umass.edu/

University of Massachusetts Dartmouth

North Dartmouth, Massachusetts

State-supported, coed. Suburban campus. Total enrollment: 9,080. Art program established 1964.

Degrees Bachelor of Arts in the area of art history; Bachelor of Fine Arts in the areas of visual design, painting, sculpture, artisanry, art education. Majors and concentrations: art education, art history, ceramics, digital media, graphic design, illustration, jewelry and metalsmithing, painting, photography, sculpture, textile design/fiber arts. Graduate degrees offered: Master of Art Education in the area of art education; Master of Fine Arts in the areas of visual design, artisanry, fine arts. Cross-registration with University of Massachusetts System, Southeastern Association for Cooperation in Higher Education in Massachusetts. Program accredited by NASAD.

Enrollment 647 total; 559 undergraduate, 88 graduate.

Art Student Profile 64% females, 36% males, 10% minorities, 1% international.

Art Faculty 43 total (full-time), 23 total (part-time). 77% of full-time faculty have terminal degrees. Graduate students teach a few undergraduate courses. Undergraduate student–faculty ratio: 11:1.

Student Life Student groups/activities include Metals Guild, Sculpture Club, Communicatus.

Expenses for 2007–2008 Application fee: $40. State resident tuition: $1417 full-time. Nonresident tuition: $11,999 full-time. Mandatory fees: $7175 full-time. Full-time tuition and fees vary according to program and reciprocity agreements. College room and board: $8432. College room only: $5670. Room and board charges vary according to board plan and housing facility. Special program-related fees: $343 per semester for CVPA fee.

Financial Aid Program-specific awards: Clement Yeager Scholarships for visual or performing art students ($700–$2500), 1 Barbara Eckhardt Memorial Scholarship for fiber arts students ($1500–$2000), 1 Emil "Smokey" Ameen Endowment Scholarship for CVPA students ($200), 1 David and Alfrede Myerson Scholarship for CVPA students ($600), 1 Alda Alves and Bruce Yenawine Scholarship for CVPA students ($1000), 4 Ayuko Ito Scholarships for CVPA students ($1000), 1 Lillian Telles Jenkins Scholarship for CVPA students ($400), 1 Samuel Gamburd Memorial Art Scholarship for design or fine arts students ($750).

Application Procedures Students admitted directly into the professional program freshman year. Deadline for freshmen and transfers: continuous. Notification date for freshmen and transfers: continuous. Required: high school transcript, college transcript(s) for trans-

University of Massachusetts Dartmouth (continued)

fer students, minimum 2.0 high school GPA, portfolio, SAT or ACT test scores, slides of portfolio. Recommended: essay, minimum 3.0 high school GPA, 3 letters of recommendation. Portfolio reviews held continuously on campus; the submission of slides may be substituted for portfolios (required).

Web Site http://www.umassd.edu/CVPA

Undergraduate Contact Mr. Steven T. Briggs, Director of Admissions, University of Massachusetts Dartmouth, 285 Old Westport Road, North Dartmouth, Massachusetts 02747-2300; 508-999-8606, fax: 508-999-8755, e-mail address: admissions@umassd.edu

Graduate Contact Ms. Carol Novo, Staff Assistant, Graduate Admissions, University of Massachusetts Dartmouth, 285 Old Westport Road, North Dartmouth, Massachusetts 02747-2300; 508-999-8604, fax: 508-999-8183, e-mail address: graduate@umassd.edu

More About the College

The College of Visual and Performing Arts (CVPA) is a fully accredited, comprehensive arts college, with bachelor's and master's degree programs that prepare students for careers in the arts. Unlike most professional art schools, which are independent, CVPA is an active component of a comprehensive university, with all of the educational resources that implies.

CVPA offers a breadth of high-level programs. Students can study art education, art history, illustration, graphic design/letterform, photographic/electronic imaging, ceramics, jewelry/metals, textile design, fiber arts, painting/2-D studies, sculpture/3-D studies, and music—which includes classical music, world music, technology, jazz studies, music education, and composition. The visual arts Foundation Program introduces students to visual concepts and practices and is required of all first-year studio majors.

The Campus Noted architect Paul Rudolf created a dramatic design for UMass Dartmouth's 710-acre main campus. CVPA's studios and classrooms are located there and in the exciting new Star Store campus. Formerly a department store in nearby downtown New Bedford, the Star Store has been converted into a modern urban arts complex with spacious studios, galleries, and state-of-the-art equipment. CVPA is located just minutes from the Atlantic Ocean; about 30 minutes from Cape Cod or Providence, Rhode Island; and 1 hour from Boston.

Facilities Located on both the North Dartmouth and New Bedford campuses of the University, the facilities and equipment available to students in the College of Visual and Performing Arts are among the finest in New England. CVPA encourages applicants to attend its Open House or to schedule a campus visit to tour the College's artist studios, ample classroom spaces, state-of-the-art computer labs, artisanry workshops, photography and printmaking studios, music practice rooms, recital hall, and the many additional features the University has to offer.

Faculty CVPA faculty members are artists, musicians, composers, and educators—each distinguished in his or her field. Many are recipients of such prestigious awards as the National Endowment for the Arts, Massachusetts Cultural Council grants, Fulbright fellows, and national and international arts fellowships. Faculty members exhibit in galleries and museums regionally and nationally and perform on concert stages and smaller venues both in the United States and abroad.

Exhibition Opportunities CVPA's significant contribution to the regional arts scene is evident in its dynamic presence within the southcoast communities. The College is active in downtown New Bedford, participating in the monthly AHA! Night venues and exhibiting work in local storefronts. The College's galleries maintain a high caliber of exhibitions on the Dartmouth campus in the Campus Gallery and Gallery One and in New Bedford at the University Art Gallery and Gallery 244.

The University Art Gallery is devoted to showing the work of international and national artists. The CVPA Campus Gallery and Gallery One feature frequently changing exhibitions of CVPA student and faculty work that is curated by college faculty members. Gallery 244 is a student-run gallery, featuring work by graduate students—emerging artists in their own right.

Special Programs Study abroad is encouraged; current programs in Scotland, Portugal, and Sicily offer excellent opportunities to expand a student's experience. Internships and experiential learning are also encouraged; recent placements have included Graphics Express; WGBH; the Museum of Fine Arts, Boston; the Smithsonian; Guilford of Maine; and the Walt Disney Studios.

University of Massachusetts Lowell

Lowell, Massachusetts

State-supported, coed. Urban campus. Total enrollment: 11,635. Art program established 1982.

Web Site http://www.uml.edu/

University of Michigan

Ann Arbor, Michigan

State-supported, coed. Suburban campus. Total enrollment: 41,042. Art program established 1954.

Degrees Bachelor of Fine Arts in the area of art and design. Majors and concentrations: art, art and design, ceramics, electronic media, fibers, graphic design, industrial design, installation art, jewelry and metalsmithing, painting/drawing, photography, printmaking, scientific illustration, sculpture, sound art. Graduate degrees offered: Master of Fine Arts in the area of art and design. Program accredited by NASAD.

Enrollment 496 total; 470 undergraduate, 26 graduate.

Art Student Profile 65% females, 35% males, 14% minorities, 3% international.

Art Faculty 34 total (full-time), 40 total (part-time). 95% of full-time faculty have terminal degrees. Graduate students do not teach undergraduate courses. Undergraduate student–faculty ratio: 18:1.

Student Life Student groups/activities include Society of Art Students, Industrial Design Society of America Student Chapter, American Institute of Graphic Arts. Special housing available for art students.

Expenses for 2007–2008 Application fee: $40. State resident tuition: $10,258 full-time. Nonresident tuition: $31,112 full-time. Mandatory fees: $189 full-time. Full-time tuition and fees vary according to course load, degree level, location, program, and student level. College room and board: $8190. Room and board charges vary according to board plan and housing facility. Special program-related fees: $250–$500 per semester for materials fee.

Financial Aid Program-specific awards: 1 Shipman Scholarship for those demonstrating academic achievement and artistic ability.

Application Procedures Students admitted directly into the professional program freshman year. Deadline for freshmen and transfers: February 1. Notification date for freshmen and transfers: May 1. Required: essay, high school transcript, college transcript(s) for transfer students, minimum 3.0 high school GPA, portfolio, SAT or ACT test scores (minimum composite ACT score of 25). Recommended: interview. Portfolio reviews held 10 times plus ad hoc on campus; the submission of slides may be substituted for portfolios if accompanied by an index sheet detailing each piece and sufficient return postage.

Web Site http://www.art-design.umich.edu

Undergraduate Contact Joann McDaniel, Director of Undergraduate Academic Services, School of Art and Design, University of Michigan, 2000 Bonisteel Boulevard, Ann Arbor, Michigan 48109-2069; 734-764-0397, fax: 734-936-0469, e-mail address: a&d@umich.edu

Graduate Contact Wendy Dignan, Director of Graduate Academic Services, School of Art and Design, University of Michigan, 2000 Bonisteel Boulevard, Ann Arbor, Michigan 48109-2069; 734-764-0397, fax: 734-936-0469, e-mail address: a&dgradinfo@umich.edu

University of Minnesota, Duluth

Duluth, Minnesota

State-supported, coed. Suburban campus. Total enrollment: 11,184. Art program established 1947.

Web Site http://www.d.umn.edu/

University of Minnesota, Twin Cities Campus

Minneapolis, Minnesota

State-supported, coed. Urban campus. Total enrollment: 50,883. Art program established 1950.

Degrees Bachelor of Fine Arts in the area of art. Majors and concentrations: ceramics, paint-

University of Minnesota, Twin Cities Campus (continued)

ing/drawing, photography, printmaking, sculpture, time and interactivity. Graduate degrees offered: Master of Fine Arts in the area of art.

Enrollment 490 total; 50 undergraduate, 40 graduate, 400 nonprofessional degree.

Art Student Profile 52% females, 48% males, 18% minorities, 6% international.

Art Faculty 22 undergraduate (full-time), 20 undergraduate (part-time), 22 graduate (full-time). 95% of full-time faculty have terminal degrees. Graduate students teach a few undergraduate courses.

Student Life Student groups/activities include Arts Collective. Special housing available for art students.

Expenses for 2007–2008 Application fee: $45. One-time mandatory fee: $1000. State resident tuition: $7950 full-time. Nonresident tuition: $19,580 full-time. Full-time tuition varies according to program and reciprocity agreements. College room and board: $7062. College room only: $4184. Room and board charges vary according to board plan, housing facility, and location. Special program-related fees: $15–$250 per class for materials fees.

Application Procedures Students apply for admission into the professional program by junior year. Deadline for freshmen: December 15; transfers: June 1. Notification date for freshmen: January 15; transfers: July 15. Required: high school transcript, college transcript(s) for transfer students, SAT or ACT test scores, minimum 2.8 high school GPA.

Web Site http://art.umn.edu

Undergraduate Contact Office of Admissions, University of Minnesota, Twin Cities Campus, 240 Williamson, 231 Pillsbury Avenue SE, Minneapolis, Minnesota 55455; 800-752-1000.

Graduate Contact Director of Graduate Studies, Department of Art, University of Minnesota, Twin Cities Campus, 405 21st Avenue South, Minneapolis, Minnesota 55455; 612-625-8096, fax: 612-625-7881, e-mail address: artdept@umn.edu

University of Mississippi

University, Mississippi

State-supported, coed. Small town campus. Total enrollment: 15,129. Art program established 1948.

Degrees Bachelor of Fine Arts in the area of art. Majors and concentrations: studio art. Graduate degrees offered: Master of Fine Arts in the area of art. Program accredited by NASAD.

Enrollment 263 total; 35 undergraduate, 13 graduate, 215 nonprofessional degree.

Art Student Profile 29% females, 71% males, 9% minorities, 1% international.

Art Faculty 11 total (full-time), 13 total (part-time). 100% of full-time faculty have terminal degrees. Graduate students teach a few undergraduate courses. Undergraduate student–faculty ratio: 3:1.

Student Life Student groups/activities include Student Art Association, Mud Daubers, American Institute of Graphic Arts, Vasari Society (art history student organization), Kappa Pi.

Expenses for 2007–2008 Application fee: $50. State resident tuition: $4932 full-time. Nonresident tuition: $11,436 full-time. College room and board: $6578. College room only: $3300. Room and board charges vary according to board plan and housing facility. Special program-related fees: $20 per credit hour for materials fees.

Financial Aid Program-specific awards: 10–15 art merit scholarships for portfolio students ($200–$800).

Application Procedures Students apply for admission into the professional program by sophomore, junior year. Deadline for freshmen and transfers: July 25. Notification date for freshmen and transfers: continuous. Required: high school transcript, college transcript(s) for transfer students, minimum 2.0 high school GPA, ACT test score only (minimum composite ACT score of 18), portfolio for transfer applicants and for acceptance into the BFA program upon completion of 18 semester hours in studio art. Portfolio reviews held once on campus; the submission of slides may be substituted for portfolios.

Web Site http://www.olemiss.edu/depts/art

Undergraduate Contact Dr. Nancy L. Wicker, Chair, Art Department, University of Mississippi, 116 Meek Hall, University, Mississippi 38677; 662-915-7193, fax: 662-915-5013, e-mail address: art@olemiss.edu

Graduate Contact Dr. Nancy L. Wicker, Graduate Coordinator, Art Department, University of Mississippi, 116 Meek Hall, University, Mississippi 38677; 662-915-7193, fax: 662-915-5013, e-mail address: art@olemiss.edu

University of Missouri–Columbia

Columbia, Missouri

State-supported, coed. Suburban campus. Total enrollment: 28,477. Art program established 1979.

Degrees Bachelor of Fine Arts in the area of art. Majors and concentrations: ceramics, drawing, fibers, graphic design, painting, photography, printmaking, sculpture, watercolors. Graduate degrees offered: Master of Fine Arts in the area of art. Cross-registration with Mid-Missouri Associated Colleges and Universities.

Enrollment 249 total; 85 undergraduate, 18 graduate, 146 nonprofessional degree.

Art Student Profile 60% females, 40% males, 5% minorities, 3% international.

Art Faculty 19 total (full-time), 11 total (part-time). 90% of full-time faculty have terminal degrees. Graduate students teach about a quarter of undergraduate courses. Undergraduate student–faculty ratio: 10:1.

Student Life Student groups/activities include Imprint (graphics club), Muck (ceramics club), Student Art Community. Special housing available for art students.

Expenses for 2007–2008 Application fee: $45. State resident tuition: $7077 full-time. Nonresident tuition: $17,733 full-time. Mandatory fees: $1022 full-time. Full-time tuition and fees vary according to course load, program, and reciprocity agreements. College room and board: $7002. College room only: $3752. Room and board charges vary according to board plan and housing facility. Special program-related fees: $40–$100 per course for lab fees.

Financial Aid Program-specific awards: 1 Hennessey Scholarship for program majors demonstrating financial need ($2500), 1 William Ittner Award for program majors ($500), 1 Cox Scholarship for ceramics students ($500), 1 McNair Fellowship for program majors demonstrating financial need, 1 Radford Michael Perrine Scholarship for program majors, 1 Hazel (Pat) Steele Burney Endowment for program majors-undergraduate and graduate.

Application Procedures Students admitted directly into the professional program freshman year. Deadline for freshmen: May 1; transfers: July 1. Notification date for freshmen and transfers: continuous. Required: high school transcript, college transcript(s) for transfer students, SAT or ACT test scores, minimum 3.0 high school GPA in studio art courses.

Web Site http://art.missouri.edu

Undergraduate Contact Deborah Huelsbergen, Director of Undergraduate Studies, Department of Art, University of Missouri–Columbia, A 126 Fine Arts, Columbia, Missouri 65211-6090; 573-882-9444, fax: 573-884-6807, e-mail address: huelsbergend@missouri.edu

Graduate Contact James H. Calvin, Director of Graduate Studies, Department of Art, University of Missouri–Columbia, A 126 Fine Arts, Columbia, Missouri 65211-6090; 573-882-9440, fax: 573-884-6807, e-mail address: calvinjh@missouri.edu

The University of Montana

Missoula, Montana

State-supported, coed. Total enrollment: 13,858. Art program established 1957.

Degrees Bachelor of Fine Arts in the area of art. Majors and concentrations: art education, art/fine arts, ceramics, painting/drawing, photography, printmaking, sculpture. Graduate degrees offered: Master of Arts in the area of art history; Master of Fine Arts in the area of art. Program accredited by NASAD.

Enrollment 424 total; 306 undergraduate, 14 graduate, 104 nonprofessional degree.

Art Student Profile 53% females, 47% males, 1% minorities, 1% international.

Art Faculty 13 total (full-time), 11 total (part-time). 100% of full-time faculty have terminal degrees. Graduate students teach a few undergraduate courses. Undergraduate student–faculty ratio: 20:1.

Student Life Student groups/activities include Artists' Collective, Gallery of Visual Arts, Montana Museum of Arts and Culture.

Expenses for 2008–2009 Application fee: $30. State resident tuition: $3739 full-time. Nonresident tuition: $15,014 full-time. Mandatory fees: $1441 full-time. College room and board:

The University of Montana (continued)

$6258. College room only: $2808. Special program-related fees: $18–$65 per course for materials and supplies.

Financial Aid Program-specific awards: 2 Wallace Awards for sophomore or junior program majors ($1000), 1 Pat Williams Scholarship for sophomore or junior program majors ($500), 1 Walter Hook Scholarship for sophomore or junior program majors ($1000), 1 Diggs Scholarship for sophomore or junior program majors ($500), 1 Thomas Wickes Award for sophomore or junior art majors ($2500).

Application Procedures Students apply for admission into the professional program by sophomore year. Deadline for freshmen and transfers: continuous. Required: high school transcript, SAT or ACT test scores, minimum 2.5 high school GPA. Recommended: portfolio. Portfolio reviews held twice on campus; the submission of slides may be substituted for portfolios.

Web Site http://www.sfa.umt.edu

Undergraduate Contact New Student Services, The University of Montana, Lommasson Center #103, Missoula, Montana 59812; 406-243-6266, fax: 406-243-4087.

Graduate Contact Graduate School, The University of Montana, Lommasson Center, Missoula, Montana 59812; 406-243-2572, fax: 406-243-4593, e-mail address: gradschl@mso.umt.edu

University of Montevallo

Montevallo, Alabama

State-supported, coed. Small town campus. Total enrollment: 2,948.

Degrees Bachelor of Fine Arts in the area of studio art. Majors and concentrations: ceramic art and design, graphic design, new media, painting/drawing, photography, printmaking, sculpture. Cross-registration with Birmingham Area Consortium for Higher Education (BACHE). Program accredited by NASAD.

Enrollment 300 total; 208 undergraduate, 92 nonprofessional degree.

Art Student Profile 61% females, 39% males, 12% minorities, 2% international.

Art Faculty 11 undergraduate (full-time), 3 undergraduate (part-time). 100% of full-time faculty have terminal degrees. Graduate students do not teach undergraduate courses. Undergraduate student–faculty ratio: 17:1.

Student Life Student groups/activities include Kappa Pi, "College Night" Performance.

Expenses for 2007–2008 Application fee: $25. State resident tuition: $5850 full-time. Nonresident tuition: $11,700 full-time. Mandatory fees: $230 full-time. Full-time tuition and fees vary according to course load. College room and board: $4360.

Financial Aid Program-specific awards: 1–2 Dean's Fine Arts Awards for freshmen and transfers ($2000), 2 endowed scholarships for juniors and seniors ($600), 1 Jefferson County Alumni Scholarship for freshmen ($2500), 1 Joan Gregory Art Scholarship for freshmen and transfer students ($800), 1–2 Southern Progress/Graphic Design Awards for freshmen and transfer students ($500).

Application Procedures Students admitted directly into the professional program freshman year. Deadline for freshmen and transfers: July 26. Notification date for freshmen and transfers: September 2. Required: high school transcript, college transcript(s) for transfer students, minimum 2.0 high school GPA, SAT or ACT test scores, minimum 2.0 college GPA for transfer students, portfolio for scholarship consideration and for transfers. Recommended: minimum 3.0 high school GPA, 3 letters of recommendation, interview, portfolio. Portfolio reviews held by appointment on campus; the submission of slides may be substituted for portfolios whenever needed.

Web Site http://www.montevallo.edu

Undergraduate Contact Dr. Clifton Pearson, Chair, Department of Art, University of Montevallo, Station 6400, Montevallo, Alabama 35115; 205-665-6400, fax: 205-665-6383, e-mail address: pearsonc@montevallo.edu

University of Nebraska–Lincoln

Lincoln, Nebraska

State-supported, coed. Urban campus. Total enrollment: 22,973. Art program established 1918.

Degrees Bachelor of Fine Arts in the area of studio art. Majors and concentrations: art history, ceramics, drawing, graphic design, illustration, painting, photography, printmaking, sculpture, studio art. Graduate degrees offered: Master of Fine Arts in the area of studio art. Cross-registration with University of Nebraska at Omaha, University of Nebraska at Kearney. Program accredited by NASAD.

Enrollment 337 total; 250 undergraduate, 33 graduate, 54 nonprofessional degree.

Art Student Profile 58% females, 42% males, 8% minorities, 2% international.

Art Faculty 21 total (full-time), 10 total (part-time). 100% of full-time faculty have terminal degrees. Graduate students teach a few undergraduate courses. Undergraduate student–faculty ratio: 14:1.

Student Life Student groups/activities include Annual Juried Undergraduate Exhibition, Rotunda Gallery Exhibitions, Fame Awards.

Expenses for 2007–2008 Application fee: $45. State resident tuition: $5085 full-time. Nonresident tuition: $15,105 full-time. Mandatory fees: $1130 full-time. Full-time tuition and fees vary according to course load. College room and board: $6523. College room only: $3441. Room and board charges vary according to board plan and housing facility. Special program-related fees: $15–$150 per semester for lab fees.

Financial Aid Program-specific awards: 38 endowed scholarships for program majors ($3000).

Application Procedures Students admitted directly into the professional program freshman year. Deadline for freshmen and transfers: June 30. Required: high school transcript, college transcript(s) for transfer students, minimum 2.0 high school GPA, SAT or ACT test scores (minimum composite ACT score of 22). Recommended: interview, portfolio.

Web Site http://www.unl.edu

Undergraduate Contact Admission Office, University of Nebraska–Lincoln, Alexander Building, 1410 O Street, Lincoln, Nebraska 68588-0417; 402-472-2023, fax: 402-472-0670.

Graduate Contact Prof. Santiago Cal, Chairperson, Graduate Committee, Department of Art and Art History, University of Nebraska–Lincoln, 120 Richards Hall, Lincoln, Nebraska 68588-0114; 402-472-2102, fax: 402-472-9746.

University of New Mexico
Albuquerque, New Mexico

State-supported, coed. Urban campus.

Degrees Bachelor of Fine Arts in the area of studio art; Bachelor of Arts in Fine Arts in the areas of studio art, art history. Majors and concentrations: art history, studio art. Graduate degrees offered: Master of Arts in the area of art history; Master of Fine Arts in the area of studio art. Doctor of Philosophy in the area of art history.

Enrollment 394 total; 185 undergraduate, 85 graduate, 124 nonprofessional degree.

Art Student Profile 63% females, 37% males, 28% minorities.

Art Faculty 30 total (full-time), 15 total (part-time). 100% of full-time faculty have terminal degrees. Graduate students teach about a quarter of undergraduate courses. Undergraduate student–faculty ratio: 35:1.

Student Life Student groups/activities include Art Student Association Gallery.

Expenses for 2007–2008 Application fee: $20. State resident tuition: $4571 full-time. Nonresident tuition: $14,942 full-time. College room and board: $7020. College room only: $4100. Room and board charges vary according to board plan and housing facility. Special program-related fees: $33–$150 for studio/art history courses for materials/technology fee.

Financial Aid Program-specific awards: 20–35 art scholarships for juniors in College of Fine Arts ($500–$1000).

Application Procedures Students apply for admission into the professional program by junior year. Deadline for freshmen and transfers: June 15. Required: high school transcript, SAT or ACT test scores, minimum 2.5 high school GPA, portfolio for transfer students. Recommended: essay. Portfolio reviews held continuously by appointment on campus; the submission of slides may be substituted for portfolios.

Web Site http://www.unm.edu/~artdept2/

Undergraduate Contact Office of Admissions, University of New Mexico, Albuquerque, New Mexico 87131-0001; 505-277-2446.

Graduate Contact Ms. Kat Heatherington, Graduate Advisor, Department of Art and Art

University of New Mexico (continued)

History, University of New Mexico, Albuquerque, New Mexico 87131-0001; 505-277-6672, fax: 505-277-5955.

University of North Alabama

Florence, Alabama

State-supported, coed. Urban campus. Total enrollment: 7,097. Art program established 1930.

Degrees Bachelor of Fine Arts in the area of art. Majors and concentrations: ceramics, digital media, painting, photography, sculpture. Cross-registration with other institutions in Alabama (specific courses only). Program accredited by NASAD.

Enrollment 158 total; 78 undergraduate, 80 nonprofessional degree.

Art Student Profile 47% females, 53% males, 5% minorities, 6% international.

Art Faculty 8 undergraduate (full-time). 100% of full-time faculty have terminal degrees. Graduate students do not teach undergraduate courses. Undergraduate student–faculty ratio: 9:1.

Student Life Student groups/activities include Student Art Association, FLORALA (student newspaper) and Diorama (yearbook), Lights and Shadows "Magazine".

Expenses for 2008–2009 Application fee: $25. State resident tuition: $4410 full-time. Nonresident tuition: $8820 full-time. Mandatory fees: $983 full-time. College room and board: $4460. Special program-related fees: $30 per semester for studio lab fee.

Financial Aid Program-specific awards: 1 endowed scholarship for program majors ($900).

Application Procedures Students apply for admission into the professional program by sophomore year. Deadline for freshmen and transfers: August 30. Notification date for freshmen and transfers: continuous. Required: high school transcript, college transcript(s) for transfer students, SAT or ACT test scores, portfolio after 45 hours for entry into BFA

program. Recommended: minimum 2.0 high school GPA. Portfolio reviews held twice on campus.

Web Site http://www.una.edu

Undergraduate Contact Dr. Sue Wilson, Dean of Enrollment Management, Admissions Office, University of North Alabama, Box 5058, Florence, Alabama 35632-0001; 256-765-4680, fax: 256-765-4329, e-mail address: swilson@unanov.una.edu

The University of North Carolina at Charlotte

Charlotte, North Carolina

State-supported, coed. Suburban campus. Total enrollment: 22,388. Art program established 1965.

Degrees Bachelor of Fine Arts in the area of art. Majors and concentrations: art history, ceramics, cross-discipline studies, fibers, graphic design, illustration, painting, photography, print media, sculpture. Cross-registration with NC consortium.

Enrollment 550 total; all undergraduate.

Art Student Profile 54% females, 46% males, 11% minorities, 2% international.

Art Faculty 26 undergraduate (full-time), 10 undergraduate (part-time). 100% of full-time faculty have terminal degrees. Graduate students do not teach undergraduate courses. Undergraduate student–faculty ratio: 16:1.

Student Life Student groups/activities include National Art Education Association Student Chapter, Art Student Association.

Expenses for 2007–2008 Application fee: $50. State resident tuition: $2460 full-time. Nonresident tuition: $12,873 full-time. Mandatory fees: $1692 full-time. Full-time tuition and fees vary according to course load. College room and board: $6034. College room only: $3064. Room and board charges vary according to board plan and housing facility.

Financial Aid Program-specific awards: 7 Mull Scholarships for freshmen ($1000–$2000).

Application Procedures Students apply for admission into the professional program by sophomore year. Deadline for freshmen and transfers: continuous. Required: essay, college transcript(s) for transfer students, portfolio,

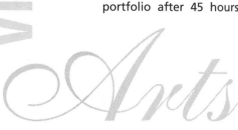

SAT or ACT test scores. Portfolio reviews held on campus; the submission of slides may be substituted for portfolios for freshmen and transfers.

Web Site http://www.uncc.edu/art/

Undergraduate Contact Prof. Malena Bergmann, Undergraduate Advisor, Department of Art and Art History, The University of North Carolina at Charlotte, 173 Rowe Building, Charlotte, North Carolina 28223; 704-687-2473, fax: 704-687-2591.

The University of North Carolina at Greensboro

Greensboro, North Carolina

State-supported, coed. Urban campus. Total enrollment: 17,157. Art program established 1936.

Degrees Bachelor of Arts in the areas of studio art, art history combined with museum studies; Bachelor of Fine Arts in the areas of studio art, art education. Majors and concentrations: art education, art history and museum studies, ceramics, design, painting/drawing, photography, printmaking, sculpture, studio art. Graduate degrees offered: Master of Fine Arts in the area of studio art. Cross-registration with Guilford College, Greensboro College, North Carolina Agricultural and Technical State University. Program accredited by NCATE.

Enrollment 450 undergraduate, 15 graduate.

Art Student Profile 68% females, 32% males, 30% minorities.

Art Faculty 12 undergraduate (full-time), 5 undergraduate (part-time), 24 graduate (full-time). 100% of full-time faculty have terminal degrees. Graduate students do not teach undergraduate courses. Undergraduate student–faculty ratio: 21:1.

Student Life Student groups/activities include Student Art League, Coraddi Art Magazine. Special housing available for art students.

Expenses for 2007–2008 Application fee: $45. State resident tuition: $2458 full-time. Nonresident tuition: $13,726 full-time. Mandatory fees: $1571 full-time. College room and board: $6051. College room only: $3427.

Financial Aid Program-specific awards: Pierce Memorial Scholarship for North Carolina residents, Maud F. Gatewood Scholarships for for painting majors demonstrating merit, Peter Agostini and Andrew Martin Scholarship for art majors with financial need, Reeves Scholarship for art majors, Mary Cochrane Austin Scholarships for art education majors, Elizabeth Jastrow Scholarship for junior art history majors.

Application Procedures Students admitted directly into the professional program freshman year. Deadline for freshmen: March 1; transfers: August 1. Required: high school transcript, college transcript(s) for transfer students, minimum 3.0 high school GPA, SAT or ACT test scores, portfolio for transfer students and for scholarship consideration. Recommended: 3.5 GPA for freshman, 1044 SAT scores (math and critical reading sections only). Portfolio reviews held continuously by appointment on campus; the submission of slides may be substituted for portfolios.

Web Site http://www.uncg.edu/art

Undergraduate Contact Undergraduate Advisor, Department of Art, The University of North Carolina at Greensboro, PO Box 26170, Greensboro, North Carolina 27402-6170; 336-334-5909, fax: 336-334-5270.

Graduate Contact Niki Blair, Associate Professor, Department of Art, The University of North Carolina at Greensboro, PO Box 26170, Greensboro, North Carolina 27402-6170; 336-334-5248, fax: 336-334-5270, e-mail address: nblair1@yahoo.com

University of North Dakota

Grand Forks, North Dakota

State-supported, coed. Urban campus. Total enrollment: 12,559. Art program established 1978.

Degrees Bachelor of Fine Arts in the area of visual arts. Majors and concentrations: ceramic art and design, fibers, jewelry and metalsmithing, new media, painting/drawing, photography, printmaking, sculpture. Graduate degrees offered: Master of Fine Arts in the area of visual arts. Program accredited by NASAD.

Enrollment 114 total; 65 undergraduate, 14 graduate, 35 nonprofessional degree.

University of North Dakota (continued)

Art Student Profile 60% females, 40% males, 3% minorities, 1% international.

Art Faculty 11 undergraduate (full-time), 8 undergraduate (part-time), 11 graduate (full-time). 100% of full-time faculty have terminal degrees. Graduate students teach about a quarter of undergraduate courses. Undergraduate student–faculty ratio: 6:1.

Student Life Student groups/activities include Ceramic Arts Organization, Art Student Collective, League of Metalsmiths.

Expenses for 2007–2008 Application fee: $35. State resident tuition: $5025 full-time. Nonresident tuition: $13,418 full-time. Mandatory fees: $1105 full-time. Full-time tuition and fees vary according to degree level, program, and reciprocity agreements. College room and board: $5203. College room only: $2137. Room and board charges vary according to board plan and housing facility. Special program-related fees: $55 per course for art materials (average fee).

Financial Aid Program-specific awards: 2 Beverly Bushaw Gulmon Scholarships ($750), 2 Stephanie Prepioria Memorial Scholarships ($600), 1 M. Anderson Scholarship ($600), 2 Friedmen Scholarships ($300–$500), 1 Mary Ellen Rogers Scholarship for sculpture students ($300), 1 Alma Anderson Scholarship ($500), 2 Haugen Scholarships ($650), 2 Rod and Carmen Gergstrom Thorpe Scholarships ($1000).

Application Procedures Students apply for admission into the professional program by sophomore year. Deadline for freshmen and transfers: continuous. Required: high school transcript, college transcript(s) for transfer students, portfolio, ACT test score only. Portfolio reviews held by appointment on campus; the submission of slides may be substituted for portfolios for large works of art or when distance is prohibitive.

Web Site http://www.und.edu/dept/arts2000

Undergraduate Contact Dr. Arthur F. Jones, Chair, Department of Art, University of North Dakota, Box 7099, Grand Forks, North Dakota 58202; fax: 701-777-2903, e-mail address: art.jones@und.nodak.edu

Graduate Contact Ms. Anita Monsebroten, Associate Professor, Department of Art, University of North Dakota, Box 7099, Grand Forks, North Dakota 58202; fax: 701-777-2903, e-mail address: anita_monsebroten@und.nodak.edu

University of Northern Iowa

Cedar Falls, Iowa

State-supported, coed. Small town campus. Total enrollment: 12,692. Art program established 1895.

Web Site http://www.uni.edu/

University of North Florida

Jacksonville, Florida

State-supported, coed. Urban campus. Total enrollment: 16,406. Art program established 1972.

Web Site http://www.unf.edu/

University of North Texas

Denton, Texas

State-supported, coed. Suburban campus. Total enrollment: 34,153. Art program established 1894.

Degrees Bachelor of Arts in the area of art history; Bachelor of Fine Arts in the areas of studio art, visual art studies, interior design, communication design, fashion design. Majors and concentrations: art history, ceramics, communication design, fashion design, fibers, interior design, jewelry and metalsmithing, new media, painting/drawing, photography, printmaking, sculpture, visual arts, watercolors. Graduate degrees offered: Master of Arts in the areas of art history, art education; Master of Fine Arts in the areas of art education, art history, ceramics, communication design, drawing and painting, fashion design, fibers, interior design, metalsmithing and jewelry, photography, printmaking, sculpture. Doctor of Philosophy in the area of art education. Program accredited by CIDA.

Enrollment 2,443 total; 2,295 undergraduate, 148 graduate.

Art Student Profile 62% females, 38% males, 19% minorities, 4% international.

Art Faculty 39 total (full-time), 54 total (part-time). 95% of full-time faculty have

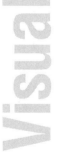

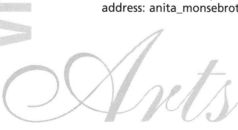

terminal degrees. Graduate students teach about a quarter of undergraduate courses. Undergraduate student–faculty ratio: 25:1.

Student Life Student groups/activities include Clay Guild, National Art Education Association (NAEA) Student Chapter, Interior Design Student Chapter. Special housing available for art students.

Expenses for 2007–2008 Application fee: $40. State resident tuition: $4390 full-time. Nonresident tuition: $12,730 full-time. Mandatory fees: $1930 full-time. Full-time tuition and fees vary according to course load. College room and board: $5490. Room and board charges vary according to board plan and housing facility. Special program-related fees: $25–$75 per course for materials fee.

Financial Aid Program-specific awards: 1 John D. Murchison Sr. Scholarship for undergraduate art majors with a minimum 3.0 GPA ($1000), 3 Helen Voertman Memorial Scholarships for full-time undergraduate (sophomore level or higher) art majors with minimum 3.0 GPA ($1000), 1 Cora E. Stafford Scholarship for full-time undergraduate (sophomore level or higher) art majors with minimum 3.0 GPA ($500), 1 Roger Thomason Scholarship for full-time undergraduate (sophomore level or higher) fibers majors with minimum 3.0 GPA ($1000), 6 Jean Andrews Scholarships for undergraduate art majors with a minimum 3.0 GPA ($1000–$1500), 1 Edward and Betty Mattil Scholarship for undergraduate art majors with a minimum 3.0 GPA ($500), 1 J. Robert Egar Scholarship for undergraduate photography majors with a minimum 3.0 GPA ($750), 3 Mack Mathes Scholarships for full-time undergraduate (sophomore level or higher) art majors with minimum 3.0 GPA ($500), 1 Barney Budow Scholarship for undergraduate fashion design majors with a minimum 3.0 GPA ($1000), 1 William J. Lee Scholarship for undergraduate fashion design majors with a minimum 3.0 GPA ($500), 4 SOVA Bloggers awards for full-time students ($1000).

Application Procedures Students apply for admission into the professional program by freshman, sophomore year. Deadline for freshmen and transfers: June 15. Required: high school transcript, college transcript(s) for transfer students, SAT or ACT test scores, minimum 2.5 high school GPA, portfolio for entry into BFA program. Portfolio reviews held on campus; the submission of slides may be substituted for portfolios (electronic media may also be used).

Web Site http://www.art.unt.edu

Undergraduate Contact Ms. Marian O'Rourke-Kapla, Associate Dean for Academic and Student Affairs, School of Visual Arts, University of North Texas, PO Box 305100, Denton, Texas 76203-5100; 940-565-2216, fax: 940-565-4717.

Graduate Contact Ms. Marian O'Rourke-Kaplan, Associate Dean for Academic and Student Affairs, School of Visual Arts, University of North Texas, PO Box 305100, Denton, Texas 76203-5100; 940-565-2216, fax: 940-565-4717.

University of Notre Dame
Notre Dame, Indiana

Independent Roman Catholic, coed. Suburban campus. Total enrollment: 11,733. Art program established 1842.

Degrees Bachelor of Fine Arts in the areas of studio art, design. Majors and concentrations: art/fine arts, ceramic art and design, computer graphics, graphic arts, industrial design, painting/drawing, photography, printmaking, sculpture, studio art. Graduate degrees offered: Master of Arts in the area of art history; Master of Fine Arts in the areas of studio art, design. Program accredited by NASAD.

Enrollment 292 total; 42 undergraduate, 24 graduate, 226 nonprofessional degree.

Art Student Profile 76% females, 24% males, 21% minorities, 30% international.

Art Faculty 17 total (full-time), 7 total (part-time). 100% of full-time faculty have terminal degrees. Graduate students teach about a quarter of undergraduate courses. Undergraduate student–faculty ratio: 2:1.

Student Life Student groups/activities include student exhibitions.

Expenses for 2007–2008 Application fee: $65. Comprehensive fee: $44,477 includes full-time tuition ($34,680), mandatory fees ($507), and college room and board ($9290). Special program-related fees: $15–$100 per course for studio materials.

Application Procedures Students apply for admission into the professional program by

University of Notre Dame (continued)

sophomore year. Deadline for freshmen and transfers: January 4. Notification date for freshmen and transfers: April 10. Required: essay, high school transcript, minimum 3.0 high school GPA, 2 letters of recommendation. Recommended: interview, slide portfolio. Portfolio reviews held by request on campus; the submission of slides may be substituted for portfolios (slides or CD preferred).

Web Site http://www.nd.edu/~art

Undergraduate Contact Admissions Office, University of Notre Dame, 113 Main Building, Notre Dame, Indiana 46556; 574-631-7505.

Graduate Contact Ms. Martina Lopez, Graduate Director, Department of Art, Art History, and Design, University of Notre Dame, 306 Riley Hall of Art, Notre Dame, Indiana 46556; 574-631-4272, fax: 574-631-6312, e-mail address: lopez.29@nd.edu

University of Oregon

Eugene, Oregon

State-supported, coed. Urban campus. Total enrollment: 20,332. Art program established 1929.

Degrees Bachelor of Fine Arts in the areas of painting, sculpture, ceramics, fibers, metalsmithing and jewelry, printmaking, photography, digital arts. Majors and concentrations: animation, ceramics, computer graphics, digital art, fibers, jewelry and metalsmithing, multimedia, painting/drawing, photography, printmaking, sculpture. Graduate degrees offered: Master of Fine Arts in the areas of painting, sculpture, ceramics, fibers, metalsmithing and jewelry, printmaking, photography, digital arts. Program accredited by NASAD.

Enrollment 665 total; 70 undergraduate, 45 graduate, 550 nonprofessional degree.

Art Student Profile 50% females, 50% males, 10% minorities, 3% international.

Art Faculty 18 total (full-time), 20 total (part-time). 90% of full-time faculty have terminal degrees. Graduate students teach a few undergraduate courses. Undergraduate student–faculty ratio: 4:1.

Student Life Special housing available for art students.

Expenses for 2007–2008 Application fee: $50. One-time mandatory fee: $250. State resident tuition: $4494 full-time. Nonresident tuition: $17,250 full-time. Mandatory fees: $1542 full-time. Full-time tuition and fees vary according to class time, course load, program, and reciprocity agreements. College room and board: $7849. Room and board charges vary according to board plan and housing facility. Special program-related fees: $5–$80 per course for material fees, $25 per course for studio fees, $125 per term for major program fee.

Financial Aid Program-specific awards: 1 Eugene Weavers' Guild Scholarship for continuing weaving students ($150), 4 Phillip Johnson Scholarships for continuing painting and printmaking students ($200–$400), 1 LaVerne Krause Scholarship for continuing printmaking students ($300–$750), 4 David McCosh Painting Scholarships for continuing painting students ($200–$400), 1 Jack Wilkinson Paint Award for continuing painting students ($200–$400), 1 Molly Muntzel Award for continuing painting students ($200–$400).

Application Procedures Deadline for freshmen and transfers: March 1. Notification date for freshmen and transfers: April 1. Required: letter of recommendation, portfolio, statement of interest, college transcript(s) for 2nd degree students. Portfolio reviews held once (digital arts), 3 times (all others) on campus; the submission of slides may be substituted for portfolios (slides preferred).

Web Site http://art-uo.uoregon.edu

Undergraduate Contact Ms. Heidi Howes, Admissions, Department of Art, University of Oregon, 5232 University of Oregon, Eugene, Oregon 97403-5232; 541-346-3610, fax: 541-346-3626, e-mail address: hhowes@uoregon.edu

Graduate Contact Ms. Bonnie Lawrence, Graduate Program Coordinator, Department of Art, University of Oregon, 5232 University of Oregon, Eugene, Oregon 97403-5232; 541-346-3618, fax: 541-346-3626, e-mail address: blawrenc@uoregon.edu

University of Regina

Regina, Saskatchewan, Canada

Province-supported, coed. Urban campus. Total enrollment: 11,819. Art program established 1915.

Web Site http://www.uregina.ca/

University of South Carolina

Columbia, South Carolina

State-supported, coed. Total enrollment: 27,272. **Web Site** http://www.sc.edu/

Roski School of Fine Arts
University of Southern California

Los Angeles, California

Independent, coed. Urban campus. Total enrollment: 33,408. Art program established 1895.

Degrees Bachelor of Fine Arts in the area of studio arts. Majors and concentrations: advertising design and communication, art, art and business, art and design, art/fine arts, ceramics, clay, communication design, computer imaging, digital media, digital photography, drawing, fine art photography, fine art studio, game art and design, graphic design, intaglio, multimedia, new genres, painting, painting/drawing, photography, photography/digital media, printmaking, public art studies, sculpture, studio art, video art. Graduate degrees offered: Master of Fine Arts in the area of studio arts; Master of Public Art Studies; Master of Public Art Studies/Master of Planning; Master of Public Art Studies/Master of Arts in Jewish Communal Service.

Enrollment 350 total; 100 undergraduate, 50 graduate, 200 nonprofessional degree.

Art Student Profile 60% females, 40% males, 20% minorities, 16% international.

Art Faculty 20 undergraduate (full-time), 40 undergraduate (part-time), 6 graduate (full-time), 8 graduate (part-time). 85% of full-time faculty have terminal degrees. Graduate students do not teach undergraduate courses. Undergraduate student–faculty ratio: 4:1.

Student Life Student groups/activities include American Institute of Graphic Arts, Animation Club, Students of Fine Arts Association. Special housing available for art students.

Expenses for 2007–2008 Application fee: $65. Comprehensive fee: $46,668 includes full-time tuition ($35,212), mandatory fees ($598), and college room and board ($10,858). College room only: $5992. Full-time tuition and fees vary according to program. Room and board charges vary according to board plan and housing facility. Special program-related fees: $55 per course for lab/studio materials fee.

Financial Aid Program-specific awards: 30 Fine Art Talent Scholarships for program majors ($2000).

Application Procedures Students admitted directly into the professional program freshman year. Deadline for freshmen: January 10; transfers: February 1. Notification date for freshmen: April 1; transfers: June 1. Required: essay, high school transcript, college transcript(s) for transfer students, portfolio, SAT or ACT test scores, 2 letters of recommendation for transfer applicants, minimum 3.3 college GPA for transfer applicants. Recommended: interview, minimum 3.5 high school GPA. Portfolio reviews held continuously on campus and off campus in various; the submission of slides may be substituted for portfolios (or digital images on CD).

Web Site http://roski.usc.edu

Contact Ms. Penelope Jones, Director of Admissions, Roski School of Fine Arts, University of Southern California, Watt Hall 104, Los Angeles, California 90089-0292; 213-740-9153, fax: 213-740-8938, e-mail address: finearts@usc.edu

University of Southern Maine

Portland, Maine

State-supported, coed. Suburban campus. Total enrollment: 10,453. Art program established 1976.

Degrees Bachelor of Arts in the area of studio art and entrepreneurial studies; Bachelor of Fine Arts in the areas of studio art, art education. Majors and concentrations: art education, ceramics, digital art, drawing, painting, photography, printmaking, sculpture. Cross-registration with Maine College of Art, University of New England, St. Joseph's College, Westbrook College, Southern Maine Technical College. Program accredited by NASAD.

Enrollment 290 total; all undergraduate.

University of Southern Maine (continued)

Art Faculty 12 undergraduate (full-time), 12 undergraduate (part-time). 100% of full-time faculty have terminal degrees. Graduate students do not teach undergraduate courses. Undergraduate student–faculty ratio: 13:1.

Student Life Student groups/activities include Union of the Visual Arts, Union of Art Students, Printmaking Collective. Special housing available for art students.

Expenses for 2007–2008 Application fee: $40. State resident tuition: $5940 full-time. Nonresident tuition: $16,410 full-time. Mandatory fees: $926 full-time. Full-time tuition and fees vary according to course load, degree level, and reciprocity agreements. College room and board: $8038. College room only: $4140. Room and board charges vary according to board plan, housing facility, and location. Special program-related fees: $10–$120 per semester for supplies for some studio and lecture courses.

Application Procedures Students apply for admission into the professional program by freshman year. Deadline for freshmen: August 1; transfers: continuous. Notification date for freshmen and transfers: July 15. Required: essay, high school transcript, college transcript(s) for transfer students, letter of recommendation, portfolio, SAT or ACT test scores. Recommended: minimum 2.0 high school GPA, interview. Portfolio reviews held twice on campus.

Web Site http://www.usm.maine.edu

Undergraduate Contact Dee Gardner, Director of Admissions, University of Southern Maine, 37 College Avenue, Gorham, Maine 04038; 207-780-5670, fax: 207-780-5640.

University of Southern Mississippi

Hattiesburg, Mississippi

State-supported, coed. Suburban campus. Total enrollment: 14,592. Art program established 1947.

Degrees Bachelor of Arts in the area of museum studies; Bachelor of Fine Arts in the area of art; Bachelor of Science in the area of interior design. Majors and concentrations: art education, graphic communication, museum studies, painting/drawing, three-dimensional studies. Graduate degrees offered: Master of Art Education. Program accredited by NASAD, CIDA, NCATE.

Enrollment 296 total; 280 undergraduate, 9 graduate, 7 nonprofessional degree.

Art Student Profile 60% females, 40% males, 13% minorities, 1% international.

Art Faculty 12 undergraduate (full-time), 5 undergraduate (part-time), 3 graduate (full-time). 100% of full-time faculty have terminal degrees. Graduate students do not teach undergraduate courses. Undergraduate student–faculty ratio: 23:1.

Student Life Student groups/activities include Student Art Club, American Institute of Graphic Arts Student Chapter, Student Chapter: ASID, IIDA, & NKBA, National Council for Accreditation of Teacher Education (NCATE) Student Chapter. Special housing available for art students.

Expenses for 2008–2009 Application fee: $25. State resident tuition: $4914 full-time. Nonresident tuition: $11,692 full-time. College room and board: $5040. College room only: $2826. Special program-related fees: $35–$40 per course for expendable materials.

Financial Aid Program-specific awards: 7 endowed scholarships for program majors ($1250), 1 Mississippi Gulf Coast Scholarship for program majors ($600–$900), 1 Maude Sherrod Scholarship for program majors ($700).

Application Procedures Students apply for admission into the professional program by freshman year. Deadline for freshmen and transfers: continuous. Notification date for freshmen and transfers: continuous. Required: high school transcript, college transcript(s) for transfer students, ACT test score only (minimum composite ACT score of 18), portfolio for scholarship consideration. Portfolio reviews held by appointment on campus; the submission of slides may be substituted for portfolios (slides preferred).

Web Site http://www.arts.usm.edu/

Undergraduate Contact Jara Naquin, Executive Secretary, Department of Art, University of Southern Mississippi, Box 5033, Hattiesburg, Mississippi 39406-5011; 601-266-4972, fax: 601-266-6379, e-mail address: jara.naquin@usm.edu

Graduate Contact Dr. Carley Causey, Director of Art Education, Graduate Admissions, University of Southern Mississippi, Box 10066, Hattiesburg, Mississippi 39406; 601-266-5137, fax: 601-266-5138, e-mail address: carley.causey@usm.edu

The University of Tennessee

Knoxville, Tennessee

State-supported, coed. Urban campus. Total enrollment: 29,937. Art program established 1947.

Degrees Bachelor of Fine Arts in the areas of studio art, graphic design. Majors and concentrations: art history, ceramics, drawing, graphic design, media arts, painting, printmaking, sculpture, watercolors. Graduate degrees offered: Master of Fine Arts in the area of studio art. Cross-registration with Arrowmont School of Art and Crafts. Program accredited by NASAD.

Enrollment 635 total; 450 undergraduate, 35 graduate, 150 nonprofessional degree.

Art Student Profile 58% females, 42% males, 2% minorities, 2% international.

Art Faculty 27 total (full-time), 12 total (part-time). 100% of full-time faculty have terminal degrees. Graduate students teach a few undergraduate courses. Undergraduate student–faculty ratio: 17:1.

Student Life Student groups/activities include University of Tennessee Potters, Student Art History Association, Sculpture Club, University of Tennessee Print Club, AIGA-American Institute of Graphic Arts Student Group.

Expenses for 2008–2009 Application fee: $30. State resident tuition: $5376 full-time. Nonresident tuition: $18,216 full-time. Mandatory fees: $812 full-time. College room and board: $6676. College room only: $3516. Special program-related fees: $10–$100 per course for lab fees.

Financial Aid Program-specific awards: 1–3 Orin B. and Erma G. Graff Scholarships for freshmen ($2000), 1–2 Buck Ewing Undergraduate Scholarships for juniors and seniors ($2000), Mary Louise Seilaz Awards for program students ($1000), T. H. Jeanette Gillespie Awards for juniors and seniors ($500), 1 Mary Lynn Glustoff Memorial Scholarship for program students ($1000), 1 Rod Norman Memorial Scholarship for program students ($500), 1–3 Dorothy Dille Materials/Travel Awards ($1000), 1–2 freshmen scholarships ($2000).

Application Procedures Students apply for admission into the professional program by freshman year. Deadline for freshmen and transfers: June 2. Required: high school transcript, college transcript(s) for transfer students, minimum 3.0 high school GPA, SAT or ACT test scores.

Web Site http://art.utk.edu

Undergraduate Contact Dr. Suzanne E. Wright, Associate Director, School of Art, The University of Tennessee, 1715 Volunteer Boulevard, Knoxville, Tennessee 37996-2410; 865-974-3407, fax: 865-974-3198, e-mail address: swright5@utk.edu

Graduate Contact Tom Riesing, Graduate Coordinator, School of Art, The University of Tennessee, 1715 Volunteer Boulevard, Knoxville, Tennessee 37996-2410; 865-974-3407, fax: 865-974-3198, e-mail address: triesing@utk.edu

The University of Tennessee at Martin

Martin, Tennessee

State-supported, coed. Small town campus. Total enrollment: 7,173. Art program established 1999.

Degrees Bachelor of Fine Arts in the area of fine and performing arts. Majors and concentrations: art education, graphic design, visual arts.

Enrollment 110 total; all undergraduate.

Art Student Profile 60% females, 40% males, 12% minorities, 3% international.

Art Faculty 5 undergraduate (full-time), 3 undergraduate (part-time). 100% of full-time faculty have terminal degrees. Graduate students do not teach undergraduate courses. Undergraduate student–faculty ratio: 16:1.

Student Life Student groups/activities include Visual Arts Society.

Expenses for 2007–2008 Application fee: $30. State resident tuition: $4150 full-time. Nonresident tuition: $14,190 full-time. Mandatory fees: $855 full-time. College room and board:

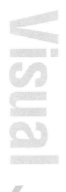

The University of Tennessee at Martin (continued)

$4446. College room only: $2160. Room and board charges vary according to board plan and housing facility.

Financial Aid Program-specific awards: 2 Endowment for the Arts Scholarships for art design majors ($1000), 1 David Wechsler Scholarship for art/design majors ($1000).

Application Procedures Students admitted directly into the professional program freshman year. Deadline for freshmen and transfers: continuous. Required: high school transcript, college transcript(s) for transfer students, SAT or ACT test scores, ACT score of 21 and high school GPA of 2.50 or ACT score of 18 and high school GPA of 2.85.

Web Site http://www.utm.edu/departments/finearts/music

Undergraduate Contact Mr. Douglas J. Cook, Chair, Department of Visual and Theatre Arts, The University of Tennessee at Martin, 102 Fine Arts Building, Martin, Tennessee 38238; 731-881-7400, fax: 731-881-7415, e-mail address: dcook@utm.edu

The University of Texas at Arlington

Arlington, Texas

State-supported, coed. Urban campus. Total enrollment: 25,095.

Degrees Bachelor of Arts in the area of art history; Bachelor of Fine Arts in the area of art. Majors and concentrations: art history, ceramic art and design, film, glass, graphic arts, jewelry and metalsmithing, painting/drawing, photography, printmaking, screenwriting, sculpture, teacher certification. Graduate degrees offered: Master of Fine Arts in the area of art. Program accredited by NASAD.

Enrollment 601 total; all undergraduate.

Art Student Profile 55% females, 45% males, 37% minorities, 2% international.

Art Faculty 29 undergraduate (full-time), 16 undergraduate (part-time). 93% of full-time faculty have terminal degrees. Graduate students do not teach undergraduate courses. Undergraduate student–faculty ratio: 20:1.

Student Life Student groups/activities include Student Art Association, Student Film and Video Organization, Art History Student Union, Eye Candy Visual Communication.

Expenses for 2007–2008 Application fee: $35. State resident tuition: $7194 full-time. Nonresident tuition: $15,534 full-time. Full-time tuition varies according to course level, course load, and program. College room and board: $6180. College room only: $3296. Room and board charges vary according to board plan and housing facility. Special program-related fees: $25–$100 per course for materials fee.

Financial Aid Program-specific awards: 9 Ideas in Art Awards for all students ($1000), 4 Wishful Wings Awards for all students ($500), 3 Arlington Arts League Awards for all students ($400), 3 Mark Baum Awards for all students ($1500).

Application Procedures Students apply for admission into the professional program by sophomore year. Deadline for freshmen and transfers: continuous. Required: high school transcript, college transcript(s) for transfer students, minimum 2.0 high school GPA, SAT or ACT test scores.

Web Site http://www.uta.edu/art

Undergraduate Contact Office of Admissions, The University of Texas at Arlington, Box 19111, Arlington, Texas 76019-0111; 817-272-2118, fax: 817-272-3435.

Graduate Contact Ms. Nancy Palmeri, Graduate Advisor, Associate Professor, Art and Art History, The University of Texas at Arlington, Box 19089, Arlington, Texas 76019; 817-272-2871, fax: 817-272-2805, e-mail address: art@uta.edu

The University of Texas at Austin

Austin, Texas

State-supported, coed. Urban campus. Total enrollment: 50,170. Art program established 1938.

Degrees Bachelor of Fine Arts in the areas of studio art, design. Majors and concentrations: design, studio art. Graduate degrees offered: Master of Fine Arts in the areas of studio art, design. Program accredited by NASAD.

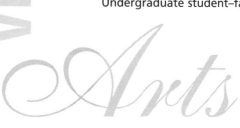

Enrollment 766 total; 432 undergraduate, 45 graduate, 289 nonprofessional degree.

Art Student Profile 70% females, 30% males, 33% minorities, 4% international.

Art Faculty 61 total (full-time), 5 total (part-time). 97% of full-time faculty have terminal degrees. Graduate students teach a few undergraduate courses.

Student Life Student groups/activities include Fine Arts Student Council, Art Students Association, Undergraduate Art History Association.

Expenses for 2007–2008 Application fee: $60. State resident tuition: $7670 full-time. Nonresident tuition: $24,544 full-time. Full-time tuition varies according to course load and program. College room and board: $8576. Room and board charges vary according to board plan, housing facility, and location. Special program-related fees for to maintain studio labs, for to supplement course instruction.

Financial Aid Program-specific awards: 6 department scholarships for currently enrolled students ($1000).

Application Procedures Students admitted directly into the professional program freshman year. Deadline for freshmen: February 1; transfers: March 1. Notification date for freshmen and transfers: April 15. Required: essay, high school transcript, college transcript(s) for transfer students, SAT or ACT test scores, portfolio for transfer applicants. Recommended: minimum 3.0 high school GPA, 3 letters of recommendation, portfolio, portfolio for freshman applicants. Portfolio reviews held 4 times on campus and off campus; the submission of slides may be substituted for portfolios (we only accept slide portfolio, not acutal work).

Web Site http://www.finearts.utexas.edu/aah/

Undergraduate Contact Mr. Shane Sullivan, Undergraduate Coordinator, Department of Art and Art History, The University of Texas at Austin, ART 3.340, Austin, Texas 78712-1285; 512-475-7718, fax: 512-471-7801, e-mail address: shanesullivan@mail.utexas.edu

Graduate Contact Ms. Judy Clack, Graduate Coordinator, Department of Art and Art History, The University of Texas at Austin, ART 3.320, Austin, Texas 78712-1285; 512-471-3377, fax: 512-471-7801, e-mail address: jclack@mail.utexas.edu

The University of Texas at El Paso

El Paso, Texas

State-supported, coed. Urban campus. Total enrollment: 20,154. Art program established 1958.

Web Site http://www.utep.edu/

The University of Texas at San Antonio

San Antonio, Texas

State-supported, coed. Suburban campus. Total enrollment: 28,533. Art program established 1974.

Degrees Bachelor of Fine Arts in the area of art. Majors and concentrations: art. Graduate degrees offered: Master of Arts in the area of art history and criticism; Master of Fine Arts in the area of art. Program accredited by NASAD.

Enrollment 436 total; 284 undergraduate, 28 graduate, 124 nonprofessional degree.

Art Faculty 13 undergraduate (full-time), 13 undergraduate (part-time), 13 graduate (full-time), 13 graduate (part-time). 100% of full-time faculty have terminal degrees. Graduate students teach a few undergraduate courses. Undergraduate student–faculty ratio: 12:1.

Student Life Student groups/activities include Photo Exposure Club, Clay Bodies, Fine Arts Association.

Expenses for 2007–2008 Application fee: $40. State resident tuition: $4530 full-time. Nonresident tuition: $12,780 full-time. Mandatory fees: $2147 full-time. Full-time tuition and fees vary according to course load. College room and board: $8169. College room only: $5616. Room and board charges vary according to board plan and housing facility. Special program-related fees: $35 per course for studio materials.

Financial Aid Program-specific awards: 3 art scholarships ($500).

Application Procedures Students admitted directly into the professional program freshman year. Deadline for freshmen and transfers: July 1. Required: high school transcript, col-

The University of Texas at San Antonio (continued)

lege transcript(s) for transfer students, minimum 2.0 high school GPA, SAT or ACT test scores (minimum composite ACT score of 20), Texas Academic Skills Program test, portfolio for transfer students with junior standing and above. Portfolio reviews held as needed on campus; the submission of slides may be substituted for portfolios when original work is not available or for large works of art.

Web Site http://art.utsa.edu

Undergraduate Contact Mr. Kent T. Rush, Chair, Department of Art and Art History, The University of Texas at San Antonio, One UTSA Circle, San Antonio, Texas 78249; 210-458-4352, fax: 210-458-4356, e-mail address: kent-rush@utsa.edu

Graduate Contact Mr. Ken Little, Graduate Advisor of Record, Department of Art and Art History, The University of Texas at San Antonio, 6900 North Loop 1604 West, San Antonio, Texas 78249-1130; 210-458-4352, fax: 201-458-4356, e-mail address: klittle@utsa.edu

The University of the Arts

Philadelphia, Pennsylvania

Independent, coed. Total enrollment: 2,396. Art program established 1876.

Degrees Bachelor of Fine Arts in the areas of graphic design, painting, printmaking, sculpture, illustration, photography, animation, ceramics, wood, multimedia, writing for film and television; Bachelor of Science in the areas of industrial design, communication. Majors and concentrations: animation, crafts, film and video production, film studies, graphic design, illustration, industrial design, multimedia, painting/drawing, photography, printmaking/book arts, sculpture. Graduate degrees offered: Master of Arts in the areas of art education, museum education, museum communication; Master of Arts in Teaching in the area of visual art; Master of Fine Arts in the areas of museum exhibition planning and design, book arts/printmaking, painting, sculpture, ceramics; Master of Industrial Design in the area of industrial design. Cross-registration with schools sponsored by American Independent Colleges of Art and Design. Program accredited by NASAD, IDSA.

Enrollment 1,603 total; 1,428 undergraduate, 175 graduate.

Art Student Profile 59% females, 41% males, 21% minorities, 3% international.

Art Faculty 68 total (full-time), 193 total (part-time). 84% of full-time faculty have terminal degrees. Graduate students do not teach undergraduate courses.

Student Life Student groups/activities include Student Government. Special housing available for art students.

Expenses for 2008–2009 Application fee: $60. Tuition: $29,500 full-time. Mandatory fees: $1100 full-time. College room only: $7047. Special program-related fees for various lab fees (depending on the curriculum).

Financial Aid Program-specific awards: 75 merit scholarships for program students ($1000–$12,000).

Application Procedures Students apply for admission into the professional program by sophomore year. Deadline for freshmen and transfers: continuous. Notification date for freshmen and transfers: September 1. Required: essay, high school transcript, college transcript(s) for transfer students, minimum 2.0 high school GPA, letter of recommendation, portfolio, SAT or ACT test scores. Recommended: minimum 3.0 high school GPA, interview. Portfolio reviews held continuously by appointment on campus and off campus at National Portfolio Days; the submission of slides may be substituted for portfolios when distance is prohibitive.

Web Site http://www.uarts.edu

Contact Susan Gandy, Director of Admission, The University of the Arts, 320 South Broad Street, Philadelphia, Pennsylvania 19102; 800-616-ARTS ext. 6049, fax: 215-717-6045, e-mail address: admissions@uarts.edu

More About the University

Located on The Avenue of the Arts in Center City Philadelphia, The University of the Arts (UArts) is the only school in the country devoted to all the arts and communication. Composed of the College of Art and Design, the College of Performing Arts, and the College of Media and Communication, UArts offers intensive concentration within each major as well as other creative opportunity for further artistic exploration and growth.

More than 2,300 undergraduate and graduate students from forty states and thirty countries are enrolled. UArts educates professional artists, performers, and communicators—people who make their living creating, designing, communicating, and performing. Active Internship Programs offer students opportunities to gain hands-on experience in their field during the academic year.

The College of Art and Design offers a full range of programs in the visual arts. It includes dynamic programs such as Animation, Crafts, Film/Animation, Film/Digital Video, Graphic Design, Illustration, Industrial Design, Painting/Drawing, Photography, Printmaking/Book Arts, and Sculpture. These programs share both exceptionally high standards and a supportive, personal environment to explore and grow as a creative individual.

The College of Performing Arts combines both the exhilaration of performance and the diligent commitment to practice and rehearsal to sharpen technique and shape vision. It includes the Schools of Dance, Music, and Theater Arts. The College offers outstanding opportunities to perform as well as the chance to grow as an artist through rigorous training.

The College of Media and Communications explores new ideas and concepts in a changing world. Video games, the Internet, interactive television, and virtual reality are just a few examples of the emerging forms that are featured in the challenging and exciting curriculum. Offering majors in writing for film and television, multimedia, and communication, the College celebrates the interdisciplinary nature of these new forms of creative expression.

Program Facilities UArts offers excellent facilities to support all of its programs in an environment rich with opportunities to encounter art and artistic inspiration. The studios, shops, theaters, recital halls, labs, galleries, and libraries are housed nearby in Hamilton Hall, the Terra Building, the Merriam Theater, the Arts Bank, and Anderson Hall—the nine-story studio building.

The facilities in the College of Art and Design include a broad range of studios and equipment: woodworking and metal shops, including a foundry; printmaking shops and digital pre-press labs; fine arts, crafts, design, and film/animation studios; and digital imaging labs. Four gas and several electric kilns are available for work in ceramics, as is a forge for sculpture. A large weaving shop offers dozens of looms and a dyeing room. Facilities supporting work in film, video, photography, and animation are extensive and first-class. A 3-D printer and scanner for student use is available and used primarily by industrial design and jewelry design students to

develop mock-ups of their ideas faster and less expensively than the traditional way of hand molding wax or foam.

The School of Dance offers a rigorous studio experience, and its home is the newly renovated Terra Building. Dance studios are bright, well-lit, and fully equipped with barres and mirrors, responsive suspension floors, beautiful windows, ceiling fans, pianos, and audio systems. In addition to the 1,800-seat Merriam Theater, student performances are held in the 240-seat UArts Dance Theater.

The School of Music at UArts has three big bands, twenty small jazz ensembles, seven vocal ensembles, and ten traditional ensembles. In addition to performance opportunities in recital halls and theaters, facilities include fully equipped music studios, practice rooms, and a class piano laboratory. The MIDI and Recording Studio is a modern recording and music technology facility with a complete 32-input recording studio, MIDI and computer labs, computer and synthesizer workstation labs, and an audio-for-video dubbing and editing room. Most practice rooms are equipped with grand pianos, and a suite of fully equipped percussion studios is also available for student practice.

Students in the College of Media and Communication have ready access to state-of-the-art audio and video systems; highly portable equipment; preproduction and postproduction studios; PC-, Mac-, and UNIX-based systems; and industry-standard software used for audio, video, and Web work. The College supports a student-run Webzine and Web radio and hosts a number of student- and alumni-produced Web sites. UArts is a member of the New Media Centers (NMC), an organization of leading universities and corporations dedicated to innovative uses of technology.

Faculty, Residential Artists, and Alumni Numbering 500 full- and part-time members, the faculty is the driving force of the UArts programs. They are practicing professionals, most with advanced degrees, who are committed to both their own creative expression and the development of their students. The student-faculty ratio is 10:1, so students can be assured of individual attention and guidance.

Proud alumni include Philadelphia Orchestra violinist Michael Ludwig, Alvin Ailey Dance member Antonio Carlos Scott, artist Sidney Goodman, Tony Award–winning dancer/actress Rhonda LaChanze Sapp, illustrator Arnold Roth, jazz artist/composer Stanley Clarke, director Joe Dante, illustrator Charles Santore, dancer/choreographer Judith Jamison, ALMA Award–winning actress Ana Ortiz, concert pianist

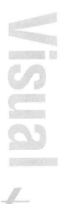

The University of the Arts (continued)

Lydia Artymiw, children's book authors/illustrators Jan and Stan Berenstain, and filmmakers the Quay Brothers.

Student Performance/Exhibit Opportunities

Events include exhibitions in UArts galleries, ensemble productions, student composition concerts featuring original choreography, repertory concerts, an annual freshmen inter-arts project, recitals, and appearances with visiting artists.

Special Programs Programs include student exchanges with other schools and colleges, foreign and summer studies, pre-College Summer Institute for talented and motivated high school students, career planning and placement, personal counseling, academic support, professional and peer tutoring, services for students with disabilities, and international student services.

University of the Pacific

Stockton, California

Independent, coed. Suburban campus. Total enrollment: 6,235. Art program established 1980.

Degrees Bachelor of Fine Arts in the areas of graphic design, studio arts. Majors and concentrations: graphic design, studio art. Program accredited by NASAD.

Enrollment 90 total; 65 undergraduate, 25 nonprofessional degree.

Art Student Profile 65% females, 35% males, 45% minorities, 5% international.

Art Faculty 8 undergraduate (full-time), 3 undergraduate (part-time). 100% of full-time faculty have terminal degrees. Graduate students do not teach undergraduate courses. Undergraduate student–faculty ratio: 8:1.

Student Life Student groups/activities include Undergraduate Research Conference, Associated Student Union of Pacific, AIGA-American Institute of Graphic Arts Student Chapter.

Expenses for 2007–2008 Application fee: $60. Comprehensive fee: $38,190 includes full-time tuition ($28,480), mandatory fees ($500), and college room and board ($9210). College room only: $4610. Room and board charges vary according to board plan and housing facility. Special program-related fees: $25–$100 per course for studio materials.

Financial Aid Program-specific awards: 10–20 endowed scholarships for art majors: studio arts graphic design ($2000–$5000).

Application Procedures Students admitted directly into the professional program freshman year. Deadline for freshmen: March 1. Notification date for freshmen: April 15. Required: essay, high school transcript, minimum 2.0 high school GPA, letter of recommendation, SAT or ACT test scores. Recommended: minimum 3.0 high school GPA, portfolio. Portfolio reviews held continuously for transfer students on campus; the submission of slides may be substituted for portfolios (or CD ROM with detailed list).

Web Site http://www.pacific.edu/cop/art/

Undergraduate Contact Office of Admissions, University of the Pacific, 3601 Pacific Avenue, Stockton, California 95211-0197; 800-959-2867, fax: 209-946-2413, e-mail address: admissions@uop.edu

University of Utah

Salt Lake City, Utah

State-supported, coed. Urban campus. Total enrollment: 28,025. Art program established 1890.

Degrees Bachelor of Fine Arts in the area of art. Majors and concentrations: art education, ceramics, digital imaging, graphic design, illustration, intermedia, painting/drawing, photography, printmaking, sculpture. Graduate degrees offered: Master of Fine Arts in the area of art.

Enrollment 610 total; 460 undergraduate, 26 graduate, 124 nonprofessional degree.

Art Student Profile 50% females, 50% males, 12% minorities, 10% international.

Art Faculty 21 total (full-time), 21 total (part-time). 100% of full-time faculty have terminal degrees. Graduate students do not teach undergraduate courses. Undergraduate student–faculty ratio: 13:1.

Student Life Student groups/activities include cross-discriminary classes and fine arts technology events, intercollegiate and interregional traveling exhibitions, Carmen Morton Christensen Visiting Artist/Scholar Lecture Series. Special housing available for art students.

Expenses for 2007–2008 Application fee: $35. State resident tuition: $4269 full-time. Nonresident tuition: $14,945 full-time. Mandatory fees: $717 full-time. Full-time tuition and fees vary according to course level, course load, degree level, program, reciprocity agreements, and student level. College room and board: $5778. College room only: $2890. Room and board charges vary according to board plan and housing facility. Contact university directly for part-time tuition costs. Special program-related fees: $30–$75 per course for tools and equipment maintenance, materials.

Financial Aid Program-specific awards: 5 departmental tuition scholarships for freshmen and continuing students ($4000), 2 Ann Cannon Scholarships for continuing students ($1000), 1 Ethel A. Rolapp Award for graduating students ($2000), 1 E. J. Bird Memorial Scholarship for continuing students ($4000), 14 C. M. Christensen Scholarships for freshmen and continuing students ($1800), 1 Florence Ware Scholarship for continuing students ($1500), 1 freshman tuition scholarship for freshmen ($4000), 1 Grace Durkee Meldrum Scholarship for continuing students ($2500), 1 Paul Davis Travel Award for continuing students ($500), 1 outstanding high school award for incoming high school students ($500), 2 Howard Clark Scholarships for continuing students ($1500), 1 Jack and Florence Sears Scholarship for continuing students ($1500), 1 Antista-Fairclough Scholarship for continuing students ($2000).

Application Procedures Students apply for admission into the professional program by freshman year. Deadline for freshmen and transfers: continuous. Required: high school transcript, college transcript(s) for transfer students, minimum 2.0 high school GPA, SAT or ACT test scores (minimum composite ACT score of 18), portfolio for transfer students and for scholarship consideration. Recommended: minimum 3.0 high school GPA. Portfolio reviews held as needed on campus; the submission of slides may be substituted for portfolios for large works of art.

Web Site http://www.art.utah.edu/

Undergraduate Contact Ms. Nevon Bruschke, Undergraduate Advisor, Department of Art and Art History, University of Utah, 375 South 1530 E Room 161, Salt Lake City, Utah 84112-0380; 801-581-8677, fax: 801-585-6171, e-mail address: n.bruschke@utah.edu

Graduate Contact Prof. John O'Connell, Graduate Director of MFA Program, Department of Art and Art History, University of Utah, 375 South 1530 E Room 161, Salt Lake City, Utah 84112-0380; 801-581-8677, fax: 801-585-6171, e-mail address: j.oconnell@utah.edu

University of Washington

Seattle, Washington

State-supported, coed. Urban campus. Total enrollment: 40,218. Art program established 1867.

Degrees Bachelor of Arts in the areas of design studies, art history; Bachelor of Fine Arts in the areas of art, design. Majors and concentrations: art history, ceramics, design art, fibers, industrial design, interdisciplinary studies, painting/drawing, photography, sculpture, visual communication design. Graduate degrees offered: Master of Arts in the area of art history; Master of Fine Arts in the areas of art, design. Doctor of Philosophy in the area of art history.

Enrollment 1,450 total; 800 undergraduate, 100 graduate, 550 nonprofessional degree.

Art Student Profile 65% females, 35% males, 10% minorities, 10% international.

Art Faculty 38 total (full-time), 2 total (part-time). 94% of full-time faculty have terminal degrees. Graduate students teach a few undergraduate courses. Undergraduate student–faculty ratio: 14:1.

Student Life Student groups/activities include MFA Thesis Exhibit, School of Art Open House, Career Discovery Week.

Expenses for 2007–2008 Application fee: $50. State resident tuition: $6385 full-time. Nonresident tuition: $22,131 full-time. Full-time tuition varies according to course load. College room and board: $8337. Room and board charges vary according to board plan and housing facility. Special program-related fees: $35–$110 per course for materials fee.

Financial Aid Program-specific awards: 56 School of Art Scholarships for program majors ($1000).

Application Procedures Students apply for admission into the professional program by freshman, sophomore, junior year. Deadline for freshmen: February 1; transfers: April 1. Notification date for freshmen: March 15. Required: essay, high school transcript, college transcript(s) for transfer students, SAT or ACT test scores, portfolio for transfer applicants

University of Washington (continued)

(for some majors). Portfolio reviews held continuously on campus; the submission of slides may be substituted for portfolios whenever needed.

Web Site http://art.washington.edu

Undergraduate Contact Admissions Office, University of Washington, Box 355840, Seattle, Washington 98195-5840; 206-543-9686.

Graduate Contact Autumn Yoke, Adviser, School of Art, University of Washington, Box 353440, Seattle, Washington 98195-3440; 206-543-0646, fax: 206-685-1657, e-mail address: gradart@u.washington.edu

University of West Florida

Pensacola, Florida

State-supported, coed. Suburban campus. Total enrollment: 10,358. Art program established 1980.

Web Site http://uwf.edu/

University of Wisconsin–Madison

Madison, Wisconsin

State-supported, coed. Urban campus. Total enrollment: 42,041.

Degrees Bachelor of Fine Arts in the area of art; Bachelor of Science in the areas of art, art education. Majors and concentrations: art education, art/fine arts, graphic design. Graduate degrees offered: Master of Arts in the areas of art, art education; Master of Fine Arts in the area of art. Doctor of Philosophy in the area of art education. Program accredited by NASAD.

Enrollment 475 total; 375 undergraduate, 100 graduate.

Art Student Profile 60% females, 40% males, 10% minorities, 1% international.

Art Faculty 30 total (full-time), 4 total (part-time). 100% of full-time faculty have terminal degrees. Graduate students teach a few undergraduate courses. Undergraduate student–faculty ratio: 10:1.

Student Life Student groups/activities include Arts Night Out, Student Art Exhibit, Student art organizations.

Expenses for 2007–2008 Application fee: $44. State resident tuition: $7188 full-time. Nonresident tuition: $21,440 full-time. Mandatory fees: $859 full-time. Full-time tuition and fees vary according to degree level, program, and reciprocity agreements. Special program-related fees: $10–$300 per course for expendable supplies.

Financial Aid Program-specific awards: 4 Edith Gilbertson Scholarships for continuing program students ($5000), 2 Ethel Odegaard Scholarships for continuing program students ($3000), 1 Carrie Jones Cady Scholarship for continuing program students/applied art ($7500), 2 Butor Scholarships for continuing program students ($2000), 2 Frazier Scholarships for continuing program students ($1250), 2 Hokin Scholarships for continuing program students ($2000), 1 Regan Scholarship for continuing program students ($500), 2 Austin Scholarships for continuing program students from Milwaukee High School ($7500), 1 Ebling Scholarship for continuing program students from Wisconsin ($1500), 1 Faculty Scholarship for continuing program students ($800), 1 Krug Scholarship for continuing program students ($1000), 1 Marten Scholarship for continuing program students/art education ($1000), 1 Logan Scholarship for continuing program students/art education ($4500), 1 Hooper Scholarship for continuing program students/printmaking ($1500), 1 Wartmann Scholarship for continuing program students/printmaking ($3500), 3 Art Metals Scholarships for continuing program students/printmaking ($7500).

Application Procedures Students admitted directly into the professional program freshman year. Deadline for freshmen and transfers: February 1. Required: essay, high school transcript, college transcript(s) for transfer students, minimum 3.0 high school GPA, SAT test score only.

Web Site http://art.wisc.edu

Undergraduate Contact Julie Ganser, Undergraduate Advisor, Art Department, University of Wisconsin–Madison, 455 North Park Street, 6241 Humanities C, Madison, Wisconsin 53706; 608-262-8831, e-mail address: ganser@education.wisc.edu

Graduate Contact Ms. Teri Van Genderen, Student Status Examiner, Art Department, University of Wisconsin–Madison, 455 North Park Street, 6241 Humanities, Madison, Wisconsin 53706; 608-262-1660.

Peck School of the Arts
University of Wisconsin–Milwaukee

Milwaukee, Wisconsin

State-supported, coed. Urban campus. Total enrollment: 29,338. Art program established 1961.

Degrees Bachelor of Fine Arts in the areas of art, art with teacher certification. Majors and concentrations: art education, ceramics, digital art, fibers, graphic design, jewelry and metalsmithing, painting/drawing, photography, printmaking, sculpture. Graduate degrees offered: Master of Arts in the area of art; Master of Fine Arts in the area of art.

Enrollment 865 total; 775 undergraduate, 30 graduate, 60 nonprofessional degree.

Art Student Profile 61% females, 39% males, 8% minorities, 1% international.

Art Faculty 20 undergraduate (full-time), 47 undergraduate (part-time), 20 graduate (full-time). 100% of full-time faculty have terminal degrees. Graduate students teach a few undergraduate courses. Undergraduate student–faculty ratio: 39:1.

Expenses for 2007–2008 Application fee: $35. State resident tuition: $6960 full-time. Nonresident tuition: $16,686 full-time. Mandatory fees: $767 full-time. Full-time tuition and fees vary according to location, program, and reciprocity agreements. College room only: $3620. Room charges vary according to housing facility. Special program-related fees: $35–$75 per course for art supplies, $60 per course for infrastructure, technology, instruction.

Financial Aid Program-specific awards: 10 Layton Scholarships ($500–$1000), 1–2 Harold A. Levin Memorial Scholarships for program majors ($500–$1000), 10 Visual Arts Scholarships ($500–$1000), 3–4 Elsa Ulbricht Memorial Scholarships for program majors ($500–$1000), 1 Rorabeck Memorial Scholarship for painting and drawing majors ($1000), 1 Clarice George

Logan Travel Scholarship for juniors only ($2500), 1 Racine Art Guild Scholarship for program majors who are residents of Racine, WI ($500), 2–3 Mary E. Van Deven Scholarships for juniors (renewable in senior year) ($500–$1000), 1 Lawrence Rathsack Scholarship for painting and drawing majors ($1000), 1–2 Ester C. Waldheim Scholarships for graphic design majors ($900).

Application Procedures Students apply for admission into the professional program by sophomore year. Deadline for freshmen and transfers: continuous. Required: essay, high school transcript, college transcript(s) for transfer students, 2 letters of recommendation, portfolio, ACT score for state residents, SAT or ACT score for out-of-state residents. Recommended: minimum 3.0 high school GPA. Portfolio reviews held on campus; the submission of slides may be substituted for portfolios with permission of graphic design faculty for graphic design program; slides or CD required for freshmen.

Web Site http://www.uwm.edu/Dept/SFA/

Undergraduate Contact Ms. Kelly Beisbier, Administrative Program Manager, Department of Visual Art, University of Wisconsin–Milwaukee, PO Box 413, 2400 East Kenwood Boulevard, Milwaukee, Wisconsin 53201; 414-229-6054, fax: 414-229-2973, e-mail address: beis@uwm.edu

Graduate Contact Prof. Marna Brauner, Director, Graduate Studies, Department of Visual Art, University of Wisconsin–Milwaukee, PO Box 413, 2400 East Kenwood Boulevard, Milwaukee, Wisconsin 53201; 414-229-6053, fax: 414-229-2973, e-mail address: marnab@uwm.edu

University of Wisconsin–Oshkosh

Oshkosh, Wisconsin

State-supported, coed. Suburban campus. Total enrollment: 12,693.

Degrees Bachelor of Fine Arts in the areas of art education, studio/fine arts, graphic communications. Majors and concentrations: applied design, art education, ceramics, drawing, fibers, graphic communication, metals, painting, photography, printmaking, sculpture.

University of Wisconsin–Oshkosh (continued)

Enrollment 370 total.

Art Faculty 13 total (full-time), 7 total (part-time). 100% of full-time faculty have terminal degrees. Graduate students do not teach undergraduate courses. Undergraduate student–faculty ratio: 20:1.

Student Life Student groups/activities include Priebe Gallery Board, SOFA (Students Organized for Art).

Expenses for 2007–2008 Application fee: $35. State resident tuition: $5693 full-time. Nonresident tuition: $13,266 full-time. College room and board: $5746. College room only: $3162. Special program-related fees: $10–$30 per course per semester for lab fees.

Financial Aid Program-specific awards: 2 Pride of Oshkosh Art Student Scholarships for any art majors, 1 Joann Kindt Scholarship for female non-traditional art students, 1 Charles Charonis Scholarship for junior or senior art education majors, 1 Milton Gardener Sculpture Scholarship for junior or senior sculpture students, 1 Bill Neiderberger Scholarship for junior or senior art students, Willcockson Scholarships for incoming freshmen, 1 William Leffin Scholarship for program majors.

Application Procedures Students admitted directly into the professional program freshman year. Deadline for freshmen and transfers: continuous. Notification date for freshmen and transfers: continuous. Required: high school transcript, college transcript(s) for transfer students, standing in top half of graduating class or minimum ACT score of 22.

Web Site http://www.uwosh.edu

Undergraduate Contact Chair, Department of Art, University of Wisconsin–Oshkosh, 900 Algoma Boulevard, Oshkosh, Wisconsin 54901; 920-424-0492, fax: 920-424-1738.

University of Wisconsin–Stevens Point

Stevens Point, Wisconsin

State-supported, coed. Small town campus. Total enrollment: 8,888.

Web Site http://www.uwsp.edu/

University of Wisconsin–Stout

Menomonie, Wisconsin

State-supported, coed. Small town campus. Total enrollment: 8,327.

Degrees Bachelor of Fine Arts in the area of art; Bachelor of Science in the area of art education. Majors and concentrations: art education, graphic design, industrial design, interior design, multimedia design, studio art. Program accredited by NASAD, CIDA.

Enrollment 802 total; all undergraduate.

Art Student Profile 61% females, 39% males, 5% minorities, 1% international.

Art Faculty 28 undergraduate (full-time), 8 undergraduate (part-time). 95% of full-time faculty have terminal degrees. Graduate students do not teach undergraduate courses. Undergraduate student–faculty ratio: 15:1.

Student Life Student groups/activities include Industrial Design Society of America Student Chapter (IDSA), American Society of Interior Designers (ASID) Student Chapter, Graphic Design Association Student Chapter (GDA), International Interior Design Association, Fine Arts Association, SIGGRAPH Student Chapter.

Expenses for 2007–2008 Application fee: $35. State resident tuition: $5367 full-time. Nonresident tuition: $13,113 full-time. Mandatory fees: $1905 full-time. Full-time tuition and fees vary according to reciprocity agreements. College room and board: $4994. College room only: $3100. Room and board charges vary according to board plan and housing facility.

Financial Aid Program-specific awards: 1 John and Frances Furlong Art Scholarship for art/art education majors ($1000), 2 Bud and Betty Micheels Student Artist-in-Residence Grants for undergraduates ($1500), 1 Larsen Design Scholarship for art/graphic design or multimedia design majors ($1000).

Application Procedures Students admitted directly into the professional program freshman year. Deadline for freshmen and transfers: continuous. Notification date for freshmen and transfers: continuous. Required: portfolio.

Web Site http://www.uwstout.edu/programs/bfaa

Undergraduate Contact Dr. Cynthia Gilberts, Director of Admissions, University of Wisconsin–

Stout, 124 Bowman Hall, Menomonie, Wisconsin 54751; 715-232-1232, fax: 715-232-1667, e-mail address: gilbertsc@uwstout.edu

University of Wisconsin–Superior

Superior, Wisconsin

State-supported, coed. Suburban campus. Total enrollment: 2,753. Art program established 1922.
Web Site http://www.uwsuper.edu/

Utah State University

Logan, Utah

State-supported, coed. Urban campus. Total enrollment: 14,893. Art program established 1908.
Web Site http://www.usu.edu/

Valdosta State University

Valdosta, Georgia

State-supported, coed. Small town campus. Total enrollment: 11,280.
Degrees Bachelor of Fine Arts in the areas of art, art education, interior design. Majors and concentrations: art education, art/fine arts, interior design. Graduate degrees offered: Master of Art Education. Program accredited by NASAD.
Enrollment 300 total; 270 undergraduate, 30 nonprofessional degree.
Art Student Profile 74% females, 26% males, 19% minorities, 3% international.
Art Faculty 16 total (full-time), 5 total (part-time). 100% of full-time faculty have terminal degrees. Graduate students do not teach undergraduate courses. Undergraduate student–faculty ratio: 16:1.
Student Life Student groups/activities include National Art Education Association Student Chapter, American Society of Interior Designers (ASID).
Expenses for 2008–2009 Application fee: $40. State resident tuition: $2958 full-time. Nonresident tuition: $11,830 full-time. Mandatory

fees: $1080 full-time. College room and board: $5990. College room only: $3050. Special program-related fees: $20 per course for materials purchase in lab classes.
Financial Aid Program-specific awards: 3 freshman art scholarships for incoming majors ($700–$1000), 2 Fortner Scholarships for continuing majors ($1275), 1–5 Art Department Assistantships for program majors ($1000), 1 Lee Bennet Scholarship for continuing majors ($2800).
Application Procedures Students admitted directly into the professional program freshman year. Deadline for freshmen and transfers: continuous. Required: high school transcript, college transcript(s) for transfer students, SAT or ACT test scores, completion of college preparatory curriculum or equivalent, minimum re-centered SAT scores of 440 verbal and 410 math or ACT English 18 and ACT Math 17. Recommended: minimum 2.0 high school GPA, portfolio. Portfolio reviews held once on campus; the submission of slides may be substituted for portfolios whenever needed.
Web Site http://www.valdosta.edu/art/
Undergraduate Contact Mr. Walter Peacock, Director, Admissions Office, Valdosta State University, 1500 North Patterson Street, Valdosta, Georgia 31698; 229-333-5791, e-mail address: wpeacock@valdosta.edu
Graduate Contact Dr. J. Stephen Lahr, Professor/Art Education, Department of Art, Valdosta State University, 1500 North Patterson Street, Valdosta, Georgia 31698-0110; 229-333-5835, fax: 229-259-5121, e-mail address: jslahr@valdosta.edu

Virginia Commonwealth University

Richmond, Virginia

State-supported, coed. Urban campus. Total enrollment: 31,907. Art program established 1928.
Degrees Bachelor of Arts in the areas of fashion merchandising, cinema, art history; Bachelor of Fine Arts in the areas of film, art education, communication arts, crafts/material studies, fashion design, interior design, painting/printmaking, sculpture, photography, graphic design, kinetic imaging. Majors and

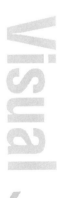

*Virginia Commonwealth University
(continued)*

concentrations: animation, art education, art history, communication arts, communication design, craft/material studies, crafts, digital imaging, fashion design, fashion merchandising, film, furniture design, glassworking, graphic arts, graphic design, illustration, interior design, jewelry and metalsmithing, kinetic imaging, medical illustration, painting/drawing, photography, printmaking, sculpture, textile arts, video art, woodworking design. Graduate degrees offered: Master of Arts in the area of art history; Master of Art Education; Master of Fine Arts in the areas of glass, jewelry/metal, interior environments, ceramics, fiber, painting/printmaking, photography, sculpture, film, kinetic imaging, furniture design, visual communication. Doctor of Philosophy in the areas of art history (media, art and text). Program accredited by NASAD, NCATE, CIDA.

Enrollment 3,323 total; 3,022 undergraduate, 301 graduate.

Art Student Profile 66% females, 34% males, 28% minorities, 17% international.

Art Faculty 132 total (full-time), 160 total (part-time). 97% of full-time faculty have terminal degrees. Graduate students teach a few undergraduate courses. Undergraduate student–faculty ratio: 13:1.

Student Life Student groups/activities include Annual Juried Student Exhibitions at the Anderson Gallery. Special housing available for art students.

Expenses for 2007–2008 Application fee: $40. State resident tuition: $4482 full-time. Nonresident tuition: $16,858 full-time. Mandatory fees: $1714 full-time. College room and board: $7567. College room only: $4497. Room and board charges vary according to board plan. Special program-related fees: $257 per semester for comprehensive arts fee.

Financial Aid Program-specific awards: 15–16 Visual Arts Scholarships for current students ($500–$1000), 1–2 Doris Lansing Scholarships for entering freshmen ($1000–$2500), university scholarship for entering freshmen ($500–$3000).

Application Procedures Students apply for admission into the professional program by freshman year. Deadline for freshmen and transfers: February 1. Notification date for freshmen and transfers: continuous. Required: high school transcript, college transcript(s) for transfer students, letter of recommendation, portfolio, SAT or ACT test scores, 12-16 images of art created in the past 2 years or 10 projects - exercises described in application. Recommended: essay, minimum 2.0 high school GPA. Portfolio reviews held continuously on campus and off campus; the submission of slides may be substituted for portfolios.

Web Site http://www.vcu.edu/arts

Undergraduate Contact Ms. Carolyn Henne, Assistant Dean for Student Affairs, School of the Arts, Virginia Commonwealth University, PO Box 842519, Richmond, Virginia 23284-2519; 866-534-3201, fax: 804-828-6469, e-mail address: chenne@vcu.edu

Graduate Contact Mr. Joseph Seipel, Senior Associate Dean for Academic Affairs and Director of Graduate Studies, School of the Arts, Virginia Commonwealth University, PO Box 842519, Richmond, Virginia 23284-2519; 804-828-6827, fax: 804-828-6469, e-mail address: jseipel@vcu.edu

Virginia Intermont College

Bristol, Virginia

Independent, coed. Small town campus. Total enrollment: 635.

Web Site http://www.vic.edu/

Washburn University

Topeka, Kansas

City-supported, coed. Urban campus. Total enrollment: 6,901. Art program established 1897.

Degrees Bachelor of Fine Arts. Majors and concentrations: art education, art history, visual arts. Program accredited by NASAD.

Enrollment 110 total; 50 undergraduate, 60 nonprofessional degree.

Art Student Profile 56% females, 44% males, 2% minorities, 2% international.

Art Faculty 6 undergraduate (full-time), 7 undergraduate (part-time). 100% of full-time faculty have terminal degrees. Graduate students do not teach undergraduate courses. Undergraduate student–faculty ratio: 9:1.

Student Life Student groups/activities include Washburn Art Student Association, Mulvane Art Museum.

Expenses for 2007–2008 Application fee: $20. State resident tuition: $5550 full-time. Nonresident tuition: $12,600 full-time. Mandatory fees: $86 full-time. College room and board: $5281. College room only: $2941. Room and board charges vary according to board plan and housing facility.

Financial Aid Program-specific awards: 20 Art Department Scholarship Awards for art majors ($1200–$1800), 1 Pollak Art Purchase Award for junior or senior art majors ($1300).

Application Procedures Students apply for admission into the professional program by sophomore year. Deadline for freshmen and transfers: continuous. Required: high school transcript, college transcript(s) for transfer students, ACT test score only (minimum composite ACT score of 17), minimum 2.0 high school GPA for out-of-state applicants. Recommended: portfolio for transfer applicants. Portfolio reviews held twice during sophomore year on campus; the submission of slides may be substituted for portfolios for transfer applicants.

Web Site http://www.washburn.edu/cas/art/index.html

Undergraduate Contact Ms. Glenda Taylor, Chair, Department of Art, Washburn University, 1700 College Street, Topeka, Kansas 66621; 785-670-2238, fax: 785-670-1089, e-mail address: glenda.taylor@washburn.edu

Washington State University

Pullman, Washington

State-supported, coed. Rural campus. Total enrollment: 24,396. Art program established 1910.

Degrees Bachelor of Fine Arts in the areas of painting, sculpture, printmaking, ceramics, photography, computer art, drawing. Majors and concentrations: art/fine arts, ceramics, computer graphics, painting/drawing, photography, printmaking, sculpture, studio art. Graduate degrees offered: Master of Fine Arts in the areas of painting, sculpture, printmaking, ceramics, photography, computer art, drawing. Cross-registration with institutions in the state of Washington, University of Idaho.

Enrollment 470 total; 300 undergraduate, 20 graduate, 150 nonprofessional degree.

Art Student Profile 60% females, 40% males, 30% minorities, 10% international.

Art Faculty 9 total (full-time), 8 total (part-time). 100% of full-time faculty have terminal degrees. Graduate students teach more than half of undergraduate courses. Undergraduate student–faculty ratio: 25:1.

Student Life Student groups/activities include Art Student Union, Undergraduate Exhibition Hall.

Expenses for 2007–2008 Application fee: $50. State resident tuition: $5812 full-time. Nonresident tuition: $16,126 full-time. Mandatory fees: $1054 full-time. Full-time tuition and fees vary according to location and reciprocity agreements. College room and board: $7316. College room only: $3556. Room and board charges vary according to board plan, housing facility, and location. Special program-related fees: $25–$60 for materials.

Financial Aid Program-specific awards: 1 John Ludwig Memorial Scholarship for program majors ($300–$500), 2–3 James Balyeat Awards for program majors ($200–$300), 3 Fine Arts Development Fund Scholarships for program majors ($200–$500), 2 Fine Arts Faculty Fund Scholarships for program majors ($200–$300).

Application Procedures Students apply for admission into the professional program by sophomore, junior year. Deadline for freshmen and transfers: continuous. Required: high school transcript, college transcript(s) for transfer students, minimum 2.0 high school GPA. Portfolio reviews held whenever needed on campus.

Web Site http://www.wsu.edu/~finearts

Contact Kathy Parkins, Support Supervisor, Fine Arts Department, Washington State University, 5072 Fine Arts Center, Pullman, Washington 99164-7450; 509-335-8686, fax: 509-335-7742, e-mail address: lparkins@wsu.edu

Visual *Arts*

Washington University in St. Louis

St. Louis, Missouri

Independent, coed. Suburban campus. Total enrollment: 13,382.

Web Site http://www.wustl.edu/

Watkins College of Art and Design

Nashville, Tennessee

Independent, coed. Urban campus. Total enrollment: 393. Art program established 1978.

Degrees Bachelor of Fine Arts in the areas of film, fine arts, graphic design, interior design, photography. Majors and concentrations: ceramics, cinematography, directing, drawing, editing, graphic design, interior design, painting, photography, printmaking, producing, screenwriting, sculpture. Program accredited by NASAD, CIDA.

Enrollment 360 undergraduate.

Art Student Profile 57% females, 43% males, 19% minorities, 2% international.

Art Faculty 18 undergraduate (full-time), 21 graduate (full-time). 98% of full-time faculty have terminal degrees. Graduate students do not teach undergraduate courses. Undergraduate student–faculty ratio: 11:1.

Student Life Student groups/activities include Screenwriters Association, AISD, Nashville Advertising Association.

Expenses for 2008–2009 Application fee: $50. Tuition: $13,200 full-time. Mandatory fees: $960 full-time. College room only: $6000.

Financial Aid Program-specific awards: 100 Institutional Scholarships for students demonstrating merit ($1500), 50 Cent. Student Awards for those students demonstrating merit and need ($1000).

Application Procedures Students admitted directly into the professional program freshman year. Deadline for freshmen and transfers: July 15. Notification date for freshmen and transfers: August 1. Required: essay, high school transcript, college transcript(s) for transfer students, minimum 2.0 high school GPA, letter of recommendation, portfolio, SAT or ACT test scores (minimum combined SAT score of 1500, minimum composite ACT score of 20). Recommended: minimum 3.0 high school GPA, interview. Portfolio reviews held as needed on campus and off campus; the submission of slides may be substituted for portfolios if requested by applicant.

Web Site http://www.watkins.edu

Undergraduate Contact Ms. Linda Schwab, Admissions, Watkins College of Art and Design, 2298 MetroCenter Boulevard, Nashville, Tennessee 37228; 615-383-4848, fax: 615-383-4849, e-mail address: admissions@watkins.edu

Wayne State University

Detroit, Michigan

State-supported, coed. Urban campus. Total enrollment: 33,240.

Degrees Bachelor of Arts in the areas of fashion design and merchandising, art history, art; Bachelor of Fine Arts in the area of art; Bachelor of Science in the area of fashion design and merchandising. Majors and concentrations: apparel design, art history, ceramic art and design, drawing, electronic arts, fashion design, fashion merchandising, fibers, graphic design, industrial design, interior design, jewelry and metalsmithing, painting, painting/drawing, photography, printmaking, sculpture. Graduate degrees offered: Master of Arts in the areas of fine arts, art history, fashion design and merchandising; Master of Fine Arts in the area of art. Cross-registration with University of Windsor (Canada).

Enrollment 926 total; 875 undergraduate, 51 graduate.

Art Student Profile 60% females, 40% males, 25% minorities, 5% international.

Art Faculty 32 total (full-time), 39 total (part-time). 100% of full-time faculty have terminal degrees. Graduate students teach a few undergraduate courses. Undergraduate student–faculty ratio: 23:1.

Student Life Student groups/activities include Fashion Design and Merchandising Club, Art Student Art Organization.

Expenses for 2007–2008 Application fee: $30. State resident tuition: $6783 full-time. Nonresident tuition: $15,534 full-time. Mandatory fees: $1061 full-time. Full-time tuition and fees vary according to course load and student level. College room and board: $6702. Room and board charges vary according to board plan and housing facility. Special program-related fees: $15–$275 per course for materials, model fees, special course expenses.

Financial Aid Program-specific awards: 4 talent awards for program majors ($1600), 1 Becker Award for program majors ($1500), 10 endowed scholarships for program majors ($1300), 2 endowed travel scholarships for program majors ($2000).

Application Procedures Students admitted directly into the professional program freshman year. Deadline for freshmen and transfers: continuous. Required: high school transcript, college transcript(s) for transfer students, minimum 2.0 high school GPA, SAT or ACT test scores (minimum composite ACT score of 21), possible portfolio review for graphic design, interior design, or industrial design for transfer students.

Web Site http://www.art.wayne.edu

Undergraduate Contact Michele Porter, Academic Services Officer II, Department of Art and Art History, Wayne State University, 150 Art Building, Detroit, Michigan 48202; 313-577-2980, fax: 313-577-3491, e-mail address: aa2961@wayne.edu

Graduate Contact Stanley Rosenthal, Graduate Advisor, Department of Art and Art History, Wayne State University, 150 Art Building, Detroit, Michigan 48202; 313-577-2980, fax: 313-577-3491.

Weber State University

Ogden, Utah

State-supported, coed. Urban campus. Total enrollment: 18,081. Art program established 1965.

Web Site http://weber.edu/

Leigh Gerdine College of Fine Arts
Webster University

St. Louis, Missouri

Independent, coed. Suburban campus. Total enrollment: 8,430. Art program established 1960.

Degrees Bachelor of Arts in the areas of studio art, art history and criticism, art education K-12 certification; Bachelor of Fine Arts in the areas of studio art, graphic design. Majors and concentrations: art education, art history, art therapy, ceramic art and design, ceramics, graphic design, media arts, media performance, painting/drawing, photography, printmaking, sculpture. Graduate degrees offered: Master of Arts in the areas of studio art, art history and criticism. Cross-registration with various colleges in St. Louis.

Enrollment 195 total; 180 undergraduate, 15 graduate.

Art Student Profile 60% females, 40% males, 11% minorities, 4% international.

Art Faculty 10 total (full-time), 21 total (part-time). 100% of full-time faculty have terminal degrees. Graduate students do not teach undergraduate courses. Undergraduate student–faculty ratio: 10:1.

Student Life Student groups/activities include Art Council, Graduate Art Council.

Expenses for 2007–2008 Application fee: $35. Comprehensive fee: $27,550 includes full-time tuition ($19,330) and college room and board ($8220). College room only: $4100. Full-time tuition varies according to program. Room and board charges vary according to board plan and housing facility. Special program-related fees: $50–$150 per course for studio lab fee.

Financial Aid Program-specific awards: Sr. Gabriel Mary Hoare Scholarship for visual arts students.

Application Procedures Students apply for admission into the professional program by junior year. Deadline for freshmen and transfers: continuous. Notification date for freshmen and transfers: August 15. Required: essay, high school transcript, college transcript(s) for transfer students, minimum 2.0 high school GPA, 2 letters of recommendation, interview, portfolio, SAT or ACT test scores (minimum combined SAT score of 1500, minimum composite ACT score of 21). Recommended: minimum 3.0 high school GPA. Portfolio reviews held 12 times on campus and off campus in Vienna, Austria; the submission of slides may be substituted for portfolios when distance is prohibitive.

Web Site http://www.webster.edu/depts/finearts/art

Webster University (continued)

Undergraduate Contact Carrie Indelicato, Portfolio Review Coordinator, Office of Admissions, Webster University, 470 East Lockwood Avenue, St. Louis, Missouri 63119-3194; 314-968-7001, fax: 314-968-7115, e-mail address: cgeorge@webster.edu

Graduate Contact Dr. Jeffrey A. Hughes, Graduate Program Coordinator, Department of Art, Webster University, 470 East Lockwood Avenue, St. Louis, Missouri 63119-3194; 314-968-7159, fax: 314-968-7139, e-mail address: hughes@webster.edu

West Chester University of Pennsylvania

West Chester, Pennsylvania

State-supported, coed. Suburban campus. Total enrollment: 13,219.

Degrees Bachelor of Arts in the area of art; Bachelor of Fine Arts in the area of studio art. Majors and concentrations: art/fine arts, ceramics, computer graphics, painting/drawing, sculpture.

Enrollment 225 total; all undergraduate.

Art Student Profile 60% females, 40% males.

Art Faculty 12 undergraduate (full-time), 3 undergraduate (part-time). 100% of full-time faculty have terminal degrees. Graduate students do not teach undergraduate courses. Undergraduate student–faculty ratio: 10:1.

Student Life Student groups/activities include Print Club, Art Association, American Institute of Graphic Arts.

Expenses for 2007–2008 Application fee: $35. One-time mandatory fee: $1499. State resident tuition: $5177 full-time. Nonresident tuition: $12,944 full-time. Mandatory fees: $1499 full-time. Full-time tuition and fees vary according to course load and student level. College room and board: $6590. College room only: $4388. Room and board charges vary according to board plan and housing facility.

Financial Aid Program-specific awards: 2 McKinney Scholarships for junior painting majors ($1000), 1 Bessie Grubb Scholarship for junior graphic design majors ($1000), 1 Hawthorne Scholarship for painting majors ($1000).

Application Procedures Students admitted directly into the professional program freshman year. Deadline for freshmen and transfers: continuous. Required: essay, high school transcript, college transcript(s) for transfer students, minimum 2.0 high school GPA, SAT or ACT test scores. Recommended: minimum 3.0 high school GPA.

Web Site http://www.wcupa.edu/

Undergraduate Contact Mr. John Baker, Chair, Art Department, West Chester University of Pennsylvania, Mitchell Hall, West Chester, Pennsylvania 19383; 610-436-2755, e-mail address: jbaker@wcupa.edu

Western Carolina University

Cullowhee, North Carolina

State-supported, coed. Rural campus. Total enrollment: 9,056. Art program established 1964.

Degrees Bachelor of Fine Arts in the areas of studio art, graphic design. Majors and concentrations: book arts, ceramic art and design, graphic design, painting/drawing, photography, printmaking, sculpture. Graduate degrees offered: Master of Art in Education; Master of Arts in Teaching; Master of Fine Arts in the area of fine arts. Cross-registration with Penland School of Crafts.

Enrollment 313 total; 296 undergraduate, 4 graduate, 13 nonprofessional degree.

Art Student Profile 50% females, 50% males, 3% minorities, 1% international.

Art Faculty 15 total (full-time), 13 total (part-time). 100% of full-time faculty have terminal degrees. Graduate students teach a few undergraduate courses. Undergraduate student–faculty ratio: 15:1.

Student Life Student groups/activities include Annual Student Exhibition, Nomad (student art and literature publication), Art Students League.

Expenses for 2008–2009 Application fee: $40. State resident tuition: $2078 full-time. Nonresident tuition: $11,661 full-time. Mandatory fees: $2336 full-time. College room and board: $5626. College room only: $2916.

Financial Aid Program-specific awards: 1 Lorraine Stone Scholarship for non-traditional students ($1000), 4 departmental scholarships for program students ($500).

Application Procedures Students admitted directly into the professional program freshman year. Deadline for freshmen and transfers: continuous. Notification date for freshmen and transfers: August 1. Required: high school transcript, college transcript(s) for transfer students, minimum 2.0 high school GPA, 3 letters of recommendation, SAT or ACT test scores. Recommended: interview, portfolio. Portfolio reviews held continuously on campus; the submission of slides may be substituted for portfolios (slides preferred).

Web Site http://www.wcu.edu/as/arts

Undergraduate Contact Mr. Richard Tichich, Director, Department of Art, Western Carolina University, Cullowhee, North Carolina 28723; 828-227-2464, fax: 828-227-7505, e-mail address: rtichich@wcu.edu

Graduate Contact Mr. Richard Tichich, Director, School of Art and Design, Western Carolina University, Cullowhee, North Carolina 28723; 828-227-2464, fax: 828-227-7505, e-mail address: rtichich@wcu.edu

Western Illinois University

Macomb, Illinois

State-supported, coed. Small town campus. Total enrollment: 13,331. Art program established 1938.

Degrees Bachelor of Arts in the area of teacher education; Bachelor of Fine Arts in the area of art. Majors and concentrations: art education, ceramics, graphic design, metals, painting/drawing, printmaking, sculpture, studio art, watercolors. Cross-registration with Spoon River College.

Enrollment 149 total; 52 undergraduate, 97 nonprofessional degree.

Art Student Profile 58% females, 42% males, 11% minorities, 1% international.

Art Faculty 16 undergraduate (full-time), 2 undergraduate (part-time). 100% of full-time faculty have terminal degrees. Graduate students do not teach undergraduate courses. Undergraduate student–faculty ratio: 10:1.

Student Life Student groups/activities include Student Art League, National Art Education

Association Student Chapter, Clay Club. Special housing available for art students.

Expenses for 2008–2009 Application fee: $30. State resident tuition: $6456 full-time. Nonresident tuition: $9684 full-time. Mandatory fees: $1816 full-time. College room and board: $7210. College room only: $4350. Special program-related fees: $75–$100 per semester for material fees.

Financial Aid Program-specific awards: 4 Bulkeley Scholarships for program majors ($600), 10 talent grants for program majors ($3300), 20 tuition waivers for program majors ($1400), 4 freshman scholarships for incoming freshmen program majors ($500), 1 Purdum Scholarship for art education majors ($1000).

Application Procedures Students admitted directly into the professional program freshman year. Deadline for freshmen and transfers: August 10. Notification date for freshmen and transfers: continuous. Required: high school transcript, college transcript(s) for transfer students, SAT or ACT test scores (minimum combined SAT score of 920, minimum composite ACT score of 20), ACT score of 18, SAT score of 850, if in upper 40% of high school graduating class, minimum 2.5 high school GPA. Recommended: portfolio. Portfolio reviews held continuously on campus; the submission of slides may be substituted for portfolios when distance is prohibitive or for large work.

Web Site http://www.wiu.edu

Undergraduate Contact Ms. Jan Clough, Chair, Department of Art, Western Illinois University, 32 Garwood Hall, Macomb, Illinois 61455; 309-298-1549, fax: 309-298-2605, e-mail address: jb-clough@wiu.edu

Frostic School of Art
Western Michigan University

Kalamazoo, Michigan

State-supported, coed. Urban campus. Total enrollment: 24,433.

Degrees Bachelor of Fine Arts in the areas of painting, ceramics, sculpture, photography, graphic design, printmaking. Majors and concentrations: art education, art history, art/fine

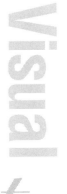

Western Michigan University (continued)

arts, ceramics, graphic design, metals and jewelry, painting, photography, photography and intermedia, printmaking, sculpture. Graduate degrees offered: Master of Arts in the area of art education. Cross-registration with Michigan colleges and universities and community colleges. Program accredited by NASAD.

Enrollment 668 total; 385 undergraduate, 8 graduate, 275 nonprofessional degree.

Art Student Profile 70% females, 30% males, 10% minorities, 1% international.

Art Faculty 21 total (full-time), 18 total (part-time). 100% of full-time faculty have terminal degrees. Graduate students teach a few undergraduate courses. Undergraduate student–faculty ratio: 25:1.

Student Life Student groups/activities include Students in Design, Michigan Art Education Association.

Expenses for 2007–2008 Application fee: $35. One-time mandatory fee: $300. State resident tuition: $6570 full-time. Nonresident tuition: $16,116 full-time. Mandatory fees: $690 full-time. Full-time tuition and fees vary according to course load, location, and student level. College room and board: $7042. College room only: $3725. Room and board charges vary according to board plan. Special program-related fees: $25–$150 per class for studio fees.

Financial Aid Program-specific awards: 1 departmental scholarship for freshmen with outstanding portfolios ($500), 5 James Kerr and Rose Netzorg Kerr Awards for outstanding students ($400), 9 Art Star Awards for junior/senior art majors ($200), 2 Elizabeth Smutz Awards for outstanding art education majors ($600), 2 Haig and Janette Tashjian Scholarships for outstanding art education majors demonstrating need ($1100), 2 Walter F. Enz Memorial Awards for outstanding art students ($1000), 7 Angie Gayman Carmer Art Scholarships for art students with minimum 3.5 GPA demonstrating financial need ($1400), 4 foundation scholarships for outstanding students in foundation courses ($375), 20 enrichment grants for full-time art students ($600).

Application Procedures Students apply for admission into the professional program by freshman, sophomore year. Deadline for freshmen and transfers: March 14. Notification date for freshmen and transfers: April 1. Required: essay, high school transcript, college transcript(s) for transfer students, minimum 2.0 high school GPA, letter of recommendation, portfolio, ACT test score only. Recommended: minimum 3.0 high school GPA. Portfolio reviews held once for graphic design majors and 2 times for other program majors on campus; the submission of slides may be substituted for portfolios on a case-by-case basis.

Web Site http://www.wmich.edu/art

Undergraduate Contact John Kollig, Academic Advisor, Department of Art, Western Michigan University, 2104 Richmond Center, Kalamazoo, Michigan 49008-5213; 269-387-2440, fax: 269-387-2477, e-mail address: john.kollig@wmich.edu

Graduate Contact Ellen Armstrong, Academic Advisor, Department of Art, Western Michigan University, 2104 Richmond Center, Kalamazoo, Michigan 49008-5213; 269-387-2440, fax: 269-387-2477, e-mail address: ellen.armstrong@wmich.edu

Rider University
Westminster College of the Arts of Rider University

Princeton, New Jersey

Independent, coed. Small town campus.

Degrees Bachelor of Arts in the area of fine arts. Majors and concentrations: art/fine arts.

Application Procedures Students admitted directly into the professional program freshman year. Required: essay, high school transcript, college transcript(s) for transfer students, 2 letters of recommendation, SAT or ACT test scores, TOEFL score and certification of finances (international students only). Recommended: minimum 3.0 high school GPA.

Web Site http://www.rider.edu/westminster

Undergraduate Contact Ms. Katherine Shields, Senior Associate Director of Admission, Westminster College of the Arts of Rider University, 101 Walnut Lane, Princeton, New

Jersey 08540-3899; 609-921-7100 ext. 8103, fax: 609-921-2538, e-mail address: kshields@ rider.edu

West Texas A&M University

Canyon, Texas

State-supported, coed. Small town campus. Total enrollment: 7,502. Art program established 1953.

Degrees Bachelor of Fine Arts in the areas of studio art, graphic design. Majors and concentrations: ceramics, computer art, glassworking, graphic design, jewelry and metalsmithing, painting/drawing, printmaking, sculpture. Graduate degrees offered: Master of Arts in the area of art; Master of Fine Arts in the area of studio art.

Enrollment 106 total; 80 undergraduate, 21 graduate, 5 nonprofessional degree.

Art Student Profile 48% females, 52% males, 10% minorities, 3% international.

Art Faculty 5 total (full-time), 3 total (part-time). 100% of full-time faculty have terminal degrees. Graduate students teach a few undergraduate courses. Undergraduate student–faculty ratio: 16:1.

Student Life Student groups/activities include Art This.

Expenses for 2008–2009 Application fee: $25. Special program-related fees: $7–$30 per course for lab fees.

Financial Aid Program-specific awards: 2 Levi Margaret Cole Endowment Awards for program majors ($200–$500), 1 Charles Hohmann Endowment Award for graphic design majors ($400), 1 Mary Moody Northen Endowment Award for program majors ($200–$500), 1 Isabel Robinson Scholarship for program majors ($200–$500), 1 Emmit Smith Art Scholarship for studio art students ($200–$500), 12 Foundation for Fine Arts Awards for program majors ($200–$500), 6 Sybil Harrington Scholarships for program majors ($500–$1000), 4 Harrington Bequest Awards for program majors ($200–$500), 1 Georgia O'Keefe Scholarship for program majors ($500–$600).

Application Procedures Students admitted directly into the professional program freshman year. Deadline for freshmen and transfers: continuous. Required: high school transcript, college transcript(s) for transfer students, SAT or ACT test scores. Recommended: 2 letters of recommendation, interview, portfolio. Portfolio reviews held once and as needed on campus; the submission of slides may be substituted for portfolios when distance is prohibitive.

Web Site http://www.wtamu.edu

Undergraduate Contact Mr. Royal Brantley, Head, Department of Art, Theater and Dance, West Texas A&M University, WTAMU Box 60747, Canyon, Texas 79016; 806-651-2799, fax: 806-651-2818, e-mail address: rbrantley@ mail.wtamu.edu

Graduate Contact Mr. David Rindlisbacher, Graduate Program Coordinator, Department of Art, Theater and Dance, West Texas A&M University, WTAMU Box 60747, Canyon, Texas 79016; 806-651-2792, fax: 806-651-2818, e-mail address: drindlisbacher@mail.wtamu.edu

West Virginia University

Morgantown, West Virginia

State-supported, coed. Small town campus. Total enrollment: 28,113. Art program established 1897.

Degrees Bachelor of Fine Arts. Majors and concentrations: art education, ceramics, graphic design, intermedia, painting/drawing, printmaking, sculpture. Graduate degrees offered: Master of Arts in the areas of art education, studio art; Master of Fine Arts in the areas of painting, printmaking, sculpture, ceramics, intermedia graphic design. Program accredited by NASAD.

Enrollment 328 total; 310 undergraduate, 18 graduate.

Art Student Profile 55% females, 45% males, 6% minorities, 4% international.

Art Faculty 16 total (full-time), 3 total (part-time). 98% of full-time faculty have terminal degrees. Graduate students teach a few undergraduate courses. Undergraduate student–faculty ratio: 17:1.

Student Life Student groups/activities include Student Art Association, National Art Education Association Student Chapter. Special housing available for art students.

Expenses for 2007–2008 Application fee: $25. State resident tuition: $4722 full-time. Nonresi-

West Virginia University (continued)

dent tuition: $14,600 full-time. Full-time tuition varies according to location, program, and reciprocity agreements. College room and board: $7046. Room and board charges vary according to board plan, housing facility, and location. Special program-related fees: $75 per 3 credit hours for expendable supplies for studio courses.

Financial Aid Program-specific awards: 12 Fine Arts Awards for program students ($2000–$6000), 3 Loyalty Permanent Endowment Awards for state residents ($1000), 1 Gabriel Fellowship for state residents ($1000), 6 Mesaros Scholarships for junior and senior art majors ($500–$2000).

Application Procedures Students apply for admission into the professional program by sophomore year. Deadline for freshmen and transfers: February 1. Notification date for freshmen and transfers: March 1. Required: high school transcript, college transcript(s) for transfer students, minimum 2.0 high school GPA, letter of recommendation, portfolio, SAT or ACT test scores, minimum combined SAT scores 910 (state residents), minimum combined SAT scores 950 (non-residents), minimum composite ACT scores-19 (state residents), minimum composite ACT scores-20 (non-residents). Recommended: interview. Portfolio reviews held 3 times on campus; the submission of slides may be substituted for portfolios if original work is not available or distance is prohibitive.

Web Site http://www.wvu.edu/~ccarts

Undergraduate Contact Ms. Kristina Olson, Associate Chair, Division of Art, West Virginia University, College of Creative Arts, PO Box 6111, Morgantown, West Virginia 26506-6111; 304-293-4841 ext. 3210, fax: 304-293-5731, e-mail address: kristina.olson2@mail.wvu.edu

Graduate Contact Ms. Alison Helm, Interim Chair, Division of Art, West Virginia University, College of Creative Arts, PO Box 6111, Morgantown, West Virginia 26506-6111; 304-293-4841 ext. 3138, fax: 304-293-5731.

Williams Baptist College

Walnut Ridge, Arkansas

Independent Southern Baptist, coed. Rural campus. Total enrollment: 629 (2007). Art program established 1994.

Degrees Bachelor of Arts in the area of studio art. Majors and concentrations: ceramics, painting, printmaking.

Enrollment 5 total; all undergraduate.

Art Student Profile 100% females.

Art Faculty 1 undergraduate (full-time), 1 undergraduate (part-time). 100% of full-time faculty have terminal degrees. Graduate students do not teach undergraduate courses. Undergraduate student–faculty ratio: 3:1.

Student Life Student groups/activities include museum trips.

Expenses for 2007–2008 Application fee: $20. Comprehensive fee: $15,070 includes full-time tuition ($9700), mandatory fees ($670), and college room and board ($4700). Special program-related fees: $75 per course for studio fee.

Financial Aid Program-specific awards: 4 art scholarships for program majors ($500).

Application Procedures Students admitted directly into the professional program freshman year. Deadline for freshmen and transfers: continuous. Required: high school transcript, college transcript(s) for transfer students, portfolio, SAT or ACT test scores. Recommended: interview, minimum 2.5 high school GPA. Portfolio reviews held once per semester after completion of foundation courses on campus; the submission of slides may be substituted for portfolios when distance is prohibitive.

Web Site http://www.wbcoll.edu

Undergraduate Contact Dr. David Midkiff, Chairman, Department of Art, Williams Baptist College, PO Box 3681 WBC, Walnut Ridge, Arkansas 72476; 870-759-4141, fax: 870-886-3924, e-mail address: dmidkiff@wbcoll.edu

Wright State University

Dayton, Ohio

State-supported, coed. Suburban campus. Total enrollment: 16,151. Art program established 1964.

Degrees Bachelor of Fine Arts in the areas of art education, fine arts. Majors and concentrations: art education, painting, photography, printmaking, sculpture.

Enrollment 206 total; 139 undergraduate, 67 nonprofessional degree.

Art Student Profile 70% females, 30% males, 21% minorities, 4% international.

Art Faculty 11 undergraduate (full-time), 7 undergraduate (part-time). 100% of full-time faculty have terminal degrees. Graduate students do not teach undergraduate courses. Undergraduate student–faculty ratio: 8:1.

Student Life Student groups/activities include Graphic Arts Club.

Expenses for 2007–2008 Application fee: $30. State resident tuition: $7278 full-time. Nonresident tuition: $14,004 full-time. College room and board: $7180. Special program-related fees: $35–$120 per course for materials fee.

Financial Aid Program-specific awards: 10–20 Art Department Merit Scholarships for program majors ($1800), 1–2 Arts Gala Scholarships for entering program majors ($5000).

Application Procedures Students apply for admission into the professional program by sophomore year. Deadline for freshmen and transfers: continuous. Required: high school transcript, college transcript(s) for transfer students, SAT or ACT test scores.

Web Site http://www.wright.edu

Undergraduate Contact Dr. Linda Caron, Chair, Department of Art and Art History, Wright State University, Creative Arts Center A-226, Colonel Glenn Highway, Dayton, Ohio 45435; 937-775-2896, fax: 937-775-3049, e-mail address: linda.caron@wright.edu

York University

Toronto, Ontario, Canada

Province-supported, coed. Urban campus. Total enrollment: 51,420. Art program established 1969.

Degrees Bachelor of Design in the area of communications design; Bachelor of Fine Arts in the area of visual arts. Majors and concentrations: design, drawing, new media, painting, photography, printmaking, sculpture. Graduate degrees offered: Master of Fine Arts in the area of visual arts; Master of Design in Designed Objects in the areas of graphic, communications design. Mandatory cross-registration with Sheridan College (BDes program only).

Enrollment 1,256 total; 1,037 undergraduate, 35 graduate, 184 nonprofessional degree.

Art Student Profile 77% females, 23% males, 3% international.

Art Faculty 39 total (full-time), 39 total (part-time). 88% of full-time faculty have terminal degrees. Graduate students teach a few undergraduate courses. Undergraduate student–faculty ratio: 12:1.

Student Life Student groups/activities include Visual Arts Student Council, Creative Arts Students Association, Design Students Association.

Expenses for 2007–2008 Application fee: $175 Canadian dollars. Tuition, fee, and room and board charges are reported in Canadian dollars. Comprehensive fee: $11,664 includes full-time tuition ($5278) and college room and board ($6386). College room only: $3986. Full-time tuition varies according to course load, degree level, and program. Room and board charges vary according to board plan and housing facility. International student tuition: $15,278 full-time. Special program-related fees: $15–$150 per semester for lab fees for photography, sculpture, printmaking, and new media.

Financial Aid Program-specific awards: 6 talent awards for applicants with outstanding portfolios ($1000), 5 Harry Rowe Bursaries for those demonstrating achievement or potential in artistic or scholarly work ($1000–$2000), Fine Arts Bursaries for academically qualified applicants demonstrating financial need, 6 Jack Bush Scholarships for those demonstrating merit in studio work ($800), 1 L.L. Odette Sculpture Scholarship for juniors or seniors showing excellence in sculpture ($2000), 2 Michael Plexman Awards for juniors or seniors demonstrating creative innovation and need ($2000), 1 Department of Visual Arts Award for those demonstrating financial need and with B average ($1000), Joseph Drapell Award for those demonstrating financial need and academic and artistic excellence.

Application Procedures Students admitted directly into the professional program freshman year. Deadline for freshmen and transfers: March 1. Notification date for freshmen: June 30; transfers: July 15. Required: high school transcript, college transcript(s) for transfer students, minimum 3.0 high school GPA, portfolio, SAT, ACT or Canadian equivalent, interview for applicants within a reasonable distance, questionnaire. Recommended: interview. Portfolio reviews held 15 times on

York University (continued)

campus; the submission of slides may be substituted for portfolios when distance is prohibitive or for large works of art.

Web Site http://www.yorku.ca/finearts/visa/

Undergraduate Contact Susan Wessels, Coordinator, Recruitment and Liaison, Student and Academic Services, York University, 201R Goldfarb Centre for Fine Arts, Toronto, Ontario M3J 1P3, Canada; 416-736-2100 ext. 77141, fax: 416-736-5447, e-mail address: swessels@yorku.ca

Graduate Contact Yvonne Singer, Graduate Director, Department of Visual Arts, York University, 235 GCFA, 4700 Keele Street, Toronto, Ontario M3J 1P3, Canada; 416-736-5533, fax: 416-736-5875.

Youngstown State University

Youngstown, Ohio

State-supported, coed. Urban campus. Total enrollment: 13,489. Art program established 1927.

Degrees Bachelor of Arts in the area of art history; Bachelor of Fine Arts in the area of studio art; Bachelor of Science in the area of art education. Majors and concentrations: art and technology, art education, art history, general studio, graphic design, individualized major, painting, photography, printmaking, spatial arts. Program accredited by NASAD.

Enrollment 313 total; 307 undergraduate, 6 graduate.

Art Student Profile 55% females, 45% males, 9% minorities, 2% international.

Art Faculty 16 undergraduate (full-time), 20 undergraduate (part-time). 95% of full-time faculty have terminal degrees. Graduate students do not teach undergraduate courses. Undergraduate student–faculty ratio: 13:1.

Student Life Student groups/activities include Student Art Association, American Institute of Graphic Arts Student Chapter, Spatial Arts Alliance.

Expenses for 2007–2008 Application fee: $30. State resident tuition: $6492 full-time. Nonresident tuition: $12,165 full-time. Mandatory fees: $229 full-time. Full-time tuition and fees vary according to course load. College room and board: $6740. Room and board charges vary according to board plan and housing facility. Special program-related fees: $45 per course for art history classes, $60 per course for studio lab fees.

Financial Aid Program-specific awards: Beecher Talent Scholarships for freshmen (renewable) ($1000), Scholastics Portfolio Award for freshmen (renewable) ($2000), Trumbull County Scholarship for freshmen (renewable) ($300), Cubbison Painting Award for freshmen ($2500).

Application Procedures Students apply for admission into the professional program by sophomore year. Deadline for freshmen and transfers: continuous. Required: high school transcript, college transcript(s) for transfer students, portfolio for scholarship consideration. Recommended: SAT or ACT test scores. Portfolio reviews held twice on campus; the submission of slides may be substituted for portfolios.

Web Site http://www.fpa.ysu.edu/art/index.html

Undergraduate Contact Chair, Department of Art, Youngstown State University, 1 University Plaza, Youngstown, Ohio 44555; 330-941-3627, fax: 330-941-7183, e-mail address: art@cc.ysu.edu

Appendixes

Summer Programs in Art

This list of summer programs is not exhaustive but will help you in thinking about some wonderful opportunities in the visual arts, since taking advantage of summer study is important.

ABBEY ROAD OVERSEAS PROGRAMS

Pre-College: Art History and Studio Art–Florence

Dr. Arthur Kian
Managing Director
8904 Rangely Avenue
West Hollywood, CA 90048
Phone: 888-462-2239
Fax: 866-488-4642
E-mail: info@goabbeyroad.com
Web site: www.goabbeyroad.com/florence.htm

ACADEMY OF ART UNIVERSITY

Summer Pre-College

Admissions Department
79 New Montgomery Street, 4th Floor
San Francisco, CA 94105-3410
Phone: (800) 544–2787 x6558
Fax: 415-618-6287
E-mail: admissions@academyart.edu
Web site: www.academyart.edu/degrees/summer_artexperience.html

AMERICAN COLLEGIATE ADVENTURES

American Collegiate Adventures–Italy

Jason Lubar
Director of Summer Programs
1811 W. North Avenue
Suite 201
Chicago, IL 60422
Phone: 800-509-7867 (toll-free)
Fax: 773-342-0246
E-mail: info@acasummer.com
Web site: www.acasummer.com

APPEL FARM ARTS AND MUSIC CENTER

Appel Farm Summer Arts Camp

Ms. Jennie Quinn
Camp Director
PO Box 888
457 Shirley Road
Elmer, NJ 08318-0888
Phone: 856-358-2472
Fax: 856-358-6513
E-mail: appelcamp@aol.com
Web site: www.appelfarm.org

ATELIER DES ARTS

Francia Tobacman
Director
55 Bethune Street, B645
New York, NY 10014
Phone: 212-727-1756
Fax: 212-691-0631
E-mail: info@atelierdesarts.org
Web site: www.atelierdesarts.org

BELVOIR TERRACE

Summer Contact: Ms. Nancy S. Goldberg
Director
80 Cliffwood Street
Lenox, MA 01240
Phone: 413-637-0555
Fax: 413-637-4651
E-mail: info@belvoirterrace.com
Web site: www.belvoirterrace.com

Winter Contact: Ms. Nancy S. Goldberg
Director
101 West 79th Street
New York, NY 10024
Phone: 212-580-3398
Fax: 212-579-7282
E-mail: info@belvoirterrace.com
Web site: www.belvoirterrace.com

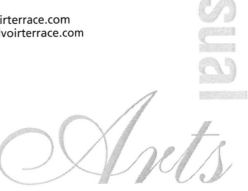

BUCK'S ROCK PERFORMING AND CREATIVE ARTS CAMP

Ms. Laura Morris
Director
59 Buck's Rock Road
New Milford, CT 06776
Phone: 860-354-5030
Fax: 860-354-1355
E-mail: info@bucksrockcamp.com
Web site: www.bucksrockcamp.com

CALIFORNIA STATE SUMMER SCHOOL FOR THE ARTS/INNER SPARK

Summer Contact: Neil Brillante
Office Technician
1010 Hurley
Suite 185
Sacramento, CA 95825
Phone: 916-274-5815
Fax: 916-274-5814
E-mail: application@innerspark.us
Web site: www.innerspark.us

Winter Contact: Neil Brillante
Office Technician
PO Box 1077
Sacramento, CA 95812-1077
Phone: 916-274-5815
Fax: 916-274-5814
E-mail: application@innerspark.us
Web site: www.innerspark.us

CAPITOL REGION EDUCATION COUNCIL

Center for Creative Youth

Nancy Wolfe
Director
Wesleyan University
350 High Street
Middletown, CT 06459
Phone: 860-685-3307
Fax: 860-685-3311
E-mail: ccy@wesleyan.edu
Web site: www.wesleyan.edu/CCY/home.html

CARNEGIE MELLON UNIVERSITY

Carnegie Mellon University Pre-College Program in the Fine Arts

Office of Admission, Pre-College Programs
5000 Forbes Avenue
Pittsburgh, PA 15213-3890
Phone: 412-268-2082
Fax: 412-268-7838
E-mail: precollege@andrew.cmu.edu
Web site: www.cmu.edu/enrollment/pre-college

CHAUTAUQUA INSTITUTION

Chautauqua School of Art

Sarah Malinoski, Coordinator of Student Services
PO Box 1098
Chautauqua, NY 14722
Phone: 800–836-ARTS (toll-free)
716-357-6233
Fax: 716-357-9014
E-mail: art@ciweb.org
Web site: www.ciweb.org

CHOATE ROSEMARY HALL

Choate Rosemary Hall Summer Arts Conservatory–Visual Arts Program

Mrs. Randi J. Brandt
Admissions Director, Arts Conservatory
Paul Mellon Arts Center
333 Christian Street
Wallingford, CT 06492
Phone: 203-697-2423
Fax: 203-697-2396
E-mail: rbrandt@choate.edu
Web site: www.choate.edu/summerprograms

DUKE YOUTH PROGRAMS–DUKE UNIVERSITY CONTINUING STUDIES

EXPRESSIONS! Duke Fine Arts Camp

Duke Continuing Studies
201 Bishop's House
Box 90700
Durham, NC 27708-0700
Phone: 919-684-6259
Fax: 919-681-8235
E-mail: learnmore@duke.edu
Web site: www.learnmore.duke.edu/youth

Visual *Arts*

EMMA WILLARD SCHOOL
GirlSummer at Emma Willard School

Director
285 Pawling Avenue
Troy, NY 12180
Phone: 866-397-2267 (toll-free)
Fax: 718-237-8862
E-mail: girlsummer@emmawillard.org
Web site: www.emmawillard.org/summer/
residential

**THE EXPERIMENT IN INTERNATIONAL LIVING–
WORLD LEARNING**

Brazil: Arts and Community Service

France: Art and Adventure In Provence

France: Homestay and Photography

Mexico: Mayan Arts and Culture

**United Kingdom—Filmmaking Program and
Homestay**

Enrollment Director
Summer Abroad
1 Kipling Road
PO Box 676
Brattleboro, VT 05302-0676
Phone: 800-345-2929 (toll-free)
Fax: 802-258-3428
E-mail: info@worldlearning.org
Web site: www.usexperiment.org

HOLLINS UNIVERSITY

Hollinsummer Program

Director of Admissions
PO Box 9707
Roanoke, VA 24020-1707
Phone: 800-456-9595 (toll-free)
Fax: 540-362-6218
E-mail: huadm@hollins.edu
Web site: www.hollins.edu/

HUMANITIES SPRING IN ASSISI

**Interdisciplinary Travel-Study Programs in
New York and Assisi, Italy**

Ms. Jane R. Oliensis
Director
Santa Maria di Lignano, 2
Assisi 06081, Italy
Phone: 39–075–802400
Fax: 39–075–802400
E-mail: info@humanitiesspring.com
Web site: www.humanitiesspring.com

IDYLLWILD ARTS FOUNDATION

Idyllwild Arts Summer Program

Diane Dennis
Registrar, Summer Program
PO Box 38
Idyllwild, CA 92549
Phone: 951-659-2171 Ext. 2365
Fax: 951-659-4552
E-mail: summer@idyllwildarts.org
Web site: www.idyllwildarts.org

INTERLOCHEN CENTER FOR THE ARTS

Interlochen Arts Camp

Kelye Modarelli
Director of Admissions
PO Box 199
Interlochen, MI 49643
Phone: 231-276-7472
Fax: 231-276-7464
E-mail: admissions@interlochen.org
Web site: www.interlochen.org/

INTERN EXCHANGE INTERNATIONAL, LTD.

**IEI–Art Gallery and Auction House
Internship Programme**

**Media and Design Workshops: Digital Media,
Fashion & Design, Photography**

Nina Miller Glickman
Director
1858 Mallard Lane
Villanova, PA 19085
Phone: 610-527-6066
Fax: 610-527-5499
E-mail: info@internexchange.com
Web site: www.internexchange.com

LEYSIN AMERICAN SCHOOL IN SWITZERLAND

Summer in Switzerland

Mr. Tim Sloman
Director of Summer in Switzerland
Admissions Office
Leysin American School
Leysin 1854, Switzerland
Phone: 41–24–493–3777
Fax: 41–24–494–1585
E-mail: admissions@las.ch
Web site: www.las.ch/summer

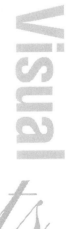

Visual Arts

MASSACHUSETTS COLLEGE OF ART

Art New England Summer Workshops

Certificate and International Programs

In the Studio: A Pre-College Course for College Credit

Studios for Teens in Art and Design

Graduate and Continuing Education
Tower Building, 2nd Floor
621 Huntington Avenue
Boston, MA 02115
Phone: 617-879-7200
Fax: 617-879-7171
E-mail: continuing_education@massart.edu
Web site: www.massartplus.org

MOORE COLLEGE OF ART & DESIGN

Summer Art & Design Institute: Pre-College Residency Program for High School Women—Programs in Animation, Fashion Design, and Fine Arts

Moore College of Art & Design
20th Street and The Parkway
Philadelphia, PA 19103
Phone: 215-965-8573
Fax: 215-965-4047
E-mail: sadimoore.edu
Web site: www.moore.edu

NATIONAL STUDENT LEADERSHIP CONFERENCE

Inside the Arts–New York City

Admissions
414 North Orleans Street
Suite LL8
Chicago, IL 60610-1087
Phone: 312-322-9999
800-994-6752 (toll-free)
Fax: 312-765-0081
E-mail: info@nslcleaders.org
Web site: www.nslcleaders.org

THE NEW HAMPSHIRE INSTITUTE OF ART

Pre-College Workshop

Diane Vesci
148 Concord Street
Manchester, NH 03104
Phone: 603-836-2513
Fax: 603-641-1832
E-mail: dvescinhia.edu
Web site: www.nhia.edu

NEW YORK FILM ACADEMY

The New York Film Academy, Disney-MGM Studios, FL

The New York Film Academy, Harvard University, Cambridge, MA

The New York Film Academy in Florence, Italy

The New York Film Academy/Saint Catherine's College at Oxford University

The New York Film Academy in Paris

The New York Film Academy, Universal Studios, Hollywood, CA

Admissions
100 East 17th Street
New York, NY 10003
Phone: 212-674-4300
Fax: 212-477-1414
E-mail: film@nyfa.com
Web site: www.nyfa.com

NEW YORK UNIVERSITY, TISCH SCHOOL OF THE ARTS

Tisch School of the Arts–International High School Program–Dublin

Tisch School of the Arts–International High School Program–Paris

Tisch School of the Arts–Summer High School Programs

Mr. Josh Murray
Assistant Director of Recruitment
Special Programs
721 Broadway
12th Floor
New York, NY 10003
Phone: 212-998-1500
Fax: 212-995-4610
E-mail: tisch.special.info@nyu.edu
Web site: specialprograms.tisch.nyu.edu

NORTHWESTERN UNIVERSITY

National High School Institute at Northwestern University

Summer Programs for High School Students
Northwestern University
617 Noyes St.
Evanston, IL 60208-4165
Phone: 847-491-3026
Fax: 847-467-1057
E-mail: nhsi@northwestern.edu
Web site: www.northwestern.edu/nhsi

OXBRIDGE ACADEMIC PROGRAMS

The Cambridge Tradition

La Academia de España

L'Académie de France

L'Académie de Paris

The Oxford Tradition

Admissions
601 Cathedral Parkway, Suite 7R
New York, NY 10025-2186
Phone: 212-932-3049
800-828-8349 (toll-free in U.S. and Canada)
Fax: 212-663-8169
E-mail: info@oxbridgeprograms.com
Web site: www.oxbridgeprograms.com

PARSONS THE NEW SCHOOL FOR DESIGN

Parsons Pre-College Academy

Summer Intensive Studies–New York

Summer Intensive Studies–Paris

Summer Studies in Architecture

Director
Pre-Enrollment Programs
66 Fifth Avenue, Room 200
New York, NY 10011
Phone: 212-229-8925
Fax: 212-336-8437
E-mail: academy@newschool.edu
Web site: www.parsons.edu/summer

THE PUTNEY SCHOOL

The Putney School Summer Arts Program

Susan Farber
Administrative Coordinator
Elm Lea Farm
418 Houghton Brook Road
Putney, VT 05346
Phone: 802-387-6276
Fax: 802-387-6216
E-mail: summer@putneyschool.org
Web site: www.putneyschool.org/summer

RENSSELAER POLYTECHNIC INSTITUTE

Summer@Rensselaer

Mr. Michael L. Gunther
Program Manager for Recruitment
CII Low Center, Suite 4011
110 8th Street
Troy, NY 12180-3590
Phone: 518-276-8351
Fax: 518-276-8738
E-mail: gunthm@rpi.edu
Web site: www.summer.rpi.edu

RHODE ISLAND SCHOOL OF DESIGN

Summer Pre-College Program

Pre-College Program
RISD Continuing Education
Two College Street
Providence, RI 02903-2787
Phone: 401-454-6200
800-364-7473 (toll-free outside local calling
   area)
Fax: 401-454-6218
E-mail: cemail@risd.edu
Web site: www.risd.edu/precollege.cfm

RINGLING SCHOOL OF ART AND DESIGN

Ringling School of Art and Design Pre-College Perspective

Director of Continuing Studies and Special
   Programs
2700 North Tamiami Trail
Sarasota, FL 34234-6895
Phone: 941-955-8866
Fax: 941-955-8801
E-mail: cssp@ringling.edu
Web site: www.ringling.edu/precollege

RUSTIC PATHWAYS

International Programs in Art and Photography

Admissions
P.O. Box 1150
Willoughby, Ohio 44096
Phone: 440-975-9691
800-321-4353 (toll-free)
Fax: 440-975-9694
E-mail: rustic@rusticpathways.com
Web site: www.rusticpathways.com

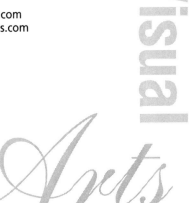

Visual *Arts*

SAGE SUMMER LEARNING ADVENTURES
Arts and Religions of India

Summer SAGE Program
19 Old Town Square
Suite 238
Fort Collins, CO 80524
Phone: 888–997-SAGE (toll-free)
Fax: 970-482-0251
E-mail: info@sageprogram.org
Web site: http://sageprogram.org

SALEM ACADEMY AND COLLEGE
Salem Spotlight

Douglas Murphy
Executive Director
PO Box 10578
Winston-Salem, NC 27108-1753
Phone: 800-883-1753 (toll-free)
E-mail: spotlight@salem.edu
Web site: http://spotlight.salem.edu

SARAH LAWRENCE COLLEGE
Sarah Lawrence College Summer High School Programs

Liz Irmiter
Director of Special Programs
1 Mead Way
Bronxville, NY 10708
Phone: 914-395-2693
Fax: 914-395-2694
E-mail: specialprograms@sarahlawrence.edu
Web site: www.sarahlawrence.edu/summer

SAVANNAH COLLEGE OF ART AND DESIGN
Rising Star
SCAD Summer Seminars

Admission Department
PO Box 2072
Savannah, GA 31402-2072
Phone: 800-869-7223 (toll-free)
Fax: 912-525-5986
E-mail: admission@scad.edu
Web site: www.scad.edu/summer

SCHOOL OF THE MUSEUM OF FINE ARTS, BOSTON
Pre-College Summer Studio

Debra Samdperil
Director, Continuing Education and Artist's Resource Center
230 The Fenway
Boston, MA 02115
Phone: 617-267-1219
Fax: 617-369-3679
E-mail: coned@smfa.edu
Web site: www.smfa.edu/precollege

SKIDMORE COLLEGE
Pre-College Program in the Liberal and Studio Arts
Summer Studio Arts Program

Ms. Marianne Needham
Coordinator
Saisselin Art Building
815 North Broadway
Saratoga Springs, NY 12866
Phone: 518-580-5052
Fax: 518-580-5029
E-mail: mneedham@skidmore.edu
Web site: www.skidmore.edu/summer

SPOLETO STUDY ABROAD
Summer Arts and Humanities Programs

Nancy Langston
Marketing Director
PO Box 13389
Charleston, SC 29422-3389
Phone: 843-822-1248
E-mail: spoleto@mindspring.com
Web site: www.spoletostudyabroad.com

SUFFIELD ACADEMY
The Summer Academy at Suffield

Tony O'Shaughnessy
Director, Summer Academy Admissions
185 North Main Street
Suffield, CT 06078
Phone: 860-668-7315
Fax: 860-668-2966
E-mail: summer@suffieldacademy.org
Web site: www.suffieldacademy.org

Visual

Arts

SYRACUSE UNIVERSITY

Syracuse University Summer College

Program Manager
700 University Avenue
Syracuse, NY 13244-2530
Phone: 315-443-3225
Fax: 315-443-4174
E-mail: sumcoll@syr.edu
Web site: www.summercollege.syr.edu/

TASIS

The TASIS Summer Programs in England, France, and Switzerland

The TASIS Schools, U.S. Office
1640 Wisconsin Avenue, NW
Washington, D.C. 20007
Phone: 202-965-5800
800-442-6005 (toll-free)
Fax: 202-965-5816
E-mail: usadmissions@tasis.com
Web site: http://summer.tasis.com

UCLA SUMMER SESSIONS AND SPECIAL PROGRAMS

UCLA Summer Experience: Institutes

Dr. Susan Pertel Jain
Director of Academic Program Development
Box 951418
Los Angeles, CA 90095
Phone: 310-825-4101
Fax: 310-825-1528
E-mail: spjain@summer.ucla.edu
Web site: www.summer.ucla.edu

UNION COLLEGE

FivePoints Summer Residential Program

Comics and Storyboarding

Architecture 101

Office of Special Events
807 Union Street
Schenectady, New York 12308
Phone: 800-883-2540 (toll-free)
E-mail: fivepoints@union.edu
Web site: www.union.edu/fivepoints

UNIVERSITY OF MARYLAND, OFFICE OF SUMMER AND WINTER TERMS

Young Scholars Program

Student Services
Mitchell Building, 1st Floor
University of Maryland
College Park, MD 20742
Phone: 301-314-8240
Fax: 301-314-1282
Web site: www.summer.umd.edu/s/taam

UNIVERSITY OF PENNSYLVANIA

Art and Architecture at Penn

Julie Schneider, M.F.A.
Director, Undergraduate Chair, Fine Arts
School of Design
University of Pennsylvania
Philadelphia, PA 19104
Phone: 215-898-6757
Fax: 215-573-8127
E-mail: saecker@design.upenn.edu
Web site: www.aasapenn.org/

THE UNIVERSITY OF THE ARTS

Pre-College Summer Institute

Director
Pre-College Programs
320 South Broad Street
Philadelphia, PA 19102
Phone: 215-717-6430
800–616-ARTS (toll-free outside Pennsylvania)
Fax: 215-717-6433
E-mail: precollege@uarts.edu
Web site: www.uarts.edu/precollege

USDAN CENTER FOR THE CREATIVE AND PERFORMING ARTS

Dale Lewis
Executive Director
Usdan Long Island Office
185 Colonial Springs Road
Wheatley Heights, NY 11798
Phone: 631–643–7900
212-772-6060
Web site: www.usdan.org

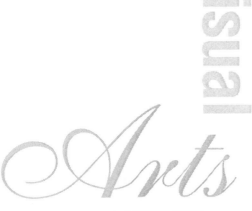

WASHINGTON UNIVERSITY IN ST. LOUIS

Portfolio Plus Program

Maurico Bruce
Senior Coordinator, Special Undergraduate
    Programs
Sam Fox School of Design & Visual Arts
Campus Box 1031
One Brookings Drive
St. Louis, MO 63130
Phone: 314-935-6500
Fax: 314-935-4643
E-mail: mbruce@wustl.edu
Web site: www.samfoxschool.wustl.edu/
    Summer_Programs

WORLD HORIZONS INTERNATIONAL

United Kingdom: Service and Arts Program

Mr. Stuart L. Rabinowitz
Executive Director
P.O. Box 662
Bethlehem, CT 06751
Phone: 800-262-5874 (toll-free)
Fax: 203-266-6227
E-mail: worldhorizons@att.net
Web site: www.world-horizons.com

Scholarships for Artists

AACE INTERNATIONAL

AACE International Competitive Scholarship

Charla Miller, Staff Director, Education and Administration
AACE International
209 Prairie Avenue, Suite 100
Morgantown, WV 26501
Phone: 304-296-8444 Ext. 113
Fax: 304-291-5728
E-mail: cmiller@aacei.org
Web site: http://www.aacei.org

ACADEMY FOUNDATION OF THE ACADEMY OF MOTION PICTURE ARTS AND SCIENCES

Academy of Motion Pictures Arts and Science Student Academy Awards

Academy of Motion Picture Student Academy Award-Honorary Foreign Film

Richard Miller, Awards Administration Director
Academy Foundation of the Academy of Motion Picture Arts and Sciences
8949 Wilshire Boulevard
Beverly Hills, CA 90211-1972
Phone: 310-247-3000
Fax: 310-859-9619
E-mail: rmiller@oscars.org
Web site: http://www.oscars.org/saa

ACADEMY OF TELEVISION ARTS AND SCIENCES FOUNDATION

Academy of Television Arts and Sciences College Television Awards

Nancy Robinson, Programs Coordinator
Academy of Television Arts and Sciences Foundation
5220 Lankershim Boulevard
North Hollywood, CA 91601
Phone: 818-754-2839
Fax: 818-761-8524
E-mail: collegeawards@emmys.org
Web site: http://www.emmysfoundation.org

ADC RESEARCH INSTITUTE

Jack Shaheen Mass Communications Scholarship Award

Mr. Nawar Shora, Director of Diversity and Law Enforcement Outreach
ADC Research Institute
1732 Wisconsin Avenue, NW
Washington, DC 20007
Phone: 202-244-2990
Fax: 202-244-3196
E-mail: nshora@adc.org
Web site: http://www.adc.org

AIA NEW JERSEY/THE NEW JERSEY SOCIETY OF ARCHITECTS

AIA New Jersey Scholarship Program

Robert Zaccone, President
AIA New Jersey/The New Jersey Society of Architects
414 River View Plaza
Trenton, NJ 08611-3420
Phone: 201-767-9575
Fax: 201-767-5541
E-mail: rzaarchitect@earthlink.net
Web site: http://www.aia-nj.org

ALLIANCE FOR YOUNG ARTISTS AND WRITERS INC.

Scholastic Art and Writing Awards-Art Section

Scholastic Art and Writing Awards-Writing Section Scholarship

General Information
Alliance for Young Artists and Writers Inc.
557 Broadway
New York, NY 10012-1396
Phone: 212-343-7791
Fax: 212-389-3939
E-mail: a&wgeneralinfo@scholastic.com
Web site: http://www.artandwriting.org

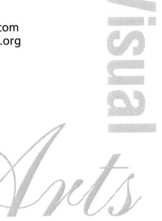

AMERICAN ARCHITECTURAL FOUNDATION

American Institute of Architects Minority/Disadvantaged Scholarship

Mary Felber, Director of Scholarship Programs
American Architectural Foundation
1735 New York Avenue, NW
Washington, DC 20006-5292
Phone: 202-626-7511
Fax: 202-626-7509
E-mail: mfelber@archfoundation.org
Web site: http://www.archfoundation.org

AMERICAN ART THERAPY ASSOCIATION

Myra Levick Scholarship Fund

Doris Arrington, Scholarship Committee
American Art Therapy Association
1202 Allanson Road
Mundelein, IL 60060-9808
Phone: 888-290-0878
Fax: 708-566-4580
E-mail: daarrington@sbcglobal.net
Web site: http://www.arttherapy.org

AMERICAN FOREIGN SERVICE ASSOCIATION

American Foreign Service Association (AFSA)/AAFSW Merit Award Program

Lori Dec, Scholarship Director
American Foreign Service Association
2101 East Street NW
Washington, DC 20037
Phone: 202-944-5504
Fax: 202-338-6820
E-mail: dec@afsa.org
Web site: http://www.afsa.org

AMERICAN INSTITUTE OF ARCHITECTS

American Institute of Architects/American Architectural Foundation Minority/Disadvantaged Scholarships

Mary Felber, Scholarship Chair
American Institute of Architects
1735 New York Avenue, NW
Washington, DC 20006-5292
Phone: 202-626-7511
Fax: 202-626-7509
E-mail: mfelber@aia.org
Web site: http://www.aia.org

AMERICAN INSTITUTE OF ARCHITECTS, NEW YORK CHAPTER

Douglas Haskell Award for Student Journalism

Marcus Bleyer, Scholarship Committee
American Institute of Architects, New York Chapter
536 LaGuardia Place
New York, NY 10012
Phone: 212-358-6117
E-mail: mbleyer@aiany.org
Web site: http://www.aiany.org

Women's Architectural Auxiliary Eleanor Allwork Scholarship Grants

Marcus Bleyer, Coordinator
American Institute of Architects, New York Chapter
536 LaGuardia Place
New York, NY 10012
Phone: 212-358-6117
E-mail: mbleyer@aiany.org
Web site: http://www.aiany.org

AMERICAN INSTITUTE OF ARCHITECTS, WEST VIRGINIA CHAPTER

AIA West Virginia Scholarship Program

Roberta Guffey, Executive Director
American Institute of Architects, West Virginia Chapter
223 Hale Street
Charleston, WV 25301
Phone: 304-344-9872
Fax: 304-343-0205
E-mail: roberta.guffey@aiawv.org
Web site: http://www.aiawv.org

AMERICAN INSTITUTE OF POLISH CULTURE INC.

Harriet Irsay Scholarship Grant

Scholarship Committee
American Institute of Polish Culture Inc.
1440 79th Street Causeway, Suite 117
Miami, FL 33141-3555
Phone: 305-864-2349
Fax: 305-865-5150
E-mail: info@ampolinstitute.org
Web site: http://www.ampolinstitute.org

AMERICAN LEGION AUXILIARY DEPARTMENT OF WASHINGTON

American Legion Auxiliary Department of Washington Florence Lemcke Memorial Scholarship in Fine Arts

Nicole Ross, News Department Secretary
American Legion Auxiliary Department of Washington
3600 Ruddell Road
Lacey, WA 98503
Phone: 360-456-5995
Fax: 360-491-7442
E-mail: alawash@qwest.net
Web site: http://www.walegion-aux.org

AMERICAN LEGION, PRESS CLUB OF NEW JERSEY

American Legion Press Club of New Jersey and Post 170 Arthur Dehardt Memorial Scholarship

Dorothy Saunders, Scholarship Chairman
American Legion, Press Club of New Jersey
Three Lewis Street
Wayne, NJ 07470-4716
Web site: http://www.walegion-aux.org

AMERICAN PHILOLOGICAL ASSOCIATION

Minority Student Summer Scholarship

Adam Blistein, Executive Director
American Philological Association
University of Pennsylvania, 249 South 36th Street, 292 Logan Hall
Philadelphia, PA 19104-6304
Phone: 215-898-4975
Fax: 210-573-7874
E-mail: apaclassics@sas.upenn.edu
Web site: http://www.apaclassics.org

AMERICAN SCHOOL OF CLASSICAL STUDIES AT ATHENS

ASCSA Summer Sessions Open Scholarships

Charles M. Edwards Scholarship

Mary Darlington, Executive Assistant
American School of Classical Studies at Athens
6-8 Charlton Street
Princeton, NJ 08540-5232
Phone: 609-683-0800
Fax: 609-924-0578
Web site: http://www.ascsa.edu.gr

AMERICAN SOCIETY OF HEATING, REFRIGERATING, AND AIR CONDITIONING ENGINEERS INC.

ASHRAE Region IV Benny Bootle Scholarship

Lois Benedict, Scholarship Administrator
American Society of Heating, Refrigerating, and Air Conditioning Engineers Inc.
1791 Tullie Circle, NE
Atlanta, GA 30329
Phone: 404-636-8400
Fax: 404-321-5478
E-mail: lbenedict@ashrae.org
Web site: http://www.ashrae.org

AMERICAN SOCIETY OF INTERIOR DESIGNERS (ASID) EDUCATION FOUNDATION INC.

ASID Educational Foundation/Yale R. Burge Competition

Lisa Armstrong, Education Department
American Society of Interior Designers (ASID) Education Foundation Inc.
608 Massachusetts Avenue, NE
Washington, DC 20002-6006
Phone: 202-546-3480
Fax: 202-546-3240
E-mail: education@asid.org
Web site: http://www.asid.org

ART DIRECTORS CLUB

Art Directors Club National Scholarships

Education Coordinator
Art Directors Club
106 West 29th Street
New York, NY 10009
Phone: 212-643-1440 Ext. 16
Fax: 212-643-4293
E-mail: isabel@adcglobal.org
Web site: http://www.adcglobal.org

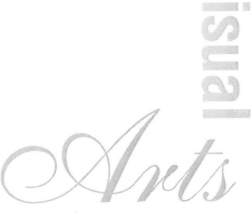

ARTIST-BLACKSMITH'S ASSOCIATION OF NORTH AMERICA INC.

Artist's-Blacksmith's Association of North America Inc Affiliate Visiting Artist Grant Program

Heather Hutton, Central Office
Administrator
Artist-Blacksmith's Association of North
America Inc.
PO Box 3425
Knoxville, TN 37927-3425
Phone: 865-546-7733
Fax: 865-546-9964
E-mail: abana@abana.org
Web site: http://www.abana.org

ASIAN AMERICAN JOURNALISTS ASSOCIATION

Asian-American Journalists Association Scholarship

Kim Mizuhara, Programs Coordinator
Asian American Journalists Association
1182 Market Street, Suite 320
San Francisco, CA 94102
Phone: 415-346-2051 Ext. 102
Fax: 415-346-6343
E-mail: programs@aaja.org
Web site: http://www.aaja.org

ASPRS, THE IMAGING AND GEOSPATIAL INFORMATION SOCIETY

Robert E. Altenhofen Memorial Scholarship

Jesse Winch, Program Manager
ASPRS, The Imaging and Geospatial
Information Society
5410 Grosvenor Lane, Suite 210
Bethesda, MD 20814-2160
Phone: 301-493-0290 Ext. 101
Fax: 301-493-0208
E-mail: scholarships@asprs.org
Web site: http://www.asprs.org

ASSOCIATION FOR WOMEN IN ARCHITECTURE FOUNDATION

Association for Women in Architecture Scholarship

Mary Werk, Scholarship Chair
Association for Women in Architecture
Foundation
22815 Frampton Avenue
Torrance, CA 90501-5034
Phone: 310-534-8466
Fax: 310-257-6885
E-mail: scholarship@awa-la.org
Web site: http://www.awa-la.org

AUTHOR SERVICES INC.

L. Ron Hubbard's Illustrators of the Future Contest

Contest Administrator
Author Services Inc.
PO Box 3190
Los Angeles, CA 90078
Phone: 323-466-3310
Fax: 323-466-6474
E-mail: contests@authorservicesinc.com
Web site: http://www.writersofthefuture.
com

BAY AREA BLACK JOURNALISTS ASSOCIATION SCHOLARSHIP CONTEST

Luci S. Williams Houston Memorial Scholarship

Young Journalists Scholarship

Scholarship Committee
Bay Area Black Journalists Association
Scholarship Contest
1714 Franklin Street, Suite 100-260
Oakland, CA 94612
Phone: 510-986-9390
Fax: 510-382-1980
E-mail: info@babja.org
Web site: http://www.babja.org

BMI FOUNDATION INC.

BMI Student Composer Awards

Mr. Ralph N. Jackson, Director
BMI Foundation Inc.
320 West 57th Street
New York, NY 10019
Phone: 212-586-2000
Fax: 212-245-8986
E-mail: classical@bmi.com
Web site: http://www.bmifoundation.org

CALIFORNIA CHICANO NEWS MEDIA ASSOCIATION (CCNMA)

CCNMA Scholarships

Julio Moran, Executive Director
California Chicano News Media Association (CCNMA)
300 South Grand Avenue, Suite 3950
Los Angeles, CA 90071-8110
Phone: 213-437-4408
Fax: 213-437-4423
E-mail: ccnmainfo@ccnma.org
Web site: http://www.ccnma.org

CENTRAL INTELLIGENCE AGENCY

Central Intelligence Agency Undergraduate Scholarship Program

Van Patrick, Chief, College Relations
Central Intelligence Agency
Recruitment Center, L 100 LF7
Washington, DC 20505
Phone: 703-613-8388
Fax: 703-613-7676
E-mail: ivanilp0@ucia.gov
Web site: http://www.cia.gov

CHARLES & LUCILLE KING FAMILY FOUNDATION INC.

Charles and Lucille King Family Foundation Scholarships

Michael Donovan, Educational Director
Charles & Lucille King Family Foundation Inc.
366 Madison Avenue, Tenth Floor
New York, NY 10017
Phone: 212-682-2913
Fax: 212-949-0728
E-mail: info@kingfoundation.org
Web site: http://www.kingfoundation.org

CHRISTOPHER PETTIET SCHOLARSHIP FUND

Christopher Pettiet Memorial Fund

Scholarship Committee
Christopher Pettiet Scholarship Fund
The Actors Circle, 4475 Sepulveda Boulevard
Culver City, CA 90230
Phone: 310-837-4536
E-mail: workshops@theactorscircle.com
Web site: http://www.theactorscircle.com/chris.html

CHRISTOPHERS

Poster Contest for High School Students

Video Contest for College Students

David Dicerto, Youth Coordinator
Christophers
5 Hanover Square, 11th Floor
New York, NY 10014
Phone: 212-759-4050
Fax: 212-838-5073
E-mail: youth@christophers.org
Web site: http://www.christophers.org

CINCINNATI LITHO CLUB

Bill Staudt/Al Hartnett Scholarship

Day International Scholarship

Scholarship Administrator
Cincinnati Litho Club
6550 Donjoy Drive
Cincinnati, OH 45242
Phone: 910-575-0399
Web site: http://www.cincylithoclub.org

CIRI FOUNDATION (TCF)

CIRI Foundation Susie Qimmiqsak Bevins Endowment Scholarship Fund

Susan Anderson, President and Chief Executive Officer
CIRI Foundation (TCF)
3600 San Jeronimo Drive, Suite 256
Anchorage, AK 99508-2870
Phone: 907-793-3575
Fax: 907-793-3585
E-mail: tcf@thecirifoundation.org
Web site: http://www.thecirifoundation.org

COLLEGEBOUND FOUNDATION

Janet B. Sondheim Scholarship

Jamie Crouse, Scholarship Program Administrator
CollegeBound Foundation
300 Water Street, Suite 300
Baltimore, MD 21202
Phone: 410-783-2905 Ext. 207
Fax: 410-727-5786
E-mail: jcrouse@collegeboundfoundation.org
Web site: http://www.collegeboundfoundation.org

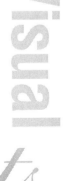

Visual *Arts*

COLLEGE PHOTOGRAPHER OF THE YEAR

College Photographer of the Year Competition

Rita Ann Reed, Program Director
College Photographer of the Year
University of Missouri
School of Journalism
107 Lee Hills Hall
Columbia, MO 65211
Phone: 573-882-2198
Fax: 573-884-4999
E-mail: info@cpoy.org
Web site: http://www.cpoy.org

COMMUNITY FOUNDATION FOR GREATER ATLANTA INC.

James M. and Virginia M. Smyth Scholarship

Kristina Morris, Program Associate
Community Foundation for Greater
  Atlanta Inc.
50 Hurt Plaza, Suite 449
Atlanta, GA 30303
Phone: 404-688-5525
Fax: 404-688-3060
E-mail: scholarships@atlcf.org
Web site: http://www.atlcf.org

CONNECTICUT CHAPTER OF SOCIETY OF PROFESSIONAL JOURNALISTS

Connecticut SPJ Bob Eddy Scholarship Program

Debra Estock, Scholarship Committee
  Chairman
Connecticut Chapter of Society of Profes-
  sional Journalists
71 Kenwood Avenue
Fairfield, CT 06430
Phone: 203-255-2127
E-mail: destock963@aol.com
Web site: http://www.ctspj.org

COSTUME SOCIETY OF AMERICA

Adele Filene Travel Award

Noel Liccardi, Program Contact
Costume Society of America
203 Towne Center Drive
Hillsborough, NJ 08844
Phone: 800-272-9447
Fax: 908-450-1118
E-mail: national.
  office@costumesocietyamerica.com
Web site: http://www.
  costumesocietyamerica.com

Stella Blum Research Grant

Noel Liccardi, Program Contact
Costume Society of America
203 Towne Center Drive
Hillsborough, NJ 08844
Phone: 800-272-9447
Fax: 908-450-1118
E-mail: national.
  office@costumesocietyamerica.com
Web site: http://www.
  costumesocietyamerica.com

DAYTON FOUNDATION

Larry Fullerton Photojournalism Scholarship

Diane Timmons, Vice President, Grants and
  Programs
Dayton Foundation
2300 Kettering Tower
Dayton, OH 45423
Phone: 937-222-0410
Fax: 937-222-0636
E-mail: dtimmons@daytonfoundation.org
Web site: http://www.daytonfoundation.
  org

ELECTRONIC DOCUMENT SYSTEMS FOUNDATION

Electronic Document Systems Foundation Scholarship Awards

Ms. Brenda Kai, Executive Director
Electronic Document Systems Foundation
1845 Precinct Line Road, Suite 212
Hurst, TX 76054
Phone: 817-849-1145
Fax: 817-849-1185
E-mail: brenda.kai@edsf.org
Web site: http://www.edsf.org

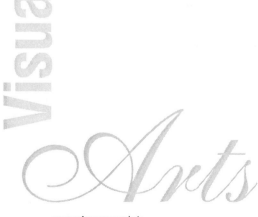

ELIZABETH GREENSHIELDS FOUNDATION
Elizabeth Greenshields Award/Grant

Diane Pitcher, Applications Coordinator
Elizabeth Greenshields Foundation
1814 Sherbrooke Street, W, Suite 1
Montreal, QC H3H IE4
Canada
Phone: 514-937-9225
Fax: 514-937-0141
E-mail: greenshields@bellnet.ca
Web site: http://www.edsf.org

FLORIDA EDUCATIONAL FACILITIES PLANNERS' ASSOCIATION

FEFPA Assistantship

Robert Griffith, Selection Committee Chair
Florida Educational Facilities Planners'
 Association
Florida International University, University
 Park, CSC 142A
Miami, FL 33199
Phone: 305-348-4070 Ext. 4002
Fax: 305-348-4091
E-mail: griffith@fiu.edu
Web site: http://www.fefpa.org

FLORIDA PTA/PTSA

Florida PTA/PTSA Fine Arts Scholarship

Janice Bailey, Executive Director
Florida PTA/PTSA
1747 Orlando Central Parkway
Orlando, FL 32809
Phone: 407-855-7604
Fax: 407-240-9577
E-mail: janice@floridapta.org
Web site: http://www.floridapta.org

FORT COLLINS SYMPHONY ASSOCIATION

Fort Collins Symphony Association Young Artist Competition, Junior Division

Carol Kauffman, Office Manager
Fort Collins Symphony Association
214 South College Avenue
PO Box 1963
Fort Collins, CO 80524
Phone: 970-482-4823
Fax: 970-482-4858
E-mail: yac@fcsymphony.org
Web site: http://www.fcsymphony.org

GENERAL FEDERATION OF WOMEN'S CLUBS OF MASSACHUSETTS

General Federation of Women's Clubs of Massachusetts Pennies For Art Scholarship

Joan Shanahan, Arts Chairman
General Federation of Women's Clubs of
 Massachusetts
PO Box 703
Upton, MA 01568-0703
E-mail: cmje@aol.com
Web site: http://www.gfwcma.org

GETTY GRANT PROGRAM

Library Research Grants

Kathleen Johnson, Program Associate
Getty Grant Program
1200 Getty Center Drive, Suite 800
Los Angeles, CA 90049-1685
Phone: 310-440-7320
Fax: 310-440-7703
E-mail: researchgrants@getty.edu
Web site: http://www.getty.edu/grants

GOLDEN KEY INTERNATIONAL HONOUR SOCIETY

Visual and Performing Arts Achievement Awards

Scholarship Program Administrators
Golden Key International Honour Society
PO Box 23737
Nashville, TN 37202
Phone: 800-377-2401
Web site: http://www.goldenkey.org

GRAVURE EDUCATION FOUNDATION

GEF Resource Center Scholarships

Gravure Catalog and Insert Council Scholarship

Gravure Education Foundation Corporate Leadership Scholarships

Hallmark Graphic Arts Scholarship

Leon C. Hart Memorial Scholarship

Werner B. Thiele Memorial Scholarship

Robert Sheridan, Director of Development
Gravure Education Foundation
1200 A Scottsville Road
Rochester, NY 14624
Phone: 518-589-5153
Fax: 585-436-7689
E-mail: rbsheridan@gaa.org
Web site: http://www.gaa.org

GREAT FALLS ADVERTISING FEDERATION
College Scholarship
High School ART Scholarship

Christine Depa, Administrative Assistant
Great Falls Advertising Federation
609 Tenth Avenue South, Suite B
Great Falls, MT 59405
Phone: 406-761-6453
Fax: 406-453-1128
E-mail: gfaf@gfaf.com
Web site: http://www.gfaf.com

GREAT LAKES COMMISSION
Carol A. Ratza Memorial Scholarship

Christine Manninen, Program Manager
Great Lakes Commission
Eisenhower Corporate Park, 2805 South
   Industrial Highway, Suite 100
Ann Arbor, MI 48104-6791
Phone: 734-971-9135
Fax: 734-971-9150
E-mail: manninen@glc.org
Web site: http://www.glc.org

HELLENIC UNIVERSITY CLUB OF PHILADELPHIA
Dimitri J. Ververelli Memorial Scholarship for Architecture and/or Engineering

Zoe Tripolitis, Scholarship Chairman
Hellenic University Club of Philadelphia
PO Box 42199
Philadelphia, PA 19101-2199
Phone: 215-483-7440
E-mail: hucphila@yahoo.com
Web site: http://www.hucphila.org

HEMOPHILIA FEDERATION OF AMERICA
Artistic Encouragement Grant

Scholarship Committee
Hemophilia Federation of America
1405 West Pinhook Road, Suite 101
Lafayette, LA 70503
Phone: 337-261-9787
E-mail: info@hemophiliafed.org
Web site: http://www.hemophiliaed.org

HISPANIC COLLEGE FUND INC.
Denny's/Hispanic College Fund Scholarship
El Nuevo Constructor Scholarship Program

Fernando Barrueta, Chief Executive Officer
Hispanic College Fund Inc.
1301 K Street, NW, Suite 450-A West
Washington, DC 20005
Phone: 202-296-5400
Fax: 202-296-3774
E-mail: hcf-info@hispanicfund.org
Web site: http://www.hispanicfund.org

HISPANIC SCHOLARSHIP FUND
HSF/McNamara Family Creative Arts Project Grant

John Schmucker, Scholarship Coordinator
Hispanic Scholarship Fund
55 Second Street, Suite 1500
San Francisco, CA 94105
Phone: 877-473-4636
E-mail: scholar1@hsf.net
Web site: http://www.hsf.net

ILLUMINATING ENGINEERING SOCIETY OF NORTH AMERICA
Robert W. Thunen Memorial Scholarships

Phil Hall, Chairman
Illuminating Engineering Society of North
   America
120 Wall Street
New York, NY 10005-4001
Phone: 510-864-0204
Fax: 510-864-8511
E-mail: mrcatisbac@aol.com
Web site: http://www.iesna.org

ILLUMINATING ENGINEERING SOCIETY OF NORTH AMERICA–GOLDEN GATE SECTION
Alan Lucas Memorial Educational Scholarship

Phil Hall, Scholarship Committee
Illuminating Engineering Society of North
   America–Golden Gate Section
1514 Gibbons Drive
Alameda, CA 94501
Phone: 510-864-0204
Fax: 510-864-8511
E-mail: iesggthunenfund@aol.com
Web site: http://www.iesgg.org

INSTITUTE FOR HUMANE STUDIES
Film and Fiction Scholarship

Keri Anderson, Program Coordinator
Institute for Humane Studies
3301 North Fairfax Drive, Suite 440
Arlington, VA 22201-4432
Phone: 703-993-4880
Fax: 703-993-4890
E-mail: ihs@gmu.edu
Web site: http://www.theihs.org

INTERNATIONAL COMMUNICATIONS INDUSTRIES FOUNDATION
ICIF Scholarship for Dependents of Member Organizations
International Communications Industries Foundation AV Scholarship

Shana Rieger, Social Media Program Manager
International Communications Industries Foundation
11242 Waples Mill Road, Suite 200
Fairfax, VA 22030
Phone: 703-273-7200 Ext. 3690
Fax: 703-278-8082
E-mail: membership@infocomm.org
Web site: http://www.infocomm.org/ scholarships

INTERNATIONAL FOODSERVICE EDITORIAL COUNCIL
International Foodservice Editorial Council Communications Scholarship

Carol Lally, Executive Director
International Foodservice Editorial Council
PO Box 491
Hyde Park, NY 12538-0491
Phone: 845-229-6973
Fax: 845-229-6993
E-mail: ifec@aol.com
Web site: http://www.ifeconline.com

INTERNATIONAL FURNISHINGS AND DESIGN ASSOCIATION
Charles D. Mayo Scholarship
IFDA Student Scholarship
Ruth Clark Scholarship

Earline Feldman, Director
International Furnishings and Design Association
150 South Warner Road, Suite 156
King of Prussia, PA 19406
Phone: 610-535-6422
Fax: 610-535-6423
E-mail: tapis2@bellsouth.com
Web site: http://www.ifdaef.org

INTERNATIONAL INTERIOR DESIGN ASSOCIATION (IIDA) FOUNDATION
Kimball Office Scholarship Fund

Jocelyn Pysarchuk, Senior Director, Communications and Marketing
International Interior Design Association (IIDA) Foundation
222 Merchandise Mart Plaza
Chicago, IL 60654-1104
Phone: 312-467-1950
Fax: 312-467-0779
E-mail: jpysarchuk@iida.org
Web site: http://www.iida.org

JACK J. ISGUR FOUNDATION
Jack J. Isgur Foundation Scholarship

Charles Jensen, Attorney at Law
Jack J. Isgur Foundation
c/o Charles F. Jensen, Stinson, Morrison, Hecker LLP
1201 Walnut Street, 28th Floor
Kansas City, MO 64106
Phone: 816-691-2760
Fax: 816-691-3495
E-mail: cjensen@stinson.com
Web site: http://www.iida.org

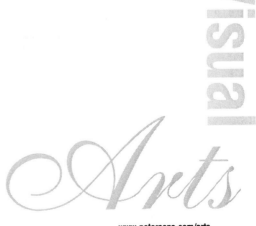

Visual Arts

JOHN F. AND ANNA LEE STACEY SCHOLARSHIP FUND

John F. and Anna Lee Stacey Scholarship Fund

Ed Muno, Art Curator
John F. and Anna Lee Stacey Scholarship Fund
1700 Northeast 63rd Street
Oklahoma City, OK 73111
Phone: 405-478-2250
Fax: 405-478-4714
E-mail: emuno@nationalcowboymuseum.org
Web site: http://www.nationalcowboymuseum.org

JUNIOR ACHIEVEMENT

Walt Disney Company Foundation Scholarship

Denise Terry, Scholarship Coordinator
Junior Achievement
One Education Way
Colorado Springs, CO 80906-4477
Phone: 719-540-6134
Fax: 719-540-6175
E-mail: dterry@ja.org
Web site: http://www.ja.org

KARMEL SCHOLARSHIP

KarMel Scholarship

Scholarship Committee
KarMel Scholarship
PO Box 70382
Sunnyvale, CA 94086
E-mail: karen@karenandmelody.com
Web site: http://www.karenandmelody.com

KE ALI'I PAUAHI FOUNDATION

Bruce T. and Jackie Mahi Erickson Grant

Native Hawaiian Visual Arts Scholarship

Elizabeth Stevenson, Development Manager
Ke Ali'I Pauahi Foundation
567 South King Street, Suite 160
Honolulu, HI 96813
Phone: 808-534-3966
Fax: 808-534-3890
E-mail: scholarships@pauahi.org
Web site: http://www.pauahi.org

KNIGHTS OF PYTHIAS

Knights of Pythias Poster Contest

Alfred Saltzman, Supreme Secretary
Knights of Pythias
Office of Supreme Lodge
59 Coddington Street, Suite 202
Quincy, MA 02169-4150
Phone: 617-472-8800
Fax: 617-376-0363
E-mail: kop@earthlink.net
Web site: http://www.pythias.org

LADIES AUXILIARY TO THE VETERANS OF FOREIGN WARS

Young American Creative Patriotic Art Awards Program

Judith Millick, Administrator of Programs
Ladies Auxiliary to the Veterans of Foreign Wars
406 West 34th Street
Kansas City, MO 64111
Phone: 816-561-8655
Fax: 816-931-4753
E-mail: jmillick@ladiesauxvfw.org
Web site: http://www.ladiesauxvfw.org

LIBERTY GRAPHICS INC.

Annual Liberty Graphics Art Contest

Mr. Jay Sproul, Scholarship Coordinator
Liberty Graphics Inc.
3 Main Street, PO Box 5
Liberty, ME 04949
Phone: 207-589-4596
Fax: 207-589-4415
E-mail: jay@lgtees.com
Web site: http://www.lgtees.com

LIQUITEX ARTIST MATERIALS PURCHASE AWARD PROGRAM

Liquitex Excellence in Art Purchase Award Program

Liquitex Excellence in Art Purchase Award Program-Secondary Category

Mrs. Renee Hile, Vice President Marketing
Liquitex Artist Materials Purchase Award Program
11 Constitution Avenue
PO Box 1396
Piscataway, NJ 08855-1396
Phone: 732-562-0770
Fax: 732-562-0941
Web site: http://www.liquitex.com

Visual

Arts

MAINE GRAPHICS ARTS ASSOCIATION

Maine Graphics Art Association

Angie Dougherty, Director
Maine Graphics Arts Association
PO Box 874
Auburn, ME 04212-0874
Phone: 207-883-9525
Fax: 207-883-3158
E-mail: edpougher@maine.rr.com
Web site: http://www.megaa.org

MARYLAND ARTISTS EQUITY FOUNDATION

Maryland Artists Equity Foundation Visual Arts Annual Scholarship Competition

Mark Coates, Scholarship Chair
Maryland Artists Equity Foundation
PO Box 17050
Baltimore, MD 21297
Phone: 410-313-6634
Fax: 410-313-6634
E-mail: mark_coates@hcpss.org
Web site: http://www.maef.org

MEDIA ACTION NETWORK FOR ASIAN AMERICANS

MANAA Media Scholarships for Asian American Students

Scholarship Coordinator
Media Action Network for Asian Americans
PO Box 11105
Burbank, CA 91510
E-mail: manaaletters@yahoo.com.
Web site: http://www.manaa.org

METAVUE CORPORATION

FW Rausch Arts and Humanities Paper Contest

Michael Rufflo, Scholarship Committee
Metavue Corporation
1110 Surrey Drive
Sun Prairie, WI 53590
Phone: 608-577-0642
Fax: 512-685-4074
E-mail: rufflo@metavue.com
Web site: http://www.metavue.com

MINNESOTA COMMUNITY FOUNDATION

ASID Minnesota Chapter Scholarship Fund

Frank Chaney Memorial Scholarship

Donna Paulson, Administrative Assistant
Minnesota Community Foundation
55 Fifth Street East, Suite 600
St. Paul, MN 55101-1797
Phone: 651-325-4212
E-mail: dkp@mncommunityfoundation.org
Web site: http://www.
mncommunityfoundation.org

MINNESOTA HIGHER EDUCATION SERVICES OFFICE

Minnesota Academic Excellence Scholarship

Ginny Dodds, Manager
Minnesota Higher Education Services
Office
1450 Energy Park Drive, Suite 350
St. Paul, MN 55108-5227
Phone: 651-642-0567
Fax: 651-642-0675
E-mail: ginny.dodds@state.mn.us
Web site: http://www.getreadyforcollege.
org

NATIONAL ART MATERIALS TRADE ASSOCIATION

National Art Materials Trade Association Art Scholarship

Karen Brown, Administrative Assistant
National Art Materials Trade Association
15806 Brookway Drive, Suite 300
Huntersville, NC 28078
Phone: 704-892-6244
Fax: 704-892-6247
E-mail: kbrown@namta.org
Web site: http://www.namta.org

NATIONAL ASSOCIATION OF BLACK JOURNALISTS

National Association of Black Journalists Non-Sustaining Scholarship Awards

Visual Task Force Scholarship

Irving Washington, Manager
National Association of Black Journalists
8701-A Adelphi Road
Adelphi, MD 20783-1716
Phone: 301-445-7100
Fax: 301-445-7101
E-mail: iwashington@nabj.org
Web site: http://www.nabj.org

Visual Arts

NATIONAL ASSOCIATION OF HISPANIC JOURNALISTS (NAHJ)

National Association of Hispanic Journalists Scholarship

Newhouse Scholarship Program

Virginia Galindo, Program Assistant
National Association of Hispanic Journalists (NAHJ)
1000 National Press Building
529 14th Street, NW
Suite 1000
Washington, DC 20045-2001
Phone: 202-662-7145
Fax: 202-662-7144
E-mail: vgalindo@nahj.org
Web site: http://www.nahj.org

NATIONAL ASSOCIATION OF WOMEN IN CONSTRUCTION

NAWIC Undergraduate Scholarships

Scholarship Committee
National Association of Women in Construction
327 South Adams Street
Fort Worth, TX 76104
Phone: 817-877-5551
Fax: 817-877-0324
Web site: http://www.nawic.org

NATIONAL FEDERATION OF THE BLIND

Howard Brown Rickard Scholarship

Anil Lewis, Chairman, Scholarship Committee
National Federation of the Blind
315 West Ponce De Leon Avenue
Decatur, GA 30030
Phone: 404-371-1000
E-mail: alewis@nfbga.org
Web site: http://www.nfb.org

National Federation of the Blind Humanities Scholarship

Peggy Elliot, Chairman, Scholarship Committee
National Federation of the Blind
805 Fifth Avenue
Grinnell, IA 50112-1653
Phone: 641-236-3369
Web site: http://www.nfb.org

NATIONAL FOUNDATION FOR ADVANCEMENT IN THE ARTS

youngARTS

Carla Hill, Programs Department
National Foundation for Advancement in the Arts
444 Brickell Avenue, Suite R14
Miami, FL 33133
Phone: 800-970-2787
Fax: 305-377-1149
E-mail: nfaa@nfaa.org
Web site: http://www.youngARTS.org

NATIONAL OPERA ASSOCIATION

NOA Vocal Competition/Legacy Award Program

Robert Hansen, Executive Secretary
National Opera Association
2403 Russell Long Boulevard, PO Box 60869
Canyon, TX 79016-0001
Phone: 806-651-2857
Fax: 806-651-2958
E-mail: hansen@mail.wtamu.edu
Web site: http://www.noa.org

NATIONAL PRESS PHOTOGRAPHERS FOUNDATION INC.

Bob East Scholarship

Chuck Fadely, Scholarship Committee
National Press Photographers Foundation Inc.
The Miami Herald, One Herald Plaza
Miami, FL 33132
Phone: 305-376-2015
Web site: http://www.nppa.org

National Press Photographers Foundation Still Photographer Scholarship

Bill Sanders, Photo Editor
National Press Photographers Foundation Inc.
Asheville Citizen-Times, PO Box 2090
Asheville, NC 28802
E-mail: wsanders@citizen-times.com
Web site: http://www.nppa.org

National Press Photographers Foundation Television News Scholarship

Ed Dooks, Scholarship Committee
National Press Photographers Foundation Inc.
Five Mohawk Drive
Lexington, MA 02421-6217
Phone: 781-861-6062
E-mail: dooks@verizon.net
Web site: http://www.nppa.org

Reid Blackburn Scholarship

Fay Blackburn, Manager
National Press Photographers Foundation Inc.
The Columbian, PO Box 180
Vancouver, WA 98666
Phone: 360-759-8027
E-mail: fay.blackburn@columbian.com
Web site: http://www.nppa.org

NATIONAL SCULPTURE SOCIETY

National Sculpture Society Alex J. Ettl Grant

National Sculpture Society Scholarships

Gwen Pier, Executive Director
National Sculpture Society
237 Park Avenue
New York, NY 10017
Phone: 212-764-5645 Ext. 15
Fax: 212-764-5651
E-mail: gwen@nationalsculpture.org
Web site: http://www.nationalsculpture.org

NEBRASKA PRESS ASSOCIATION

Nebraska Press Association Foundation Inc. Scholarship

Allen Beermann, Executive Director
Nebraska Press Association
845 South Street
Lincoln, NE 68508-1226
Phone: 402-476-2851
Fax: 402-476-2942
E-mail: abeermann@nebpress.com
Web site: http://www.nebpress.com

NEW ENGLAND PRINTING AND PUBLISHING COUNCIL

New England Graphic Arts Scholarship

Jay Smith, Scholarship Chair
New England Printing and Publishing Council
166 New Boston Street
Woburn, MA 01801
Phone: 781-944-1116
Fax: 781-944-3905
E-mail: jay@mhcp.com
Web site: http://www.ppcne.org

NEW YORK STATE EDUCATION DEPARTMENT

Regents Professional Opportunity Scholarship

Lewis Hall, Supervisor
New York State Education Department
89 Washington Avenue, Room 1078 EBA
Albany, NY 12234
Phone: 518-486-1319
Fax: 518-486-5346
E-mail: scholar@mail.nysed.gov
Web site: http://www.highered.nysed.gov

OREGON STUDENT ASSISTANCE COMMISSION

Homestead Capital Housing Scholarship

Director of Grant Programs
Oregon Student Assistance Commission
1500 Valley River Drive, Suite 100
Eugene, OR 97401-7020
Phone: 800-452-8807 Ext. 7395
Web site: http://www.osac.state.or.us

OUTDOOR WRITERS ASSOCIATION OF AMERICA

Outdoor Writers Association of America Bodie McDowell Scholarship Award

Kevin Rhoades, Executive Director
Outdoor Writers Association of America
121 Hickory Street, Suite 1
Missoula, MT 59801
Phone: 406-728-7434
Fax: 406-728-7445
E-mail: owaa@montana.com
Web site: http://www.owaa.org

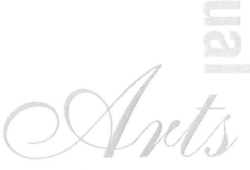
Visual *Arts*

PALM BEACH ASSOCIATION OF BLACK JOURNALISTS

Palm Beach Association of Black Journalists Scholarship

Christopher Smith, Scholarship Chair
Palm Beach Association of Black Journalists
PO Box 19533
West Palm Beach, FL 33416
Web site: http://www.pbabj.org

P. BUCKLEY MOSS SOCIETY

Buckley Moss Endowed Scholarship

Brenda Simmons, Administrative Assistant
P. Buckley Moss Society
20 Stoneridge Drive, Suite 102
Waynesboro, VA 22980
Phone: 540-943-5678
Fax: 540-949-8408
E-mail: brenda@mosssociety.org
Web site: http://www.mosssociety.org

PHI DELTA THETA EDUCATIONAL FOUNDATION

Francis D. Lyon Scholarships

Mrs. Carmalieta Jenkins, Assistant to the President
Phi Delta Theta Educational Foundation
Two South Campus Avenue
Oxford, OH 45056-1801
Phone: 513-523-6966
Fax: 513-523-9200
E-mail: carmalieta@phideltatheta.org
Web site: http://www.phideltatheta.org

PLAYWRIGHTS' CENTER

Many Voices Residency Program

Kevin McLaughlin, Fellowships Technology and Space Manager
Playwrights' Center
2301 East Franklin Avenue
Minneapolis, MN 55406-1099
Phone: 612-332-7481 Ext. 15
Fax: 612-332-6037
E-mail: info@pwcenter.org
Web site: http://www.pwcenter.org

PLUMBING-HEATING-COOLING CONTRACTORS ASSOCIATION EDUCATION FOUNDATION

Bradford White Corporation Scholarship

Delta Faucet Company Scholarship Program

PHCC Educational Foundation Need-Based Scholarship

Iva Vest, Scholarship Coordinator
Plumbing-Heating-Cooling Contractors Association Education Foundation
PO Box 6808
Falls Church, VA 22046
Phone: 800-533-7694
Fax: 703-237-7442
E-mail: vest@naphcc.org
Web site: http://www.phccweb.org

POLISH ARTS CLUB OF BUFFALO SCHOLARSHIP FOUNDATION

Polish Arts Club of Buffalo Scholarship Foundation Trust

Anne Flansburg, Selection Chair
Polish Arts Club of Buffalo Scholarship Foundation
PO Box 1362
Williamsville, NY 14231-1362
Phone: 716-626-9083
E-mail: anneflanswz@aol.com
Web site: http://www.pacb.bfn.org

PRINCESS GRACE FOUNDATION-USA

Princess Grace Scholarships in Dance, Theater, and Film

Kathleen Richards, Program Manager
Princess Grace Foundation-USA
150 East 58th Street, 25th Floor
New York, NY 10155
Phone: 212-317-1470
Fax: 212-317-1473
E-mail: grants@pgfusa.org
Web site: http://www.pgfusa.org

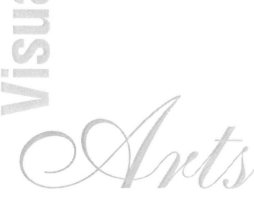

PRINT AND GRAPHIC SCHOLARSHIP FOUNDATION

Print and Graphics Scholarships

Bernadine Eckert, Scholarship
  Administrator
Print and Graphic Scholarship Foundation
200 Deer Run Road
Sewickley, PA 15143-2600
Phone: 412-741-6860
Fax: 412-741-2311
E-mail: pgsf@gatf.org
Web site: http://www.pgsf.org

PRINTING INDUSTRY OF MINNESOTA EDUCATION FOUNDATION

Printing Industry of Minnesota Education Foundation Scholarship Fund

Kristin Davis, Director of Education
  Services
Printing Industry of Minnesota Education
  Foundation
2829 University Avenue, SE, Suite 750
Minneapolis, MN 55414-3248
Phone: 651-789-5508
E-mail: kristinp@pimn.org
Web site: http://www.pimn.org

QUILL AND SCROLL FOUNDATION

Edward J. Nell Memorial Scholarship in Journalism

Vanessa Shelton, Executive Director
Quill and Scroll Foundation
School of Journalism, E346AJB
Iowa City, IA 52242-1528
Phone: 319-335-3457
Fax: 319-335-3989
E-mail: quill-scroll@uiowa.edu
Web site: http://www.uiowa.edu/~quill-sc

RADIO-TELEVISION NEWS DIRECTORS ASSOCIATION AND FOUNDATION

Carole Simpson Scholarship

Melanie Lo, Project Coordinator
Radio-Television News Directors Associa-
  tion and Foundation
1600 K Street, NW, Suite 700
Washington, DC 20006
Phone: 202-467-5218
Fax: 202-223-4007
E-mail: irvingw@rtndf.org
Web site: http://www.rtndf.org

RHODE ISLAND FOUNDATION

Constant Memorial Scholarship for Aquidneck Island Residents

J. D. Edsal Advertising Scholarship

MJSA Education Foundation Jewelry Scholarship

Libby Monahan, Funds Administrator
Rhode Island Foundation
One Union Station
Providence, RI 02903
Phone: 401-274-4564 Ext. 3117
Fax: 401-751-7983
E-mail: libbym@rifoundation.org
Web site: http://www.rifoundation.org

ROBERT H. MOLLOHAN FAMILY CHARITABLE FOUNDATION INC.

Mary Olive Eddy Jones Art Scholarship

Beth Michalec, Program Manager
Robert H. Mollohan Family Charitable
  Foundation Inc.
1000 Technology Drive, Suite 2000
Fairmont, WV 26554
Phone: 304-333-2251
Fax: 304-333-3900
E-mail: bmichalec@wvhtf.org
Web site: http://www.mollohanfoundation.
  org

SAN FRANCISCO FOUNDATION

Phelan Art Award in Filmmaking

Phelan Art Award in Video

Phelan Award in Photography

Phelan Award in Printmaking

Art Awards Coordinator
San Francisco Foundation
225 Bush Street, Suite 500
San Francisco, CA 94104
Phone: 415-733-8500
Web site: http://www.sff.org

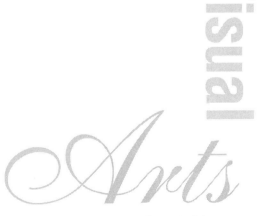

SERVICE EMPLOYEES INTERNATIONAL UNION (SEIU)

SEIU Moe Foner Scholarship Program for Visual and Performing Arts

c/o Scholarship Program Administrators, Inc.
Service Employees International Union (SEIU)
PO Box 23737
Nashville, TN 37202-3737
Phone: 615-320-3149
Fax: 615-320-3151
E-mail: info@spaprog.com
Web site: http://www.seiu.org

SISTER KENNY REHABILITATION INSTITUTE

International Art Show for Artists with Disabilities

Laura Swift, Administrative Assistant
Sister Kenny Rehabilitation Institute
800 East 28th Street
Minneapolis, MN 55407-3799
Phone: 612-863-4466
Fax: 612-863-8942
E-mail: laura.swift@allina.com
Web site: http://www.allina.com/ahs/ski.nsf

SOCIETY OF MOTION PICTURE AND TELEVISION ENGINEERS

Lou Wolf Memorial Scholarship

Student Paper Award

Sally-Ann D'Amato, Director of Operations
Society of Motion Picture and Television Engineers
Third Barker Avenue
White Plains, NY 10601
Phone: 914-761-1100 Ext. 4965
Fax: 914-761-3115
E-mail: sdamato@smpte.org
Web site: http://www.smpte.org

SOUTH DAKOTA RETAILERS ASSOCIATION

South Dakota Retailers Association Scholarship Program

Donna Leslie, Communications Director
South Dakota Retailers Association
PO Box 638
Pierre, SD 57501
Phone: 800-658-5545
Fax: 605-224-2059
E-mail: dleslie@sdra.org
Web site: http://www.sdra.org

STRAIGHTFORWARD MEDIA

StraightForward Media Art School Scholarship

StraightForward Media Liberal Arts Scholarship

StraightForward Media Media & Communications Scholarship

Scholarship Committee
StraightForward Media
2040 West Main Street, Suite 104
Rapid City, SD 57701
Phone: 605-348-3042
Fax: 605-348-3043
Web site: http://www. straightforwardmedia.com

TAG AND LABEL MANUFACTURERS INSTITUTE INC.

TLMI Four-Year Colleges/Full-Time Students Scholarship

Karen Planz, Office Manager
Tag and Label Manufacturers Institute Inc.
40 Shuman Boulevard, Suite 295
Naperville, IL 60563-8465
Phone: 630-357-9222 Ext. 11
Fax: 630-357-0192
E-mail: office@tlmi.com
Web site: http://www.tlmi.com

TECHNICAL ASSOCIATION OF THE PULP & PAPER INDUSTRY (TAPPI)

Coating and Graphic Arts Division Scholarship

Veranda Edmondson, Member Group Specialist
Technical Association of the Pulp & Paper Industry (TAPPI)
15 Technology Parkway, South
Norcross, GA 30092
Phone: 770-209-7536
Fax: 770-446-6947
E-mail: vedmondson@tappi.org
Web site: http://www.tappi.org

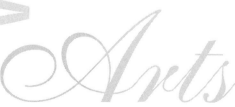

TELETOON

Teletoon Animation Scholarship

Denise Vaughan, Senior Coordinator,
Public Relations
Teletoon
BCE Place, 181 Bay Street
PO Box 787
Toronto, ON M5J 2T3
Canada
Phone: 416-956-2060
Fax: 416-956-2070
E-mail: denisev@teletoon.com
Web site: http://www.teletoon.com

TEXAS ARTS AND CRAFTS EDUCATIONAL FOUNDATION

Emerging Texas Artist Scholarship

Debbie Luce, Assistant Director
Texas Arts and Crafts Educational Foundation
4000 River Side Drive East
Kerrville, TX 78028
Phone: 830-896-5711
Fax: 830-896-5569
E-mail: info@tacef.org
Web site: http://www.tacef.org

TEXAS GRIDIRON CLUB INC.

Texas Gridiron Club Scholarships

Angie Summers, Scholarships Coordinator
Texas Gridiron Club Inc.
709 Houston Street
Arlington, TX 76012
E-mail: asummers@star-telegram.com
Web site: http://www.spjfw.org

TURNER CONSTRUCTION COMPANY

YouthForce 2020 Scholarship Program

Stephanie V. Burns, Community Affairs
Coordinator
Turner Construction Company
375 Hudson Street, Sixth Floor
New York, NY 10014
Phone: 212-229-6480
Fax: 212-229-6083
E-mail: sburns@tcco.com
Web site: http://www.turnerconstruction.com

UNICO NATIONAL INC.

Theodore Mazza Scholarship

Ann Tichenor, Secretary
UNICO National Inc.
271 U.S. Highway 46 West, Suite A-108
Fairfield, NJ 07004
Phone: 973-808-0035
Fax: 973-808-0043
Web site: http://www.unico.org

UNITARIAN UNIVERSALIST ASSOCIATION

Marion Barr Stanfield Art Scholarship

Pauly D'Orlando Memorial Art Scholarship

Stanfield and D'Orlando Art Scholarship

Ms. Hillary Goodridge, Program Director
Unitarian Universalist Association
PO Box 301149
Boston, MA 02130
Phone: 617-971-9600
Fax: 617-971-0029
E-mail: uufp@aol.com
Web site: http://www.uua.org

UNITED METHODIST COMMUNICATIONS

**Leonard M. Perryman Communications
Scholarship for Ethnic Minority Students**

Communications Resourcing Team
United Methodist Communications
810 12th Avenue, South
PO Box 320
Nashville, TN 37202-0320
Phone: 888-278-4862
Fax: 615-742-5485
E-mail: scholarships@umcom.org
Web site: http://www.umcom.org

UNITED NEGRO COLLEGE FUND

CDM Scholarship/Internship

Gilbane Scholarship Program

Houston Symphony/Top Ladies Scholarship

Mae Maxey Memorial Scholarship

Wells Fargo/UNCF Scholarship Fund

Director, Program Services
United Negro College Fund
8260 Willow Oaks Corporate Drive
PO Box 10444
Fairfax, VA 22031-8044
Phone: 800-331-2244
E-mail: rebecca.bennett@uncf.org
Web site: http://www.uncf.org

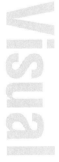

Visual Arts

UNIVERSITY FILM AND VIDEO ASSOCIATION

University Film and Video Association Carole Fielding Student Grants

Prof. Robert Johnson, Jr., Chair
University Film and Video Association
Framingham State College, 100 State
   Street
Framingham, MA 01701-9101
Phone: 508-626-4684
Fax: 508-626-4847
E-mail: rjohnso@frc.mass.edu
Web site: http://www.ufva.org

USA FILM FESTIVAL

Family Award

Grand Prize

Special Jury Award

Student Award

Texas Award

Ann Alexander, Director of Operations
USA Film Festival
6116 North Central Expressway, Suite 105
Dallas, TX 75206
Phone: 214-821-6300
Fax: 214-821-6364
E-mail: usafilmfestival@aol.com
Web site: http://www.usafilmfestival.com

U.S. FISH AND WILDLIFE SERVICE

Federal Junior Duck Stamp Conservation and Design Competition

Elizabeth Jackson, Program Coordinator
U.S. Fish and Wildlife Service
4401 North Fairfax Drive, Suite 4073
Arlington, VA 22203-1622
Phone: 703-358-2073
E-mail: elizabeth_jackson@fws.gov
Web site: http://www.fws.gov/duckstamps

VALLEY PRESS CLUB

Valley Press Club Scholarships, The Republican Scholarship, Channel 22 Scholarship

Robert McClellan, Scholarship Committee
   Chair
Valley Press Club
PO Box 5475
Springfield, MA 01101
Phone: 413-783-3355
Web site: http://www.valleypressclub.com

VARIAZIONE MIXED MEDIA ARTISTS' COLLECTIVE

Learning Scholarship

Scholarship Coordinator
VariaZioNE Mixed Media Artists' Collective
1152 Crellin Road
Pleasanton, CA 94566
Web site: http://www.zneart.com

VESALIUS TRUST FOR VISUAL COMMUNICATION IN THE HEALTH SCIENCES

Student Research Scholarship

Wendy Hiller Gee, Student Grants and
   Scholarships
Vesalius Trust for Visual Communication in
   the Health Sciences
1100 Grundy Lane
San Bruno, CA 94066
Phone: 650-244-4320
E-mail: wendy.hillergee@krames.com
Web site: http://www.vesaliustrust.org

WATERBURY FOUNDATION

Lois McMillen Memorial Scholarship Fund

Josh Carey, Program Officer
Waterbury Foundation
43 Field Street
Waterbury, CT 06702-1216
Phone: 203-753-1315
Fax: 203-756-3054
E-mail: jcarey@conncf.org
Web site: http://www.conncf.org

WEST VIRGINIA SOCIETY OF ARCHITECTS/AIA

West Virginia Society of Architects/AIA Scholarship

Ms. Roberta Guffey, Executive Director
West Virginia Society of Architects/AIA
223 Hale Street
Charleston, WV 25323
Phone: 304-344-9872
Fax: 304-343-0205
E-mail: roberta.guffey@aiawv.org
Web site: http://www.aiawv.org

WOMEN IN FILM AND TELEVISION (WIFT)

WIF Foundation Scholarship

Gayle Nachlis, Executive Director
Women in Film and Television (WIFT)
8857 West Olympic Boulevard, Suite 201
Beverly Hills, CA 90211
Phone: 310-657-5144 Ext. 28
Fax: 310-657-5154
E-mail: gnachlis@wif.org
Web site: http://www.wif.org

WOMEN'S JEWELRY ASSOCIATION

WJA Scholarship Program

Scholarship Committee
Women's Jewelry Association
7000 West Southwest Highway, Suite 202
Chicago Ridge, IL 60415
Phone: 708-361-6266
Fax: 708-361-6166
E-mail: info@womensjewelry.org
Web site: http://www.womensjewelry.org

WORLDFEST INTERNATIONAL FILM AND VIDEO FESTIVAL

Worldfest Student Film Award

Hunter Todd, Executive Director
Worldfest International Film and Video
Festival
9898 Blssonnet Street, Suite 650
PO Box 56566
Houston, TX 77256-6566
Phone: 713-965-9955
Fax: 713-965-9960
E-mail: hunter@worldfest.org
Web site: http://www.worldfest.org

WORLDSTUDIO FOUNDATION

Special Animation and Illustration Scholarship

Maria Emmighausen, Scholarship
Coordinator
Worldstudio Foundation
200 Varick Street, Suite 507
New York, NY 10014
Phone: 212-807-1990
Fax: 212-807-1799
E-mail: scholarship@aiga.org
Web site: http://www.aiga.org/

Worldstudio AIGA Scholarships

Leah Rico, Project Manager
Worldstudio Foundation
164 Fifth Avenue
New York, NY 10010
Phone: 212-807-1990
Fax: 212-807-1799
E-mail: scholarship@aiga.org
Web site: http://www.aiga.org/

Worldstudio Foundation Scholarship Program

Maria Emmighausen, Scholarship
Coordinator
Worldstudio Foundation
200 Varick Street, Suite 507
New York, NY 10014
Phone: 212-807-1990
Fax: 212-807-1799
E-mail: scholarship@aiga.org

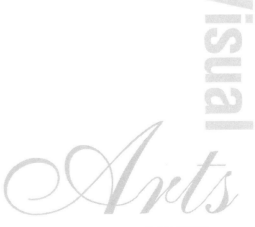

Visual Arts

Additional Resources

AMERICAN SOCIETY OF INTERIOR DESIGNERS (ASID)

608 Massachusetts Ave., NE
Washington, DC 20002-6006
Phone: 202-546-3480
Fax: 202-546-3240
Web site: www.asid.org

FOUNDATION FOR INTERIOR DESIGN EDUCATION RESEARCH (FIDER)

146 Monroe Center NW, Suite 1318
Grand Rapids, MI 49503-2822
Phone: 616-458-0400
Fax: 616-458-0460
E-mail: fider@fider.org
Web site: www.fider.org

NATIONAL ART HONOR SOCIETIES

A Program of the National Art Education
Association
1916 Association Drive
Reston, VA 20191-1590
Phone: 703-860-8000
Fax: 703-860-2960
Web site: www.naea-reston.org

NATIONAL ASSOCIATION OF SCHOOLS OF ART AND DESIGN (NASAD)

11250 Roger Bacon Drive, Suite 21
Reston, VA 20190-5248
Phone: 703-437-0700
Fax: 703-437-6312
E-mail: info@arts-accredit.org
Web site: http://nasad.arts-accredit.org

NATIONAL FOUNDATION FOR ADVANCEMENT IN THE ARTS (NFAA)

Arts Recognition and Talent Search®
(ARTS)
444 Brickell Avenue, P-14
Miami, FL 33131
Phone: 305-377-1140
Fax: 305-377-1149
Web site: www.artsawards.org

NATIONAL PORTFOLIO DAY ASSOCIATION (NPDA)

Web site: www.npda.org

THE SOCIETY OF ILLUSTRATORS

128 East 63rd Street
New York, NY 10021-7303
Phone: 212-838-2560
Fax: 212-838-2561
E-mail: info@societyillustrators.org
Web site: www.societyillustrators.org

VISUAL AND PERFORMING ARTS COLLEGE FAIRS

National Association for College Admission
Counseling (NACAC)
1631 Prince Street
Alexandria, Virginia, 22314
Phone: 703-836-2222
Fax: 703-836-8015
Web site: www.nacacnet.org/memberportal/
events/collegefairs/

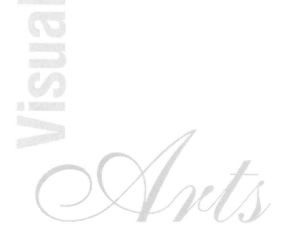

Indexes

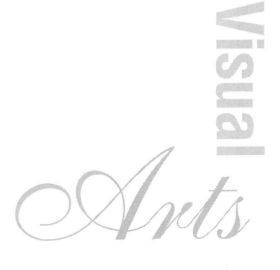

Majors and Concentrations

Accessories design and fabrication
Fashion Institute of Technology *166*

Acting
Academy of Art University *111*

Advertising
Art Center College of Design *121*
The Art Institute of Portland *128*
Minneapolis College of Art and Design *203*
Seton Hall University *260*

Advertising art direction
Columbia College Chicago *154*

Advertising design
Academy of Art University *111*
The Art Institute of Dallas *127*
College for Creative Studies *147*
Cornish College of the Arts *160*
Fashion Institute of Technology *166*
Ohio Northern University *220*
Otis College of Art and Design *223*
Ringling College of Art and Design *241*
Savannah College of Art and Design *251*
School of Visual Arts *258*
Syracuse University *269*

Advertising design and communication
University of Southern California *303*

Advertising graphic design
Cazenovia College *144*
Central State University *144*

Advertising illustration
The Art Institute of Boston at Lesley
   University *124*

Alternative forms
Columbia College Chicago *154*

Animation
Academy of Art University *111*
The Art Institute of Boston at Lesley
   University *124*
Ball State University *130*
Brigham Young University *135*

California College of the Arts *136*
California Institute of the Arts *139*
Collins College: A School of Design and
   Technology *151*
Cornish College of the Arts *160*
Kansas City Art Institute *179*
Laguna College of Art & Design *184*
Maryland Institute College of Art *194*
Massachusetts College of Art and Design *197*
Memphis College of Art *198*
Minneapolis College of Art and Design *203*
Pratt Institute *234*
Radford University *238*
Rocky Mountain College of Art & Design *244*
Savannah College of Art and Design *251*
School of the Museum of Fine Arts, Boston *257*
School of Visual Arts *258*
University of Oregon *302*
The University of the Arts *308*
Virginia Commonwealth University *315*

Animation and illustration
State University of New York at Fredonia *266*

Animation and interactive media
Montserrat College of Art *206*

Apparel accessory design
The Art Institute of Portland *128*

Apparel design
The Art Institute of Portland *128*
Rhode Island School of Design *239*
Wayne State University *318*

Applied art
Memphis College of Art *198*

Applied design
Daemen College *161*
University of Wisconsin–Oshkosh *313*

Applied photography
Northern Kentucky University *218*

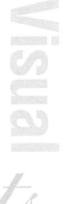

359

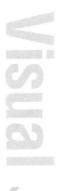

Visual Arts

Art history

Art history and curatorial practice

Art history and museum studies

Art therapy

Arts administration

Arts management

Audio for visual media

Audio production

Book arts

Visual

Arts

Visual Arts

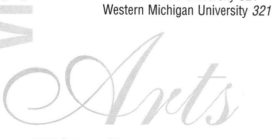

International Academy of Design & Technology *175*
Miami International University of Art & Design *200*
Missouri State University *205*
Ringling College of Art and Design *241*

Computer animation and interactive media
Cornish College of the Arts *160*
Fashion Institute of Technology *166*
Milwaukee Institute of Art and Design *202*

Computer art
Academy of Art University *111*
Brooklyn College of the City University of New York *136*
The College of New Rochelle *150*
Jacksonville University *178*
Syracuse University *269*
West Texas A&M University *323*

Computer art/animation/visual effects
School of Visual Arts *258*

Computer graphics
Illinois Wesleyan University *173*
Lindenwood University *187*
Louisiana Tech University *188*
Manhattanville College *192*
Memphis College of Art *198*
Miami University *200*
Millikin University *202*
New York Institute of Technology *213*
Southern Illinois University Edwardsville *264*
Temple University *274*
The University of Arizona *277*
University of Dayton *282*
University of Notre Dame *301*
University of Oregon *302*
Washington State University *317*
West Chester University of Pennsylvania *320*

Computer imaging
Lehman College of the City University of New York *186*
Metropolitan State College of Denver *200*
University of Southern California *303*

Construction management
Pratt Institute *234*

Craft/material studies
Virginia Commonwealth University *315*

Crafts
California State University, Fullerton *141*
College for Creative Studies *147*
The University of the Arts *308*
Virginia Commonwealth University *315*

Creative arts and therapy
Russell Sage College *246*

Creative writing
California College of the Arts *136*
Kansas City Art Institute *179*

Critical studies
Columbia College Chicago *154*

Cross-discipline studies
The University of North Carolina at Charlotte *298*

Curatorial studies
Moore College of Art & Design *208*

Design
The Art Institute of Portland *128*
Barton College *131*
Lindenwood University *187*
The University of Iowa *289*
The University of North Carolina at Greensboro *299*
The University of Texas at Austin *306*
York University *325*

Design and management
Parsons The New School for Design *226*

Design and technology
San Francisco Art Institute *248*

Design art
University of Washington *311*

Design communication
Belmont University *131*
Texas A&M University–Commerce *270*

Design technology
Parsons The New School for Design *226*

Designed objects
School of the Art Institute of Chicago *253*

Developmental art
University of Calgary *279*

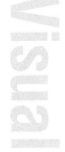

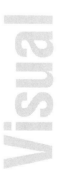

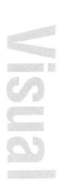

Drexel University *162*
School of Visual Arts *258*
The University of the Arts *308*

Film animation
Laguna College of Art & Design *184*

Film studies
Massachusetts College of Art and Design *197*
The University of the Arts *308*

Film/animation/video
Edinboro University of Pennsylvania *164*
Rhode Island School of Design *239*

Film/photography/visual arts
Ithaca College *177*

Film/video/new media
School of the Art Institute of Chicago *253*

Filmmaking
Minneapolis College of Art and Design *203*

Fine art photography
Columbia College Chicago *154*
University of Southern California *303*

Fine art studio
Milwaukee Institute of Art and Design *202*
University of Southern California *303*

Foundry
New Mexico Highlands University *211*

Furniture design
California College of the Arts *136*
Edinboro University of Pennsylvania *164*
Kendall College of Art and Design of Ferris State
  University *183*
Minneapolis College of Art and Design *203*
Rhode Island School of Design *239*
Savannah College of Art and Design *251*
Virginia Commonwealth University *315*

Game art and design
The Art Institute of Atlanta *123*
The Art Institute of Portland *128*
The Art Institute of Seattle *128*
The Art Institute of Tampa *128*
The Art Institute of Washington *129*
Collins College: A School of Design and
  Technology *151*
The Illinois Institute of Art–Chicago *172*
The Illinois Institute of Art–Schaumburg *173*

Ringling College of Art and Design *241*
University of Southern California *303*

General studio
Youngstown State University *326*

General visual arts studies
University of Florida *284*

Glass
Alberta College of Art & Design *114*
Alfred University *115*
California College of the Arts *136*
California State University, Chico *141*
California State University, Fullerton *141*
The Cleveland Institute of Art *146*
Kent State University *184*
Massachusetts College of Art and Design *197*
The Ohio State University *221*
Rhode Island School of Design *239*
Salisbury University *248*
Southern Illinois University Carbondale *263*
Temple University *274*
Tennessee Technological University *118*
The University of Texas at Arlington *306*

Glassblowing
Boston University *133*

Glassworking
Emporia State University *165*
Virginia Commonwealth University *315*
West Texas A&M University *323*

Graphic and interactive communication
Ringling College of Art and Design *241*

Graphic arts
American University *116*
Drake University *162*
Emmanuel College *164*
Illinois Wesleyan University *173*
Maryland Institute College of Art *194*
Massachusetts College of Art and Design *197*
Memphis College of Art *198*
Minnesota State University Mankato *204*
Parsons The New School for Design *226*
Temple University *274*
University of Dayton *282*
University of Illinois at Chicago *287*
University of Louisville *290*
University of Notre Dame *301*
The University of Texas at Arlington *306*

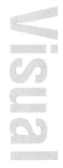

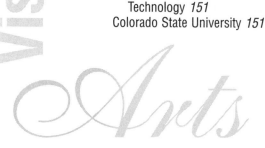

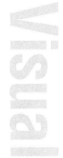

School of the Museum of Fine Arts, Boston *257*
University of Washington *311*

Interior architecture
Academy of Art University *111*
Lawrence Technological University *186*
Rhode Island School of Design *239*
School of the Art Institute of Chicago *253*

Interior architecture and design
Columbia College Chicago *154*
Milwaukee Institute of Art and Design *202*

Interior design
Abilene Christian University *111*
Arcadia University *119*
The Art Institute of Atlanta *123*
The Art Institute of Atlanta–Decatur *123*
The Art Institute of Austin *123*
The Art Institute of Charleston *127*
The Art Institute of Dallas *127*
The Art Institute of Houston *127*
The Art Institute of Jacksonville *127*
The Art Institute of Michigan *128*
The Art Institute of Portland *128*
The Art Institute of Seattle *128*
The Art Institute of Tampa *128*
The Art Institute of Tennessee–Nashville *129*
The Art Institute of Washington *129*
The Art Institutes International Minnesota *129*
California College of the Arts *136*
California State University, Chico *141*
Cazenovia College *144*
The Cleveland Institute of Art *146*
College for Creative Studies *147*
Collins College: A School of Design and
    Technology *151*
Columbus College of Art & Design *155*
Corcoran College of Art and Design *156*
Cornish College of the Arts *160*
Drexel University *162*
Fashion Institute of Technology *166*
Harding University *171*
Harrington College of Design *171*
The Illinois Institute of Art–Chicago *172*
The Illinois Institute of Art–Schaumburg *173*
International Academy of Design &
    Technology *175*
Iowa State University of Science and Technology
    176

Kendall College of Art and Design of Ferris State
    University *183*
Maryville University of Saint Louis *196*
Miami International University of Art &
    Design *200*
Moore College of Art & Design *208*
New York School of Interior Design *213*
Otis College of Art and Design *223*
Paier College of Art, Inc. *226*
Parsons The New School for Design *226*
Pratt Institute *234*
Ringling College of Art and Design *241*
Rocky Mountain College of Art & Design *244*
Rosemont College *245*
Savannah College of Art and Design *251*
School of Visual Arts *258*
Stephens College *267*
Suffolk University *268*
Syracuse University *269*
University of Bridgeport *278*
University of Georgia *285*
University of Louisville *290*
University of North Texas *300*
University of Wisconsin–Stout *314*
Valdosta State University *315*
Virginia Commonwealth University *315*
Watkins College of Art and Design *318*
Wayne State University *318*

Intermedia
Arizona State University *119*
Northern Kentucky University *218*
The University of Iowa *289*
University of Utah *310*
West Virginia University *323*

Interrelated media
Massachusetts College of Art and Design *197*

Jewelry
New Mexico Highlands University *211*

Jewelry and metalsmithing
Abilene Christian University *111*
Alberta College of Art & Design *114*
Arcadia University *119*
Ball State University *130*
California College of the Arts *136*
California State University, Fullerton *141*
East Carolina University *163*
Edinboro University of Pennsylvania *164*

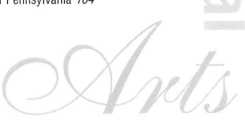

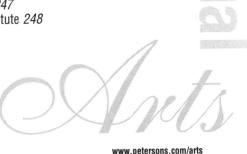

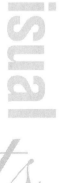

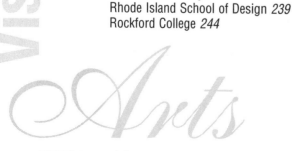

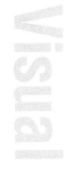

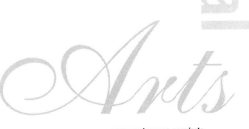

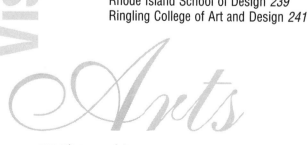

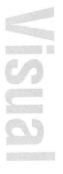

Studio art (continued)

University of Southern California *303*
The University of Texas at Austin *306*
University of the Pacific *310*
University of Wisconsin–Stout *314*
Washington State University *317*
Western Illinois University *321*

Studio art/emerging practices
University at Buffalo, the State University of New York *274*

Surface design
East Carolina University *163*
Syracuse University *269*
Tennessee Technological University *118*

Teacher certification
The University of Texas at Arlington *306*

Text and image art
School of the Museum of Fine Arts, Boston *257*

Textile arts
California College of the Arts *136*
East Carolina University *163*
Indiana University Bloomington *174*
Kent State University *184*
Massachusetts College of Art and Design *197*
Moore College of Art & Design *208*
School of the Art Institute of Chicago *253*
Southern Illinois University Edwardsville *264*
Tennessee Technological University *118*
The University of Arizona *277*
Virginia Commonwealth University *315*

Textile design
Syracuse University *269*

Textile design/fiber arts
University of Massachusetts Dartmouth *291*

Textile/surface design
Fashion Institute of Technology *166*

Textiles
NSCAD University *220*
Rhode Island School of Design *239*

Theory and criticism
School of the Art Institute of Chicago *253*

Three-dimensional studies
Harding University *171*
Manhattanville College *192*
Moore College of Art & Design *208*
Salisbury University *248*
Seton Hill University *260*
University of Cincinnati *280*
University of Louisville *290*
University of Southern Mississippi *304*

Time and interactivity
University of Minnesota, Twin Cities Campus *293*

Time arts
Northern Illinois University *217*

Toy design
Fashion Institute of Technology *166*
Otis College of Art and Design *223*

Traditional animation
Columbia College Chicago *154*

Transportation design
Academy of Art University *111*
Art Center College of Design *121*
College for Creative Studies *147*
Lawrence Technological University *186*

Two-dimensional studies
Manhattanville College *192*
Moore College of Art & Design *208*
Salisbury University *248*
Seton Hill University *260*
University of Cincinnati *280*
University of Louisville *290*

Urban design
Savannah College of Art and Design *251*

Urban studies
San Francisco Art Institute *248*

Video and sonic arts
Alfred University *115*

Video art
Cornish College of the Arts *160*
Maharishi University of Management *191*
Maryland Institute College of Art *194*
Otis College of Art and Design *223*
School of the Art Institute of Chicago *253*
School of the Museum of Fine Arts, Boston *257*

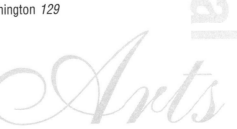

Alphabetical Listing of Schools

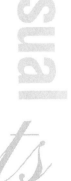

Visual *Arts*

Visual

Arts

Visual

Arts

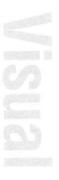

NOTES

NOTES

NOTES

NOTES

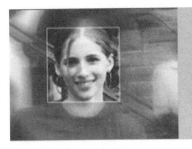

Peterson's
Book Satisfaction Survey

Give Us Your Feedback

Thank you for choosing Peterson's as your source for personalized solutions for your education and career achievement. Please take a few minutes to answer the following questions. Your answers will go a long way in helping us to produce the most user-friendly and comprehensive resources to meet your individual needs.

When completed, please tear out this page and mail it to us at:

Publishing Department
Peterson's, a Nelnet company
2000 Lenox Drive
Lawrenceville, NJ 08648

You can also complete this survey online at **www.petersons.com/booksurvey.**

1. **What is the ISBN of the book you have purchased? (The ISBN can be found on the book's back cover in the lower right-hand corner.)** _____

2. **Where did you purchase this book?**
   - ❑ Retailer, such as Barnes & Noble
   - ❑ Online reseller, such as Amazon.com
   - ❑ Petersons.com
   - ❑ Other (please specify) _____

3. **If you purchased this book on Petersons.com, please rate the following aspects of your online purchasing experience on a scale of 4 to 1 (4 = Excellent and 1 = Poor).**

	4	3	2	1
Comprehensiveness of Peterson's Online Bookstore page	❑	❑	❑	❑
Overall online customer experience	❑	❑	❑	❑

4. **Which category best describes you?**
   - ❑ High school student
   - ❑ Parent of high school student
   - ❑ College student
   - ❑ Graduate/professional student
   - ❑ Returning adult student
   - ❑ Teacher
   - ❑ Counselor
   - ❑ Working professional/military
   - ❑ Other (please specify) _____

5. **Rate your overall satisfaction with this book.**

Extremely Satisfied	Satisfied	Not Satisfied
❑	❑	❑

6. Rate each of the following aspects of this book on a scale of 4 to 1 (4 = Excellent and 1 = Poor).

	4	3	2	1
Comprehensiveness of the information	❏	❏	❏	❏
Accuracy of the information	❏	❏	❏	❏
Usability	❏	❏	❏	❏
Cover design	❏	❏	❏	❏
Book layout	❏	❏	❏	❏
Special features (e.g., CD, flashcards, charts, etc.)	❏	❏	❏	❏
Value for the money	❏	❏	❏	❏

7. This book was recommended by:
- ❏ Guidance counselor
- ❏ Parent/guardian
- ❏ Family member/relative
- ❏ Friend
- ❏ Teacher
- ❏ Not recommended by anyone—I found the book on my own
- ❏ Other (please specify) _____

8. Would you recommend this book to others?

Yes	Not Sure	No
❏	❏	❏

9. Please provide any additional comments.

_____

_____

_____

_____

_____

Remember, you can tear out this page and mail it to us at:

Publishing Department
Peterson's, a Nelnet company
2000 Lenox Drive
Lawrenceville, NJ 08648

or you can complete the survey online at **www.petersons.com/booksurvey.**

Your feedback is important to us at Peterson's, and we thank you for your time!

If you would like us to keep in [ ] products and services, please include your e-mail address here: _____